FINALE® 2005
P O W E R !

✳ ✳ ✳

By Mark Johnson

Important: Thomson Course Technology PTR cannot provide software support. Please contact the appropriate software manufacturer's technical support line or Web site for assistance.

Thomson Course Technology PTR and the author have attempted throughout this book to distinguish proprietary trademarks from descriptive terms by following the capitalization style used by the manufacturer.

Information contained in this book has been obtained by Thomson Course Technology PTR from sources believed to be reliable. However, because of the possibility of human or mechanical error by our sources, Thomson Course Technology PTR, or others, the Publisher does not guarantee the accuracy, adequacy, or complete-ness of any information and is not responsible for any errors or omissions or the results obtained from use of such information. Readers should be particularly aware of the fact that the Internet is an ever-changing entity. Some facts may have changed since this book went to press.

Educational facilities, companies, and organizations interested in multiple copies or licensing of this book should contact the publisher for quantity discount information. Training manuals, CD-ROMs, and portions of this book are also available individually or can be tailored for specific needs.

ISBN: 1-59200-536-5
Library of Congress Catalog Card Number: 2004108529
Printed in the United States of America
04 05 06 07 08 BH 10 9 8 7 6 5 4 3 2 1

THOMSON

COURSE TECHNOLOGY

Professional ■ Trade ■ Reference

Thomson Course Technology PTR,
a division of Thomson Course Technology
25 Thomson Place
Boston, MA 02210
http://www.courseptr.com

SVP, Thomson Course Technology PTR:
Andy Shafran

Publisher:
Stacy L. Hiquet

Senior Marketing Manager:
Sarah O'Donnell

Marketing Manager:
Heather Hurley

Manager of Editorial Services:
Heather Talbot

Senior Acquisitions Editor:
Todd Jensen

Senior Editor:
Mark Garvey

Associate Marketing Managers:
Kristin Eisenzopf and
Sarah Dubois

Project Editor/Copy Editor:
Dan Foster, Scribe Tribe

Technical Reviewer:
Kami Miller

Course Technology PTR Market Coordinator:
Elizabeth Furbish

Interior Layout Tech:
Shawn Morningstar

Cover Designer:
Mike Tanamachi

Indexer:
Sharon Shock

Proofreader:
Kim Benbow

Dedication

I dedicate this book to my parents and family.
Your continued encouragement and support is always an inspiration.

Acknowledgments

I would like to thank the wonderful people at MakeMusic! for their continued support, expertise, and for Finale. It's truly an honor to write about a product of such high quality. Also, a special thanks to the superb staff at Thomson Course Technology, who are great at what they do and always a real pleasure to work with.

About the Author

Mark Johnson is the author of the original *Finale Power!* and has been an avid Finale user for more than 8 years. He is currently an employee of MakeMusic! and has worked among Finale's product development staff as a technical support representative, quality assurance technician, and technical writer. He has a B.A. in music theory and composition from St. Olaf College, and has both composing and engraving experience with Finale. He continues to use Finale on a daily basis.

Contents at a Glance

Contents

3 Basic Note Entry, Articulations, and Expressions   47

4 Advanced Note Entry, Chords, and Lyrics   83

5 Clefs, Key Signatures, and Time Signatures   109

6 Slurs, Hairpins, Other Smart Shapes, and Repeats   133

7 Creating and Working with Multiple-Staff Scores   159

8 Alternate Notation, Staff Styles, and Guitar Tablature   183

9 Editing Your Music   213

10 Fine Tuning: the Details   237

11 Measure Numbers, Graphics, Part Extraction, and Printing   269

12 Tricks for Specific Projects and Composing with Finale   293

13 Customizing Finale, Scanning, and Tricks for Music Educators   325

14 Playback and the MIDI Tool

353

15 Integrating Finale with the Web and Other Programs

385

Introduction

Welcome to the fabulous world of Finale 2005. You are about to embark on a quest through the most powerful music notation software in existence and have plenty of fun along the way.

In this book, you'll learn all about creating professional-quality sheet music with Finale, and if you already know how to do this, you'll learn how to do it *faster*. You'll begin by establishing a solid understanding of Finale's framework and then mastering the everyday shortcuts and tricks that make Finale a breeze to use. I'll then take you through every step of the score creation process, from starting a new document, to entering and spacing your music, to layout, extracting parts, and, finally, printing your score.

Finale once had a notorious reputation for being difficult—often described as having a "high learning curve." Leave all of that behind. Today, Finale is as easy to learn and use as any professional publishing program. The complexity of music notation itself is the main demon here, and Finale is the ultimate tool for conquering it. That's where this book comes in. You will be presented with a musical topic and then given a tutorial explaining the many ways to create and customize the musical elements using one or several of Finale's tools or options. In other words, you don't need to know anything about Finale to get the most out of this book; just a basic knowledge of music theory and terminology.

If you are a regular Finale user, you will learn how to quicken your pace using special tricks, new features in Finale 2005, little-known options, and supplemental third-party plug-ins. If you have used older versions of Finale, you may be astounded to discover the time-saving improvements built into Finale in the last few versions. Many tasks that involved complicated workarounds in the past can now be done with just a few simple commands.

Over the past several years, Finale has evolved into a program with more power than ever before, and you can learn to harness it. This book will show you how.

What You'll Find in This Book

The goal of this book is to teach you the skills you need to know to make the most out of Finale. This book is neither a quick start-up guide (like the Finale Installation and Tutorials manual) nor a detailed explanation of menu items and dialog boxes (like the Finale user manual). *Finale 2005 Power!* bridges the gap and integrates the simplicity of a tutorial with virtually all of Finale's tools, including advanced features and plug-ins that you might have overlooked or never thought you had a reason to use.

After reading this book, you will know how to

* Begin and set up a new score with any number of staves, each defined for any instrument or transposition you wish.
* Quickly enter music into your score using Finale's entry methods, both with and without a MIDI keyboard. You'll even learn how to use a MIDI guitar or acoustic instrument for input.
* Add, define, and edit articulations, dynamic markings, rehearsal letters, slurs, and other markings to your music.
* Change clefs, key signatures, and time signatures at any point in your score, as well as customize these items in just about any way imaginable.

❋ Easily define repeat markings for display and playback.

❋ Create staff groups, edit barlines, and work efficiently with multiple-staff scores overall.

❋ Edit any element of your score, including beams, music spacing, noteheads, tuplets, and measure numbers, individually or throughout your document.

❋ Lay out your measures, systems, and pages for printing.

❋ Extract parts from a score, and even explode a multi-part staff into two or more parts.

❋ Compose with Finale, and learn how to create specific types of scores such as lead sheets, guitar TAB, and chant.

❋ Open scanned sheet music in Finale and integrate Finale with other programs such as MIDI sequencers, Finale Performance Assessment, and SmartMusic, and even open files in earlier Finale versions.

❋ Use Finale's plug-ins as well as plug-ins created by third-party developers to boost efficiency.

❋ Take advantage of Finale's sophisticated Human Playback capabilities, how to manage SoundFonts, and also how to save as an MP3, WAV, or AIFF file.

❋ Use Finale as an educational tool, and quickly create custom, technique-building exercises as well as musical examples and worksheets. You will even learn how to create a solo to be evaluated with Finale Performance Assessment.

❋ Use the many subtle features, new and old, that make your time spent with Finale efficient, productive, and fun.

Who This Book Is For

This book is for anyone who wants to get the most out of Finale 2005. If you have never used Finale, this book is a great introduction to the program. The first part of this book will take you step-by-step through the very basics, establishing a solid foundation that will prepare you for the more advanced techniques you will learn in later chapters. If you have already been using Finale, prepare to revolutionize your Finale experience with innovative procedures, tips, and tricks, using everything Finale has to offer in addition to third-party plug-ins and even external programs. Whether you are just becoming familiar with this program or want to become a Finale power user, this book is for you.

How This Book Is Organized

This book contains 15 chapters, as summarized below.

❋ **Chapter 1: Getting Started.** First, you'll be introduced to Finale's framework, how it is organized, and how it works. Here, you will become acquainted with fundamental tricks and terminology that will prepare you for the chapters to come.

❋ **Chapter 2: Beginning a New Score.** You'll learn the variety of ways to begin a new project and how to choose the right one. I'll cover how to create a new score from scratch or easily generate a new custom document with the Setup Wizard. You'll learn how to customize all of the elements generated by the Setup Wizard from within the document, and you'll learn the basics of editing any new score.

❋ **Chapter 3: Basic Note Entry, Articulations, and Expressions.** This chapter covers the two most common note entry methods, Simple Entry and Speedy Entry, and how to use a MIDI keyboard for note entry. Also, you'll learn how to enter articulations and expressions. By the end of this chapter, you will be prepared to score an instrumental solo with dynamic markings and articulations.

❋ **Chapter 4: Advanced Note Entry, Chords, and Lyrics.** You'll learn more ways to enter music into your score, including real-time entry with a MIDI keyboard (HyperScribe). I'll also describe how to add lyrics and chord symbols. By the end of this chapter, you will be prepared to create a lead sheet with chord symbols and lyrics.

❋ **Chapter 5: Clefs, Key Signatures, and Time Signatures.** Here, you'll learn how to add clefs and meter and time changes at any point in your score. I'll also move into more advanced techniques for manipulating the appearance of clefs, key signatures, and time signatures.

❋ **Chapter 6: Slurs, Hairpins, Other Smart Shapes, and Repeats.** You'll learn how to create and customize all of these items. Highlights of this chapter include how to tell Finale to adjust slurs for you automatically and how to most easily define repeat barlines and text.

❋ **Chapter 7: Creating and Working with Multiple-Staff Scores.** Here you'll learn how to handle scores with many staves—for example, how to create and edit staff groups, barlines, and even select certain staves for viewing. This chapter shows you how to eliminate empty staves in systems (optimize) and how to make changes to all staves in your score at once.

❋ **Chapter 8: Alternate Notation, Staff Styles, and Guitar Tablature.** You'll learn how to create staves with alternate notation styles, such as slash, rhythmic, and tablature notation, and then learn how to apply these styles, or any staff attribute, to any region of a staff. At the end of this chapter, use the skills you have learned to create a guitar part with TAB.

❋ **Chapter 9: Editing Your Music.** Here, I'll cover the many ways to edit your score *en mass*. Copy, paste, transpose, or choose from many other options to edit any region of your score. You'll also learn how to fine-tune music spacing and manage fonts.

❋ **Chapter 10: Fine Tuning: the Details.** You'll learn how to align and position just about any item in your score with great precision as well as how to make fine adjustments to beams, stems, noteheads, accidentals, augmentation dots, and ties.

❋ **Chapter 11: Measure Numbers, Graphics, Part Extraction, and Printing.** You'll learn how to finalize your score by defining the measure numbering, inserting graphics, creating parts from the score, and printing.

❋ **Chapter 12: Tricks for Specific Projects and Composing with Finale.** Here, I'll focus on techniques for creating particular types of notation including chant, figured bass, and cross-staff notation. You'll also become acquainted with Finale's compositional utilities such as the Composer Assistant plug-ins, and orchestration utilities such as the MiBAC Jazz Rhythm Section Generator and Band-in-a-Box Auto Harmonizing plug-in.

❋ **Chapter 13: Customizing Finale, Scanning, and Tricks for Music Educators.** You'll learn how to customize the Finale program to fit your personal working style by managing Finale's program options. You'll also learn the best ways to open a scanned file into Finale and how to use Finale as an educational tool.

❊ **Chapter 14: Playback and the MIDI Tool.** You'll learn how to manage Finale's powerful Human Playback capabilities to make your piece sound like a live human performance. You'll also learn how to spot-check your music for accuracy using the many built-in tricks for defining playback of staves and regions, and how to manually edit MIDI data using the MIDI Tool and other features and plug-ins designed to customize playback.

❊ **Chapter 15: Integrating Finale with the Web and Other Programs.** You'll learn how to share files online and transfer Finale files to other programs including SmartMusic and Finale Performance Assessment. You'll also learn how to expand Finale's capabilities using the many available third-party plug-ins.

What's New in This Latest Edition of *Finale Power!?*

The first edition of *Finale Power!* was based on Finale 2003, and *plenty* has changed since then. Here are some of the most exciting enhancements that MakeMusic! has made in Finale versions 2004 and 2005, and where you'll find more about them in this book.

❊ All new Simple Entry. Yes, you can still point and click, but using your computer or MIDI keyboard to enter notes, articulations, expressions, and even clef, key, and time changes has never been faster. See Chapter 3.

❊ You can now mix fonts in expressions (great for tempo markings) and easily align expressions above or below the staff using baselines. See Chapter 3.

❊ Finale's revolutionary Human Playback is like handing your piece over to an accomplished performer. Choose from several playback styles, apply Human Playback to regions of your score, and even mix your own MIDI data with Human Playback's interpretation. Finale's included SoundFont gives your music a realistic sound without the need for an expensive synthesizer. See Chapter 14.

❊ Record sustain pedal and other continuous data during a HyperScribe session. See Chapter 4.

❊ Finale's all new repeat design makes creating repeats defined for playback easy. Also, assign repeat text and ending brackets to specific staves with staff lists and check the playback route. See Chapter 6.

❊ Easily extend beams over barlines using the Beam Over Barlines plug-in. See Chapter 10.

❊ Create cross-staff notation in seconds using the Cross Staff plug-in. See Chapter 12.

❊ TWAIN supported scanning now allows you to acquire sheet music directly from your scanner and import it into Finale using SmartScore Lite. See Chapter 13.

❊ Word extensions and hyphens are now automatic and can adjust to music spacing changes. See Chapter 4.

❊ Finale Performance Assessment (FPA) allows you to evaluate a live performance by comparing it to its notated solo line. This is a separate application included with Finale 2005 and is also available as a free download from www.finalemusic.com. Finale's Assessment Wizard guides you through setting up new FPA files. See Chapter 15.

❊ You can now save as an audio file. You can create a compressed MP3 or uncompressed WAV or AIFF file to burn to a CD. See Chapter 15.

❋ You can use the FinaleScript plug-in to automate complex procedures or edit many documents at a time. See Chapter 15.

❋ Begin new SmartMusic accompaniment files with the new SmartMusic Accompaniment Wizard. Then use the new Add SmartMusic Markers feature to specify pauses, repeats, and other performance markings. See Chapter 15.

❋ Many other small changes have been made that are reflected throughout the book. In several cases, such as defining repeats for playback and cross-staff notation, Finale's design improvements have cut the number of steps in half.

Finale has become easier to use with each new version and continues to hold true to its reputation for complete user control. New features such as Enhanced Tuplets and Smart Word Extensions make your music look great automatically without any need for editing, although you can always customize these items with complete precision. This guide illustrates the best way to approach a task and isolates the places where you're most likely to need some manual tweaking (without muddying the water with commands you'll probably never need). By the time you've finished reading this book, you will have a comprehensive understanding of Finale as well as the resources you'll need to efficiently manage almost any project.

1

GETTING STARTED

Okay, it's time to start the journey to Finale proficiency! If you are familiar with programs similar to Finale, some of the basics might come easy for you. If not, this chapter will be extremely useful for nailing down the way Finale is organized and how it works. If you consider yourself an experienced Finale user, there are tricks and procedures here that will help boost your productivity on a program-wide level. If you haven't had much experience with Finale, don't worry; this chapter is particularly important for the individual who has never used Finale at all. In any case, the terminology and general concepts described in this chapter will lay the groundwork for topics I'll be discussing later on.

Here's a summary of what you will learn in this chapter:

* ❀ How to register your copy of Finale
* ❀ How to install and set up Finale for use with MIDI
* ❀ How to get around in Finale
* ❀ Finale file types

Before You Begin

First, I will assume that you already own a copy of Finale 2005. If you own an earlier version, some of the instructions in this book will not apply. If you are considering an upgrade, I recommend downloading the Finale 2005 demo available at www.makemusic.com. The Finale demo is a fully functional copy of the latest Finale version but lacks the ability to save and limits printing to one page. You might wish to use the Finale demo in conjunction with this book to decide whether an upgrade is right for you.

Registering Finale

Registering is easy. Just click Register Now when prompted upon first starting Finale 2005, or, from the Help Menu, choose Register Finale. Then follow the instructions to register by phone, Internet or fax. Registration entitles you to free maintenance updates and customer support. You have 30 days to register Finale 2005 before printing and saving are disabled. You can install Finale on up to two machines at a time. The Finale Installation disk is a hybrid (Windows and Macintosh), so you could install Finale 2005 on, for example, one Windows machine and one Macintosh. If you need to install Finale on a different machine after you have used up both slots, you'll need to call MakeMusic! Customer Support.

Your Version of Finale

There are many versions of Finale scattered about. In the late 1980s, MakeMusic! (then called Coda Music Software) released Finale 1.0; since then there have been over 14 large-scale product upgrades. Each upgrade contains useful new features, bug fixes, and interface improvements. In the last few years particularly, Finale has become much easier to learn and also far better at handling many of the complex tasks that required awkward workarounds in the past. In fact, to explain how to do everything described in this book would take twice as many pages for an older version of Finale. Finale 2005 owners benefit from about 15 years of design improvements, many inspired by customer requests.

In addition to owning the most recent Finale version, it is also important to get the latest product update. After each upgrade release, MakeMusic! continues to add new features and fix bugs that crop up. Registered owners can either download the latest update from MakeMusic!'s Web site (www.makemusic.com) or contact their customer service department for an update CD. This update is free, and you should consider it part of the software you purchased. Check MakeMusic!'s Web site periodically to be sure you have the most recent update.

Each time a new version of Finale comes out, all changes and bug fixes are documented in the Read Me file. To make sure you're up to date with the most recent changes, I recommend reading through this file whenever you upgrade or update Finale. The Read Me file is located in your Finale folder.

Your Finale Package

Whether or not you are new to Finale, it's a good idea to become familiar with the resources that came with your Finale package. These include the Installation and Tutorials manual, QuickStart Video Tips, Quick Reference Card, and the User Manual. Following is a brief description of these resources and how to use them most effectively as you work with Finale.

Installation and Tutorials

Although I will cover the fundamentals of Finale in this book, you will find the Installation and Tutorials manual a valuable resource, especially if you are new to Finale. Use this manual for help with installation and MIDI setup, as there are step-by-step instructions for these at the beginning. Run through the tutorials to get a good feel for many of the basic features. This is especially beneficial for learning how to use the most common tools in the context of real-world situations.

QuickStart Video Tips

Once you have installed Finale, you may also want to take a look at the QuickStart Video Tips. These are short video clips that introduce several key features, such as entering with Simple Entry, Scanning, HyperScribe, page layout, and much more. There are over 60 QuickStart Videos. You can access these videos from the Launch Window (or under the Help menu).

Quick Reference Card

The Quick Reference Card is a small pamphlet-like book containing information that you may want to access quickly instead of hunting through the User Manual. In it you will find all the keyboard shortcuts, font characters, and a visual index of the tools you will need to use for a variety of musical figures. Keep your Quick Reference Card near your computer any time you are working with Finale. It can save you a lot of time.

The User Manual

The Finale User Manual (formally known as the On-Line Documentation) is in PDF format and available from the Help menu and the Launch Window. Veteran Finale users will discover that this is the replacement to those three bulky volumes that used to accompany the software. You will find this electronic format very convenient as you jump between chapters easily while investigating any topic right from your computer screen. It is heavy in content, describing the functionality of each dialog box in great detail, and is a valuable resource for the new and expert user alike. You will benefit most from the User Manual by treating it as a reference to a specific subject. For instance, say you want to modify your measure numbers. Click the Help menu and choose "Index" from the User Manual submenu. Find "Measure Numbers" from the alphabetical list and click it to get directly to the chapter describing measure numbers. Do not attempt to read through the User Manual as you would the tutorial (or this book). You may not need to know all the information given on a certain topic to complete the task at hand. Also, there may be other valuable time-saving methods and tricks from other areas of the program you might be missing. To take best advantage of Finale, you will need to develop an approach to each individual project and incorporate many of Finale's tools. There is even a small description for how best to use the User Manual within the User Manual. Once you have the program started, click the Help menu and choose How to Use the User Manual from the User Manual submenu.

Your Finale 2005 Power! Online Resource

Visit www.finalepower.com (and click "Links" on the right side of the page) to find a list of valuable third-party plug-ins and resources, including the JW plug-ins, TGTools plug-in collection, Dolet for Finale, and SharpEye. These are all supplemental plug-ins that have been designed to give your Finale package even more power. They make many complicated tasks easy, and include shortcuts for playback, spacing, part extraction, and many other tasks. The JW plug-ins are yours for free. TGTools, the Patterson Collection, Dolet, and SharpEye are full-featured demo versions you can use at no cost for a limited time. Throughout the book, I'll reference these plug-ins where appropriate, so you won't have to do things the long way when you don't have to. Following is a short description of the available third-party plug-ins.

TGTools

TGTools, created by Tobias Giesen, is a set of third-party plug-ins you can use to enhance your Finale software. After installing TGTools, you will see a new item in the menu bar at the top of your screen, "TGTools," which contains over 60 additional features. This plug-in set includes utilities for expression management, music spacing, playback, part extraction, and much more. They have become a staple for many professional Finale users, and I highly recommend incorporating them into your Finale repertoire. Some of the TGTools plug-ins are already included with Finale 2005. From the Plug-ins menu, choose the TGTools submenu to see them. Throughout this book, you will be directed to the TGTools plug-ins where appropriate.

To install a demo of the full featured TGTools plug-in set, visit www.tgtools.de where you can download a demo version. Follow the instructions on the site to download and install TGTools.

The TGTools plug-in set is a full-featured 30-day trial version. After 30 days, you can use only one TGTools dialog per Finale session. You can extend your evaluation period by requesting a registration code from Tobias Giesen, developer of TGTools. To do this, or to purchase a registered version of TGTools, visit www.tgtools.de. Also, these plug-ins are improved regularly, so be sure to check the site every once in a while to make sure you have the most recent version.

Patterson Plug-In Collection

The Patterson plug-ins, created by Robert Patterson, include several useful utilities. The following is from the Patterson plug-ins download page, http://robertgpatterson.com/-fininfo/finmain.html: "These plug-ins provide automated editing of ties, tuplets, and beams, with numerous configuration options to suit any taste. Also available is a vastly improved equivalent of Mass Edit for moving note-attached items. Finally, tools for managing measure numbers (including repeated measures), file settings, page shifting, and staff views round out the collection."

You can find a "Lite" version of the Patterson plug-ins in the Finale 2005 Plug-ins menu. Choose Plug-ins > Note, Beam, and Rest Editing > Patterson Plug-ins Lite. Patterson Beams can improve the appearance of beams throughout your score, and Beam Over Barlines allows you to easily extend a beam across a barline (which is an arduous task if done manually).

JW Plug-ins

The JW plug-ins are developed and distributed for free by third-party plug-in developer Jari Williamsson. Among them are

* **JW Tempo**. Define accelerandos and ritardandos for playback easily. All you need to do is select a region, set the beginning and ending tempo, and click OK.
* **JW Search and Replace**. Search for any type of text (text blocks, expressions, staff names, etc.), and replace all occurrences quickly and easily.
* **JW Playback**. Tell Finale to play back any number of staves, groups, or a measure region without having to go into the Instrument List.

These are just a few of the plug-ins available. You can download all of the freeware JW plug-ins at www.jwmusic.nu/freeplugins/index.html.

Dolet

Dolet is a utility you can use to export and import files in MusicXML format on the Windows platform only. If you own Finale 2005, you already have access to the Dolet Lite plug-in, which can be used to export or import MusicXML files. The full version of Dolet is compatible back to Finale 2000, and therefore offers a method of compatibility among these Finale versions. By exporting a file from Finale 2005 in MusicXML format and importing it into Finale 2000 (for example), you have essentially achieved backwards compatibility with a good deal of accuracy.

You can also use the MusicXML import feature to open files created in any other program that supports the MusicXML format. One program that supports the MusicXML file format is the SharpEye scanning utility.

SharpEye

On Windows, you can use SharpEye to open scanned sheet music and convert it to MusicXML for import into Finale. Many have found that this process offers a very accurate solution for converting sheet music into a Finale file. A fully functional trial version of SharpEye is available at their Web site (www.visiv.co.uk/dload.htm). You can find instructions for converting scanned sheet music into a Finale file using SharpEye in Chapter 13.

Other Resources

If you're ever curious about the functionality of one of the dialog boxes, simply click the Help button. There is a Help button in just about every dialog box—on Windows, usually to the right of the Cancel button; on

Macintosh, the Help button looks like a square box with a question mark. Clicking the Help button will open a window containing a description of the dialog box and links to related material. Click the Find tab in the upper left to search though the help topics.

> **TIP**
> On Windows, press the F1 key to open the context help at any time. On Macintosh, click the Help button in any dialog box to open the context help.

It would be cumbersome to cover all of the common troubleshooting tips in this book. I will do my best to cover the most common ones, but if you run into something and can't find the solution here, go to www.makemusic.com and search the Finale Knowledge Base. The articles in this searchable database were compiled by MakeMusic! Customer Support and cover all of the common problems they are used to hearing all the time. If you can't find the answer there, you could also contact MakeMusic! Customer Support at macsupport@makemusic.com (Macintosh users) or winsupport@makemusic.com (Windows users), or call them by phone—check the Finale About Box for specific contact information. On Windows, go to the Help menu and select About Finale. On Mac, go to the Finale 2005 menu and select About Finale. To be eligible for technical support, you must own a registered copy of Finale. You can also go to the www.finalemusic.com Web site and log on to the user forum to discuss Finale with other Finale users.

Installation and MIDI Setup

There are good installation and MIDI setup instructions available at the beginning of the Installation and Tutorials manual. I recommend using these instructions to get started. Instead of hashing through the same detailed step-by-step procedure, this section will focus on common problems people encounter during the installation and MIDI setup process.

Installation

Nine times out of ten, installation should be a breeze. Pop in the CD and just keep clicking Next, OK, or Accept, and everything should work like a charm. Unfortunately, when something goes wrong things can get a little complicated. Following are some helpful tips to avoid or solve potential installation problems. Since many of the common problems are platform specific, I'll cover Windows and Macintosh installations separately.

Installation on Windows

Here are some tricks to a smooth installation on the Windows platform:

1. If you plan on uninstalling an older version of Finale, remove all older versions of Finale from your system before installing the new version. (Uninstalling an old Finale version may remove Finale's fonts, which you will need to view your music after installing Finale 2005). When you do this, make sure you spare any files you have created and saved in the Finale folder. Your new version of Finale will be able to open all files saved from any earlier version. Note that if you use the Windows Add/Remove Programs utility to remove a version of Finale, fonts will not be removed.

2. If you are unable to install Finale, try this: Before installation, close all programs running on your computer. This includes any programs running in the background, such as antivirus software. For Windows 2000 or XP, Press Ctrl-Alt-Del once and click Task Manager. Click the Applications tab and click End Task on all of the items there. Click on the Processes tab. This lists every process that is running on the system. Click on User Name or User Group to reorganize the list. Start at the top, highlight a process, and click the End Process button. There are some processes that Windows will not let you shut down, so when you reach one of these processes, you may exit the Task Manager. (Windows 2000 users, do not end Explorer). For Windows 98 or ME, press Ctrl-Alt-Del once to bring up the Close Program/Task Manager dialog box. This lists every process that is running on the system. Explorer and Systray are always running, so leave them alone. If you see anything other than those two, click on any one of the others and click End Task. When that goes away, press Ctrl-Alt-Del again and End Task on another one in the list. (If a program remains on the list after you have tried to End Task on it, click on it, click and hold End Task for 10 seconds, then release it. If a "This program is not responding..." message appears, click End Task in it). Repeat the process until only Explorer and Systray are left. Then begin the installation.

3. While installing on a machine running Windows, you may get an error message that complains about a missing DLL (dynamic-link library) file. The error message will say something like "The dynamic link library MSVCP60.DLL could not be found in the specified path." To resolve this problem, either update your copy of Windows or run a search online and download the missing DLL file. Generally, you will want the most recent DLL updates available. You can also try using a DLL updater application already included on the Finale 2005 CD. Navigate to the file "dllupdateb" and double-click it to replace DLLs that require updating on some machines.

4. After installation, restart your computer. Though you may not be prompted to do this, it is still a good idea. By doing this you also restart all of the tasks you closed down before installation.

5. If, following installation, you open Finale and see a bunch of strange characters on the screen, you may be missing your Finale music fonts. To reinstall them, run the Finale installation again and when you see a window for Install Type, choose Custom and click Next. Put a checkmark on "TrueType" or "PostScript." Click Next until the installation is completed. Then restart your computer.

Installation on Macintosh

Installation problems are less frequent on Macintosh computers. In fact, I'm willing to bet that as long as you are installing on a Machine running OS X 10.2.x or greater (the minimum system requirements for Finale) you'll be just fine.

MIDI Setup

Again, use the Finale Installation and Tutorials manual for basic MIDI setup instructions. If you are having problems, here are some things to try. First, make sure your MIDI cables are connected properly.

Hooking Up the MIDI Cables

If you want to use an external MIDI instrument (like a MIDI keyboard) with Finale, make sure the MIDI input device is properly connected to the computer. As simple as it sounds, incorrectly connecting the MIDI cables is a common mistake. If you have a Windows computer and are using a MIDI cable connected to the 15-pin jack at the back of your computer, you should connect the MIDI OUT cable to the MIDI IN port on your keyboard and the MIDI IN cable to the MIDI OUT port on your keyboard. If you are using a MIDI interface (this includes most Mac users) then one cable should connect to the MIDI OUT on the interface and MIDI IN on the keyboard. Likewise, the other cable should connect the MIDI IN on the interface and the MIDI OUT on the keyboard. In other words, the MIDI that comes OUT of the MIDI input device should go IN to the computer or interface.

Some synthesizers have several modes, so if you're having trouble playing a file, make sure your synthesizer is set to receive and transmit MIDI data. Consult the synthesizer's manual if you do not know how to do this.

MIDI Setup on Windows

After you have checked the cables, you will need to tell Finale to use the drivers for MIDI IN and MIDI OUT. MIDI input refers to the information coming into the computer from the MIDI keyboard (note entry into Finale), and MIDI output refers to information sent to the keyboard from the computer (playback from Finale). In Finale, click the MIDI menu and choose MIDI Setup. On the left, select the MIDI driver for your MIDI IN device. To see what choices you have available, click the drop-down arrow to see various installed drivers. If you have a Sound Blaster card, for example, you might select the driver in that list that says "SB16 MIDI IN." On the right side of the MIDI Setup dialog box, choose the driver for your MIDI output. If you want your music to play through a synthesizer, look for an option with "MPU" or "MIDI OUT" in its name. If you are using your soundcard (internal sounds) for output, look for an option with "Synth" or "FM" in its name. By default, Finale's included sound font, "SmartMusic SoftSynth," which provides high quality General MIDI instrument sounds, is defined for MIDI OUT.

If you do not see these drivers in the MIDI Setup window, they have not been installed on your machine or they have a problem. You may need to reinstall the drivers for your soundcard or MIDI interface. Contact the manufacturer of your soundcard or interface for more information on reinstalling the device drivers. Once your soundcard is set up properly with your computer, it will work in Finale.

MIDI Setup on Macintosh

To get MIDI working on your Mac, ensure you have installed any MIDI devices (MIDI interfaces, etc.) properly. You'll find helpful installation instructions with your MIDI device. Once your devices are installed, you will be able to choose them in Finale's MIDI Setup dialog box (MIDI menu > MIDI Setup). For more control over your MIDI devices, you can use Apples Audio MIDI Setup utility. To do this, go to your hard drive and choose Applications > Utilities > Audio MIDI Setup. Now click the MIDI Devices tab to add, name, and configure your MIDI device (see page xv of the Finale Installation and Tutorials manual for more details). Once you've got your devices set up, you'll be able to specify an input and output device in Finale's MIDI Setup dialog box (you'll see a button for Audio MIDI Setup from here, too).

NOTE

If you have used Finale on a Macintosh running OS 9 (or earlier) in the past, you may remember complex steps were often necessary to configure MIDI helper software (i.e., OMS and FreeMIDI) to use your MIDI device. The Audio MIDI Setup feature of OS X replaces these helper programs and takes a lot of the hassle out of getting your MIDI system up and running.

Getting Around in Finale

Let's get acquainted with the outlying structure of Finale and general navigation skills. Many instructions throughout this book make the assumption that you are familiar with the following subjects, so it is important to learn about them in preparation for other chapters. Some of this information may seem rudimentary at first, but there are also some pleasant surprises at this level that could have easily slipped by a regular Finale user.

To prepare for this section, launch Finale. You will see a gleaming new Launch Window (it's new to Finale 2005). Click Default Document. This will open a single staff document that you can use to experiment with the following subjects.

A Tool-Based Program

At the core of Finale lies the Main Tool Palette (see Figure 1.1). Just about everything you do in Finale is in the context of one of these 27 main tools (on Windows, this palette is split into the Main and Advanced Tools Palettes). For example, to enter an articulation, first click the Articulation Tool. To add a staff, first click the Staff Tool. As you work on your score, you can usually make a good guess as to which tool you will need to use, but sometimes it isn't completely clear. For example, you may want to enter tempo marking at the beginning of your piece. To do this you would click the Mass Mover Tool, choose a plug-in from the Plug-ins menu, then edit the tempo marking with the Expression Tool. The new Finale user then asks, "So what's the Tempo Tool for?," thus beginning the downward spiral of frustration that has accompanied the novice Finale user for years. Don't worry, that's what this book is for. The chapters are organized by musical subject, so you'll often jump around to different tools to complete similar notation tasks.

Figure 1.1
The Main Tool Palette

When you click a tool in the Main Tool Palette, two things can change on your screen. You may see another tool palette appear that you can use to specify a certain task. For instance, when you click the Simple Entry Tool, the Simple Entry Palette appears. You can choose a tool in the Simple Entry Palette to specify a rhythmic value to click into your staff. When you click a tool in the Main Tool Palette, you may also see a new menu item appear at the top of your screen. From this menu, you can customize the way the tool works or customize items related to the tool. Click the Staff Tool to see the Staff menu appear at the top of your screen, as shown in Figure 1.2.

Working with Palettes

You can show or hide any palette with the Window menu. Click the Window menu. The palettes currently visible have a check box to the left of them. Click a checked palette name to hide it from the screen, or click one of the unchecked palettes to display it. In many cases, you won't have to worry about manually turning these palettes on or off because Finale automatically displays them when appropriate.

TIP
In Windows, right-click on the area surrounding a docked palette (the blank area), or a scroll bar, to easily choose the tool palettes you want to display.

Figure 1.2

Some main tools, like the Staff
Tool, are accompanied by a
corresponding menu.

Staff Tool

Staff menu

Instead of hiding a palette, you may simply want to move it out of the way. On Mac, the tool palettes are "floating." These palettes can be repositioned and reshaped by dragging with your mouse. On Windows, when you first launch Finale, the tool palettes are located near the top of your screen. In this state, they are said to be "docked." You can tear off each one individually (undock it) by dragging the small vertical bar located at the left edge of each palette. You will now notice a title bar at the top of the palette bearing its name. To change its shape, move your cursor to the edge of the palette so you can see a small line with two arrows pointing in opposite directions. Now click and drag to change the shape however you prefer. To hide it, simply click the "X" in the upper-right corner. If you drag the palette back to the top of the screen, it will become docked wherever you decide to place it. To return any undocked palette back to its most recent docked position, just double-click it. You can also dock palettes at the bottom or at either side of your screen. Just drag the palette to the edge of your screen until the gray outline changes shape. Release the mouse button, and the palette will dock into place.

TIP

Windows users can remove rarely used tools from a palette to save space. On Windows, click the View menu, choose Customize Palettes, and then select the palette you want to remove or customize.

Message Bar (Mac) or Status Bar (Windows)

On Windows, any time you move your cursor over any Finale icon, you will see a brief description of the icon in the Message Bar (Mac) or Status Bar (Windows). To see a description of the tool in the Message Bar on Mac, click on the tool. On Windows, the Status Bar is located at the bottom of your screen (see Figure 1.3). On Macintosh, the Message Bar is directly above your score (see Figure 1.4). The short description can be especially handy for keyboard shortcut reminders. Click one of the tools now to see the name of the active tool and its description in the Status/Message Bar.

Figure 1.3

On Windows, notice the Status Bar in the lower-left corner of your screen

Figure 1.4

On Macintosh, notice the Message Bar located just above your score

Tool Tips

If you're using Windows, move the cursor over a tool and leave it stationary for a moment. A small box will appear containing the name of the tool. These are called "Tool Tips" and are available on all tools in any tool palette. Look in the Status Bar for keyboard shortcuts you can use to access the tool more easily.

{ **TIP**

As you work, you will find yourself switching between tools a lot. On Windows, to easily select tools you use often, program them to function keys. To do this, simply click the tool you desire to program, hold down Shift and press a function key (F2–F12). On Mac, hold down Control and Option and press a key between F and the comma key. Highlight the tool you wish to associate with that key and click OK. To access the tool, press Control and the key you programmed (F-comma). This information is saved with the document, so it will be usable any time you open the document in the future. (Later, you will learn to customize your default files or templates so that new documents will contain your settings.)

The Menus

Notice the menu items at the top of the screen (see Figure 1.5). Each of these is a set of controls that govern the document, the program, or the tool selected. The Help menu, which provides informative resources, is the only exception. Nine of these menus will always be visible. These include the File, Edit, View, Options, MIDI, Plug-ins, Tools, Window, and Help menus. The other menu(s) will appear only if their corresponding tool is chosen (click the Staff Tool and the Staff menu appears). As with the main tools, I'll direct you to a menu item when describing a subject that calls for it.

Figure 1.5

The menus

Many menu items can be accessed easily with keyboard shortcuts. There are certain menu items you might find yourself using frequently (in my case Undo is a common one). Click the Edit menu and look to the right of the Undo command. You will see the keystroke Ctrl-Z (Cmd-Z on Mac). Instead of clicking the menu item every time you want to undo, simply use this keyboard shortcut. Refer to the menus for other keyboard shortcuts to save you time as you work.

TIP

On Windows, you can program any menu item to a keyboard shortcut. To do this, click the Plug-ins menu, choose TGTools, and click Menu Shortcuts.

TIP

On Windows, you can use keystrokes to open any menu item. Hold down the Alt key and type the underlined letter in the menu name (e.g., Alt-T to open the Tools menu). Then use the underlined letter of the menu item to select it. This is an alternative to clicking the item with your mouse cursor.

Basic Finale Vocabulary

There is some general terminology used throughout this book that you will need to know. Some of these terms are common to other programs, and some are unique to Finale.

Handles

Handles are small boxes that appear near items in your score that are available for editing (see Figure 1.6). Anytime you want to edit an articulation, text block, or expression (for example), click the corresponding tool, or double-click the item with the Selection Tool, to see this box appear. You will then be able to click and drag or nudge (with the arrow buttons) the handle to move the item.

Figure 1.6

Notice the handle at the lower left of this expression

Often handles can be double-clicked to open a dialog box for more editing options, or context-clicked (Windows, right-click; Mac, Ctrl-click) to open a context menu containing options specific to that item. You will become more familiar with these procedures as we apply them for certain tasks.

The Cursor

You will find that the state of the cursor can be an informative tool. It can tell you which staff or note an item will be attached to, the exact item that will be entered, or whether Finale is processing something. As you work through the program, take note of when the cursor changes and use it to your advantage. There will be descriptions of these cursor changes throughout this book.

The Scroll Bars

On the bottom and right side of your Finale window you will see vertical and horizontal scroll bars. Click and drag the box within the scroll bars in Page View or Scroll View to adjust the viewable area of the page.

Scroll View

There are two ways to view your score in Finale: Scroll View and Page View. When you first open a document, it appears in Page View. From the View menu, choose Scroll View. In this view, you will see one system extending horizontally all the way to the last measure without interruption. This view is great for entering and editing your music without having to flip through pages. Many Finale users prefer to use Scroll View exclusively while entering music, and do not even visit Page View until it's time to layout the score for printing. Use the scroll bar at the bottom of your screen to navigate through your score, or type a number in the entry field to the left of the scroll bar to move to a specific measure.

Page View

Now click the View menu and choose Page View. Page View is a representation of how the document will look if printed. Items specific to pages, such as the title, page numbers, and staff systems are now visible. Use the arrows located at the bottom of the screen to move forward or backward through pages. You can also move to a specific page by typing the page number in the entry field. To easily switch between Scroll View and Page View, press Ctrl-E (Windows) or Opt-Cmd-`(Mac).

TIP

If you want to set up measures to access quickly in Scroll View or Page View, set up Bookmarks. Click the View menu, choose Bookmarks, and then Add Bookmark (or press Ctrl/Command-B).

Display Colors

You may have noticed already the array of colored items in Finale. In addition to contributing to aesthetic appeal, these actually do serve a purpose. The color of an item allows you to see, at a glance, what tool created it. As you work in Finale, note the color of items and which type of item relates to which color. To see a breakdown of all the colors associated with each element in your score, click the View menu and choose Select Display Colors. You can also use this dialog box to modify the display colors as you wish.

TIP
You can easily edit any item on your screen with the Selection Tool. In older Finale versions, to edit any item, you first had to find and click the item's corresponding tool before you could edit it. Now, you can move or delete most items in your score by simply clicking the Selection Tool and then clicking the item. Press the Esc key to choose the Selection Tool at any time.

Navigation Tools

Quickly navigating around your score is key to working with Finale efficiently. You can easily adjust the viewable area of your score, zoom in and out, move quickly to a specific measure, or even set up bookmarks to common locations. Changing the viewable area of your screen has no effect on the printout.

Zooming

While working on your document, you may want to zoom in to make fine adjustments or zoom out to see more of your score. While in Page View or Scroll View, click the View menu, open the Scale View To submenu, and choose a different view percentage—try 200%. Notice the staves become larger. Instead of going all the way to the View menu, you can also use keyboard shortcuts to change your view percentage:

* Crtl/Cmd-= = Zoom In
* Crtl/Cmd—(minus) = Zoom Out
* Crtl/Cmd-1 = 100%
* Crtl/Cmd-2 = 200%
* Crtl/Cmd-4 = 400%
* Crtl/Cmd-5 = 50%
* Crtl/Cmd-0 = Other (to enter a different percentage)
* Crtl/Opt-Cmd-] = Fit Width
* Crtl/Opt-Cmd-[= Fit In Window

For more control over viewing various sections of your score, use the Zoom Tool. Click the Zoom Tool and then click a section of your score to zoom in or Ctrl/Option-click to zoom out. In Page View, to specify an area to enlarge, click and drag your cursor diagonally. Notice that a dashed box appears. When you release the mouse button, the enclosed area will enlarge to fit the entire viewable area.

TIP
On Windows, Shift-right-click at any time to zoom in; Ctrl-Shift-right-click to zoom out. On Mac, Shift-Control-Command-click to zoom in and Shift-Control-Option-Command-click to zoom out.

The Hand Grabber Tool

In addition to zooming in and out, you also need a way to move the viewable region. This is the purpose of the Hand Grabber Tool. Click the Hand Grabber Tool. Now click and drag to move the page or systems around.

CAUTION

In Scroll View, only use the Hand Grabber to move the viewable area *vertically*. Use the scroll bar exclusively to move around *horizontally*. You will always want to see the left edge of your staves in Scroll View.

TIP

On Windows, the Hand Grabber Tool can be used at almost any time by right-clicking and dragging. On Mac, Option-Command-click and drag.

Redrawing Your Screen

While editing your score, you may find that portions of your screen are whited out, or artifacts of items remain on the screen after you delete them. This is a common nuisance that has been around in Finale for ages. When this happens, simply hold down the Ctrl/Command key and press D. This key command will redraw your screen and restore the integrity of the viewable area.

Measurement Units

There are many cases where you might be asked to enter a value to specify a certain distance. For example, you may want to place your title an inch, centimeter, or millimeter from the top page margin. To choose your unit of measurement, click the Options menu, choose Measurement Units, and click one of the available options. Table 1.1 shows an explanation of the relationship between all of the available measurement units.

Table 1.1

Measurement Units Comparison Table

EVPUs	Spaces	Inches	Centimeters	Millimeters	Points	Picas
24	1	.083	.212	2.12	6	.667
1	.042	.0035	.009	.09	.25	.042
288	12	1	2.54	25.4	72	6
113	4.708	.392	1 (.997)	10	28.25	2.3622
11	.458	.038	.1 (.097)	1	2.75	.2362
4	.167	.014	.035	.35	1	.083
48	2	.167	.423	4.23	12	1

In addition to spatial units of measurement, Finale also uses a system of rhythmic or durational measurement. All rhythmic durations (quarter note, eighth note, etc.) can also be expressed in EDUs (ENIGMA Durational Units). Table 1.2 describes the EDU equivalent for each rhythmic duration.

Table 1.2

EDU to Rhythmic Value Equivalents

Rhythmic Value	EDU	Rhythmic Value	EDU	Rhythmic Value	EDU
double whole	8192	quarter	1024	dotted 32nd	192
dotted whole	6144	dotted eighth	768	triplet 16th	171
whole	4096	triplet quarter	683	32nd	128
dotted half	3072	eighth	512	dotted 64th	96
half	2048	dotted sixteenth	384	64th	64
dotted quarter	1536	triplet eighth	341	dotted 128th	48
half note triplet	1365	sixteenth	256	128th	32

Document and Program Options

There are two general types of settings in Finale: document options and program options. Document options are saved with the document and affect only the document you are working on. They are designed for global changes to your music or layout. Click the Options menu and choose Document Options. Here you will be able to set up a variety of document-wide specifications relating to music spacing, beaming, page format, and many others. I will cover many of these document options throughout this book.

Program options affect the general operation of the program and will not have any effect on the music in a document. Click the Options menu and choose Program Options (see Figure 1.7). Here you can customize how Finale behaves based on your own preferences. Following are some helpful program options that are good to know. You can also find more ways to customize the Finale program using the program options in Chapter 13.

Figure 1.7

Make all program-wide settings in the Program Options dialog box.

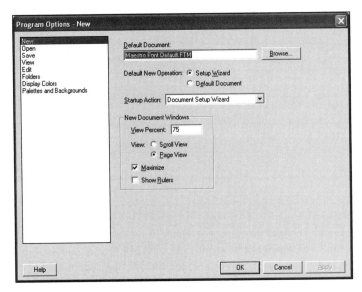

Auto Save

Although you will want to get into the habit of saving often, if you want, you can tell Finale to save your document automatically at regular intervals. This feature adds some insurance in case of a crash, freeze, power outage, etc. In the Program Options dialog box, click the Save option on the left side. Check Auto Save Files(s) and then enter the number of minutes. I like to set this to 10 minutes, but you might prefer to save more or less frequently based on the reliability of your computer and other factors.

After you have activated Auto Save, you should then specify a folder in which to put the files that are saved automatically. Click the Folders section of the Program Options dialog box and find the Auto Save option. Click the Browse or Select button to the right and specify a folder. If you ever need to find your Auto Save files, you can look here to find the path. The files saved by Auto Save are not standard Finale files. On Windows, they will have the extension .ASV. On Macintosh, the word "copy" is appended to the file name. To open them, launch Finale, click the File menu, choose Open, and navigate to the folder you have chosen for Auto Save. In the Open dialog box, be sure to display all file types. Then double-click the Auto Save file to open it.

Make Backups when Saving Files

Each time you save a file, Finale also creates a backup copy of your file. This backup file is the last saved version of the file you were working on (not including auto saves). If you save a file and then find that you have saved undesirable changes, you can rely on your backup file to go back to the previously saved version. Note that you will have only one backup file per Finale file. This file is continually being overwritten with each Save command. Make Backups when Saving Files is turned on by default. If you would like to turn it off, click Save in the left side of the Program Options dialog box and uncheck Make Backups when Saving Files.

If you have Make Backups when Saving Files turned on, you should specify a folder for your backup files. Look in the Folders section of the Program Options dialog box and find the Backup option. Click the Browse or Select button to the right and specify a folder. If you ever need to find your backup files, you can look here to find the path. The backup files you save are not standard Finale files. On Windows, they will have the extension .BAK. On Macintosh, the word "copy" is appended to the file name. To open them, launch Finale, click the File menu, choose Open, and navigate to the folder you have chosen for backup files. In the Open dialog box, be sure to display all file types. Then double-click the backup file to open it.

Startup Action

Finale automatically opens the Launch Window each time you launch Finale. From here you can choose from several ways to begin or open existing documents. To change the behavior of Finale during startup, click New on the left side of the Program Options dialog box, then click the drop-down arrow after Startup Action.

To quickly open the type of new document you have selected for Default New Operation, hold down the Ctrl/Command key and press N to begin either the Setup Wizard or a new default document.

TIP

To set the initial type of view (Scroll/Page View) and the view percentage for any new document, click New in the Program Options dialog box and make your selections.

Your Default Music Folder

By default, each time you choose to save a new file, Finale automatically prompts you to save in the Finale folder. You are also prompted to choose a file from the Finale folder every time you want to open an existing file. If you want to save and open all of your files from a folder other than the Finale folder, select Folders in the Program Options. Click the Browse or Select button to the right of the Music field and select the desired folder. Now, every time you choose Save or Open from the File menu, Finale will automatically take you to the music folder you specified.

Save Preferences at Exit

When this box is checked, any changes you make in the Program Options will also apply after you close and reopen Finale. In most cases, it is advised to leave this box checked. However, if you want the program options to apply only to a single Finale session, uncheck this check box.

Preferences and the Finale.INI File

All of the settings you make in Program Options are saved to a file on your computer. On Mac, this is the "Finale 2005 Preferences" file, which is located in your Users/Library/Preferences folder. If you want to restore your Finale program back to the way it was when you first installed, simply navigate to the Preferences folder and drag the Finale 2005 Preferences file into the Trash.

On Windows, all of your preferences are saved to the Finale.INI file (sometimes it will just say Finale and have a text file icon), which is basically a text file located in your Finale folder. If you want to restore your Finale program back to the way it was when you first installed, navigate to your Finale Folder and delete the Finale.INI.

File Types

Several types of files can be saved from or opened in Finale. Each type is represented with a different icon on your operating system. In addition, in Windows, each individual file type will conclude with its own three-letter extension. You may want to become familiar with these file types and what they are used for. For information on Finale's ability to import files in formats other than the ones described here, see Chapter 13.

Finale Files (.MUS)

Files saved normally from Finale are in Finale Notation File format. Any Finale file can be opened in the version of Finale with which it was created or any newer version. Finale files are not backward compatible, so you won't be able to open a new file in an older version of Finale. However, Finale files will open cross-platform (Windows to Macintosh or Macintosh to Windows). Also, since Finale 2001, the file size has decreased considerably from files saved in earlier versions due to automatic file compression while saving.

 TIP
If you are saving a file on Macintosh that you intend to open on Windows, be sure that the .MUS extension appears at the end of the file name. This allows Windows to associate the file with Finale. In the Save As dialog box, make sure Append File Extensions is checked. In versions of Finale before version 2002, simply type .MUS at the end of the file name.

TIP

If you want to share a Finale file with someone who does not have a version of Finale as current as yours, have them download Finale NotePad from www.makemusic.com. NotePad is a free, simplified notation program that can open any Finale file because it is based on the newest Finale version. You will be able to play files, make minor edits, transpose, save, start new files, and even print using this software. Oh, and did I mention, it's free!

Enigma Transportable Files (.ETF)

This type of file was originally designed for opening files across platforms (from Macintosh to Windows and vice versa). In current versions of Finale, it is no longer necessary to save ETF files for the purpose of cross-platform file sharing. ETF files are much larger in size than Finale binary files because they are not compressed. They are basically Finale documents in the form of a text file, so they are somewhat less prone to corruption if sent as an e-mail attachment. If you plan on e-mailing your files to friends, I recommend using WinZip (Windows) or Stuffit (Mac) to compress a Coda Notation file (.MUS) to guard against file corruption as opposed to saving an ETF, though sending a zipped or stuffed ETF is another option to try if all else fails. To save a file in ETF format, click the File menu and choose Save As. For Files of Type, choose ENIGMA Transportable File, then enter a file name and click Save.

NOTE:

In Finale, the acronym "ENIGMA" stands for Environment for Notation utilizing Intelligent Graphic Music Algorithms (in case you were wondering).

Template Files (.FTM)

Finale comes with about 50 template files, each containing a default setup for certain types of projects. For instance, if you want to start a piece for concert band, you can save time by opening the Full Concert Band template file that contains a blank concert band score. These pre-set documents are located in the Templates folder (within the Finale folder). On Windows, these files have the extension FTM. Template files are handled differently on Windows than on Macintosh. On Windows, template files are different than regular Coda Notation files. They always open as Untitled documents in Finale, so you will not be prompted to overwrite them when you save. In this way, the original template file is preserved. On Macintosh, a template file is the same kind of file as a Coda Notation file, but can be opened as an Untitled document by choosing New > Document from Template from the File menu. On Macintosh, any file can be opened as an Untitled document by using the Document from Template command. In these ways, template files can be used over and over again.

On Windows, to save your own template, click the File menu and choose Save As. For Files of Type, choose Coda Template file, then enter a file name and click Save. On Mac, choose Save As, give your template a name and save your template in the Coda Notation File format. Then, choose File > New > Document from Template to open it.

MIDI Files (.MID)

Files in MIDI format are basically standard music files that are transferable among almost all music software. They are very small in size and will open cross-platform. In the context of Finale, they are generally a representation of the playback. When you save a MIDI file from Finale, only the playback information will be retained in the file. When you open a MIDI file in Finale, you will see a translation of the playback information in the form of notation, but all information (page formatting, text, etc.) will be lost. See Chapter 15 for more information on saving and opening MIDI files in Finale.

TIP

On Windows, you might want to associate .ETF, .FTM, or maybe even .MID files with Finale. Once Finale is associated to a file type, any time you double-click the file's icon it will open in Finale automatically (typically, *.ETF and *.FTM are automatically assigned to Finale when you install). To do this, open Windows Explorer (double-click the My Computer icon on your desktop) and find a file type you would like to associate with Finale. Then right-click the file icon. In the context menu, choose Open With. When you see a list of applications, choose Finale and click OK. Now you can open that file type simply by double-clicking it while working in Windows.

Library Files (.LIB)

Virtually all elements of a document you can define yourself, such as articulations, expressions, shapes, and many others, are organized into libraries. When you open a new default document, Finale offers a collection of default libraries that contain common markings that you can access from various places in Finale. When you select an articulation from the Articulation Selection dialog box, for example, you are choosing a character that exists in the document's Articulation library. When you define a new articulation, Finale saves the new articulation in the document's Articulation library so it will always be available while working with the document. You can use libraries to transfer elements you have defined in one document to any other document. Throughout this book, you will learn how to do this for a wide variety of items.

Lesson Files (.LSN)

Lesson files are groups of exercises and an ensemble of instruments. You can save and open .LSN files within Finale's Exercise Wizard. See Chapter 13 for more information on creating custom technique building exercises.

SmartMusic Accompaniment Files (.SMP)

You can save full featured SmartMusic accompaniments with Finale. SmartMusic is another software program developed by MakeMusic! that features intelligent accompaniment, which listens to your performance and follows spontaneous tempo changes as you play your wind instrument or sing. To save a SmartMusic accompaniment, choose the File menu, Save as Special, and then Save as SmartMusic Accompaniment. There will be more information on saving SmartMusic accompaniments in Chapter 15.

Finale Performance Assessment Files (.FPA)

Finale Performance Assessment, which was introduced in Finale 2005, is a free application, installed with Finale, that listens to a live performance played into a computer microphone (or with a MIDI keyboard) and assesses its accuracy by comparing it to the notated solo line. This solo notation is created in Finale and saved in .FPA format. You can open an .FPA file and edit it in Finale, but you must open it from within Finale by choosing File > Open (if you double-click the file, the Finale Performance Assessment application will launch and open the file).

NOTE:

You can also download Finale Performance Assessment for free at www.finalemusic.com.

2

BEGINNING
A NEW SCORE

Now that you have a feel for how Finale works, it's time to move ahead into the first step for any project, starting a new document. There are several ways to begin your score in Finale. The one you choose will depend on the type of project and how much customization you want control over from the start. Do you want to add and define your staves manually or have Finale do it for you? In most cases, the Document Setup Wizard will suit your needs just fine, though you might also find one of the existing templates ideal for your project. If you want more control over your score from the start, you could use Finale's default document or a document without libraries. In this chapter, you will learn how to decide which method to use for the type of project you want to start as well as other helpful tips that apply to almost any new document.

Here's a summary of what you will learn in this chapter:

- ❋ How to start a score with the Document Setup Wizard
- ❋ How to customize your staves
- ❋ How to enter and modify text (title, page number, copyright)
- ❋ The fundamentals of working with the Mass Edit Tool
- ❋ The basics of page layout

Opening a New Document

When you first start Finale, the Launch Window appears on your screen as shown in Figure 2.1. This window provides easy access to the common methods for starting new documents and opening existing ones. While working in Finale, to open the Launch Window at any time, press Ctrl-Shift-N on Windows, or Command-Shift-N on Mac (or choose Launch Window from the File menu). From here, you can do anything from acquiring a file from your scanner to opening a MIDI file. Whenever you start working, you'll probably get your document up fastest with the Launch Window (if only by a mouse click or two, but every bit counts).

For most projects, I recommend starting with the Document Setup Wizard. You will find this method the easiest for defining all elements critical to a new score, including title, instrument(s), key signature, time signature, and tempo.

Figure 2.1

Use the Launch Window to begin new or open existing documents

Starting a Score with the Document Setup Wizard

To start the Setup Wizard, click Setup Wizard in the Launch Window (or click the File menu, choose New, and then Document With Setup Wizard). You can also hold down the Ctrl/Command key and press N to begin the Setup Wizard. Let's start the Setup Wizard now. If you haven't changed any of your program options, simply launch Finale and, in the Launch Window, click Setup Wizard. If you already have Finale open, hold down Ctrl/Command and press N.

Page 1: Title, Composer, Copyright, and Page Size

Any time you start the Setup Wizard you will see this page (see Figure 2.2). Here, enter the title, composer, and copyright of your piece. To move between fields, you can either click on them or press the Tab key.

Figure 2.2

On page 1 of the Setup Wizard, enter the title, composer, copyright, and page size

If you haven't thought of a title yet, don't worry, you can leave any of these fields blank if you like. In the Copyright field, you may want to enter a copyright symbol (©). To do this on Windows, hold down the Alt key and type 0169 on the numeric keypad (with Num Lock on). On Macintosh, hold down the Option key and press the letter G. When you are ready to move ahead, click the Next button.

Page 2: Choose Your Parts

Now choose the instruments you want in your piece. In the left column, choose the instrument family, then double-click the instrument you want to add in the second column. You will see the instrument appear in the third column in orchestral score order regardless of the order in which you choose them (see Figure 2.3). Each instrument you add will become one staff in your Finale score (except in the case of keyboard instruments), so if you want four trumpet staves, add four trumpets.

Figure 2.3
On page 2 of the Setup Wizard, add the parts

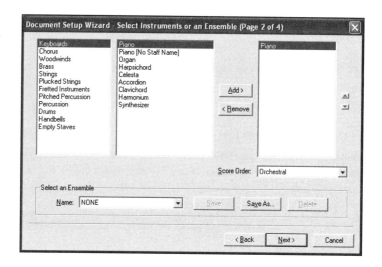

To change the order of your instruments, click the Score Order drop-down arrow beneath the third column and choose from the available options. To change the order of your instruments manually, highlight the instrument you would like to move (in the third column), then click the up or down arrows on the right to change their positioning. Double-click any instrument in the third column to remove it. Finale will automatically group staves of similar instrumental sections (with group brackets) in the score upon completing the Setup Wizard. Finale will even number like instruments incrementally, so you need not worry about adding a 1, 2, 3, or 4 to the trumpet names, for example. When you have chosen all of your instruments and placed them in the order you like, click the Next button to continue to the next page. You can click the Back button at any time to make any changes to the previous page. The Setup Wizard will retain all of your settings.

If you find yourself using the same group of instruments regularly, save an ensemble. On page 2 of the Setup Wizard, add the desired instruments, and then click Save As. Enter a name for your ensemble and click OK. Now, you can choose this ensemble anytime you reach page 2 of the Setup Wizard. Finale saves this info to the ensembles.txt file in the Finale/Component files folder (so if that file gets deleted or moved, you'll lose your ensemble).

Page 3: Specify Key and Time Signatures

On page 3 of the Setup Wizard, you can specify the key and time signatures of your piece (see Figure 2.4).

Figure 2.4

On page 3 of the Setup Wizard, choose the time signature and key signature

To select a key signature, click the up or down arrow of the vertical scroll bar to the right of the key signature display in the lower portion of this dialog box. Clicking the up arrow will add a sharp to your key signature (or take away a flat) and clicking the down arrow will add a flat to your key signature (or take away a sharp). Then choose Major or Minor from the drop-down menu to the right of the key signature display. Don't worry about instrument transposition here, just select the concert key of your piece.

To select a time signature, click one of the available time signature buttons in the upper portion. If the time signature you want to use is not available, click the far-right button (with the question marks) to specify a custom key signature. You will see the dialog box shown in Figure 2.5.

Figure 2.5

In the Time Signature dialog box, specify a meter for your piece

For Number of Beats, click the left or right arrow to increase or decrease the number of beats per measure in your time signature. For Beat Duration, click the left or right arrow to increase or decrease the rhythmic value of each beat. Click OK to choose your custom time signature. You will find information on more advanced time signature options in Chapter 5.

Once you have chosen a key and time signature, click the Next button to continue.

Page 4: Define Tempo Marking, Pickup, and Music Font

Finalize your customized score on page 4 by specifying an initial tempo marking, pickup measure, and default music font for your score (see Figure 2.6).

Figure 2.6

On page 4 of the Setup Wizard, specify a tempo marking, pickup measure, and music font

If you have a specific tempo marking in mind, check Specify Initial Tempo Marking, then enter the number of quarter note beats per minute in the entry field below, after "Tempo." In the text field, you can enter "Allegro," "Largo," or another tempo indication. If you would like to specify a different rhythmic value for your tempo indication, click the quarter note and choose a different note value from the drop-down menu (see Figure 2.7).

Figure 2.7

Choose the duration of the pickup measure from the drop-down menu

If you would like a pickup measure before the first measure of your piece, check Specify Pickup Measure. Then choose the value of your pickup measure from one of the boxes to the right.

Finally, you may want to change the general appearance of your music. Finale allows you to choose between two default music fonts. In the preview window, you currently see a representation of the standard Maestro font. If you would like your music to appear as though it was handwritten, you may want to use the Jazz font. Under Default Music Font, click the Jazz radio button to see a representation of the Jazz font in the preview window. Once you have selected the default music font, click Finish. Finale will open a document using all of the information you provided in the Setup Wizard.

New Default Document

You can begin a new, basic, single-staff document by choosing Default Document in the Launch Window (or by choosing File > New > Default Document). This will open a treble clef staff in the key of C, and in common time. This might be an attractive option for a lead sheet or solo document. Or if you are composing and haven't yet figured out what kind of instrument or key you might be using, a new default document might be the way to go.

TIP

If you find yourself making the same changes to the default document every time you open it, customize it to save yourself time. From the File Menu, choose New > Default Document, make your changes, and then choose Save As from the File menu. Name the file "Maestro Font Default.FTM" (on Mac, just "Maestro Font Default"), then save the file to your Finale folder and replace the existing default file. Now these settings will apply any time you open a new default document.

Document from Template

As mentioned in Chapter 1, Finale comes with over 30 pre-set templates you can use to get a head-start while starting a new project. If the score you are working on has a common instrumentation (brass quintet, piano grand staff, etc.) try starting with a template. Click Templates in the Launch Window (or click File > New > Document from Template). Then browse through the folders to see the available options.

Document without Libraries

If you want to start a completely empty document without any presets or libraries, click File > New > Document Without Libraries. (They don't let us choose this option from the Launch Window). You will see a document with a single measure and no text at all (brings back fond memories of Finale 2.0). You will also find that there are no articulations or expressions to choose from. Use this option to start a document only if you feel comfortable setting up your score and loading all libraries from scratch. For information on loading articulation and expression libraries, see Chapter 3.

Exercise Wizard

This feature was built specifically to allow music educators to create customized, technique-building exercises quickly and easily for a rehearsal warm-up (for example). The Exercise Wizard will ask you to choose from a variety of scales, twisters, keys, and articulations for each exercise. Then, you can print the exercise (or number of exercises) for any ensemble while Finale takes care of the transposition and articulation placement. The whole process takes about 10 minutes or so (depending on the speed of your printer) and can be a great utility for any conductor in an educational setting. You can find more specific information on creating exercises with the Exercise Wizard in Chapter 13.

Other New Document Types

The Launch Window brings to light a few more options worth mentioning. Here's a quick breakdown. Click Scanning to acquire a file from your scanner using Finale's TWAIN support (new to 2005). Your scanner software is configured to the optimum settings for Finale Import. You'll learn more about scanning and importing sheet music in Chapter 13. (TWAIN support is expected be available for Macintosh in a maintenance release).

The FPA Wizard is there to help you create a Finale Performance Assessment file. FPA is an application installed with Finale 2005 that assesses a performance by comparing it to its corresponding notation. You create the solo for assessment in Finale. FPA is a stepchild of SmartMusic (intelligent accompaniment software, which is also developed by MakeMusic!), and both products use the same advanced pitch-recognition technology to hear everything you play into your computer's microphone. Speaking of SmartMusic, notice the SmartMusic Wizard option in the Launch Window. You can start creating a new SmartMusic Accompaniment or SmartMusic Assessment file by clicking this button. You'll learn more about FPA and SmartMusic in Chapter 15.

TIP

If you have the original sheet music, don't import a MIDIScan (.MND) file. Generally speaking, this Finale feature is practically useless. Use Finale's Acquire feature to scan the page(s), and import the file with Finale's new (much better) SmartScore Lite utility.

To open an existing file, choose one of the three options on the right: Open or Open Recent File to work on an existing Finale file, or Import to convert a file of one of the formats listed to a Finale file.

Customize Your Document

Regardless of the method you used to begin your document, you may find that you want to change your key signature, time signature, or other element. The following section covers how to safely change these settings at any point while working on your score, as well as other techniques you should know for any document.

Add, Remove, or Insert Measures

After opening a new document with the Setup Wizard or a default document, you will have 31 measures. Your piece will probably be either longer or shorter than this. To add a measure to the end of your score at any time, simply double-click the Measure Tool. To add a specific number of measures, click the Measure Tool and then click the Measure menu and choose Add (or Ctrl/Option-click the Measure Tool). You will see the Add Measures dialog box (Figure 2.8). Enter the number of measures you would like to add here and click OK. The number of measures you specify will be added to the end of your score.

Figure 2.8

Enter the number of measures
you would like to add to the
end of the score in the Add
Measures dialog box

There are a couple ways to delete measures. With the Measure Tool selected, highlight the measures you want to delete and press the Delete key. You can also delete measures using the Mass Edit Tool. Click the Mass Edit Tool, highlight the measures you want to delete, and then press the Delete key on your keyboard. I'll cover more Mass Edit options, such as clearing or copying measures, at the end of this chapter.

To insert new measures at the beginning or in the middle of your score, click the Measure Tool and click a measure to highlight it. From the Measure menu, choose Insert. Type the number of measures and click OK. The number of measures you specify will appear, inserted to the left of the highlighted measure.

Changing the Key Signature

To change the opening key signature, click the Key Signature Tool. Double-click the first measure of your score to open the Key Signature dialog box. Use the scroll bars to specify the number of sharps or flats in the key signature and click OK. This will change the key signature at measure one for all staves proportionally. In other words, Finale will consider transposing staves and assign the appropriate key signature to each staff. I'll soon explain how to change the instrument transposition of a staff.

TIP
To change the staff attributes for all of your staves at once, use the Global Staff Attributes plug-in. Click the Plug-ins menu and choose Scoring and Arranging, and then Global Staff Attributes. Now make any settings that you want to apply to all your staves and click OK.

Changing or Hiding the Time Signature

To change the time signature of your piece, click the Time Signature Tool. Right/Control-click a measure to display the time signature context menu. Choose a new time signature from this list to change the meter.

To specify a time signature that doesn't appear in the context menu, double-click the first measure of your piece. This opens the Time Signature dialog box. For Number of Beats, click the left or right arrow to increase or decrease the number of beats per measure in your time signature. For Beat Duration, click the left or right arrow to increase or decrease the rhythmic value of each beat. Click OK to return to your score and see the new time signature. You will find information on more advanced time signature options in Chapter 5.

To hide the time signature completely for the entire staff, click the Staff Tool and double-click a measure in a staff. The Staff Attributes dialog box opens. In the Items to Display section, uncheck Time Signature. Click OK to return to your score. Do this for any other staves as necessary.

Changing or Entering a Staff Name

After you have created a document with the Setup Wizard, you will notice a staff name to the left of each of your staves. To change this name, or to enter a new one, click the Staff Tool and double-click the staff to open the Staff Attributes dialog box. To change the full staff name, click the Edit button to the right of Full Staff Name. The Edit Text dialog box opens. Change or delete the staff name here. Click OK to return to the Staff Attributes. To change the abbreviated staff name (the one that appears at the beginning of all subsequent systems), click the Edit button to the right of Abbr. Staff Name. The Edit Text dialog box opens. Change or delete abbreviated staff names here. Click OK to return to the Staff Attributes, then click OK to return to your score.

To enter a sharp, flat, or other accidental character in the staff name, use a text insert. While in the Edit Text dialog box, move the cursor to the place you want to enter the accidental. Then, from the Text menu, choose Inserts > Sharp, Flat, or Natural.

Configuring a Staff for a Transposing Instrument

Since not all instruments are in the key of C, Finale allows you to set up staves for transposing instruments, such as a Bb Clarinet or an Eb Alto Sax. If you used the Document Setup Wizard to start your score, then all of the staff transpositions are already defined for you, but if you started your score from a New Default Document, then you will have to set up the staff transpositions for the appropriate staves. To specify a transposition for a staff, click the Staff Tool and double-click the staff. Click the Select button to the right of Transposition. To the right of Key Signature, click the drop-down arrow and choose the pitch of the transposing instrument. Click OK twice to return to your score. Now, any notes in your staff will display according to the transposition you chose.

After specifying a transposition for a staff, Finale automatically calculates the appropriate key signature based on the concert key. For instance, if the concert key signature of your piece is C major, any staff set to a French horn transposition (up a perfect fifth, add one sharp), will automatically display in the key of G (one sharp), and the pitches will be displayed up a perfect fifth. Note that the Staff Transposition affects only the displayed pitches of the music and never the sounding pitches. Finale will always play back any notes in a transposed staff in concert pitch. In the case of a French horn, the sounding notes are a perfect fifth down from the written pitch, as it would sound if played by a French horn. To view all of your staves back in concert pitch, check Display in Concert Pitch from the Options menu. For information on regional staff transpositions (e.g., instrument doubling, etc.) see "Staff Styles" in Chapter 8.

Changing the Clef

You can change the opening clef of any staff with the Staff Tool. Click the Staff Tool and double-click a staff to open the Staff Attributes dialog box. In the upper-left portion, click the Select button to the left of the clef display. You can now choose one of the 18 clefs. Click OK twice to return to your score and see the new clef. For information on adding a clef change within a staff, see Chapter 5.

Changing the Tempo Marking

Instead of editing an existing tempo marking in your score, you will find it easier to simply delete it and create a new one. To delete a tempo marking, click the Selection Tool, click on the tempo marking and press the Delete key.

CHAPTER 2

To enter a new tempo marking, click the Mass Edit Tool. Highlight the first measure, click the Plug-ins menu and choose Expressions > Create Tempo Marking. This will open the Create Tempo Marking dialog box as seen in Figure 2.9.

Figure 2.9

You can use the Create Tempo Marking plug-in to specify a tempo marking to place in the score.

Now choose the rhythmic duration and type a value for the desired number of beats per minute. If you want your piece to play back at the specified tempo, check Define Expression for Playback. Click OK to return to your score. You should notice the tempo marking above the first measure.

If you have multiple staves in your score, you will see the tempo marking above all of your staves. To set the tempo marking to show on the top staff only, do this:

1. Click the Expression Tool.
2. Right/Ctrl-click one of the tempo marking handles to bring up a context menu.
3. Choose Edit Measure Expression Assignment.
4. In the Show On section choose Staff List and click the Edit button.
5. Click OK twice to return to your score.

You should now see your tempo marking above the first measure on the top staff only.

NOTE

Although the plug-in simplifies creating a tempo marking, it's almost as easy to just create the expression manually. In Finale 2004, a new expression design was introduced that allows for more than one font in the same expression. Before that, creating tempo markings wasn't easy, and we still have the plug-in to prove it! You'll learn more about defining expressions for playback in Chapter 3.

Adding or Removing a Pickup Measure

To add a pickup measure to your score, click the Options menu and choose Pickup Measure. You should now see the Pickup Measure dialog box (see Figure 2.10).

Click the box representing the duration of your pickup measure, and then click OK to return to your score. Now, Finale will treat the first measure of your score as a pickup measure of the values specified. Measure number one will be redefined to the measure after the pickup.

Figure 2.10

Define a pickup in the Pickup Measure dialog box

Showing or Hiding Measure Numbers

By default, Finale will display measure numbers at the beginning of each system. To show measure numbers on each measure, first click the Measure Tool, and then click Measure > Measure Numbers > Edit Regions (or Right/Ctrl-click the Measure Tool and choose Edit Measure Number Region). The Measure Number dialog box will appear. In the Positioning & Display section, choose Show Every. Then, in the fields to the right, enter "1" and "1" to tell Finale to show measure numbers every measure starting with measure one. Click OK to return to your score. You can now click and drag the measure number handles to position them, or click a handle and press the Delete key to delete it.

To hide all measure numbers on a staff, click the Staff Tool and double-click the staff. The Staff Attributes dialog box opens. In the Items to Display section, uncheck Measure Numbers and click OK. You will find more information on changing the font, style, and enclosure of measure numbers, as well as how to program several measure number regions, in Chapter 11.

Define a Staff for Playback with the Instrument List

If you changed the name and transposition of a staff, you may also want to change the playback instrument. To change the instrument of any staff for playback, click the Window menu and choose Instrument List. The Instrument List dialog box will appear on your screen.

Figure 2.11

Use the Instrument List to assign playback sounds to staves

Now, under the Instrument column, click the drop-down arrow in the row of the staff you want to change. In this drop-down menu, choose the new instrument for your staff.

If the instrument you want to use is not there, choose New Instrument (at the top of the drop-down menu). This will open the Instrument Definition dialog box. Name your new instrument, choose an unused channel (a channel that is not being used for any other staff or instrument), and then click the drop-down arrow to the right of General MIDI and choose the instrument sound you want to use. Click OK, and then close out of the Instrument List to return to your score. Repeat this process for any other staves as needed.

For more information on configuring a staff for playback using a non-General MIDI instrument, such as an external sound module, see Chapter 14.

TIP

For more control over playback, Windows users can try the JW Playback plug-in. With this plug-in, you can easily define any number of staves, groups, or measures for playback. Also, see Chapter 14 for more playback techniques you can use to review your score.

Enter and Modify Text (Title, Composer, Copyright)

When you open a new score, by default you will see three text blocks on your page: title, composer, and copyright. These items are *page-assigned text blocks,* and their placement will remain fixed according to the page margins (or page edge). In other words, as you edit and move measures around, these items will stay in the same place on the page. Page-attached text will always appear green on your screen by default. The use of page-assigned text blocks should generally be restricted to text that has nothing to do with the performance of the music. This includes the title, composer, copyright, and page numbers. For this section, you will need the Text Tool selected throughout.

Entering Text Blocks

The best way to enter or modify the title, composer, or copyright text of any piece is to use the File Info dialog box (Figure 2.12). To get there, click the File menu and choose File Info.

Figure 2.12

Store the title, composer, description, and other information about the document in the File Info dialog box

File Info	
Title	The Worms Don't Hear
Composer	Scott Yoho
Copyright	©1999
Description	The Auto Body Experience: A Tribute to Carhenge

	Initials	Date	Application
Created		4/11/2002	Finale 2003.a8 for Windows
Modified		---	Unknown

OK   Cancel   Statistics...   Help

Enter a new title, composer, and copyright in this dialog box, then click OK. You will probably see the new text already appear in your score in the appropriate place. If not, double-click where you want to place the title. A dashed box will appear on your score. From the Text menu, click Inserts > Title. Now the title appears in the specified location. You can also insert any of the other File Info this way by choosing Composer, Copyright, etc., from the Inserts submenu.

To enter any page-assigned text directly into the score, first make sure you are in Page View (select Page View from the View menu). Then, click the Text Tool and double-click in the score. You will see a dashed box enclosing a cursor. Type your text here. The box will expand as you type. Then, click anywhere in the score when you are finished typing to remove the dashed editing frame.

Text blocks can also be assigned to a specific measure. If your measure layout changes, the text block will move with its assigned measure. Any text block entered while working in Scroll View will automatically be measure-assigned. Measure-assigned text blocks are always red by default. In general, if you want to assign text consisting of only a single word, or just a couple of words, to a measure, you will probably want to use a measure-attached expression instead of a measure-assigned text block. You can find more information on measure-attached expressions in Chapters 3 and 7.

If you want to enter a measure-assigned text block in Page View, first click anywhere in the score so none of the text block handles are selected. Then click the Text menu and choose Assign to Measure. Now any text you enter will be measure-assigned. To revert back to entering page-assigned text, make sure no handle is selected and choose Assign to Page from the Text menu. Page-assigned text can be entered only in Page View.

Editing a Text Block

You can easily reposition or delete any text block. To move text, click the Text Tool, and then click the text block's handle. Drag it anywhere on the page or use the arrow keys to nudge it for fine adjustments. To delete it, click the text block handle and press the Delete key. Remember, you can use the Selection Tool to select any item, move it, edit it, or delete it.

Changing the Font, Size, or Style

To change the font, size, or style, click a text block handle. Click the Text menu and choose Font. This opens the Font dialog box. Select a new font, size, or style for the text block here. Click OK to return to your score.

Alignment and Positioning

If simply dragging text into place isn't precise enough, you can specify the exact location of any text block relative to the page margin, page edge, or assigned measure. Right-click (on Mac, Control-click) the title, for instance, and choose Edit Frame Attributes. This will open the Frame Attributes dialog box (see Figure 2.13).

In this box, specify the placement of the text block. On the left side of the Alignment and Positioning section, choose the general location of the chosen text block from the drop-down menus. For instance, for the title, you would probably choose Center for horizontal and Top (header) for vertical. Then, you can fine-tune the placement in the H: (horizontal) and V: (vertical) fields to the right. These values indicate any adjustment from your settings in the left side of this section. In this case, to move the title a half inch below the top page margin, enter "-.5" in the V: field. Click OK to return to your score and review the placement. Use this method to position any page-assigned text block.

Figure 2.13

Use the Frame Attributes dialog box for precise positioning of text blocks

You can also adjust the positioning of measure-assigned text blocks in the Frame Attributes dialog box. Right-click the handle on a measure-assigned text block and choose Edit Frame. Now, use the H: and V: fields to specify the distance from the beginning of the measure in the H: field and the distance above or below the top staff line in the V: field. The beginning of a measure in this case relates to the left barline, or just after a displayed key or time signature. Click OK to return to your score and review the placement.

Page Numbers

If you started your document with the Setup Wizard, Default Document, or a template, there will already be page numbers at the top of each page starting with page 2. To enter new page numbers into your score, double-click where you would like to place the page number. Then, from the Text menu, choose Inserts > Page Numbers (or press Ctrl/Command-Shift-P). You can specify the positioning of your page numbers exactly like page-assigned text blocks (as described above).

Left and Right Pages

You may want to place your page numbers on alternating sides of each page if you intend your music to end up on left and right pages of a book for instance. If you are already using the Maestro Font default file, this is already set up for you. Otherwise, to do this, first move into Page View (select Page View from the View menu), and then follow these steps:

1. Right/Control-click the handle on a page number and click Frame Attributes.

2. In the Alignment and Positioning section, choose Left for horizontal and Top for vertical.

3. In the Attach To section, after Page, choose Left Pages.

4. Enter a Page Range in the field to the right. For example "2 through 0," where "0" indicates the end of the piece (odd page numbers are always right pages and even numbers are always left pages).

5. Click OK to return to your score. Now you will see page numbers for every other page. Next, number the remaining pages.

6. Move to a right page (page without a page number).

7. Double-click anywhere on the page to open a new text block.

8. From the Text menu, choose Inserts > Page Numbers (or press Ctrl/Command-Shift-P). A page number will appear in the score.

9. Right/Control-click the handle on the page number and click Frame Attributes.

10. In the Alignment and Positioning section, choose Right for horizontal and Top for vertical.

11. In the Attach To section, after Page, choose Right Pages.

12. Enter a Page Range in the field to the right. For instance, "2 through 0," so the first page will not be numbered.

13. Click OK to return to your score.

Other Text Tool Tricks

In this section I have covered the very basics of the Text Tool. There are many other ways to modify text blocks. You can change the tracking, line spacing, baseline, and several other parameters. Many of these other features resemble functionality you may have seen before in word-processing programs. To maintain focus on music notation (and avoid redundancy with the User Manual) I won't go into every one of these features here. There may, however, be a few Text Tool tricks you might want to know about.

Entering Musical Symbols (Sharp, Flat, etc.) in a Text Block

To enter accidentals in a text block, move the cursor to the desired location within a text block. Then click the Text menu and open the Inserts submenu. Choose one of the accidentals in this submenu. The accidental will appear in your score.

If you want to add other music characters, such as rhythmic durations, you can change the font of a portion of your text block. Highlight a region of a text block, then click the Text menu and choose Font. Choose one of the music fonts (Maestro, Petrucci, etc.) and click OK. The characters will change to their corresponding music symbol. You will find a chart showing the keystrokes for all characters for every Finale music font under the Help menu (on Windows, refer to the User Manual submenu of the Help menu). For more control over editing text, you might consider using Finale's built-in text editor.

Finale's Text Editor

If you want to create a large amount of text, or perform more advanced tasks like mixing fonts within a text block, use Finale's text editor. Click the Text menu and choose Edit Text. You can use this window to enter a large amount of text at once. Use the Text menu in this window to change the font, size, style, or any other attribute of a highlighted region of text.

You can also view any text block in your score using the up and down arrows. Click the up arrow next to ID to view the next text block. This can be particularly helpful while editing large scores with many pages and/or lots of text.

Displaying a Text Block Only On Screen

If you want a text block to display on your screen but not in the printout, choose a text block by clicking its handle. Then, click the Text menu and choose Show Only On Screen. Now the text block will not appear when the document is printed.

TIP
In large documents, you may want to search and change every occurrence of a text block or other text (expression, staff name, etc.). To do this, use the Text Search and Replace Plug-in included with Finale 2005. From the Plug-ins menu choose Miscellaneous > Text Search and Replace.

Introduction to the Mass Edit Tool

Formally known as the Mass Mover Tool, the Mass Edit Tool is fundamental to working with Finale efficiently. This workhorse eliminates a great deal of redundancy, offering many powerful editing features that can be applied to any portion of your score. You will use this tool to copy music, transpose, move measures around, change beaming, tweak music spacing, and perform a variety of other tasks. For now, I'll cover the most common uses of the Mass Edit Tool and how to use it most effectively. You will find more information on applying advanced Mass Mover operations in Chapter 9. Click the Mass Edit Tool now. For this section, I'll assume that you already have the Mass Edit Tool selected.

Selecting Regions

The first step to editing with the Mass Edit Tool is selecting a region of music. First, click the Edit menu and make sure Select Partial Measures is not checked. Now click the first measure in your score. It should become highlighted, indicating it is selected. Click above measure one and drag below measure two (you'll see a dashed box appear). Release the mouse button and measures one and two will be selected. Click and drag over any region of your score to easily select multiple measures. Now, let's say you want to select measures one through five. Hold down the Shift key and click measure five. Notice the first five measures are highlighted. (This method is useful if your highlighted region needs to spans over more than one page, for example.) Hold down the Shift key and press the right arrow key. Now the selected area extends to the end of the piece. You can also use the left arrow to highlight any region to the beginning of the piece. Click anywhere outside the highlighted area to clear the selection. Hold down Ctrl/Command and press A to select the entire document (or choose Select All from the Edit menu).

TIP
At any point while working in the Mass Edit Tool, right-click (Windows)/Command-Option (Macintosh) and drag to move the viewable area of the page.

Selecting Partial Measures

You may want to edit or copy a portion of a measure, or a region that doesn't begin and end on a barline. To do this, click the Edit menu and check Select Partial Measures (the menu item should now have a checkmark next to it). Click and drag over the first half of the first measure to highlight the beginning of the measure. When there are notes or rests in a staff, you will be able to highlight any region starting with even the smallest subdivision. Double-click a measure to quickly highlight the entire measure. Also, with a partial measure selected, hold down Shift and press the right arrow to select to the end of the measure, or the left arrow to select to the beginning of the measure. Press the left or right arrow again to select to the end or beginning of the piece.

The Select Regions Dialog Box

For more control over selection, you may want to specify the exact beat or EDU to start and end your region (remember, EDUs are Finale's unit of rhythmic duration—there are 1024 EDUs in a quarter note, 512 in an eighth note, etc.). To do this, choose Select Region from the Edit menu. This will open the Select Region dialog box (see Figure 2.14).

Figure 2.14
Use the Select Region dialog box for precision in selecting a region of measures

In this dialog box, choose the beginning and end of your region down to the precise subdivision. Leave the check box empty if you want to select from the beginning of the specified measure. Click OK to return to your score with the region selected.

Copy and Clear Music

Of course, one of the great beauties of music notation with a computer is the ability to copy large sections of music from one place to another. In Finale, this is quite simple to do. Let's start by entering a few notes in the first measure of your document. Click the Simple Entry Tool, then click the Quarter Note Tool in the Simple Entry Palette and click four quarter notes on any pitch in the first measure. Now, select the Mass Edit Tool. Click the Edit menu and uncheck Select Partial Measures (if it is checked). Click the first measure so it is highlighted. Now, click on the highlighted area and drag to measure two. When you see a black border surrounding measure two, release the mouse button. You should now see the Copy Measures dialog box (Figure 2.15). For now, just click OK, and you will see your music copied to measure two.

Figure 2.15
Choose the number of times to copy a selected region in the Copy Measures dialog box

Now, say you want the same one-bar pattern throughout the first ten measures. Click and drag around the first two measures so they are highlighted. Now, click on the highlighted area and drag to the right so measures three and four are surrounded with a black border. Release the mouse button. Now, for How Many Times?, enter 4 and click OK. You should now see the two measures copied four times, filling the first ten measures of your staff.

CHAPTER 2

You may need to copy music to a location that is not visible on the screen. This makes drag-copying impossible. To copy a section of music to any measure in your score, first highlight the section you wish to copy. Use the scroll bars at the bottom and right side of your screen so that the destination measure is showing. On Windows, hold down Ctrl and Shift, and click in the destination measure. On Mac, hold down Option and Shift, and click the destination measure. Choose the number of times and click OK. Try this in the document you have been working on. Highlight a measure of music, then Ctrl·Shift/Option·Shift and click on any empty measure.

You may want to remove the original music as you copy it to a new location. To do this, highlight a measure or any region containing music. Hold down the Ctrl/Command key and press X (or choose Cut from the Edit menu). On Windows, this will open the Cut Measures dialog box as seen in Figure 2.16. On Macintosh, you will see a dialog box with identical functionality.

Figure 2.16

Choose whether to delete or clear the selected region in the Cut Measures dialog box

Leave Clear the Selected Measures, Replacing their Contents with Rests selected and click OK. On Macintosh, click Clear. The measure should now be filled with a whole rest. Highlight an empty measure. Hold down the Ctrl/Command key and press V (or choose Replace Entries from the Edit menu). The music will appear in the highlighted measure. To completely delete the original measure while copying, follow these same steps, but choose Delete the Selected Measures and Measure Contents for All Staves in the Score in the Cut Measures dialog box.

If you want to insert music between two measures, without replacing any entries, click the Mass Edit menu and choose Copy and Insert. In doing so, this will actually add measures to your document, inserted before the selected region. Now simply highlight a region and drag-copy it into place. The original music will shift to the right of the inserted music. If you Cut the original music, highlight the destination measure and choose Insert from the Edit menu.

Clear any highlighted region of note or rest entries by pressing the Backspace key on Windows, or the Clear key on Macintosh. To completely delete a measure (for example, to remove extra measures at the end of a score), highlight the measures and press the Delete key.

Introduction to Page Layout

In general, most Finale users agree that page layout should be the last stage in editing a score before printout. There are, however, a few basic principles you should be aware of as you continue to develop a working knowledge of Finale. These concepts should be adequate for finalizing small projects, particularly single staff documents such as lead sheets. I'll cover more advanced page layout topics in Chapter 11.

Page Layout Icons and Margins

Whenever the Page Layout Tool is chosen you will see system margins, page margins, and perhaps Page Layout icons appearing on your page (see Figure 2.17).

Figure 2.17

Refer to Page Layout icons and margins for layout information

If you have entered music into your score in Page View, you may have noticed measures moving from system to system automatically. This is Finale's way of maintaining consistent music spacing as you enter. Any time you specify a number of measures on a system (by using Fit Music, or even by manually moving measures between systems), Finale will lock the system, preventing Automatic Music Spacing from ever shifting the measures. Systems that are locked will be tagged with a System Lock icon that looks like a padlock (see Figure 2.17). To lock any system, highlight the measures in the system with the Mass Edit Tool and choose Lock Systems from the Mass Edit menu (to unlock systems, choose Unlock from the Mass Edit menu). Or, instead of choosing Lock Systems and Unlock Systems from the Mass Edit menu, try using the L key on Windows or Command-L on Macintosh.

The icon with two miniature staves (shown in blue) indicates a system has been optimized (see Figure 2.17). Optimization is used for hiding empty staves in a system, adjusting staves independently within a system and making other system-specific changes. There will be a description of optimization, as well as when to use it, in Chapters 7 and 11. In case you care to experiment a bit with optimization (or remove it from an existing score), here's how to apply and remove it. Click a system handle and choose Optimize Staff Systems from the Page Layout menu (or Right/Control-click anywhere within a system). Choose Optimize Staff Systems and click OK to apply Optimization. Click Remove Staff System Optimization and click OK to remove it.

The System Lock and Optimization icons will not appear in your printout; only on-screen. To show or hide these icons on your screen display, use the Show Page Layout Icons command under the View menu.

 NOTE
In large scores, you may need to hide empty staves in some of your systems. This is known as optimization, and will be covered in Chapter 11.

CHAPTER 2

Editing Staff and System Spacing

Now, it's time to learn the basics for editing the layout of staves and systems. Here, I'll cover how to space staves and systems, as well as other techniques that come into play while editing the layout of staves and systems. First, it is important to make the distinction between staves and systems.

When you look at your score in Scroll View (select Scroll View from the View menu), you will see the total number of staves in your document. Think of Scroll View as one really long system that can stretch into eternity. Only when you look at your score in Page View (select Page View from the View menu) will you be able to see your staff systems. In Page View, a system is one or more staves extending across the page that are intended to be played at the same time.

Changing the Distance between Staves

There are a few ways to adjust staff and system spacing. To demonstrate how to space staves and systems, we'll first need more than one staff in our score. First, move to Scroll View. Click the Staff Tool, then click the Staff menu and choose New Staves. In the New Staves dialog box, enter 2 and click OK. You should now see three staves in your score. Each staff will have a handle on the upper-left corner. Click this handle to drag any staff up or down. These spacing changes will also apply in Page View.

You may want to increase or decrease the amount of space between each staff in a system. To do this, click the Staff menu and choose Respace Staves. You will see the Respace Staves dialog box (Figure 2.18).

Figure 2.18

Choose the space between each staff, or scale the distance between staves in the Respace Staves dialog box

Enter a negative value after Set To and click OK to space all of your staves a specific distance apart. Choose Respace Staves from the Staff menu and choose a percentage for Scale To if you want to reduce or increase the distance between each staff proportionally, but not necessarily have the staves evenly spaced.

Changing the Distance between Systems by Dragging

You may want to manually adjust the staff systems in your score. Click the Page Layout Tool to see the dashed margins around each system. Then, simply click within any system and drag. When you drag a system, all systems beneath the one you are dragging will adjust respectively. To drag a system independently (so that systems below are not influenced), hold down the Ctrl/Option key, then click and drag. You will be able to move a system only until the margin collides with an adjacent system margin or a page margin. To move systems closer together, or closer to the top or bottom page margin, you will need to edit their margins.

You will see a handle on the upper-left and lower-right corner of each system (see Figure 2.17). Use these handles to adjust system margins. For instance, you may want to move the top staff system closer to the top page margin. To do this, click the handle on the upper-left corner of the top system margin and drag it down. Now, click on the staff lines of the top system and drag it up to the top of the page (the distance between systems below it will not change). If you want to move the second system closer to the top system, try dragging up the handle on the lower-right corner of the top system. All systems will move up toward the top system margin.

To move all systems closer together or farther apart, click a handle on the lower right of one of your systems and press Ctrl/Command-A to Select All (or choose Select All from the Edit menu). Now all bottom system margin handles should be highlighted. Drag one down to increase the distance between all systems or drag one up to decrease the distance. For more control, you can also use the arrow keys to nudge system handles.

Spacing Systems Evenly

You can easily space all systems evenly on a page so that the top and bottom systems lie against the top and bottom page margins. To do this, choose Space Systems Evenly from the Page Layout menu. In the Space Systems Evenly dialog box, choose the page, or a page range, and click OK. All systems will be spaced evenly and will more closely resemble a standard engraving layout (see Figure 2.19).

Figure 2.19

An example of Space Systems Evenly. Notice that the system margins line up with the top and bottom page margins.

Moving Measures across Systems

You can easily move measures between systems with the Mass Edit Tool. Highlight the last measure in a system and press the down arrow to move it to the next system. Highlight the first measure in a system and press the up arrow to move it to the prior system. You can also do this for several measures at once.

Fitting Selected Measures to a System

You can easily fit any number of measures to a single system. First, make sure you are in Page View (Select Page View from the View menu). Highlight the measures you want to fit on one system. Click the Mass Edit menu and choose Fit Music. Choose Lock Selected Measures into One System and click OK. The highlighted measures now all appear on one system.

CHAPTER 2

Specifying Number of Measures per System for a Selected Region

To specify a certain number of measures per system for a selected region, highlight the region you want to change (Ctrl/Command-A to select all). Then, click the Mass Edit menu and choose Fit Music. Choose Lock Layout with _ Measure(s) per System and enter a number. Click OK. Your selected region will now contain the number of measures per system you specified.

Resizing a Page

If you find all of your music is too large or small on the page, you can use the Resize Tool to reduce or enlarge your music. You can change the size of all the music on your page without changing the margins or page size. Click the Resize Tool and click an empty area of your page (outside any staves or systems). You will see the Resize Page dialog box (Figure 2.20).

Figure 2.20

Reduce or enlarge all elements on a page by choosing a percentage in the Resize Page dialog box

Enter a percentage (less than 100% will reduce the music on the page, greater than 100% will enlarge the music on the page) and choose a page range. You will probably want to keep Page 1 Through End of Piece selected so all of your pages appear at the same reduction. Click OK to return to your score and review the new sizing. You can also resize individual systems, staves, and even notes with the Resize Tool. You'll find more on the Resize Tool in Chapter 11.

Redefining Pages and Page Format for Score

If you want to revert to Finale's default page format, click the Page Layout menu and choose Redefine Pages. Choose the pages you want to redefine from the Redefine Pages submenu. You will see a message warning that all page layout information will be lost. Click OK to return to the default page layout settings. Any time you choose to redefine your pages, Finale will draw settings from the Page Format for Score dialog box found in Options > Page Format > For Score. (See Figure 2.21).

Configure settings in this dialog box to specify a default page format to revert to any time you choose Redefine Pages from the Page Layout menu. You'll find more information on this dialog box in Chapter 11.

Figure 2.21

Use the Page Format for Score dialog box to specify precise spacing for system and page margins

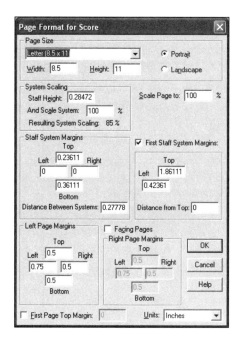

Page Size, Orientation, and Printing

When you start a score with the Default Document, for example, Finale will use a standard 8.5 × 11 page size in portrait orientation. To change the size and orientation of your page, click the Page Layout menu and choose Page Size. This will open the Page Size dialog box (see Figure 2.22).

Figure 2.22

Use the Page Size dialog box to specify page size and orientation

In this dialog box, choose a new height and width for your page. You can also change the orientation of the page by choosing Landscape or Portrait on the right. Choose the page range for which you want to apply the changes. or choose All Pages to apply these changes to all pages. Click OK to return to the score. You should now see the new page size on your screen.

Now that you have set a new page size in Finale, before you print the document you will need to modify your print settings so this information corresponds to the page size and orientation of your document. Click the File menu and choose Page Setup. You will now see the Page Setup dialog box (see Figure 2.23).

Figure 2.23

In the Page Setup dialog box, choose the page size and orientation for the printed page

Here, choose the same orientation and page size you indicated in the Page Size dialog box. Then, click the printer driver to open the settings for your print driver. Set up your printer to print the specified page size here. Consult your printer's instruction manual for specific information on how to specify a new page size. Once you have made print settings, click OK in the Page Setup dialog box. Then choose Print from the File menu to open the Print dialog box. Click Print to send your score to the printer.

The above instructions are just the basics to setting up a score for printing. A variety of other options are available in Finale, including left and right pages, tiled pages, and placing many "Finale pages" on a single printed page. Information on more advanced page layout topics can be found in Chapter 11.

3

BASIC NOTE ENTRY, ARTICULATIONS, AND EXPRESSIONS

So far, I have focused on the concepts and methods common to the first stages of any new project. Now it's time to expand the focus to the more diverse practice of entering notes, articulations, and expressions. There are differing opinions about the best way to enter these items. Some find that entering all the notes first, followed by articulations and then expressions works best. Others prefer entering all these items at the same time while progressing from measure to measure. The method you adopt should depend on the size of the project you are working with as well as the materials you have available to you. If you are composing a work from scratch, you may want to include these markings immediately to help you remember a specific phrase or musical idea. If you are copying from an existing score, entering all of your notes and then going back to enter articulations or expressions may be a faster method for you.

Finale offers many ways to enter notes into a staff. In this chapter, I'll cover the two most common: Simple Entry and Speedy Entry. First, I'll define some terminology used in this chapter. An *entry* in Finale is essentially any note or rest. Notes stacked vertically (as in a chord) are also defined as an *entry*. An *articulation* is a marking attached to a single entry. As you reposition an entry, its articulation(s) will move with it respectively. These include, but are not limited to, standard articulations such as accents and staccatos. You may also find the Articulation Tool useful for fingerings and other items. Finally, an *expression* is generally an item that affects a region of music and can be attached to a note or measure. Examples of items you will enter with the Expression Tool are dynamic markings, tempo indications, and rehearsal letters.

Here's a summary of what you will learn in this chapter:

- ❉ How to enter notes and rests with the mouse and keyboard: Simple Entry.
- ❉ How to enter notes and rests with Speedy Entry
- ❉ How to enter articulations (accents, staccato markings)
- ❉ How to enter expressions (dynamics, tempo indications, rehearsal letters)
- ❉ How to create a simple arrangement

The Simple Entry Tool

This recently renovated Simple Entry Tool is now more powerful than ever. You can use the Simple Entry Tool to enter all the basic-notation building blocks including notes, rests, chords, grace notes, tuplets, and ties. In addition, you can use the new Entry Caret feature to add articulations, expressions, and even clef, key and time signature changes into your score as you enter notes. Simple Entry is also a powerful editing tool. You can modify the pitch of any note, add accidentals and augmentation dots as well as flip stems, break/join beams, and even hide notes. Though this can be the simplest and most intuitive form of note entry, you can use its incredible versatility to perform the majority of your work. Users of any skill level will benefit greatly by learning how to harness the full potential of this tool. You'll start by getting acquainted with entering notes. Note that these instructions may not apply if you are using a Finale version earlier than 2005.

Entering Notes in Simple Entry with a Mouse

To prepare for this chapter, begin a new document. Click the File menu, choose New, and select Default Document. This provides a good canvas to experiment with basic note entry. The first time you launch Finale, the Simple Entry Tool is already selected by default. Click the Simple Entry Tool now if it isn't chosen already. You should see a note and vertical line in measure one. This is called the Simple Entry Caret, and you'll learn about it later. For now, press Esc to hide it. Click the eighth note in the Simple Entry Palette (see Figure 3.1). Notice that when you position your mouse over the staff, your cursor now looks like an eighth note. Now click the half note and the cursor changes to a half note. Your cursor will always reflect the duration chosen in the Simple Entry Palette. Click the quarter note icon, move the cursor to the middle staff line in the first measure, and click to enter a quarter note on middle line B. You can use this method to enter notes of any duration into your staff. Notice your cursor jump between the staff lines and spaces as you slowly drag over a staff. Click to place the note on the desired staff line or space.

Figure 3.1

Choose a rhythmic value, pitch alteration, grace note, triplet, tie, or a combination of these tools from the Simple Entry Palette for entry into the score

{ **TIP**
Finale is set by default to play back notes as you enter them and change their pitch. To turn off this feature, click the Simple menu, choose Simple Entry Options, and uncheck Playback.

You can specify a great deal of information before entering a note by choosing several items at once in the Simple Entry Palette. There are six categories in the Simple Palette separated with a small vertical bar. These consist of independent elements that could exist on any entry. They include note duration, augmentation dot, alteration (sharp/flat/natural), tie, tuplet, and grace note. You can choose one item from any number of these six categories before clicking into the score. Let's say you wanted to enter a dotted eighth note with a tie. From the Simple Palette, double-click the Eighth Note Tool (to deselect everything but the eighth note), and then click the Dot Tool and the Tie Tool. You can now see all of these items on your cursor. Click in the score and you will see a dotted eighth with a tie on whatever pitch you click on. To select any one tool independently, just double-click it and all other Simple Entry Tools will deactivate.

Now, let's say you have just entered a note, but it ended up on the wrong pitch. Notice the note just entered is always highlighted in purple. This note is now selected (I'll get into this more later on). Press the up and down arrows to change its pitch. You can also click the note, hold down the mouse button, and drag the note to the desired location. These techniques will come in handy anytime you misplace a note or want to change the pitch right away. To deselect a note or rest, press the Esc or Backspace key on Windows or the Clear key on Macintosh.

To enter a chord, simply click notes above or below an existing entry. You can stack up to 12 notes vertically to create thick chords. You will be able to edit the pitches of each note in a chord independently.

Select the Eraser icon and click any note to delete it. Click the stem of a chord with the Eraser Tool to delete the entire chord; click directly on a note head in a chord to remove a note from a chord. Press Ctrl/Cmd-Z to undo the most recent edit.

Entering Rests

There are a few ways to enter rests into your score with Simple Entry. You may have already noticed rests added to measures in your score. By default, Simple Entry automatically fills incomplete measures with rests after clicking into a different measure or changing tools in the Main Tool Palette. To see this for yourself, enter a quarter note into an empty measure. Then click a note into a different measure. The first measure fills with rests. If you want to disable this feature and enter all rests manually, click the Simple menu, Choose Simple Entry Options, and uncheck Fill With Rests. If you turn it off, you will still be able to go back and fill measures with rests later on with the Mass Edit Fill with Rest feature (which I'll cover later in Chapter 9).

To enter rests manually, start by opening the Simple Entry Rests Palette (Figure 3.2) if you don't see it on your screen already. Click the Window menu and choose Simple Entry Rest Palette. Notice the appearance of the new palette filled with rests of different durations.

Figure 3.2
Specify the rhythmic duration of a rest for entry into the score from the Simple Entry Rest Palette

You can treat this palette the same as the Simple Entry Palette to enter rests. However, there is a better way. Use keyboard shortcuts! To quickly choose a rest, simply hold down the Ctrl/Command key and press a duration number on the numeric pad on your keyboard. Your cursor will change to a rest of that duration. You can also press the R key to toggle between notes and rests of the same duration in your cursor. Click in a measure to enter the rest or on existing notes to change them into rests of the duration you have chosen. To change any note in your score to a rest of the same duration, Ctrl/Option-click it (it will change color) and press the R key. I'll provide a complete explanation of selection later.

Accidentals

If you enter a note without specifying an accidental, Finale will always assume you want the note entered on the diatonic pitch regardless of what key you are in. Any divergence from the key signature will need to be specified with one of the five alteration tools: Sharp, Flat, Natural, Half Step Up, or Half Step Down. To enter a note with an accidental, click the desired note duration, and then click the Sharp, Flat, or Natural icon in the Simple Palette. Now your cursor tells you the duration and the alteration (sharp/flat/natural) that will be entered after you click in the score. Click somewhere in the staff to see how this works. Choose the Half Step Up or Half Step Down Tool and click a note to raise or lower its pitch in half steps. You can add double sharps or double flats this way as well. To remove the accidental from the cursor, either click its icon again or double-click the desired note duration.

> **NOTE**
> The Sharp, Flat, and Natural Tools are said to be absolute, meaning independent from the key signature. Clicking an F# into a staff with the Sharp Tool will always result in an F#. If the alteration is already implied in the key signature (an F# in the key of G major for instance), Finale will automatically hide the accidental since it is already part of the diatonic scale. If you want to ensure that any note you enter will appear one half step above or below the diatonic pitch in any key, choose the Half Step Up or Half Step Down Tool. For example, in the key of G major, clicking an F into your staff with the Half Step Up Tool will result in an F double sharp (since F# is already part of the diatonic scale). To clarify, the only time the Sharp Tool will act differently than the Half Step Up Tool is while entering or editing notes already altered by the key signature.

Tuplets

The Simple Entry Tuplet Tool is a bit different than the others. This tool was added in Finale 2002 in response to many customer requests for an easier method of tuplet entry. In one click you can add an entire triplet, quintuplet, or any other type by specifying a custom tuplet. Let's start by entering an eighth note triplet. Click the Eighth Note icon, then the Tuplet icon. Click in an empty measure. Notice there is now an eighth note, followed by two rests, all within a tuplet bracket. You can leave both tools selected and simply click over the next two rests to finish entering your triplet. To change this figure to a quarter note–eighth note triplet, delete the middle note and change the first entry to a quarter note. You can also change three existing notes into a triplet by clicking on the first of the three with just the Simple Tuplet Tool selected.
To specify a tuplet definition other than a triplet (quintuplet, sextuplet, etc.) choose the Simple Tuplet Tool, hold down the Shift key and click in the score. In the Simple Entry Tuplet Definition dialog box, enter your settings (e.g., 6 in place of 4 for a sextuplet, etc.) and click OK. If you will be entering many custom tuplets, check Save as default Simple Entry tuplet definition in the Simple Entry Tuplet Definition dialog box to save your settings. You'll find more on defining and editing tuplets in Chapter 9.

Keyboard Shortcuts

By now you may be wondering, "Am I really going to have to click all these icons before entering each note?" The answer is no. Instead of clicking a duration tool, you can choose that tool using the numbers on your numeric keypad. For example, press 3 to select a 16th note, 4 for an eighth note, 5 for a quarter, and so on. Now press the + key and the period key (.) to add a sharp and an augmentation dot to the cursor. Choosing durations with your keypad and clicking notes into the score is one way to increase efficiency; however, that's just the tip of the iceberg, as you will see in the next section.

> **TIP**
> To select any single tool in the Simple Palette and deselect all others, double-press any keyboard shortcut (much like a double-click).

Editing Notes in Simple Entry

You may have already noticed that it is possible to select any Simple Entry icon by itself. This comes in handy when editing existing notes. Double-click the Tie icon (or double-press the letter T), for instance, and then click on any note to add or remove a tie. You can edit notes with any Simple Tool by simply selecting the appropriate item and clicking the entry. Keep in mind that all Simple Tools selected will affect the entry you click. For instance, if you have the Sharp and Half Note icons selected, any note you click will become a half note as well as sharp. Like entering notes, editing would be far more difficult if there weren't time-saving keyboard shortcuts to make your life easier. In this case, Finale does more than just offer tool selection keystrokes. You can use many keyboard commands to edit any note by selecting it!

Selecting Notes

Selection is an integral part to making the most of the Simple Entry Tool. The same keyboard shortcuts you used to choose note durations, accidentals, and the like from the Simple Palette can also be used to modify any selected note. Click a series of quarter notes into a measure. After you enter a note it is highlighted in purple automatically. Press Alt-4 on Windows or Option-4 on Mac to change it to an eighth note, or press the + key to raise by a half step. Experiment with the other shortcuts. Use the left and right arrows to move between entries. You can also select any note in your score easily by holding down Ctrl/Option and clicking an entry. To remove the selection from the note (so that keyboard shortcuts can be used for tool selection again), press the Esc or Backspace/Clear key.

Selecting Notes in Chords

You can move the selection between notes in a chord and even select several notes within an entry at once. Enter a chord of seven notes in a measure. Now hold down Ctrl/Option and use the up and down arrows to highlight any one note in the chord for editing. To select multiple notes within a chord, hold down Ctrl/Option-Shift and click all of the notes in the chord you want to select (Figure 3.3).

To select all notes in a chord, select one of the notes, press Ctrl/Cmd-A or Ctrl/Option-click above or below it. Any keystroke will now affect all highlighted notes. If you change the pitch or duration with any one note of the chord selected, all notes in the chord will change. To see all of the available keystrokes for note selection, click the Simple menu and choose Simple Navigation Commands.

Other Editing Commands for Selected Notes

In addition to note durations, accidentals, and the other commands similar to Tool Selection and Selected Note editing, there are several other commands that were built in specifically for selected notes. Select a note and press the L key to flip its stem, press the R key to change it to a rest, and press the H key to hide an entry. You can also break/join the beam between a note and the previous entry (/ on the QWERTY keyboard) or show/hide a courtesy accidental (Windows: Ctrl-Shift–[minus; use the minus key on the QWERTY keyboard] Mac: Shift-Command–[minus; use the minus key on the QWERTY keyboard]). To see a full list of the possibilities, or apply any command, click the Simple menu and choose Simple Edit Commands (Figure 3.4). A full list of the keyboard shortcuts can be found in your Quick Reference Card.

Figure 3.3

Ctrl/Option-Shift-click to select non-contiguous notes in a chord

Figure 3.4

Choose Simple Edit Commands from the Simple menu to see a list of keyboard shortcuts

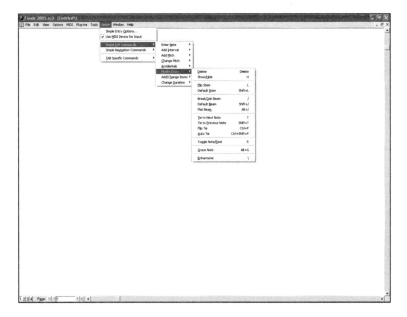

Entering Notes in Simple Entry with Your Computer Keyboard

Up to this point I've covered the basic concepts of Simple Entry; now it's time to learn how to do the same stuff faster. For Finale 2004 (and improved in 2005), the engineers at MakeMusic! implemented a new approach to Simple Entry that allows you to quickly type in all the musical elements covered so far (and more) using your computer keyboard. In fact, you can even use your MIDI keyboard, or even a wind instrument, to specify pitches in Simple Entry. In this section, you'll learn how to take advantage of these capabilities. To get started, do the following:

1. Open a new Default Document (File > New > Default Document). The Default Document opens.

2. Click the Simple Entry Tool. Notice the note with a vertical line through it at the beginning of the first measure (as shown in Figure 3-5). This is called the Simple Entry Caret. The Caret is much like a cursor in a word-processing program. The vertical line tells you where the next note will be entered. The note tells you the currently selected duration.

Figure 3.5
The Simple Entry Caret is like the cursor in a word processor.

{ **CAUTION**
Laptop users: If you are using a notebook computer without a numeric keypad, the standard keystrokes will be difficult to use. To load keystrokes designed for laptops without numeric keypads, do the following: From the Simple Menu, choose Simple Entry Options and click Edit Keyboard Shortcuts. In the drop-down menu under Keyboard Shortcut Set, choose Laptop Shortcut Table. Follow these steps using the alternative key commands (to quickly reference them, choose Simple Edit Commands from the Simple Menu. Keystrokes shown here now reflect the laptop shortcut set.)

3. On the numeric keypad, press 6, then 5, then 4. Notice that the Caret changes to a half, then a quarter, then an eighth note. (The mouse cursor and Duration Tool on the Simple Entry Palette change as well). This is how you select the duration for the next entry.

4. Now, press the up arrow and then the down arrow. Notice that the Caret moves up and down on the staff. You can use this method to select the pitch you want to add and press Enter to add the note, but it's faster to do the following.

5. Type the letters A, B, C, D, E, F, and G. These notes appear on the staff. Finale places the pitch you type on the staff position closest to the Caret. Now, for example, if you were to type E, Finale would add a top space E. But say you want to add an E on the bottom staff line.

6. Hold down Shift and press the down arrow, and then type E. An E appears on the bottom staff line. Similarly, you can press Shift-up arrow to move the Caret up an octave. So, thus far you have learned how to specify the duration and pitch. Your first measure should look like Figure 3.6.

Figure 3.6
With the Caret active, use the numeric pad to specify duration, and then use letter keys to add pitches.

Notice the last note in measure 1 is selected. You can change this note in many ways using special modifier keystrokes.

7. Press the + key on the numeric pad to raise the note you just entered a half step. Press − (minus) in the numeric pad to lower it a half step. These keystrokes increment chromatically so you can also easily add double-sharps and flats. Now let's experiment with some other modifiers.

8. Press T to add a tie, \ (backslash) to change the enharmonic spelling, and Alt/Option-G to change to a grace note. Press T again to remove the tie and Alt/Option-G again to toggle between an unslashed grace note, a slashed grace note and a regular note.

TIP

From the Simple Menu, choose Simple Entry Commands, and then Modify Entry to see a list of the modifier keystrokes. These modifiers work on any selected note. (Remember, after you enter a note with the Caret, it is selected automatically).

9. Now let's add a rest. Press 5 on the numeric pad and then 0 on the numeric pad to enter a quarter rest. (You can also press R to change a selected note to a rest after entering it.)

10. Press the F key to add an F. Say we want to create a triad (chord). There are two ways to do this. The easiest: in the QWERTY keyboard (number row), press 3 twice. Use the number row to add a note of an interval (unison through ninth) above the selected note (see Figure 3.7. Hold down Shift and press a number to add a note below the selected note). You could also hold down Shift and type the note letters to create a chord.

Figure 3.7

Use keys in the number row (or shift-pitch letter) to add intervals above or below notes

11. Now, if you want to change the pitch of the note you just entered, just hold down Alt/Option and press the up or down arrow.

12. To change the duration of a selected note, hold down Alt/Option and press a duration key on the numeric pad. For example, press Alt/Option-6 to change to a half note.

NOTE

All notes on the same beat (chords) change if you change the duration of any note in the chord. To enter notes of different durations (e.g., more than one voice) on the same beat, use a different layer. You'll learn more about layers later in this chapter.

The preceding was a crash course designed to give you a basic idea of how fast and easy entry can be with the Caret. For additional hands-on training, open the file "EntryExercise" in the Finale 2005/Tutorials folder. It's an instructional Finale file that guides you through most of Simple Entry's functionality. Highly recommended! You can also find helpful advice in the QuickStart Videos (Help menu > QuickStart Videos).

Navigating with the Caret

If you plan to use the Caret to edit your music, you'll need to know how to get around with it. Here are the keystrokes you need to know:

* Ctrl/Option-click an empty measure to display the Caret at the beginning of the measure.
* Use the left and right arrow keys to move the Caret (or selection) forward and backward in the staff.
* Press Ctrl/Command-right arrow to advance the Caret to the next measure, Ctrl/Command-left arrow to move the Caret left a measure.
* Press Ctrl/Command-down arrow to move the Caret (or selection) down one staff in the system, Ctrl/Command-up arrow to move the Caret up one staff.
* Select a note (Ctrl/Option-click) and press Enter to display the Caret to the right of the note.
* Press Esc to hide the Caret. Press Enter to redisplay the Caret.

Adding Articulations and Other Markings with the Caret

Now that you've learned to add notes, you'll also probably want to add other markings such as articulations and dynamic markings to notes as you enter them. Doing so is easy. Let's keep using the document we have open.

1. Ctrl/Option-click an empty measure to activate the Caret.
2. Enter a note (of any duration).
3. Press the * in the numeric pad. The Waiting for Input dialog box appears.
4. Press the S key to add a staccato. A staccato marking appears on the note (as shown in Figure 3.8). You just used one of many available "Metatools" to add this articulation. You could have also pressed A to add an accent ('). Press Enter to choose from a list of articulations. In the Articulation Selection dialog, the metatool key for each articulation is in parentheses.

Figure 3.8
With the Caret, press * and then S to add a staccato, A to add an accent, or Enter to choose another articulation

 NOTE
Press X instead of * to add a dynamic marking expression like f or p. You'll learn more about expressions and articulations later in this chapter.

5. Now, let's say you want an articulation to appear on the next several notes. To do this, you can use a different keystroke to make the articulation (or expression) "sticky." Hold down Ctrl/Command and press *. Press a metatool key like A or S (or press Enter, select a marking, and click OK). The marking appears on the Caret as shown in Figure 3.9.

6. Enter notes into the score. The articulation appears on each note you enter.

Figure 3.9

Use Ctrl/Command * to specify a "sticky" articulation to appear on several notes.

7. Press Ctrl/Command * to remove (or "unstick") the articulation from the Caret.

Using a MIDI Keyboard or Other MIDI Device with the Caret

If you have a MIDI keyboard (or other MIDI device) setup with your computer, you can use it to specify the pitches you want to add while using the Caret. No special setup is necessary, just choose the duration from the numeric pad, and then play the pitches on your MIDI device. Change the duration at any point from the numeric pad.

Many find using a MIDI keyboard with Simple Entry an easy way to enter music quickly. If you do this, you will need to use the \ (Backslash) key to alter the enharmonic spelling (if, for example, an F sharp appears in the score that should be spelled G flat).

Entering More Than One Voice—Layers

It is very common to see more than one melodic line, or voice, entered in the same staff. With layers, you can enter up to four independent voices in any measure (see Figure 3.10). Notice the four boxes (or pop-up menu on Mac) in the lower-left corner of the screen labeled 1, 2, 3, and 4. These are the layer selection controls. Make sure layer 1 is selected and click four quarter notes on the top staff line. Now select layer 2. Click the Eighth Note Tool, or press the 4 key, and click eighth notes into the same measure on the middle line. They are red so you will always know these notes are in layer 2 in case you want to edit them later.

The stems on your notes in layer 2 automatically flip down, so if you're using two layers, use layer 2 for the lower voice. You can flip the stems by selecting them and pressing the L key, or you can change the default stem direction for each layer of your document in the Layer Options dialog box (I'll cover this later). You can use the remaining layers to enter up to two more independent voices in this measure. They will each have their own color so you can distinguish between them (layer 3, green; layer 4, blue). You will only be able to

Figure 3.10

Enter multiple voices in your
score using layers

edit one layer at a time in Simple Entry. For example, if you want to add or edit notes in layer 1, first select
layer 1 in the lower-left corner of your screen.

TIP

You can also use keyboard shortcuts to switch between layers. On Windows, hold down Alt-Shift
and press the number of the layer you would like to select. On Macintosh, hold down Cmd-Option and
press the number of the layer you would like to select.

You may want to begin entering notes in a new layer somewhere within the measure instead of the first beat.
To do this, begin entering notes into the measure with the Caret. When you want to switch layers, Windows
users type Alt-Shift-#, and Mac users type Command-Option-# (where # is the layer number), then continue
entering in the new layer. Under the hood, hidden rests are added up until that point in the new layer.

If you want stems extending in both directions on a single note (to indicate two voices in unison), you could
enter overlapping notes in layer 1 and layer 2. Do this if you need to enter more than one layer in the
measure anyway. To apply beams in both directions in a single layer, use the Double-Split Stem Special Tool
(more on the Special Tools in Chapter 10).

Entering Notes and Rests with Speedy Entry

For all versions of Finale prior to 2004, Speedy Entry was widely viewed as the primary note entry method, and
many professionals still use it for the majority of their work. Although the Simple Entry Caret now provides the
ability to enter notes quickly with a MIDI keyboard, which was the main advantage of Speedy Entry before, it
is still a popular choice due to its speed, navigation abilities, and expanded MIDI control. In this section I will
cover the various methods of note entry within this tool both with and without a MIDI keyboard.

CHAPTER 3

Click the Speedy Entry Tool and notice the Speedy menu that appears at the top of your screen. You will be using the many features in this menu to customize the way Speedy Entry works. These features will be explained throughout this chapter as I cover the methods and tricks they apply to.

If you are using a MIDI keyboard for input, note that the first part of this chapter applies to editing in Speedy Entry with or without a MIDI keyboard. In other words, even in Speedy's MIDI entry mode, all of the non-MIDI features (besides actual note entry) are available. You may find these techniques useful for editing after entering notes with your MIDI keyboard. If you are unfamiliar with Speedy Entry, I recommend reading through the entire Speedy Entry section.

> **NOTE**
> If you are using a German or Swiss-German keyboard, consult the Finale User Manual to learn how to customize the Speedy key map.

To prepare for this section, launch the Setup Wizard (File > New > Setup Wizard). Click Next. On Page 2, add a Piano and complete the wizard. You should now see an empty grand staff score.

Navigation in Speedy Entry

While using Speedy Entry, you will be entering notes within the context of the Speedy Frame as shown in Figure 3.11.

Figure 3.11

Enter notes quickly using the Speedy Frame

Click any measure to activate the Speedy Frame. You can also show or hide the Speedy Entry Frame by pressing the number 0. When you show it this way, it will appear on the most recently active measure. There are several ways to move the Speedy Entry Frame around your score. Click any measure to activate the Speedy Frame. Move the cursor horizontally by pressing the left and right arrow keys. You can also move from measure to measure this way. Move the frame horizontally among measures by pressing the left and right bracket keys ([and]) on your computer keyboard. Move the frame to between staves in a system (from the top to bottom staff in your piano score): on Windows, hold down Shift and use the up and down arrows; on Mac, press the Return key to move down a staff and Shift-Return to move up.

Until Finale 2002, the Speedy Frame's size was fixed. Increasing the view percentage of your file did not increase the Speedy Frame size. Now the Speedy Frame's size will adjust automatically based on your view percentage. To select a fixed size or allow for a greater frame size at low view percentages, click the Speedy menu and choose Speedy Options. You will find these settings in the Frame section.

Speedy Entry without a MIDI Keyboard

The most basic way to use Speedy Entry is with the computer keyboard. Click the Speedy menu and uncheck Use MIDI Device for Input You are now ready to use your computer keyboard for note entry.

Press the up and down arrows on your keyboard and notice the small horizontal bar move up and down between the staff lines and spaces. I will refer to this horizontal bar as the Speedy Entry Cursor. Use this cursor to specify the pitch of the note you want to enter. Move the cursor to the third space C and press the 5 key to enter a quarter note. Use the same keystrokes for note durations (1-8) you used in Simple Entry. After you enter each note, the vertical bar automatically advances to the right. Now, press the down arrow twice to move the cursor down to the second space A and press the 4 key twice to enter two eighth notes. Now press the 6 key to enter a half note. Once you have filled a measure, the Speedy Frame automatically jumps to the next measure.

Using the QWERTY Keyboard to Specify Pitch

There is a faster way to move the cursor between pitches in Speedy Entry without using the arrow keys or a MIDI keyboard. If you engage Caps Lock, all of the letters on your computer keyboard will act differently. Click an empty measure with the Speedy Entry Tool chosen. Press Caps Lock and press the A key to move the cursor down to middle C. Each letter to the right corresponds to the next highest staff location: S=D, D=E, F=F, and so on. Press the Q key to start from the third space or Z to begin below the staff. Use each adjacent letter to move up or down to different pitches. This can be an effective way to quickly enter notes if you spend some time getting used to the keystrokes. Remember, to access the Speedy Entry keyboard shortcuts on the QWERTY keyboard, Caps Lock must be disengaged.

Entering Rests

After entering any note, simply press the Backspace/Clear key to change it to a rest. To change any chord to a rest, position the cursor so that it is not on a note or pitch present in the chord (otherwise, pressing Backspace/Clear will remove an individual note). Any time the Speedy Frame leaves a measure, Finale will automatically fill any space at the end with rests. To avoid this, and enter all of your rests manually, click the Speedy menu and choose Speedy Options. In the Frame section, uncheck Fill With Rests at End of Measure.

Edit as You Enter

Unlike Simple Entry, in this form of Speedy Entry, you will always add accidentals, dots, ties, etc., after entering the note. There is no "selection" necessary other than placing the cursor on or adjacent to the note. Press 5 to enter a quarter note in an empty measure, then press the + key to add a sharp, press period (.) to add an augmentation dot, or T for a tie. Now enter three more quarter notes (the frame will move to the next measure).

CHAPTER 3

Press the S key (make sure Caps Lock is off). Finale will look back across the barline and add the sharp to the last note of the previous measure. Press the T key to begin a tie on the last note of the previous measure. Also use keystrokes during entry to flip stems, break/join beams, change enharmonic spelling, etc. For a complete list of keystrokes, click the Speedy menu and choose Speedy Edit Commands (Figure 3.12).

Figure 3.12

Choose Speedy Edit Commands from the Speedy menu to see a list of keyboard commands for Speedy Entry

You may want to insert a note between existing entries. To do this, click the Speedy menu and choose Insert Notes or Rests (or on Windows, press the Insert key, and on Macintosh, press Shift-I). Now click an empty measure. You will notice black triangles at the top and bottom of the vertical insertion bar within the Speedy Frame. Enter two quarter notes in the measure. Now, press the left arrow so the cursor is covering the second quarter note. Your measure should look like Figure 3.13.

Figure 3.13

Speedy Entry in Insert mode

Press the 6 key to insert a half note between the two quarter notes. To activate or deactivate Insert Notes or Rests, you can also press the Insert key on Windows or Shift-I on Mac.

 NOTE
If you're familiar with the Speedy Edit Pitch Commands in the QWERTY keyboard as they were before Finale 2002, don't worry, they will work, too. Just make sure Caps Lock is on (and Use MIDI Keyboard is deactivated under the Speedy menu).

Accidentals

After you have entered a note, use the + or - keys to raise or lower notes incrementally (by half steps). For instance, to change a G to a G#, place the cursor over it and press +. To change it back to a G, press -. The plus and minus keys act the same as the Half Step Up and Half Step Down keys in Simple Entry. To show an accidental on any note, use the A key. To hide any accidental, press the * key (you can use these two keystrokes interchangeably in most occasions, though the A key won't hide "real" accidentals, just courtesy accidentals). Again, you can also use any of the Simple Entry commands (S, F, N, etc.) to enter accidentals as you would on a selected note in Simple Entry (with Caps lock off).

Chords

To enter a chord, simply move the cursor directly above or below a note and press the Enter key. Finale will automatically enter a note of the same duration as the existing one. To remove a single note from a chord, move the cursor directly on top of it and press Backspace/Clear. To delete an entire chord, use the Delete key. To change the chord to a rest, move the cursor over the stem (not on top of a notehead) and press the Backspace/Clear or R key.

Tuplets

Entering tuplets of any kind is easy in Speedy Entry. With the Speedy Frame active, hold down the Ctrl/Option key and press the number corresponding to the number of notes you would like to enter in the tuplet (3 for triplet, 6 for sextuplet, etc.). You will see the number appear in the upper-right corner of the Speedy Entry Window. Now enter these notes (of the same duration for now) and Finale will automatically place them within a tuplet definition. The first note you enter in the series will contain the information that tells Finale the value of the tuplet. For instance, if you press Ctl/Option-3, then enter a quarter note, Finale will assume you want a quarter note triplet. Therefore, always begin the tuplet with the value that represents the crucial subdivision. If you wish to enter a tuplet whose first note does not begin on the crucial subdivision, press Ctrl/Option-1 to open the Tuplet Definition dialog box for more advanced tuplet settings. You'll find more on defining and editing tuplets in Chapter 9.

Layers in Speedy Entry

The basic concept of layers in Speedy Entry is exactly the same as in Simple Entry. If you need to enter multiple voices or melody lines in the same staff, you will need to use multiple layers. On Windows, click the layer selection boxes in the lower-left of your screen to specify a layer; on Macintosh, click and select the Layer from the pop-up menu. To move between layers on Windows, hold down Shift and press the ' (apostrophe) key; and on Macintosh, hold down Shift and use the up and down arrows.

In the Speedy Frame, non-active layers are grayed out in the background. To hide notes in any layer, use the H or 0 key. You will also be able to specify multiple note durations on the same beat in Speedy Entry using voices.

NOTE
You can use Alt-Shift-# and Option-Shift-# to change layers at any time, just as you can with the Simple Entry Caret.

Voices

To enter multiple melodic lines, I recommend always using layers. However, when working with Speedy Entry, you have the option of using up to two voices in each layer. With voices and layers combined, you can have up to eight independent passages simultaneously in one staff! You may have already noticed the "V1" located in the upper left of the Speedy Frame. This indicates the voice you are currently working with. At any time, while working in Speedy Entry, press the ` (apostrophe) key to move to voice 2 or back to voice 1. After entering a note in voice 1, press the ` key (notice V1 changes to V2), move your cursor to the desired pitch, and enter a note of any duration. Since notes in voice 2 can be entered anywhere over an existing note in voice 1, they can come in handy for independent lines that begin somewhere other than the first beat (so you don't have to go back and hide notes in different layers).

Speedy Entry with a MIDI Keyboard

You can improve the speed of Speedy Entry dramatically with the aid of a MIDI keyboard. In this mode of Speedy, you can use your MIDI keyboard to specify all pitches and use the computer keyboard for durations, ties, etc. You will also have the option to abandon the computer keyboard almost entirely by programming MIDI pitches to durations, ties, and navigation controls. Again, it is important to note that all of the information that pertains to editing existing notes without a MIDI keyboard is still valid and may be useful for adjusting your notes once they have been entered, without changing back to non-MIDI mode.

To use a MIDI keyboard (or any external MIDI device) for input, you will need to ensure it is properly connected to the computer and set up in Finale. For complete instructions on MIDI setup, consult the Finale Installation and Tutorials manual.

TIP
To test if your MIDI keyboard is set up properly, hold down a pitch and press one of the duration numbers while the Speedy Frame is active (make sure Use MIDI Device for Input is checked under the Speedy menu). If you get a note, Finale is receiving the MIDI information from your keyboard. If you get a rest, this information is not getting through. If this is the case, consult Chapter 1 of this book for troubleshooting solutions or the Finale Installation and Tutorials manual for instructions on MIDI setup.

To configure Speedy Entry to use a MIDI keyboard, click the Speedy menu and check Use MIDI Device for Input. Now click a measure to activate the Speedy Frame. Hold down middle C on your MIDI keyboard and press the 5 key. Finale will place a quarter note into your staff on middle C. While holding down any pitch, use the standard duration keystrokes (1-8) to enter any note duration on that pitch. Finale will add accidentals automatically.

TIP

To change the enharmonic spelling of any note, use the 9 key.

Now without pressing down any notes on your MIDI keyboard, press the 5 key. You will see a quarter rest. Any time you press a number without holding down one of the keys on your MIDI keyboard, a rest of the corresponding duration will appear in your score.

You can enter several notes at once from your MIDI keyboard. Hold down as many notes as you want (up to 12) and press one of the duration keys to enter a chord into your score.

Entering tuplets into your score works almost the same way as in Speedy Entry without MIDI. With a Speedy Frame open, hold down Ctrl/Option and press the 3 key. You will see the number 3 appear in the upper-right corner of the Speedy Frame. Now hold down the first pitch and press a number for the duration of the first note of the triplet. Enter the following two notes as you would normally. Note that triplet duration information is contained in the first note.

Entering Many Notes of the Same Duration

Let's say you want to enter a passage of eighth notes without having to press the 4 key for each note. Press the Caps Lock key. Now press the 4 key, and you will see the number 4 appear in the lower-left corner of the Speedy Frame. Now every time you play a note or chord on your MIDI keyboard, Finale will enter an eighth note into your score. To start entering quarter notes, press the 5 key and begin entering notes with your MIDI keyboard. To enter a rest, simply strike three consecutive notes, half steps apart, for instance C, C#, and D. Many Finale users endorse this method as the fastest way to use Speedy Entry, especially in scores containing long strands of notes of similar duration.

NOTE

The Caps Lock method of Speedy Entry is similar to using Simple Entry with the Caret (if you opt to specify rhythmic durations prior to entering notes).

Using the Caps Lock mode of Speedy Entry with MIDI also makes entering long strands of tuplets easy. Invoke the Speedy Frame on an empty measure and press Caps Lock. Press the 4 key to specify an eighth note duration. Now hold down the Ctrl/Option key and press 3 on your computer keyboard. The number 3 appears in the upper-right corner of the Speedy Frame indicating a triplet. Now enter several notes using your MIDI keyboard. Each new set of three notes will be defined as a triplet (see Figure 3.14).

To stop entering tuplets, press the number of any note duration (the number in the upper-right corner of the Speedy Frame will disappear).

CHAPTER 3

Figure 3.14

Entering a strand of triplets in
Speedy Entry

{ **TIP**
You can enter a strand of tuplets in Simple Entry with or without a MIDI keyboard. While using the
Caret, select the Simple Entry Tuplet Tool. When you are done entering tuplets, disable the Simple
Entry Tuplet Tool.

Entry Using Your MIDI Keyboard Exclusively

You do not even need to use your computer keyboard for note entry with Speedy. Instead of using the
number keys to specify note duration, you can program them to specific MIDI pitches. To do this, use the
MIDI Modifier Key Map. (This feature was new to Finale 2002.) Click the Speedy menu and choose Speedy
Options. Click the Create Key Map button and the Edit MIDI Modifiers dialog box will open (see Figure 3.15).

Figure 3.15

Assign MIDI notes to Speedy
Entry commands with the MIDI
Modifier Key Map

To program a MIDI pitch to one of the commands, simply click the corresponding Listen button and press a note on your MIDI keyboard (choose a note used rarely or not at all in the piece you are working on). Do this for any duration or other command you would like to use in this box. Once you have finished programming, click OK twice to return to the score. Click a measure and use the notes you programmed just as you would keys on your computer keyboard for note entry.

Entering Articulations

Whether you plan to enter all of your articulations at once or during the note entry process, it is important to make the most of the time-saving tricks Finale has to offer. In this section I will describe how to most efficiently enter staccato markings, accents, fermatas, and any other articulation. I will also cover how to choose from an extended variety of articulations, how to space them properly and also define them for playback. I'll begin with the fastest way to set articulations on individual notes.

To prepare for this section, you need a document containing notes without articulations. You can use the scratch document you used in one of the previous sections or open one of the Finale tutorial files. To open a tutorial, click the File menu and choose Open. Navigate to the Finale folder and double-click the Tutorials folder. Open the file "Tutorial 2.MUS." This is an arrangement of "O, Susannah" that will suit our needs just fine.

Basic Articulation Entry

To get acquainted with the Articulation Tool, start by adding articulations to individual notes. Click the Articulation Tool (if it isn't selected already). Now click a note. The Articulation Selection dialog box will appear on your screen, as shown in Figure 3.16.

Figure 3.16

Choose articulations for entry in the Articulation Selection dialog box

This dialog box shows the items in Finale's default articulation library. For now, click the accent marking and then click the Select button. Notice the accent appears on the note you clicked. You can add any one of the

articulations in the Articulation Selection window by simply clicking a note, choosing the articulation, and clicking the Select button. If you don't like the placement, click its handle and either drag it with your mouse or nudge it using the arrow keys (I'll cover more specific placement techniques later). To delete the articulation, click its handle and press the Delete key.

To edit individual articulations, right-click/Ctrl-click an articulation handle to open the context menu. From here you can easily access the Articulation Definition dialog box to edit that particular articulation. (Of course, it's easier to just double-click the handle.) I will cover the usage of this dialog box in this section. You can also delete any articulation from the context menu (and it's easier to highlight the handles and press Delete). You can click and drag, or Shift-click to select multiple handles.

Metatools

Metatools are time-saving shortcuts available in many areas of Finale, and are integral to using the program most effectively. Learning to use articulation metatools is a great introduction to this concept. You will see more discussion of metatools throughout this book.

Usually, while working on a score you will find yourself entering some articulations quite often and others not at all. To click a common articulation into your score without even entering the Articulation Selection dialog box, use a metatool. Click a note in your score to open the Articulation Selection dialog box. Notice the numbers or letters in parentheses in the upper-right corner on some of the articulation boxes. These are preset metatool assignments. Take note of the staccato marking in the far upper-left, metatool (S). Click the Cancel button to close the Articulation Selection dialog box. Now hold down the S key and click any note to enter a staccato marking. Now hold down the A key and click another note to add an accent. Use these metatools to enter articulations quickly throughout the score. Refer to the Articulation Selection dialog box to reference all of the preset metatool assignments.

Programming a Metatool

Not all of the articulations in the Articulation Selection dialog box have a preset metatool assignment. There is a simple way to assign any letter or number to any articulation. For instance, let's say you want to use the 2 key to enter accent markings instead of the letter A. Hold down the Shift key and press the number 2. The Articulation Selection dialog box opens. Now choose the accent marking and click Select. The accent is now assigned to the 2 key. Hold down the 2 key and click any note to add an accent. If you open the Articulation Selection dialog box again, you will notice the number 2 in the upper-right corner of the accent box.

Entering an Articulation on Several Notes at Once

Finale makes it easy to add articulations to a region of notes. Simply click and drag over a region of your staff. You will notice a black square highlighting part of the staff. Encircle an area containing several notes and release the mouse button to open the Apply Articulation dialog box. Click the Select button and highlight an articulation in the Articulation Selection dialog box. Click the Select button, then OK. Finale adds the articulation you selected to all of the notes in the area you surrounded. You can also use metatools when applying articulations to a section of music. To enter an articulation to a region of notes faster, hold down a metatool key and drag over the region. To delete all articulations from any region, hold down the Delete key and drag over the region.

Adding New Articulations to the Library

If the articulation you are looking for does not exist in the Articulation Selection dialog box, you can create it. To do this, double-click a note in the score to open the Articulation Selection dialog box, and click the Create button. This brings us to the Articulation Designer, shown in Figure 3.17.

Figure 3.17

Specify the visual definition, placement, and playback for an articulation in the Articulation Designer dialog box

You will notice two buttons in the Symbol section: Main and Flipped. These refer to the articulation as it will appear above or below the staff, depending on your settings in the Symbol Options section. To select from a list of font characters, click the Main button. Find the character you want to use and click the Select button. If you want the same character to appear on the opposite side of the staff, click the Flipped button and do the same. If you can't find the character you are looking for, click the Set Font button to choose a different font. Once you have selected characters to add to your Articulation Selection, click OK and then Select to return to the score.

Finale offers several music fonts that contain articulations you might find useful. For a complete list of characters in all Finale fonts, click the Help menu on Mac (on Windows, click Help, then User Manual) and select the Engraver, Jazz, or Maestro character map. Of course, you will be able to select a character from any font that exists on your system in the Articulation Designer dialog box.

Editing Articulations

You may need to modify the size, font, or character of an existing articulation. To do this, click a note in your score to bring up the Articulation Selection dialog box. Highlight the articulation you would like to change and click the Edit button. This brings up the Articulation Designer dialog box. To modify the articulation, click the Set Font button. This launches the Font dialog box (see Figure 3.18).

Select a new size, style, or font for the articulation here. Click OK, OK, and then Select to return to your score. Any changes you make to an articulation will apply to every instance of that articulation in your score.

Figure 3.18

Choose the font, size, and style for an articulation in the Font dialog box

Using Articulations from Other Documents

If you have already created or edited articulations in another document or have a document that contains articulations you would like to use, you can transfer these articulations between documents by saving and opening an articulation library. Open the document containing the existing articulations. Click the File menu and choose Save Library. You should see the Save Library dialog box shown in Figure 3.19.

Figure 3.19

Save a library of articulations to open in any document by choosing Articulations in the Save Library dialog box

Choose Articulations and click OK. Enter a name and save the file to your Libraries folder in your Finale directory (Finale should take you there by default). Now open the document you are working on, click the File menu, and choose Open Library. You will now see the Load Library dialog box (Figure 3.20).

Double-click the library you saved to open it. Now click a note to open the Articulation Selection dialog box and all of the new articulations will be available. Finale will check for duplicate articulations, so only new ones will appear in the Articulation Selection window.

Figure 3.20

Add articulations to a document by opening an articulation library from the Open Library dialog box

Articulation Placement

If an articulation does not appear where you want it to by default, you can change its placement settings in the Articulation Designer dialog box. This will change the placement of the articulation throughout the document. With the Articulation Tool selected, click a note to bring up the Articulation Selection dialog box. Choose the articulation you would like to change and click Edit. Use the items in the Positioning section to specify the articulation's position in relation to the note.

Defining Articulations for Playback

Finale's Human Playback feature automatically interprets and performs articulations it finds in the score. If you want to define your own playback definition for an articulation, do the following: on Windows, click the speaker icon on the Playback controls to open the Playback Settings dialog box. Then, from the Human Playback drop-down menu, choose None, then Click OK. On Macintosh, click the expand arrow in the Playback Controls. Then, from the Human Playback pop-up menu, choose None. Now you can define your own playback definitions as follows.

 NOTE
You will learn more about Human Playback in Chapter 14.

There are three ways articulations can affect playback of a note or chord: when it starts (attack), how long it is (duration), and how loud it is (key velocity). To set an articulation to playback, click a note to enter the Articulation Selection, choose the articulation you would like to edit and click the Edit button. In the playback section, click the drop-down menu to choose the type of effect (see Figure 3.21). An articulation can have more than one effect—for example, an accent with a dot should be played with increased attack and decreased duration. In this case, you would change both the velocity and duration setting.

Figure 3.21

Define an articulation for playback in the Playback Effect section of the Articulation Designer

Then specify the percentage of change in the box after Top Note Value. Most of the time you can simply leave Bottom Note Value blank. Both the top and bottom note value fields will apply only to articulations that you want to scale from the bottom to top (or top to bottom) note of a chord. You can use both these settings with the Attack function to create a rolled chord.

Copying Articulations within Your Score

You can copy articulations independently by using the Mass Edit Tool. To try this, enter two measures of quarter notes and add some articulations on every note in the first of these measures. Click the Mass Edit Tool and highlight the first measure. Make sure that Select Partial Measures is turned off in the Edit menu. From the Mass Edit menu, choose Copy Entry Items. Check Articulations and click OK. Now drag the highlighted measure to the second measure. Finale will paste the original articulations on any note that lines up with the beat placement of the original articulation.

Automatically Copy Articulations to Similar Rhythmic Passages

You may have a reoccurring passage in your score that demands the same set of articulations at each occurrence throughout the piece. SmartFind and Paint allows you find and copy articulations to these passages automatically. To demonstrate this, fill a measure with a combination of eighth and quarter notes on different pitches with the Simple or Speedy Entry Tool. Click the Mass Edit Tool, highlight this measure and drag-copy it to a different measure. In the Copy Measures dialog box, type 10 and click OK. Now click the Articulation Tool and add several various articulations to the original measure. Click the Mass Edit Tool again and highlight the measure containing the articulations. Click the Mass Edit menu and choose Set SmartFind Source. Now click the Mass Edit menu again and choose Apply SmartFind and Paint. You will see the SmartFind and Paint dialog box shown in Figure 3.22.

Click the Find button and the measure containing the similar passage becomes highlighted. Click the Paint button, and the articulations appear on the notes just as they did in the original measure. This is also a great technique for copying Slurs, Smart Shapes, Note Expressions, and Measure Expressions to identical rhythmic passages throughout your score.

Figure 3.22

Choose elements to copy to similar rhythmic passages in the SmartFind and Paint dialog box

Entering Expressions

What exactly is an expression? Well, in Finale, expressions are most commonly used for dynamic markings (forte, piano, etc.). However, you will be using expressions to enter many other items, including rehearsal letters, tempo indications, style indications, and many other items. The main benefit of an expression, as opposed to a text block, is spacing and metatool assignment. While editing your score, there will usually be a good deal of spacing changes to notes and measures. Therefore, there are two basic types of expressions: note-attached and measure-attached. In addition, any note-attached or measure-attached expression can be in the form of text or a shape. We refer to these as text expressions and shape expressions. There are many situations that lend themselves to one or the other of these types depending on the type of marking, number of staves in your score, and other factors. Generally, if you plan to enter the text once and spacing isn't an issue, use the Text Tool. If you will use the text more than once, the Expression Tool is a better choice. In this section, I'll discuss the best way to enter expressions and also when to use each type.

To prepare for this section, either use the scratch document from the previous section or open tutorial number 2. To do this, click the File menu and choose Open. Navigate to the Finale folder and double-click the Tutorials folder. Open the file "Tutorial 2.MUS." This is an arrangement of "O, Susannah" that will suit our needs just fine.

Basic Expression Entry

Since dynamic markings are usually the most common expressions, let's enter some of those first. Click the Expression Tool if it isn't selected already. Double-click below the first measure of your score. This opens the Expression Selection dialog box (see Figure 3.23).

Here, you will see a list of default dynamic markings, tempo indications, and rehearsal letters. Click the forte (f) expression to highlight it, then click the Select button, and click OK.

You will be able to enter any expression in the Expression Selection dialog box this way. You can click above or below a measure to enter an expression. Make sure the arrow on the cursor is pointing to the correct staff before you click. If you don't like the placement of an expression, click its handle and either drag it with your mouse or nudge it using the arrow keys. (I'll get into more specific placement techniques later.) To delete the expression, click its handle and press the Delete key.

To edit individual expressions, right-click/Ctrl-click an expression handle to open the context menu. From here you can easily access the Expression Assignment, Expression Definition, or Font dialog boxes to edit

CHAPTER 3

Figure 3.23

Choose an expression for entry in the Expression Selection dialog box

that particular expression. I'll cover the usage of these dialog boxes throughout this section. You can also delete any expression from the context menu.

Note Expressions

As mentioned earlier, note expressions are designed to adjust accordingly with the note or rest to which they are attached. They are particularly useful when working with single-staff documents because, unlike measure expressions, they are designed to appear on one staff only and can affect playback of individual layers (I'll cover the benefits of measure expressions next). To enter a note-attached expression, move your cursor directly above or below a note or rest so you see a small quarter note appear to the upper right of your cursor. With the cursor in this state, double-click. At the bottom of the Expression Selection dialog box, you will see two radio buttons, Note Expression and Measure Expression. Make sure Note Expression is selected and click the Select button. Next you will see the Note Expression Assignment dialog box. Here you can adjust the expression's placement and on which layer you want it to affect playback. You will only see this dialog box while entering note expressions. Click OK, and the expression appears in your score. You can distinguish between note and measure-attached expressions in your score by the color. By default, note expressions are red and measure expressions are green.

Measure Expressions

Measure expressions are designed to adjust their positioning depending on the width and placement of the measure to which they are attached. As you adjust your bar lines and move measures around, the associated measure expressions move with them. To enter a measure expression, double-click above or below a measure to open the Expression Selection dialog box. Click an expression and make sure the Measure Expression radio button is selected at the bottom of this dialog box. Click Select, and you will see the Measure Expression Assignment dialog box. You will be able to specify spacing and where to affect playback here. The Show on section and the Allow Individual Positioning check box are for managing measure expressions attached to several staves. For now, just click OK to enter the expression into your score. The main benefit of measure expressions comes into play while working with multi-staff scores since they can be entered on multiple staves at the same time. This concept will be explained in detail in Chapter 7 where we focus on multiple-staff documents.

Metatools

Like Articulations, you will also be able to enter any expression with a metatool. Again, this is a much faster way to enter them into your score than opening the Selection dialog all the time. Hold down the 4 key and click underneath the second measure. A forte (f) marking will appear. Now double-click an empty space below the staff to open the Expression Selection dialog box. Notice the numbers and letters in parentheses to the right of each expression. These are the preset metatool assignments. While working on your score, hold down one of these numbers or letters and click to quickly enter its associated expression into the score.

You can also specify the type of expression (note-attached/measure-attached) to enter while using expression metatools. Click the Expression menu. Choose Metatools: Note-Attached to automatically enter note expressions, or choose Metatools: Measure-Attached to automatically enter measure expressions as you click expressions into your score. Choose Metatools: Context Sensitive to choose the type of expression based on where you click in the score.

Click the Expression menu and choose Metatools: Context Sensitive. Move your cursor directly above or below a note so you see a small quarter note appear to the upper right of your cursor. Now use a metatool to enter an expression, and it will be attached to the note. If it's a dynamic or tempo marking, it is already defined to appear on a baseline. Move your cursor so the small note vanishes from the cursor and enter another expression with a metatool into your score to specify a measure expression.

Programming an Expression Metatool

You can program your own expression metatools just like articulation metatools. Hold down the Shift key and press a number or letter key. Choose the expression you would like to assign to that key and click Select. Hold down the key you programmed and click in the score to enter the expression you chose.

On Macintosh, you can use TGTools to quickly assign expressions to metatools. From the TGTools menu, choose Select Text Expression to do this (see Chapter 15 for details). If you do not see the TGTools menu, install the TGTools demo available at www.tgtools.de. On Windows, you can use the TGTools Text Expression Browser to easily assign metatools.

Creating a Text Expression

You will want to create expressions for any text in your score that refers to the performance of the music. Tempo markings, style indications, volume or performance practice (andante, crescendo, arco, etc.) will all be added with the Expression Tool. To create an expression, double-click above or below a staff to open the Expression Selection dialog box. Click the Create button. This opens the Text Expression Designer dialog box, shown in Figure 3.24.

Type your text into the entry field. To change the size, font, or style, use the Text menu at the top of this dialog/screen. Choose Font to open the Font dialog box. Here you can choose any size, style, or font on your system. You can use multiple fonts in the same expression (for metronome markings, etc.). When you have finished, click OK, Select, and OK to return to your score. The expression will appear in the size, style, and font you specified. You will be able to enter the expression you just created at any time while working on

CHAPTER 3

Figure 3.24

Create or edit text for entry
as an expression in the Text
Expression Designer dialog box

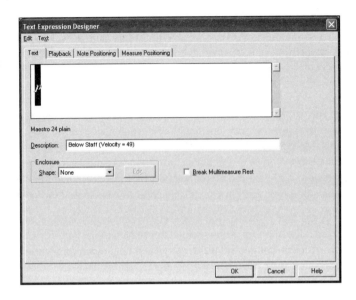

this document. Double-click above or below a staff. Scroll to the bottom of the list and notice your custom expression at the bottom. If you plan on using this expression often, program a metatool for it.

TIP
If you want to ensure that an expression will remain the same size, regardless of staff, system, or page resizing, set it to a fixed size. On Windows, you will find this check box in the Effects section of the Font dialog box while editing your expression. On Mac, it is found under Text > Size.

Editing and Creating Similar Text Expressions

There may be many expressions in your score bearing similar characteristics. To avoid the redundancy of creating each one from scratch, duplicate existing expressions and edit them. To do this, double-click above or below a staff to enter the Expression Selection dialog box. Click the expression you just created (or any existing expression) and click the Duplicate button. This adds a duplicate of the expression at the bottom of the list that will automatically be highlighted. Click the Edit button to edit this expression. Change the text or any other attribute, then click OK, OK, and Select to return to your score. You can duplicate and/or edit any expression that exists in the Expression Selection dialog box.

TIP
While editing your expression in the Text Expression Designer, you may want to define an expression to display on your screen but not in the printout. To do this, on Windows, in the Effects section of the Font dialog box, choose Hidden. On Mac, choose the Text Menu and then Style.

For Windows, there is an alternative way to manage and edit text expressions. If you have many expressions in your library, you may find the Expression Selection dialog box inadequate for quickly finding the expression you're looking for. In response to this problem, an Expression Browser has been included with TGTools for better management and availability of expressions. From the TGTools menu, choose Browser. Use this window to arrange, edit, and select your expressions (see the TGTools documentation at www.tgtools.de for more details).

Enclosing an Expression

You may want to enclose an expression within a box, circle, or rectangle. This is a common trait in rehearsal letters, but is also used for various other text in music. Double-click above or below a staff to open the Expression Selection dialog box. Click one of the existing rehearsal letters in the selection and click the Edit button to open the Text Expression Designer. Under Enclosure (see Figure 3.25), click the Shape drop-down menu and choose Square. To preview and modify the enclosure, click Edit.

Figure 3.25
Preview and edit an enclosure for an expression in the Enclosure Designer dialog box

You can change the shape of the enclosure from the drop-down menu in the upper-right corner, then use the handles in the display window to make any manual adjustments (or use the Height/Width fields to specify the size of the enclosure). Click OK, OK, and then Select and OK to return to your score and see the enclosed expression.

Creating a Shape Expression

You may want to enter a measure or note-attached item in your score that is not in the form of text, but a shape. Double-click above or below the staff to open the Expression Selection dialog box. Click the Shape radio button in the lower-right corner of this dialog box. You will now see a bunch of shapes in the display window. These are the items in your default Shape Expression Library. You can enter any of these just as you would a text expression. For access to more shapes, click the Create button. This opens the Shape Expression Designer dialog box. Click the Select button to see an expanded number of shapes (Figure 3.26). These are all of the shapes in your Shape library.

Figure 3.26

Choose a shape for entry as a
shape expression in the Shape
Selection dialog box

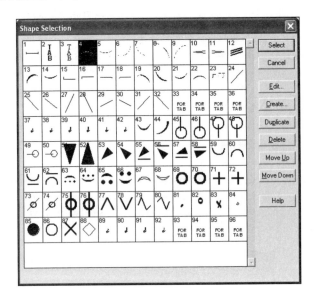

To use one of these shapes, click it, then click Select, OK, Select, and OK to return to your score. Like text
expressions, these can be defined as either measure or note-attached expressions.

You can modify any shape expression while looking at your score. Double-click the handle on the shape
expression. You will see it's now surrounded with black boxes. Click and drag these boxes to modify your
shape.

 NOTE
If you have multiple occurrences of a shape expression in your document, modifying it in the score will
change every occurrence of the shape expression. If you would like to be able to edit each shape
expression independently, enter them with metatools. Each time you use a metatool to enter a shape
expression, Finale creates a duplicate shape ID in the Shape Selection dialog box. Therefore, changes
to one shape in the score will not apply to any other occurrence of that shape.

Creating Your Own Custom Shape

You can design and enter any shape by creating or editing a shape expression. Double-click above or below
a staff to open the Expression Selection dialog box. Click the Shape radio button in the lower-right corner.
Now click the Create button. Click the Select button to display the shapes in your Shape library. To design
your own shape, click the Create button. This opens the Shape Designer dialog box shown in Figure 3.27.

Use the tools available in this box to create your own custom shapes or brackets, or even import graphics to
edit and place in your score. Once you have created your shape, to return to your score, click OK, Select,
OK, Select, and OK. Once you have created the shape, it will exist in this document's Shape library (libraries
are discussed at the end of this chapter).

Figure 3.27

Design your own shape for entry as an expression in the Shape Designer

Aligning and Positioning Expressions

If simply dragging expressions into place isn't consistent enough, you can align and position multiple expressions evenly by selecting several of them or using baselines. For example, drag a box around two or more expressions to select them, then click one of the handles and drag to move them uniformly. Or, to position many expressions at once, use the positioning arrows to adjust the expression baselines. When the Expression Tool is selected, you see four positioning arrows on the left side of the screen as shown in Figure 3.28.

Figure 3.28

Use positioning arrows to position many expressions at once.

If your score has more than one staff, click any staff to display the positioning arrows for that staff. You can use these arrows to move several expressions at once, by staff, system, or score. If you have used Finale's default expression placement (you haven't changed settings under the Note/Measure Positioning tab of the Text Expression Designer), simply choose the Expression menu and select whether you want to adjust the above or below staff baselines, and then click a staff containing the expressions you want to position. Now, do the following:

- ❋ Drag the left arrow to adjust all expressions in the score.
- ❋ Drag the second arrow to adjust all expressions in just that staff (throughout the score).
- ❋ Drag the third arrow to adjust expressions for that staff and that system only.
- ❋ Drag the fourth arrow to specify a position for the next measure expression added (you don't ever really need to use this one).

CHAPTER 3

NOTE

The same positioning arrows are also available for positioning lyrics and chords.

If you want to define an expression to always remain at the same position, and disregard any changes to the baseline, do the following:

1. Right-click (Mac: Ctrl-click) the expression's handle and choose Edit Measure > Note Text > Shape Definition (the one that says "Definition").

2. Click the Note Positioning or Measure Positioning tab (depending on whether this is a note or measure expression).

3. In the Vertical section, under Position, click the drop-down menu and choose Vertical Click Position.

NOTE

For measure expressions, choose Staff Reference Line if you would like to specify the distance from the left barline top staff for the expression.

4. Click OK. A message appears warning you that all manual positioning will be removed. That's fine, you'll just need to drag it into place. If you choose this setting prior to entering the expression, it will appear where you originally clicked.

5. Click Yes.

6. Drag the expression to the desired position. Changes to the baseline will not affect this expression.

Defining an Expression for Playback

As mentioned earlier with articulations, Finale's Human Playback feature automatically interprets and performs expressions it finds in the score. If you want to define your own playback definition for an expression, do the following: On Windows, click the speaker icon on the Playback controls to open the Playback Settings dialog box. Then, from the Human Playback drop-down menu, choose None, and click OK. On Macintosh, click the expand arrow in the Playback Controls. Then, from the Human Playback pop-up menu, choose None. Now, you can define your own playback definitions as follows.

Any expression can be manually defined to affect playback of the score. To define an expression for playback, first double-click above or below a staff to open the Expression Selection dialog box. Click the forte (f) expression, and then click the Edit button. In the Text Expression Designer, click the Playback tab to show the playback options (Figure 3.29).

Here you will see that this expression already has a playback definition assigned. This expression, like all the dynamic expressions, has a key velocity assigned to it. Key velocity is basically the volume of the MIDI note (it actually relates to the velocity of a key as it is struck on a MIDI keyboard). To increase the key velocity (make the note play back "louder") enter a higher number into the Set to Value field. You can define an expression to affect playback in many ways including tempo, pitch, panning, channel, and many others. You will find a more complete description of any shape or text expression's playback capabilities in Chapter 14.

Figure 3.29
Click the Playback tab to
define an expression for
playback

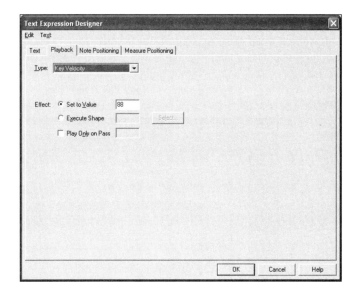

Using Expressions from Other Documents

Like articulations, you can transfer any expression between documents by saving and opening a library.
Open the document containing the existing text or shape expressions that you would like to transfer
to another document. Click the File menu and choose Save Library. Choose Text Expressions or Shape
Expressions and click OK. Enter a name and save the file to your Libraries folder in your Finale directory
(Finale should take you there by default). Now open the document you are working on, click the File
menu and choose Open Library or Load Library. Double-click the library you saved to open it. Now these
expressions will be available in this document's Expression Selection dialog box.

You may see some duplicate expressions that existed in both documents to begin with. To clean this up,
highlight the duplicates and click the Delete button. To avoid these duplicate expressions, you can delete
them from the original document before saving the library. If you do this, make sure not to save changes
when closing the file.

You can delete unused expressions with the Text Expression Sorter Plug-in available in the TGTools plug-in set.

TIP
If you want your own custom expressions available in every new default document or document
created with the Setup Wizard, customize your Maestro Font Default file. To do this, click the File
menu and choose New, then Default Document. After the file opens, load any libraries containing
expressions you want to add into the document. Now click the File menu and choose Save As. On
Windows, name the file "Maestro Font Default.FTM", on Macintosh, simply name the file "Maestro
Font Default" (without the .MUS extension.) Save the file to the Components folder in your Finale folder
and replace the existing file. Now, any time you start a new Default Document or use the Document
Setup Wizard, these expressions will be available in your Expression Selection dialog box.

Creating a Simple Arrangement

Let's apply the skills we've learned so far to create a simple score. In the following example, we'll begin a new document with the Setup Wizard, enter the notes with Simple or Speedy Entry, program metatools to enter articulations and expressions, finalize layout, and print. For this example, we'll notate an arrangement of Greensleeves. When complete, our arrangement will look like Figure 3.30.

Figure 3.30

Greensleeves arrangement

1. From the File menu, choose New > Document With Setup Wizard. For Title, enter "Greensleeves," and for Composer, enter "Arr. by" followed by your name. Then click Next to move to page 2.

2. Now, let's choose our instrument. Click Woodwinds in the leftmost column. We'll create a part for flute, so double-click Flute in the second column. Then click Next to move to page 3.

3. Our arrangement will be in 6/4. Notice this isn't one of the available time signatures on page 3 of the Setup Wizard, so we'll have to define it ourselves. Under Select a Time Signature, click the icon with two question marks. The Time Signature dialog box appears. After Number of Beats, click the right arrow twice so 6/4 appears in the display window. Then click OK to return to the Setup Wizard. Now we'll select the key of the piece. Under Select a Concert Key Signature, click the drop-down arrow to the right of the preview window and choose Minor Key (notice the preview window updates accordingly). This arrangement will be in A minor, so click Next to move to page 4.

4. Check Specify Initial Tempo Marking. Then, in the text box to the right of Tempo, enter "90." Our arrangement will also have a one beat pickup, so check Specify Pickup Measure and make sure the quarter note icon is selected to the right. Click Finish. Your new document appears as shown in Figure 3.31.

Figure 3.31

After competing the Setup
Wizard, the score is ready
for entry

5. Now, use the Simple or Speedy Entry Tool (as described earlier in this chapter) to enter notes into the first four measures as they appear in Figure 3.30.

6. Notice that measures five and six are duplicates of measures one and two. Let's save time by copying with the Mass Edit Tool. Click the Mass Edit Tool and then drag over measures one and two so they are highlighted. Then click the highlighted area and drag to measure five (you will see a black border around measures five and six). Release the mouse button and click OK.

7. Now use the Simple or Speedy Entry Tool to enter notes into measures seven through twelve.

8. Use the same procedure described in step 6 to copy measures nine and ten into measure thirteen and fourteen.

9. Enter notes into the final two measures with the Simple or Speedy Entry Tool.

10. To delete the extra measures, click the Mass Edit Tool, and then click to highlight measure seventeen (the first empty measure). Then, while holding down the Shift key, press the right arrow key to select every measure to the end of the piece. Press Delete to delete these measures (notice there is now a final barline at the end of the piece).

11. Now that we have entered notes into the score, let's enter the dynamic markings. We'll use the Expression Tool to do this. Click the Expression Tool, and then double-click beneath the pickup measure. The Expression Selection dialog box appears. Choose the *mf* expression and click Select. Then click OK. The *mf* expression appears below the staff. Now, let's use pre-defined metatools to enter the remaining two dynamic markings. While holding down the 4 key, click beneath measure nine to add the *f* marking. Then, while holding down the 5 key, click beneath measure fifteen to enter the *mf* marking. To see all of the metatool assignments, double-click anywhere in the score to open the Expression Selection dialog box. All of the metatool assignments appear to the right of each expression. Click Cancel to return to the score.

12. Now, let's enter the articulations. Click the Articulation Tool. Double-click the quarter note in the pickup measure. The Articulation Selection dialog box appears. Choose the tenuto marking (number 7; notice the E in the upper-right corner indicating the metatool assignment) and then click Select. The tenuto marking appears beneath the note. To enter the remaining tenuto marking use a metatool. While holding down the E key, click the last note in measure four. Now, hold down the A key and click each note in measure nine and thirteen to enter the accent articulations. Hold down the F key and click the last note to add the fermata. Click its handle and drag up to move it above the staff.

13. If you wish, click the Play button in the playback controls to hear your piece.

14. Now, let's finalize the layout. We have some extra space at the bottom of the page, so let's evenly space the systems on the page. Click the Page Layout Tool. Click the Page Layout menu, and choose Space Systems Evenly. Now, leave the settings alone and click OK. Notice all systems are evenly spaced on the page.

15. Your piece should now look similar to the example in Figure 3.30. To print the score, choose Print from the File menu. In the Print dialog box, Click OK/Print to print the piece.

Congratulations! You have now created a new score from scratch using Finale's entry tools and the Mass Edit Tool, and you've also added expressions and articulations quickly with metatools. These skills can be used whenever you are working on a score and provide a good foundation for more time-saving concepts you will come across in the following chapters.

ADVANCED NOTE ENTRY, CHORDS, AND LYRICS

If Simple or Speedy Entry isn't quick enough for you, there are a few more methods of note entry that could prove very effective, especially if you are a pianist. Here, I'll cover the variety of methods you can use to enter music in real time with either an external MIDI device (MIDI keyboard/MIDI guitar) or even an acoustic wind instrument. You will also learn how to easily create and enter your own chord suffixes as well as enter lyrics. By the end of this chapter, you will have covered the topics necessary to quickly produce lead sheets and most other single staff documents.

Here's a summary of what you will learn in this chapter:

* ❋ Real-time entry: HyperScribe
* ❋ Entering chord symbols
* ❋ Entering lyrics
* ❋ Creating a lead sheet

Real-Time Entry: HyperScribe

HyperScribe is Finale's tool for translating a live musical performance into sheet music. Recording into Finale with a MIDI keyboard is the most common way to do this. In this section, you will learn how to enter notes in real time while playing along with a click track or tapping the tempo with the sustain pedal. Since you are entering music without interruption, there is some more preparation involved than with Simple or Speedy Entry. However, once you find the settings that work best for you, HyperScribe can really move. While going through this chapter, you can expect a certain amount of editing needed to make finishing touches on your HyperScribe sessions. Plan on using HyperScribe in conjunction with Simple Entry or Speedy Entry to most effectively enter notes overall. In reality, the key to efficiency is finding the most comfortable combination of note entry tools as you approach each individual project.

To prepare for this chapter, set your keyboard to the most basic Piano sound (without any effects). Then open a new Default Document (File > New > Default Document).

 NOTE
To use a MIDI keyboard (or any external MIDI device) for input, you will need to ensure that it is properly connected to the computer and set up in Finale. For complete instructions on MIDI setup, consult the Finale Installation and Tutorials manual.

Playing into the Score along with a Metronome Click

We'll start by using the most common method of HyperScribe: playing over a click track.

1. Click the HyperScribe Tool, then click the HyperScribe menu and choose Click and Countoff (yes, it's already checked, but click it anyway). You should now see the Playback and/or Click dialog box as shown in Figure 4.1. This is where you will choose the beat subdivision of your score, tempo of the click track, and start signal for recording.

Figure 4.1

Specify a beat duration, tempo, and start signal for your HyperScribe session in the Playback and/or Click dialog box

2. Since we are in common time, choose the quarter note box. In the future, you might need to select a different note value depending on the time signature of your piece. In cut time, you would choose a half note, in 6/8, probably a dotted quarter note, and so on. Click the drop-down arrow to the right of Start Signal for Recording. From this list, choose Any MIDI Data. This tells Finale to begin the metronome click on a MIDI note command. For now, let's leave the tempo at 96 beats per minute.

3. Click the Click and Countoff button to open the Click and Countoff dialog box (see Figure 4.2). Here, leave both Countoff and Click fields set to While Recording. The Measures field in the upper-right corner controls the number of measures in the countoff. By default, it is set to click for two measures before recording. Leave this at 2 for now. In the future, you may want to set this to 1.

Figure 4.2

Choose the countoff and MIDI attributes for the click in the Click and Countoff dialog box

Click and Countoff				
Countoff:	While Recording		Measures	2
Click:	While Recording			
Source:	MIDI Note			
Metronome Sound				
	Channel	Note	Velocity	Duration (% of the beat)
Down Beats	10	37	127	50 % Listen
Other Beats	10	37	100	25 % Listen
	OK	Cancel	Help	

In the Metronome Sound section, you will find parameters for your metronome click. The Down Beats row indicates properties for the first click in every measure, and the Other Beats row indicates properties for, well, the other beats. The default settings should work fine, as most synthesizers will use channel ten for percussion. The Key Velocity and Duration of down beats is higher, so the first click in each measure will be more pronounced.

4. Click OK twice to return to the score.

5. When Finale records your performance, it will round off the notes you play to the nearest sixteenth note, eighth note, or other rhythmic subdivision depending on your quantization settings. Unlike other MIDI sequencers that use quantization to perfect playback, the quantization settings in Finale are used to accurately translate a performance into notation (though you can tell Finale to play back the resulting quantized music too if you want). As you record, you will find even the most rhythmically accurate performance will vary somewhat with Finale's concrete timing. For example, if you tend to anticipate the beat slightly, a perfectly accurate transcription would result in unwanted sixty-fourth notes or one-hundred twenty-eighth notes. You would probably also see a number of unwanted rests and ties scattered throughout your score. To specify a reasonable rhythmic value for Finale to use as a rounding marker during your HyperScribe session, use the Quantization Settings dialog box (see Figure 4.3).

6. Choose Quantization Settings from the Options menu.

Figure 4.3
Round your notated rhythms to the nearest eighth note or other rhythmic value by configuring the Quantization Settings dialog box

The value you choose for Smallest Note Value should generally depend on the smallest note used most frequently in the piece you are transcribing. If your piece has many small note values, you may consider choosing a slower recording tempo in the Playback and/or Click dialog box. If you intend to enter tuplets, keep in mind the duration of notes in a tuplet is smaller than the base note value. To accurately choose a tuplet duration for the Smallest Note Value, note the number of EDUs for the full duration of the tuplet and divide it by three. For instance, an eighth note tuplet is the same duration as a quarter note, 1024 EDUs. Enter 341 EDUs (one third of 1024) to specify an eight-note tuplet as the smallest note value.

Don't attempt to HyperScribe ornaments more complex than grace notes, such as trills or tremolos, in a HyperScribe session. These should be added afterwards

7. For now, click the Quarter Note box for Smallest Note Value. Leave Mix Rhythms selected and click the More Settings button. You should now see the More Quantization Settings dialog box as shown in Figure 4.4. Here, you can fine-tune your quantization settings.

Figure 4.4

Make settings for playback, treatment of rests and grace notes for a HyperScribe session in the More Quantization Settings dialog box

8. If you plan to record a number of syncopated rhythmic passages in your score, you may want Finale to eliminate ties between beats and use larger note durations. If this is the case, leave Soften Syncopations checked. If you want notes across beats tied, uncheck Soften Syncopations (see Figure 4.5).

Figure 4.5

HyperScribe results with and without Softened Syncopations

9. Click OK twice to return to your score. You are now ready to begin.

10. Click the first measure of your score. You will see the HyperScribe frame appear on the measure you clicked. Finale is now waiting for a MIDI pitch.

11. Press a note on your keyboard and Finale will begin to click, giving you two measures before recording. At the completion of the second countoff measure, begin entering quarter notes into your score. After the HyperScribe frame moves on to the subsequent measure, you will see your notes appear.

12. When you are finished, click anywhere in the score to stop recording. To enter more complicated music, click Options > Quantization Settings, and choose the eighth or sixteenth note for Smallest Note Value. Then begin your HyperScribe session again. Existing notes are overwritten when you HyperScribe over them.

TIP

You can specify the enharmonic spelling of accidentals for non-diatonic pitches entered with HyperScribe by editing the spelling tables. From the Options menu, choose Enharmonic Spelling > Edit Major and Minor Key Spellings or Edit Modal or Chromatic Key Spellings (see Chapter 10 for details).

13. After completing a HyperScribe session, you may notice extra rests where notes should be held. You can use TGTools to easily clean up your HyperScribe results with the Modify Rests plug-in. From the Plug-ins menu, choose TGTools, and then Modify Rests (this plug-in was added to the standard Finale Plug-ins menu in version 2005).

Playing into the Score while Tapping the Tempo

You can control the tempo of HyperScribe as you record. You can do this easily by tapping the tempo with the sustain pedal (or by using another MIDI signal).

1. Click HyperScribe > Beat Source > Tap. You will now see the Tap Source dialog box as shown in Figure 4.6.

Figure 4.6

Tap to specify the beat for a HyperScribe session by first setting up the Tap Source dialog box

2. At the top, choose the type of MIDI signal you will be using to send the Tap information. The most common is a standard sustain pedal. It should be chosen by default. In the Beat section, after Tap Equals, choose the rhythmic duration of each beat. Since we are in common time, choose the quarter note. For now, click OK (I'll talk about Tap States soon).

CAUTION

Finale will not record MIDI data from the controller you choose to send Tap information, even if it is selected in the Record Continuous Data dialog box.

3. Click the first measure to see the HyperScribe frame around measure 1. Finale will assume the first tap on the sustain pedal is beat 1.

4. Begin playing while tapping the tempo on the sustain pedal. Feel free to adjust the tempo while you play. Like with a click, after the HyperScribe frame moves on to the subsequent measure, you will see your notes appear. When you are finished, click anywhere in the score to stop recording.

If you want to record into a score over a meter change without having to stop and change the beat unit, (for example, record over a time signature change from 4/4 to 6/8), you can instruct the Tap Equals setting to change from a quarter note to a dotted quarter note. To do this, set up Tap States. From the HyperScribe menu, choose Beat Source > Tap. In the Tap Source dialog box, click the Select button for Tap States. This will bring up the Tap States dialog box as shown in Figure 4.7.

Figure 4.7

Switch the beat duration per tap on the fly by setting up the Tap States dialog box

Here, click the Select button to the right of Tap Equals to choose a new beat value. You will also need to set up a MIDI trigger to tell Finale to switch to the new Tap State. Then select a new Smallest Note Value. Click the Listen button, and then press a MIDI note you won't be using in your notation (perhaps a really high or low note). This will be your trigger for Tap State 1. You can program up to three Tap States. Click the spinner arrows at the top of this box to program any other Tap States you are using (you can program up to three). Click OK twice to return to your score. Now, record into the score, and just before the down beat of the new meter, stop tapping and press the appropriate trigger. Then resume with your performance while tapping along with the tempo. Click anywhere in the score to finish.

CAUTION

Once you trigger a Tap State, you will not be able to go back to your original Beat Equals setting. If you want to return to the original meter during a Tap session, program another Tap State with your original Beat Equals setting.

Recording into Two Staves at Once

Whether you are using a metronome click or are tapping the tempo, you may want to record music directly into a grand staff (both treble and bass clef) in a single HyperScribe session. To do this, click the HyperScribe menu, and choose Record Mode > Split into Two Staves. You will now see the Fixed Split Point dialog box as shown in Figure 4.8.

Figure 4.8

Tell Finale where to split between the treble and bass clef staves in a grand staff with the Fixed Split Point dialog box

The split point is the lowest pitch Finale will enter into the upper staff. Any notes entered below the split point will be entered into the lower staff. Click OK to return to your score. Now click on the first measure to begin a new HyperScribe session. Notice there is now a box surrounding both staves. Click anywhere in the score when you are finished recording. For information on more advanced topics, such as entering into more than two staves at once and cross-staff notation, see Chapter 7.

TIP

To easily open a new grand staff document, use the Setup Wizard (File > New). Choose Piano from the Keyboards category on page 2. To easily add a grand staff to an existing score, click the Staff Tool and choose New Staves (with Setup Wizard) from the Staff menu.

Using HyperScribe with a MIDI Guitar

In addition to using a MIDI keyboard for note entry, you can also use a number of other external MIDI devices such as a MIDI guitar. To use a MIDI guitar for entry, follow the same instructions above. You can use a guitar (or other MIDI device) just as you would a MIDI keyboard.

MIDI guitars require an interface between the guitar and the computer to translate the acoustic pitches into MIDI information. As a result of the extra processing necessary, there might be a slight, yet consistent delay in the time it takes from the moment the string is plucked to the time it reaches Finale. This is called latency and can cause the HyperScribe transcription to lag behind the beat. To compensate for this, you can tell Finale to leave a specific amount of time between clicks/taps and the actual recording tempo. To do this, choose MIDI Setup from the MIDI menu (and on Windows, click the Advanced button.) Enter a MIDI Latency value anywhere from 25 to 150 milliseconds (the precise amount of time will depend on your interface and hardware configuration). Once you have established the correct amount of latency, you should be able to use HyperScribe normally.

Finale comes with many new features specifically for guitar and notation of other fretted instruments. One of these is the ability to record directly into a TAB staff with HyperScribe. When you do this, Finale will even record the actual fret numbers you play during the HyperScribe session. For more information on creating and editing TAB staves, see Chapter 8.

Playback

While HyperScribe is a great way to transcribe notes into your score, it can also be used to record playback data. Finale can capture the subtle nuances of your performance, including the rhythmic feel and (new in 2005) sustain pedal and other continuous data. The result is playback that sounds like your original performance. If you want to play back your HyperScribe recordings as you played them, do the following:

1. Windows users: In the Playback Controls, click the speaker icon. The Playback Settings dialog box appears. Macintosh users: Click the expand arrow on the Playback Controls to show the advanced options.

2. Click the drop-down menu next to Human Playback Style and choose None. You are telling Finale you want to use your own (genuine) human performance instead of Finale's interpretation of the score. (If a style is chosen here, Human Playback is automatically applied for the entire score).

NOTE
You can apply Finale's Human Playback interpretation to parts of your score, or even mix your recorded MIDI data with Human Playback's using the Apply Human Playback plug-in (Plug-ins > New Plug-ins for Finale 2005 > Apply Human Playback).

3. Windows users: Click OK. Macintosh users: Minimize the Playback Controls if desired.

4. Click the HyperScribe Tool.

5. From the HyperScribe menu, choose Record Continuous Data. The Record Continuous Data dialog box appears. Here, you can choose to record any type of continuous MIDI data (effects applied with various controllers on your MIDI device like pitch wheel, sustain pedal, etc.).

6. You can relieve some of your computer's resources during a recording by specifying up to four controllers. (Click Listen and activate each controller you want to use). Or, just make sure All is selected if you want to retain all of this information.

7. Now, if you want to play back the music exactly as you performed it or exactly as it appears in the score, from the Options menu, choose Playback Options. Here you can specify playback of more individual elements of your recording. In the Options section, specify whether you want Finale to play back key velocities and note durations as you recorded them or as they appear in the score.

8. You can use the Playback Settings (or Playback Controls on Mac) to specify other parameters such as base key velocity and swing playback. On Windows, open the Playback Settings by clicking the speaker icon on the right of the Playback Controls. On Mac, click the little expander triangle on the left side of the Playback Controls to expand the dialog. If you don't see the Playback Controls on-screen, select them from the Window menu.

 NOTE
For information on more advanced playback options, see Chapter 14.

CHAPTER 4

Transcription Mode

Transcription Mode is basically Finale's built-in miniature MIDI sequencer. With this feature, you can record an entire piece into Finale with a MIDI keyboard, then go back afterwards and assign the measure and beat information. Though less popular than the other entry methods, this utility can be very useful, particularly if you are a pianist.

To record a performance in Transcription Mode and convert it into a Finale document, do the following:

1. Start a new document with the Setup Wizard, and make sure to specify the key and meter of the piece you will be playing. If you start with a Default Document, be sure to set the key signature and meter before moving on.

2. Choose the HyperScribe Tool, and then, from the HyperScribe menu, choose Transcription Mode. Click the measure you want to begin (this will be the first measure of the resulting transcription). The Transcription Window appears.

3. Click Wait Till. Finale is now waiting for a MIDI signal from you.

4. Play the piece on your MIDI keyboard.

5. When you are done, click anywhere in the window. You will see your performance expressed in horizontal bars as you would in a MIDI sequencer.

6. Now, if you want to save your performance, from the File menu, choose Save As. Any file saved from Transcription Mode is different than a regular Finale file, and on Windows will have the extension .NOT. You can open the .NOT file by choosing Open from the File menu while in Transcription Mode. This portion of Finale is like a separate program altogether. You will notice the menu commands pertain only to the Transcription Window, and do not apply to the Finale score in any way. To place your performance into the Finale score, you will need to transcribe the sequence, which I'll explain next.

7. To transcribe a recorded performance, you need to tell Finale how to organize the piece by beat and measure. To do this, we'll assign time and measure tags. From the Edit menu, choose Select All to highlight the entire performance. You are now going to tap along with the performance to tell Finale where each beat lies in the performance.

8. From the Time Tag menu, check Record Equal Durations. Then, from the Time Tag menu, choose First Tag Is > Quarter if your main beat is a quarter note (if not, choose the value of the main beat).

9. In the Keyboard section, choose Play. There are two types of information you record into the Transcription Window: the actual performance (which you already did), and the beat/time information we are about to enter. You will need to play the performance as you record the beat tags.

10. In the Time Tags section, choose Record.

11. Click Wait Till.

12. Now, tap any key along with the playback to record the beat tags. When finished, Finale will stop recording and you will see the Time Tags appear at the top of the Transcription Window (they look like notes).

13. From the Time Tag menu, choose Align Tags to Notes to "quantize" the time tags to the nearest note. The default value (200) usually works fine. Click OK.

14. From the Time Tag menu, choose Assign Measure Tags. Finale looks at the time signature you have specified in the score, and places a mark (M) to indicate each barline.

15. If you are transcribing into a grand staff (two staves), from the Transcription menu, choose Split Point > Fixed. Enter the MIDI note number of the lowest pitch you want to appear in the top staff (middle C = 60). If there is a discernable gap between both hands in your performance, you could choose Moving to tell Finale to attempt to alter the split point automatically by evaluating the movements of both hands in the performance. Click OK to return to the Transcription Window.

16. Click the Quant Settings button to choose the smallest note value you want Finale to round to in the transcription. Make any other desired quantization settings and Click OK.

17. Click Transcribe to convert the music into your Finale document. To view the transcription again in the Transcription Window, simply click the first measure of the transcribed sequence.

MicNotator

If you play a wind instrument, you may find MicNotator useful for note entry. Use this feature to record into a microphone for transcription into a staff. To use this method of entry, choose MicNotator from the MIDI menu and check the Enable MicNotator box. Also, use the Mic Level indicator to ensure you are getting a signal from the microphone (which should be plugged into the Mic In port on your computer). When you see a signal in the Mic Level indicator, click OK. Then use the HyperScribe tool just as you would with a MIDI keyboard. When you use the MicNotator, be sure to play notes as evenly and cleanly as possible for best results. The translation from acoustic pitch to MIDI can be somewhat less accurate than a direct connection to an external MIDI device. If you are using a newer Macintosh, there may not be a Mic In port available on your computer. If this is the case, visit www.griffintechnology.com/products/imic/index.html for information on a USB Mic adaptor.

 TIP
MakeMusic! sells special microphones designed for use with MicNotator that clip to your instrument or clothing. A MakeMusic! customer support representative will send you one for about $10.

The Auto-Dynamic Placement Plug-In

After entering any music using HyperScribe, you can easily tell Finale to scan the music and place dynamic markings in the score based on the recorded key velocities. To do this, click the Mass Edit Tool and press Ctrl/Command-A to Select All. From the Plug-ins menu, choose Expressions > Auto-Dynamic Placement. You will now see the Auto-Dynamic Placement dialog box containing several parameters for expression placement and spacing. You may need to adjust these depending on your results. Click OK to see dynamic markings placed in your score automatically as note-attached expressions.

Working with Chord Symbols

Chord symbols are an integral part of music notation. You find them in lead sheets, jazz charts, guitar tablature, and many other types of music. Chord symbols in Finale are basically entries of text placed on a baseline above entries in a staff. They consist of three elements: a symbol, suffix, and alternate bass. The symbol contains the bass pitch information of the chord (F sharp, B flat, etc.), and the suffix contains the quality of chord (major, minor, inversion, etc.). The suffix will also contain higher tertian information (7, 9, etc.) and their pitch alterations. An alternate bass pitch can also be added to any chord symbol. When entering chord symbols, you will always start with the symbol, and then specify a suffix and alternate bass if necessary.

Often, when creating notation for fretted instruments, fretboard diagrams accompany the chord symbols to indicate a specific fingering. You can easily include fretboard diagrams beneath each chord suffix using Finale's default fretboards, or you can define your own custom fretboard diagrams. In addition to adding chord symbols, you will also learn how to enter, and even customize fretboard diagrams.

Entering Chord Symbols

There are several ways to enter and edit chord symbols in Finale. You will be able to type them directly above a staff, define them manually for each entry, or even tell Finale to analyze the music and insert the appropriate chord symbol. You will be able to customize the font, style, and size of chord symbols, suffixes, and fretboards, and even transfer a library of custom chord symbols between documents. In this section, you will learn how to handle chord symbols efficiently in Finale.

To prepare for this section, open a new Default Document (File > New > Default Document). Unless specified otherwise, assume the Chord Tool is selected.

Type Into Score

Typing chords directly into the score is the most basic method of chord entry. It is also perhaps the fastest for entering basic chord symbols. To demonstrate this, first enter any single-line melody into a staff with the Simple Entry Tool. Then click the Chord Tool. From the Chord menu, choose Type Into Score. You will see four arrows to the left of the staff. These indicate the vertical positioning of your chords (more about them soon). Click the first note in the staff. You will see a blinking cursor above the note you clicked. Type "CMaj" to indicate a C major chord. When you first type a chord symbol, it will appear as normal text. Press the spacebar. The "CMaj" turns into a chord symbol with Maj as the suffix. To hide or show fretboards at any time, choose Show Fretboards from the Chord menu. Your cursor is now above the next note. Now, type "Abmin7/Db" and press the spacebar. Now you will see an A-flat minor seven chord over D flat (see Figure 4.9).

Figure 4.9

Elements of chords

Chord symbols are case sensitive. You can indicate the root of a minor chord by entering a lowercase letter or the root of a major chord by using an uppercase letter. The case of the root letter will affect the playback (major or minor) of the chord symbol.

While typing chords into the score, use the following method:

1. Type the letter representing the root of the chord.

2. Type the alteration of the root of the chord using "b" for flat and "#" for sharp.

3. Type the suffix abbreviation (Maj, min, 7, 9, etc.).

4. Type the Alternate Bass. Precede the alternate bass note with a forward slash (/) to place it to the right of the suffix, a bar symbol (|) to place it below and slightly to the right, and underscore (_) to place the alternate bass directly below the symbol and suffix.

In addition to using "b" for flat and "#" for sharp, you can also use keystrokes for diminished and half-diminished symbols. Use the "o" key (lowercase O, not zero) for a fully diminished symbol and the "%" key (Shift-5) for half diminished.

While typing into the score (or using manual input as we'll describe next), you can use keyboard shortcuts to easily select any of the available chord suffixes. After entering the root, type a colon (:) and then the number of the suffix as it appears in the Chord Suffix Selection dialog box. For example, type C:1 to enter Cmaj. If you don't remember the number of the suffix, type :o after the root, and then press the spacebar to view the Chord Suffix Selection dialog box. Choose the chord suffix and click the Select button to return to the score (or Chord Definition dialog box) with the suffix added.

Manual Input

To enter chords with more complicated suffixes, and for more control while entering chords, you may want to use Manual Input mode. From the Chord menu, choose Manual Input. You will now see the Chord Definition dialog box (Figure 4.10).

Figure 4.10

Choose the suffix, fretboard, and playback attributes for a chord in the Chord Definition dialog box

Enter the chord just as you would while typing into the score in the Chord Definition text box. Instead of typing the suffix, you can also choose from a list of available chord suffixes. Click the Advanced button and click the Select button in the Numeric Definition section (at the bottom). You will see a list of available chord suffixes. Click the one you want to use so it is highlighted, and then click the Select button. You will see the suffix to the right of the root in the Chord Definition text box. Click OK to see the chord appear in the score above the note you originally clicked.

TIP

By default, chords are set to playback. To silence playback for all chords symbols, uncheck Enable Chord Playback from the Chord menu.

MIDI Input

Use MIDI Input to enter chords easily with a MIDI keyboard. Choose MIDI Input from the Chord menu, and click a note in your score. You will see an ear icon appear above the staff. This means Finale is listening. Play a chord on your MIDI keyboard (in any inversion). Finale will analyze the chord you play and enter the corresponding chord suffix into the score. If Finale does not recognize the chord, you will be prompted with the Unknown Chord Suffix dialog box. Click "Let Finale do it" to tell Finale to automatically choose the closest chord symbol. Choose "I'll do it" to teach Finale the chord you played. Finale will take you to the Chord Definition dialog box to define a chord symbol for the chord you played.

You can edit the chord suffix associated with any chord played from the MIDI keyboard. To do this, choose Edit Learned Chords from the Chord menu. You will be prompted with the Edit Learned Chords dialog box as shown in Figure 4.11.

CHAPTER 4

Figure 4.11

Customize the chord to input for a combination of MIDI notes while using MIDI Input in the Edit Learned Chords dialog box

Choose a key for the learned chord and click the Learn button. Then play the chord you want to re-assign. Click the Edit button to define its associated chord symbol.

One/Two-Staff Analysis

If you already have a staff or staves with existing chords in the form of notation, Finale can analyze the music and enter the appropriate chord symbol automatically. Enter a chord into a staff. Then choose One- or Two-Staff Analysis from the Chord menu (depending on the number of staves you want to analyze). Click above a chord to tell Finale to place a chord symbol in the score automatically. If Finale cannot recognize the chord, you will see the Unknown Chord Suffix dialog box. Click "I'll do it" to define a chord symbol manually in the Chord Suffix Selection dialog box or choose "Let Finale do it" to let Finale make its best guess.

Creating and Editing Chord Suffixes

If you can't find the suffix you want to use in the Chord Suffix Selection dialog box, you can create one yourself. From the Chord menu, choose Manual Input. Click a note in the score to bring up the Chord Definition dialog box. Click the Advanced button (to extend the lower portion), and then click Select in the Numeric section to open the Chord Suffix Selection dialog box. Click the Create button (or, if you see a suffix similar to the one you are looking for, highlight it, click Duplicate, and then Edit). You will now see the Chord Suffix Editor dialog box, as shown in Figure 4.12.

Figure 4.12

Edit or create your own suffix in the Chord Suffix Editor dialog box

Enter a suffix symbol in the text box to the upper right (click the Set Font button to change the font). If the symbol is a number, check the Number box. To precede the symbol with a sharp, flat, plus, or minus, check Prefix With and select the prefix below. If you want another character, click the Next button and repeat the process. Use either the handle in the editing window or the H: (horizontal) or V: (vertical) text boxes to position each symbol.

You may want to assign the suffix (pitches relative to the defined root) for playback. To do this, click the Set Play button. This will bring up the Suffix Keynumber Offsets dialog box where you can enter MIDI Note numbers for playback. If you are using an external MIDI device (such as a MIDI keyboard), click the Listen button to enter the root and then the chord. Finale will record the MIDI information for you and calculate the offsets. Click OK, OK, Select, and OK to return to the score and review the suffix.

TIP

When you play a chord into the Suffix Keynumber Offsets dialog box, Finale will not retain the octave information, only the pitch. To raise or lower an offset an octave for playback, add or subtract 12 from the MIDI Note number (negatives are OK).

Changing Chord Fonts

You may want to change the default fonts of your chord symbols, suffixes, alterations, or fretboards. To do this, click the Options menu and choose Document Options. Then click the Fonts category. Click the drop-down menu for Chords and choose the element you want to change. Click the Set Font button to select a new font, size, and style. Do this for all elements of the chord you want to change. Click OK to return to the score. Changing the fonts for chord suffixes in the Document Options dialog box will only affect newly created ones, and will not affect suffixes already existing in the score or in your Suffix Selection. To change the font of existing chord suffixes, select the Chord Tool and choose Change Chord Suffix Fonts from the Chord menu. In the Replace With section, click the Set Font button. Choose the Font, Size, and Style and click OK. Check the Font, Size, and Style boxes (as needed) and click OK. Existing suffix fonts will change to the one you specified. If you find that the chords no longer line up on the same baseline, make sure to select Fix Baseline Positioning in the Change Chord Suffix Fonts dialog box.

Chord Metatools

Use chord metatools to quickly enter chords into a score. Choose Manual Input from the Chord menu. Hold down Shift and press any number or letter. You will now see the Chord Definition dialog box. Enter the chord symbol in the text box at the top (and make any other settings), then click OK. Now, hold down the letter you assigned and click on any note in the score to add the defined chord.

Chord Positioning

You can easily move any chord or fretboard diagram by clicking its handle and dragging or using the arrow keys to nudge it around. More than likely, however, you will want all of the chords symbols or fretboards to align to the same distance above the staff along a baseline. You can easily adjust the vertical placement (or baseline) of chord symbols by using the four positioning arrows on the left side of the screen. The arrow you use will depend on the region of chord baselines you want to position. Here is an explanation.

❋ Use the first arrow (from the left) to adjust the baseline of all chords or fretboards in the whole document.

❋ Use the second arrow to adjust the baseline of all chords or fretboards in that staff.

❋ Use the third arrow to adjust the baseline of all chords or fretboards in a particular staff in a system (in Page View).

❋ Use the fourth arrow to predetermine the baseline of the next chord or fretboard you enter.

To use the arrows for chord positioning, choose Position Chords from the Chord menu. To use the arrows for fretboard positioning, choose Position Fretboards from the Chord menu.

To space chords horizontally, you can drag them by the handle or reposition the notes they are attached to. If you find your chords and/or fretboards overlap, you can tell Finale to automatically respace your music to avoid collision of chord symbols and fretboards. To do this, from the Options menu, choose Document Options and select Music Spacing. In the Avoid Collision Of section, check Chords and click OK. Now, select the Mass Edit Tool, press Ctrl/Command-A to Select All, and then press the 4 key (to apply Note Spacing). Your music respaces to accommodate the chord symbols. There will be more information regarding Music Spacing in Chapter 9.

Fretboard Diagrams

If you are working on a score for guitar, you may want to include fretboard diagrams that display a fingering for the chord. As mentioned earlier, you can activate or deactivate the presence of fretboard diagrams on all chord symbols at once by choosing Show Fretboards under the Chord menu. If you decide to show fretboards, Finale will display them with a standard fingering for the specified chord. Since there are many ways to finger any given chord, you may want to edit a fretboard diagram so that the chord is played on a different fret (for example). To customize a fretboard, first choose Manual Input from the Chord menu. Click a note in the score to open the Chord Definition dialog box. In the Fretboard section, click Select to see any alternate fretboards that already exist for that chord in Finale's default Fretboard library. If you see the one you want, click it, then click Select and OK to return to your score. If you do not see the desired fretboard diagram, create your own. Click a note in your score to open the Chord Definition dialog box, enter the chord symbol, then click the Edit button in the Fretboard section to open the Fretboard Editor dialog box as seen in Figure 4.13.

Figure 4.13

Edit or create your own fretboard in the Fretboard Editor dialog box

Here, make modifications to the existing fretboard using the tools on the left side of the Fretboard section. You can edit the number of strings and string tuning of the fretboard instrument by clicking the Edit Instrument button. Once you have finished editing the fretboard diagram, click OK and Select to return to the Chord Definition dialog box. Click OK to return to the score and see the custom fretboard. If you find that the fretboards are too big or too small, choose Resize Fretboards from the Chord menu. Here you can enter a percentage of the original size (the higher the number the bigger the fretboard gets—set it to 100% to see the original size).

> **TIP**
> To easily access the Fretboard Editor or the Chord Definition dialog box to edit a chord individually, right/Control-click a chord suffix handle and select Edit Chord Definition or Edit Fretboard. Also use this context menu to show or hide chords and fretboards or to delete chord symbols independently.

Transferring Custom Chord Libraries between Documents

If you have already created or edited chord symbols or fretboards in another document or have a document that contains chords or fretboards you would like to use, you can transfer these between documents by saving and opening a Chord and Fretboard library. Open the document containing the existing chords. Click the File menu and choose Save Library. You should see the Save Library dialog box. Choose Chords and Fretboards and click OK. Enter a name and save the file to your Libraries folder in your Finale directory (Finale should take you there by default). Now open the document you are working on, click the File menu and choose Open Library or Load Library. You will now see the Open Library dialog box. Double-click the library you saved to open it. You will now be able to choose these chords and fretboards for entry in the new document.

Entering Lyrics

You will find entering lyrics in Finale is a breeze, as long as you use the right methods. Experimentation can get you into quite a mess if you aren't careful. I'll go over the right way to enter lyrics so as to avoid any of these unnecessary hurdles. In this section, you will learn how to type lyrics directly into the score or type the lyrics first and then click them into the score.

To prepare for this section, open any document and add a single-line melody. Then click the Lyrics Tool. In this section, assume you have the Lyrics Tool chosen unless directed otherwise.

Type Lyrics into the Score

The easiest and most intuitive way to enter lyrics is to type them directly into the score. From the Lyrics Menu, choose Type Into Score. Now click on a note to see a blinking cursor below the staff. Type a syllable and press the spacebar to advance the cursor to the next rhythmic subdivision. If you would like a hyphen between syllables, press the − (dash) key instead of the spacebar. Use the left and right arrow keys to move the cursor between letters. Use the Tab key to move to the next syllable and Shift-Tab to move to the previous syllable. Click any lyric to highlight it, or double-click it to activate the cursor. Use the Delete/Backspace key to delete syllables like you would in a word processor.

To enter a second verse, click the first lyric so it is highlighted. Press the down arrow, and you will see the cursor shift into position for the second verse. Do this to enter as many verses as you like. Press the up arrow to move to the previous verse. You can begin a new verse at any time.

TIP
You may want to change the distance between hyphens in your lyrics. To do this, click the Lyrics menu and choose Lyric Options. Here, change the value in the text box for Space Between Hyphens.

Click Assignment

Though typing into the score is adequate for simple scores, you will want to use Click Assignment in any document that contains repeating lyrics. To use this method of lyric entry, you will type all of the lyrics into a separate text window, and then click the lyrics into the score accordingly. You will be able to click the same text into the score many times, saving the trouble of retyping the same lyric. Also, you will be able to edit the lyrics once to change a phrase for every occurrence in the document. Start by opening the Edit Lyrics dialog box (Figure 4.14) where you will be entering text. Choose Edit Lyrics from the Lyrics menu.

Figure 4.14

Enter lyrics in the Edit Lyrics dialog box for entry later with Click Assignment

Here, enter your lyrics. You can treat this dialog box much like a basic word-processor. Place a hyphen at the end of a syllable to hyphenate it to the next. Simply use a space between non-hyphenated syllables. To enter verse two, click the up arrow to the right of Verse. The editing window will appear empty. Enter the second verse just as you did the first. Do this for as many verses as you need. If you don't know all the lyrics beforehand, don't worry, you can come back to the Edit Lyrics window any time. Now that you have entered some text in the Edit Lyrics box, click OK to return to the score. From the Lyrics menu, choose Click Assignment. You will see the Click Assignment dialog box appear as shown in Figure 4.15.

Figure 4.15
Click in the score to enter the leftmost syllable shown in the Click Assignment box

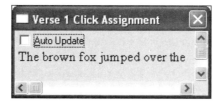

Click a note in the staff to enter the leftmost lyric. All of the lyrics in this verse will scroll to the left. The leftmost lyric always indicates the next lyric ready for entry. Use the horizontal scroll bar to advance to any lyric in the verse. Move between verses by using the vertical scroll bar. Hold down Ctrl/Option and click a note to enter all lyrics to the end of the verse automatically.

You may have noticed that in addition to verses, you can also specify choruses and sections. These are no different than verses, and can be treated the same. Use them for organization if necessary. You can enter up to 512 of each. To easily specify a current lyric (verse, section, or chorus) for entry in Type Into Score or Click Assignment, choose Specify Current Lyric from the Lyrics menu. Choose the lyric type and the number and click OK. If you want to use different fonts or styles for a verse, you can do so by entering the syllables in a chorus or section. (There is no preset visual difference between a verse, section, or chorus, and syllables will line up with the verse perfectly.)

TIP
You can easily copy text from a word-processing program into Finale for lyric entry. Highlight the text in the word-processing program with Ctrl/Command-C. Then, from the Lyrics menu, choose Edit Lyrics. Press Ctrl/Command-V to place the lyrics in the Edit Lyrics window. Then use Click Assignment to enter them into the score.

Setting or Changing the Font for Lyrics

To set the font for your lyrics before you have entered them, choose Document Options from the Options menu. On the left, click Fonts to see the font options. Click the drop-down menu for Lyrics, choose Verse, Section, or Chorus, then click the Set Font button. Set the font, size, or style here and click OK and then OK again to return to the score.

If you want to change the font of existing lyrics, use the Edit Lyrics dialog box. Choose Edit Lyrics from the Lyrics menu. Move the verse section or chorus you want to change and highlight the text (Ctrl/Command-A to Select All). From the Text menu, choose Font. Select the font, size, or style and click OK. You will see the lyrics change in the Edit Lyrics window. Click OK to return to your score and review the font change.

You can change the font of all lyrics at once by using the Change Fonts plug-in. Click the Plug-ins menu and choose Miscellaneous > Change Fonts. Click the Change button for Lyrics to open the Font dialog box. Here, choose the font, size, and style you would like to change your lyrics to. Click OK, and then click OK again to return to the score. All existing lyrics will change to the new font, size, or style you specified.

After running the Fonts plug-in, you may find that your verses overlap or that there is too much space between verses due to a new font size or style. To fix this, you can tell Finale to reset your lyric spacing automatically. From the Options menu, choose Document Options, and select Fonts. From the Lyric drop-down menu, select the type of lyric in the score, and then click the Set Font button to the right. In the Font dialog box, choose the new font and size you selected with the Change Font plug-in. Click OK twice to return to the score. Then, with the Lyrics Tool selected, go to the Lyrics menu and choose Adjust Baselines. Click Set Piece Offsets to Default Font and click OK. The vertical spacing for lyrics will be made even for all verses automatically.

Positioning Lyrics

If you change the font of your lyrics, you may want to space them out vertically. You can adjust the baseline (vertical placement) of each verse, section, or chorus independently. These baselines work much like those explained for expressions in Chapter 3. To choose the lyric you want to move, choose Specify Current Lyric from the Lyrics menu. Choose the lyric type and number, and then click OK. Notice the four arrows on the left. You can easily adjust the vertical placement (or baseline) of the chosen lyric by using the four positioning arrows on the left side of the screen just as you would for chords. The arrow you use will depend on the region of lyrics you want to position.

* Use the first arrow (from the left) to adjust the baseline of all lyrics in the whole document.

* Use the second arrow to adjust the baseline of all lyrics in the staff.

* Use the third arrow to adjust the baseline of all lyrics in a system (in Page View).

* Use the fourth arrow to predetermine the baseline of the next chord or fretboard you enter.

Like chords, to space lyrics horizontally, you will need to reposition the notes to which they are attached. Like chord symbols, avoiding overlapping syllables is most easily done with Finale's Automatic Music Spacing capabilities. From the Options menu, choose Document Options, and select Music Spacing. Under Avoid Collision Of, make sure Lyrics is checked. Click OK to return to the score. Now, select the Mass Edit Tool, press Ctrl/Command-A to Select All, and then press the 4 key (to apply Note Spacing). Your music respaces horizontally to accommodate the lyrics. You'll find more information regarding Music Spacing in Chapter 9.

You can also edit the positioning of lyrics manually. From the Lyrics menu, choose Adjust Syllables. Double-click the lyric you want to move. You will see a handle appear by the lyric. Now, click and drag, or use the arrow keys, to position the lyric manually. When you move lyrics vertically this way, you are actually separating them from their baselines. After using Adjust Syllables, you can move them back to their original position by using the Clear Lyric Positioning plug-in. Click the Mass Edit Tool. Highlight the region of lyrics you want to reset, then choose Plug-ins > Lyrics > Remove Lyric Positioning. The Backspace/Clear key will also clear the manual positioning for a single syllable.

Editing Lyrics

While you enter lyrics, there are a number of editing techniques than can come in handy. In this section I'll cover the common ways you can modify your lyrics while entering or after you have entered them.

Smart Word Extensions and Hyphens

As of Finale 2004, the word extensions and hyphens you add adjust automatically to spacing changes in the score. You may not see these adjustments as you type in lyrics (if you are using the Type Into Score method). To update the visual appearance of word extensions and hyphens, from the Edit menu, choose Update Word Extensions and Hyphens.

You can change the appearance of the offset of word extensions and line thickness, and make a variety of other settings in the Document Options dialog box (Figure 4.16). From the Options menu, choose Document Options, and then choose Lyrics (or from the Lyrics menu, choose Lyric Options). Here you can control the space between hyphens and turn off Smart Hyphens. Click Word Extensions to change the appearance of word extensions in the score.

Figure 4.16

You can change the appearance of hyphens and word extensions in the Document Options dialog box.

Shifting Lyrics

You may want to shift all or some of your lyrics to the right or left after they have been entered. Click the Lyrics menu and choose Shift Lyrics. You will see the Shift Lyrics dialog box as shown in Figure 4.17.

Figure 4.17

Shift lyrics left or right according to settings in the Shift Lyrics dialog box

Choose Shift Syllables by One note, to the End of the Lyric or Shift Syllables by One note, to the Next Open Note depending on the region of lyrics you want to shift. Then, in the drop-down menu select Left or Right depending on the direction you want to shift the lyrics. Click OK. If you chose to shift lyrics to the left, click the note to the left of the region you want to shift to move the lyrics toward the beginning of the score. If you chose to shift lyrics to the right, click the first note of the region you want to shift to move the region toward the end of the score.

Copying and Deleting Lyrics

Click Assignment, as explained above, is the best way to enter repeated lyrics to any location in a document. However, there are some other ways to copy lyrics. If you want to copy a region of music with lyrics, use the Mass Edit Tool. Click the Mass Edit Tool, highlight the region you want to copy, and drag the region to its destination. When you copy lyrics in this way, the lyrics are linked dynamically. In other words, editing lyrics in the destination region will also change lyrics in the source region respectively.

If you need to copy music to a region of your score not visible on the screen, select the measures you want to move. Then navigate to the new section of the piece, hold down Ctrl-Shift (or Option-Shift on Mac), and click on the first measure for which you'd like the selected lyrics and music to appear.

You can also copy lyrics independently with the Lyrics Tool. From the Lyrics menu, choose Clone Lyrics. Now highlight a region containing lyrics and drag it to another measure containing music. Finale will copy all syllables according to the rhythmic placement of the original lyrics (so you will need the same rhythmic passage in both measures for all lyrics to copy).

To delete a region of lyrics, first click the Mass Edit Tool. Highlight the region of music containing the unwanted lyrics. From the Mass Edit menu, choose Clear Items. Choose Only Selected Items, and then click the Entries check box. Check Lyrics and click OK. Click OK again to return to the score. Lyrics in the highlighted region will be deleted. Note that even though you've deleted the lyrics from your score, the lyrics remain in the Edit Lyrics Window.

More Than One Syllable under a Note (Elisions and Melismas)

You may need to place more than one syllable on a note. To do this, simply enter a hard space between the two syllables. Enter the first syllable, either in the score or in the Edit Lyrics window. On Windows, type Alt-0169 (type the numbers on the Num Pad). On Macintosh, type Option-spacebar. Then enter the second syllable. You can also enter a "hard hyphen" to place a hyphen between two syllables. To do this follow the same instructions, only use the keystroke Alt-0173 on Windows or Option- - (hyphen) on Macintosh.

Beam to Lyrics

In vocal music, it is common to coordinate the beaming pattern to the lyrics. Finale can do this automatically with the Mass Edit Tool. Click the Mass Edit Tool and select the region of music you want to rebeam (Ctrl/Command-A to Select All). Click Mass Edit > Rebeam > Rebeam to Lyrics. Click OK and Finale will change the beaming of notes according to the lyrics.

 TIP
You can also change the beaming of your score manually by using the Simple Entry or Speedy Entry Tool. Use the / (slash) keystroke on the QWERTY keyboard in either of these tools to beam from the previous note. You can also use the / (slash) key to remove a beam from the previous note.

Extract Lyrics Plug-In

If you want to export lyrics from Finale to another program, such as a word processor, use the Extract Lyrics plug-in. From the Plug-ins menu, choose Lyrics > Extract Lyrics. Here, you can choose a particular verse, section, or chorus for extraction, or choose to extract all lyrics at once. You can also modify the extracted lyrics by removing hyphens or line breaks. Click Extract to save the lyrics as a text file. Then copy the lyrics from the text file into the other program.

Rhymer

Finale contains a feature you can use for help in the lyric creation process—a rhyming dictionary. From the Lyrics menu, choose Rhymer. Enter a word you would like to rhyme and click the Rhyme button to generate a list of rhyming words. You can even specify the type of rhyme (ending, beginning, etc.) from the Type of Rhyme drop-down menu. Click the Options button to specify the number of syllables, letters, or the first letter in words to customize your results.

Creating a Lead Sheet

At this point, you have covered all the material necessary for creating a lead sheet with a melody, chord symbols, and lyrics. Now you can apply the skills you have learned to create your own lead sheet, all the way from starting a new document to the final printout. For this example, we'll create a lead sheet arrangement of Amazing Grace, as shown in Figure 4.18.

Figure 4.18
Amazing Grace arrangement

There are a few layout issues that apply specifically to lead sheets (like the left barline on each system, for example). To save the headache of defining these layout changes ourselves, we'll begin this process by opening the Lead Sheet template.

From the File menu, choose New > Document From Template. You should now see the contents of the Finale/Template folder. Double-click the General Templates folder, and then double-click Lead Sheet (Jazz Font) to open the Jazz Font Lead Sheet Template. The Jazz Font gives a lead sheet a nice handwritten look. If you prefer, choose the Lead Sheet Template to use Finale's standard fonts. Now, let's begin our arrangement.

1. First, we'll add the title and composer. From the File menu, choose File Info. The File Info dialog box appears. For Title, enter "Amazing Grace." Then, for composer, enter "Arr. by" followed by your name. Click OK to return to the score.

2. The meter for this piece is 3/4, so we'll need to adjust the time signature. Click the Time Signature Tool. Right/Control-click the first measure and select 3/4 from the context menu.

3. There is a one-beat pickup, so we'll need to set up a pickup measure. From the Options menu, choose Pickup Measure. The Pickup Measure dialog box appears. Choose the quarter note icon and click OK.

4. This arrangement will be in the key of F major, so we'll need to change the key. Click the Key Signature Tool and double-click the pickup measure. The Key Signature dialog box appears. To the right of the preview display, click the down arrow once so the key of F (with one flat) is displayed. Then, click OK to return to the score.

5. There are twenty-three measures in this arrangement (two more than the default twenty-one measures). Double-click the Measure Tool twice to add two measures to the end of the score (you can add a measure at any time by double-clicking the Measure Tool).

6. We'll complete setting up the template by adding a tempo marking. Click the Mass Edit Tool and highlight the pickup (first) measure. From the Plug-ins menu, choose Create Tempo Marking. The Create Tempo Marking dialog box appears. Check Define Expression for Playback. Then, in the text box, enter "90" (in place of 96). Also, make sure the quarter note icon is selected. Click OK. The tempo marking now appears as an expression above the staff. Your piece is now ready for note entry (see Figure 4.19).

Figure 4.19

Your template should now look like this. You are now ready to start entering notes.

7. In this example, the theme is repeated twice. If you have an external MIDI device (a MIDI keyboard for example), I encourage you to enter the first sixteen measures using HyperScribe. Since there are no notes under an eighth note in duration, change your quantization settings for greater accuracy. From the Options menu, choose Quantization Settings. For Smallest Note Value, choose the eighth note icon and click OK. Now begin your

HyperScribe session and enter the melody for the first sixteen measures as seen in Figure 4.18 (see the information above on the HyperScribe Tool for more details). If you do not have an external MIDI device, use Simple or Speedy Entry to enter notes into the first sixteen measures.

8. Let's use the Simple or Speedy Entry Tool to enter into measures seventeen through twenty-three. In measure seventeen, you will need to enter a triplet on the last beat of the measure. In Speedy Entry, use the Ctrl/Option-3 method to pre-define the triplet. In Simple Entry, use the Simple Entry Tuplet Tool to pre-define the triplet (see Chapter 3 for more details on entering tuplets with the Speedy and Simple Entry Tool). Enter notes into the remaining measures.

9. Now, let's put five measures on a system. Click the Mass Edit Tool, and then press Ctrl/Command-A to Select All. From the Mass Edit menu, choose Fit Music. Type "5" and click OK. Your piece now has five measures per system (besides the last system, which has three).

10. To enter the chord symbols, click the Chord Tool. From the Chord menu, make sure Manual Input is selected. Click the first note in measure one. The Chord Definition dialog box appears. F is already selected (in the future, enter the bass chord symbol here), so click OK. Now, click the first note in measure two. Click in the text box at the top of the Chord Definition dialog box so there is a cursor to the right of F. Type "7" and click OK. The "F7" chord symbol appears above the note. Continue entering chord symbols this way until you get to measure seventeen. Click the first note in measure seventeen. Now, click Advanced > Show Advanced to extend the lower section of the Chord Definition dialog box. Click the Select button on the bottom to open the Chord Suffix Selection dialog box. Choose Maj7 and click Select, then OK to return to the score. For the remaining chord symbols, when necessary, add the suffix by choosing it from the Chord Suffix Selection dialog box. After you have finished entering the chord symbols, move them closer to the staff by dragging the leftmost positioning arrow down closer to the staff. See the information above in "Entering Chord Symbols" for more chord entry and positioning techniques.

11. Now, enter the lyrics. The easiest way to enter lyrics is to type them directly into the score. Click the Lyrics Tool, and then, from the Lyrics menu, choose Type Into Score. Click the first note and type the first syllable "A," then a "-" (hyphen) followed by the spacebar to move to the next syllable. Continue entering each syllable, leaving the hyphen out where it isn't necessary. As you enter, Finale adds all the word extensions for you.

12. Now, let's make the lyrics a little bigger. From the Plug-ins menu, choose Miscellaneous > Change Fonts. After Lyrics, click the Change button and then set the size to "16." Click OK to return to the score. Your lyrics are now a little larger and more readable (adjust the lyric baseline if you wish by clicking the Lyrics Tool and using the left positioning arrow while in Type Into Score mode).

13. Now, let's make the music on the page a little bigger. Click the Resize Tool, and then click the upper-left corner of the page (away from any staves or notes). In the Resize Page dialog box, enter "112" and click OK. Everything on the page is now slightly larger and more readable.

14. Now, click the Page Layout Tool. Notice the bottom staff system extends only half-way across the page. Click the lower-right handle of the bottom system and drag it to the left to move the margin to the middle of the page. Then, make any other desired layout changes. For example, to move all the music up on the page, drag the top-left handle on the first system down a bit, and then click in the middle of the top system and drag it up to the top. You might also want to click the Text Tool and drag the title and composer up a bit to allow more space on the page for music.

You can use the above procedure as a general guide any time you create a lead sheet. After creating your own piece, you may want to add expressions, articulations, slurs, fretboard diagrams, or any number of other figures not included in the above steps. I'll be touching on most of the common notational possibilities in the remaining chapters (if you haven't seen what you're looking for already).

5

CLEFS, KEY SIGNATURES, AND TIME SIGNATURES

Chapter 2 covered most of the basics for entering and changing clefs, key signatures, and time signatures. Now it's time to isolate each one of these items and explore a variety of common editing techniques. There are a number of similarities in the way these items are handled in Finale, and for that reason they have been grouped together into one chapter. Here, you'll learn how to enter mid-measure clefs, standard and non-standard key changes, large time signatures, and how to make a variety of changes to clef, key, and time signatures on an individual or global basis.

Here's a summary of what you will learn in this chapter:

* How to work with clefs
* How to work with key signatures
* How to work with time signatures

As you read through this chapter, keep in mind that you can always use the Setup Wizard to start a document with pre-defined instruments and also choose the opening key or time signature. For more information on editing any of the settings you specify in the Document or Staff Setup Wizard, refer to Chapter 2. When you find the information in Chapter 2 isn't in-depth enough for what you're trying to do, then refer to this chapter.

TIP

Easily add clef changes, key signature changes, and time signature changes with the Simple Entry Tool. While entering with the Simple Entry Caret, type Alt/Option-Shift-C to change the clef, Alt/Option-Shift-K to change the key, and Alt/Option-Shift-T to change the time signature. (See Chapter 3 for more on the Simple Entry Caret).

Working with Clefs

To begin with, if you want to add a staff to your score with a standard clef for a specific instrument, try using the Staff Setup Wizard. Click the Staff Tool; then, from the Staff menu, choose New Staves (with Setup Wizard). Choose the instrument category in the left column and the specific instrument in the second column. Once the new instrument appears in the right column, click Finish and the staff will appear at the bottom of your score with a standard clef for that instrument. To change the opening clef, make adjustments to the Staff Attributes (as described in Chapter 2).

In addition to changing the opening clef of a staff, there are many other cases where adding or editing clefs will be necessary. You will be using the Clef Tool to make most of these changes. In this section you'll learn how to use the Clef Tool to space clefs, enter mid-measure clef changes, and even create your own custom clef. In addition, there are a variety of other settings that relate to clefs throughout your document, such as cautionary clef changes. We'll start with the most common, entering clef changes, and then move into how to modify them.

To prepare for this section, open a new Default Document (File > New > Default Document), and then enter a melody with the Simple or Speedy Entry Tool. Click the Clef Tool. For this section, assume the Clef Tool is selected unless specified otherwise.

Changing the Clef at the Beginning of a Measure

Clef changes within a staff are common, and often appear at the beginning of the measure.

1. With the Clef Tool selected, double-click the second measure of a staff. You will see the Change Clef dialog box as shown in Figure 5.1.

Figure 5.1

Enter a clef change by choosing from one of the available clefs in the Change Clef dialog box

2. Choose the new clef from the 18 available options.

3. Once the clef is highlighted, click OK to return to the score and review the clef change. It will appear to the left of the measure you clicked. All of the music after the clef change will adjust according to the new clef.

4. Now, let's say you only want the clef change to affect a single measure. Double-click measure three to open the Change Clef dialog box.

5. Choose the original clef and then click OK. You should now have a clef change back to the opening clef of the staff.

NOTE

If you have an instrument with a "Set to Clef" transposition (such as Bass Clarinet or Baritone Saxophone), and you need to change the clef, you will first need to uncheck Set to Clef in the Staff Transposition dialog box. Choose the Staff Tool, double-click the staff to open the Staff Attributes, and then click the Select button next to Transposition. Uncheck Set to Clef and click OK twice to return to the score.

You can also highlight measures to apply a clef change to a region.

1. Drag-select a few measures.

2. Double-click the highlighted region. The Clef Selection dialog box appears.

3. Double-click the clef you want to apply to that region. You return to the score. Finale adds the clef change at the beginning of the selected region, and then a clef change back to the original clef in the measure following the region.

You can also specify a return to the original clef by specifying a region in the Change Clef dialog box. If you would like the clef to appear to the right of the barline, check the Place Clef After Barline in the Change Clef dialog box after selecting the new clef.

Entering Mid-Measure Clefs

Sometimes clefs appear in the middle of a measure, most of the time at a slightly reduced size. To enter a mid-measure clef change (make sure the Clef Tool is still selected):

1. Double-click where you would like to place the clef. The Change Clef dialog box appears.

2. Choose the new clef, and then click Create a Moveable Mid-Measure Clef.

3. Click OK, and you will see the new clef appear within the measure.

4. Click and drag the handle on the mid-measure clef to move it horizontally. Notes in the measure will change staff positions accordingly as you move it.

5. To delete any mid-measure clef, click its handle and press Delete, or right/Option-click the handle and choose Delete.

Applying Clef Changes to Regions with Partial Measures

You can even apply a clef change region that begins and/or ends within the measure (instead of at the beginning). To specify clef change regions that contain mid-measure clefs, do the following:

1. From the Edit Menu, check Select Partial Measures.

2. Drag-select the region to which you want to apply the new clef (as shown in Figure 5.2).

3. Double-click the highlighted region. The Clef Selection dialog box appears.

4. Double-click the clef you want to apply to that region. You return to the score. Finale adds the clef change before the first note of the selected region, and then a clef change back to the original clef after the last note in the region.

Figure 5.2

Check Select Partial Measures under the Edit menu to easily apply a regional clef change

Editing Mid-Measure Clefs

You can easily edit mid-measure clefs, or change any mid-measure clef to a regular clef change in the Mid-Measure Clef dialog box (Figure 5.3). Right/Option click the handle on the mid-measure clef and choose Edit Clef Definition to open this dialog box.

Figure 5.3

Specify the size and placement of a mid-measure clef in the Mid-Measure Clef dialog box

Here, choose a new clef in the clef selection, or resize the clef by entering a different percentage in the Clef Size text box. In the Show Clef section, specify when you want Finale to display the clef in the score, and pinpoint the positioning of the mid-measure clef on the right under Distance from Beginning of Measure (more about these settings soon). If you want to be able to drag the clef vertically, check Allow Vertical Drag.

 CAUTION

With Allow Vertical Drag checked you will be able to drag or nudge clefs up or down in the staff. When you do this, notes will not reposition according to the vertical staff placement. To enter a clef that accurately repositions notes in a staff according to standard notation rules, choose one of the existing clefs from the clef selection or design your own clef with the Clef Designer.

If you like, you can also change the clef back to a regular clef change at the beginning of the measure. To do this, choose Revert to Single Clef. You will be taken back to the Change Clef dialog box. Make any desired settings and click OK to return to the score.

Clef Metatools

Like articulations and expressions, you can also enter mid-measure clef changes easily by using metatools.

1. Hold down the Shift key and press 1 to open the Clef Selection dialog box (Figure 5.4). In the upper-right corner, you will see the preset metatool assignments for each type of clef. For example, note the "6" in the vocal tenor clef box.

Figure 5.4

The Clef Selection dialog box

2. Click OK to return to the score.
3. Hold down the 6 key and click in the staff to enter a mid-measure vocal tenor clef. Do this for any existing clef in the Clef Selection dialog box.

You may want to assign your own clef metatools. For instance, let's say you want to use the T key to enter a treble clef instead of the number 1.

1. Hold down the Shift key and press the letter T. The Clef Selection dialog box opens.
2. Now choose the treble clef and click OK. The treble clef is now assigned to the T key.
3. Hold down the T key and click anywhere in a staff to enter a mid-measure treble clef. If you open the Clef Selection dialog box again (by holding down Shift and pressing a number or letter), you will notice the letter T in the upper-right corner of the treble clef box.
4. You can also apply a clef change to a selected region. Drag select a few measures and press the T key (or any clef metatool) to apply a clef change for the region. A clef is added at the end of the region to return to the original clef.

Clef Spacing and Placement

In addition to dragging or nudging mid-measure clefs, there are a number of ways to specify placement of clefs in a staff, globally or individually.

You may want to change the default positioning of clef changes relative to the barline. To do this, click the Options menu and choose Document Options. Choose Clefs from the column on the left to display the Clef options (see Figure 5.5).

Figure 5.5

In the Clef portion of the
Document Options dialog box,
make document-wide settings
for the appearance and spacing
of clefs

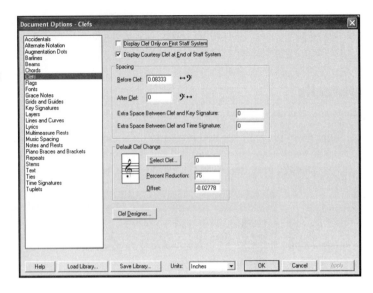

For example, specify a space "Before Clef" (between the clef and left barline) or "After Clef" (between the clef and first note) in these options and click OK to apply these settings to the entire document.

TIP

Use the "Extra Space Between Clef and Key Signature" and "Extra Space Between Clef and Time Signature" to space clefs relative to the key or time signature.

To choose the measurement unit (inches, points, EVPUs, etc.) for any parameter in the Document Options, click the drop-down menu to the right of Measurement Units and make a selection. You can find a description of all the measurement units in Table 1.1 (in Chapter 1).

You can also edit the mid-measure clef positioning manually in the Mid-Measure dialog box. Right/Option-click a mid-measure clef and choose Edit Clef Definition. Here, you can specify the desired horizontal and vertical spacing.

Showing or Hiding Clefs and Courtesy Clefs

You may want to show the clef at the beginning of the first measure only. This is common practice in certain types of documents such as lead sheets. To do this, choose Document Options from the Options menu. Click the Clefs category on the left and check Display Clef Only on First Staff System. Click OK to apply your settings and return to the score.

To hide all clefs in a staff, click the Staff Tool and double-click a staff to display the Staff Attributes. Under Items to Display, uncheck Clefs. Click OK to return to the score. All clefs in the specified staff will be hidden. Check this box in the Staff Attributes to show clefs in the staff.

TIP
You can show or hide clefs in any number of staves at once by using the Global Staff Attributes plug-in. From the Plug-ins menu, choose Global Staff Attributes. Under Items to Display, check or uncheck Clefs. Specify the staves you want to affect on the left and click OK to apply changes and return to the score. Also use this method for key signatures and time signatures.

If there is a clef change at the beginning of a system, it is customary to place a "courtesy" clef at the end of the previous system to warn the performer of the upcoming change in clef. To show or hide courtesy clefs, click the Options menu and choose Document Options. Click the Clefs category on the left and check or uncheck Display Courtesy Clef at End of Staff System. Click OK to apply your settings and return to the score.

You can also hide cautionary clefs, key signatures, and time signatures for an individual measure, or region of measures, with the Measure Tool. To hide these items individually for any region:

1. Choose the Measure Tool.
2. Double-click the measure prior to the courtesy clef change to open the Measure Attributes dialog box.
3. Check Hide Cautionary Clefs, Key and Time Signatures, and click OK.

Creating a Custom Clef (the Clef Designer)

There may be a clef you want to use that doesn't exist among the 18 available clefs in the Clef Selection dialog box. In this case, you can actually create your own clef that will contain all the properties of a legitimate clef pre-defined in Finale. To design a custom clef

1. Click the Options menu and choose Document Options. Select the Clefs category on the left and click the Clef Designer button among the options on the right. This will open the Clef Designer dialog box as seen in Figure 5.6.

Figure 5.6
Create a custom clef definition in the Clef Designer dialog box

2. First, choose the clef you want to edit from the selection boxes at the top. You will be redefining one of these clefs, so make sure you choose one you do not plan on using in this document.

3. To change the appearance of the clef, click the Select button to the right of Character. This will take you into the Symbol Selection window. Choose the character you want to use for your new clef and click Select. If you can't find the character for the clef you want to use, you could try selecting a character from a different font. To do this, click the Set Font button in the Clef Designer. This will open the Font dialog box where you can choose the new font, size, and style for your clef.

NOTE
Finale offers several music fonts that contain clef symbols you might find useful. For a complete list of characters in all Finale fonts, click the Help menu on Mac (or on Windows, click Help, then User Manual) and select the Engraver, Jazz, or Maestro character map. Of course, you can also select a character from any font that exists on your system in the Font dialog box.

4. If you cannot find a font with an existing clef, you can also design your own. In the Clef Designer, click the Shape radio button, then click the Select button. Click Create. You will now see the Shape Designer window. Use this editor to create a custom shape for your clef. You can even import existing graphics with the Graphics Tool available in this window. For more information about the Shape Designer, see Chapter 9. Click OK and then Select to return to the Shape Designer. Now it's time to configure the functional clef characteristics (how the clef will affect the notation).

5. For Middle C Position (from Top Staff Line), indicate the staff position of middle C in the clef you are defining. Enter 0 to place middle C on the top staff line. Subtract one for each line and space below the top staff line or add one for each line and space above the top staff line.

6. In the Clef Position (from Top Staff Line), use the same parameters to position the clef in the staff. You may need to adjust the Musical Baseline Offset for mid-measure (reduced) clef changes after defining a custom clef, particularly if you created a custom shape for the clef.

7. Click OK to return to your score to see your new custom clef.

Transferring Custom Clefs between Documents

Like articulations and expressions, you can transfer custom clefs (created in the Clef Designer) between documents by saving and opening a library. Open the document containing the existing clefs. Click the File menu and choose Save Library. Choose Clefs and click OK. Enter a name and save the file to your Libraries folder in your Finale directory (Finale should take you there by default). Now open the document you are working on, click the File menu, and choose Open Library. Double-click the library you saved to open it. Now your custom clefs will be available in this document's Clef Selection window.

Key Signatures

Chapter 2 touched on the basics for changing the key signature at the beginning of a document. Here you will learn how to make key changes at any measure or even create a customized key signature. Keep in mind the instructions in this section refer to changing the concert pitch of a score, therefore the key signature of a transposed staff may appear in a different key. To view your score in concert pitch at any time, select Display in Concert Pitch from the Options menu (choose the same options again to display the transposed parts).

To prepare for this section, either continue using the document from the previous section, or open a new Default Document (File > New > Default Document). You should also use the Simple or Speedy Entry Tool to enter a simple melody into the document for the purpose of demonstration. Then, click the Key Signature Tool. I'll assume you have the Key Signature Tool selected unless specified otherwise.

Entering and Changing the Key Signature

Unlike clefs, key signatures generally affect all staves in a system, so at any given measure you will only need to make one key change. Let's say you want to change to the key of A major in measure three.

1. Choose the Key Signature Tool and double-click on measure three (or right/Control-click the measure and choose Edit Key Signature). The Key Signature dialog box opens as shown in Figure 5.7.

Figure 5.7

Define a key change in the Key Signature dialog box

2. Next to the key signature preview window is a vertical scroll bar. Click the up arrow three times to add three sharps to the key signature. The display now indicates a key of A major. Since any notes in your score will transpose into the new key, you will need to choose which direction to move them.

> **TIP**
>
> At this point, if you want to change the key signature without moving the notes, you have three options. Check Hold Notes to Original Pitches and select Enharmonically to respell the notes based on the new key signature. Select Chromatically to retain the spelling. Choose Hold Notes to Same Staff Line (Modally) if you want to keep the notes where they are, but conform to the new key. (Use this setting if, for example, you forgot to set the key signature before entering notes).

3. In the Transposition Options, for Transpose Notes, click the drop-down menu and choose Up to transpose them up or Down to transpose them down.

4. Click OK to return to your score and review the key change.

In the Key Signature dialog box, you can also click the down arrow next to the display window to add flats or remove sharps from a key signature. Click the drop-down menu to the right of the preview window to specify a major, minor, or nonstandard key (I'll discuss nonstandard key signatures soon). By specifying a major or minor key from the drop-down menu, you tell Finale how to assign accidentals accurately in a HyperScribe session and also assign chord definitions properly.

Specify a region for the key signature change in the Measure Region section. Note that every time you enter the Key Signature dialog box, the setting for Measure Region will reset to Measure _ To Next Key Change, so you will need to make adjustments to this setting when necessary.

If you want to change the key of a region of your score that already contains a key change, and you want the existing key change (or any number of key changes) to adjust accordingly, check Transpose All Keys Proportionally (note that this option is not available if Measure _ To Next Key Change is selected). When you do this, all affected key changes will transpose proportionally from the new key you specify (see Figure 5.8).

Figure 5.8

Transposing keys
proportionally

A key signature that appears after transposing keys proportionally could contain unwanted double sharps or double flats. To avoid this, make sure Wrap Keys if Necessary is checked (at the bottom of the Key Signature dialog box). Click OK to return to the score.

Key Signature Metatools

If you intend to enter many key changes in a document, you may want to program Key Signature metatools. Hold down the Shift key and press the 1 key to open the Key Signature dialog box. Specify the new key here and click OK to return to the score. Hold down the 1 key and double-click a measure to enter the specified key change to a measure. Program a key signature metatool to any number or letter key on your QWERTY keyboard.

Managing Notes while Changing the Key

You may want to change the key of a region without transposing the music. To do this, double-click the measure of the key change to open the Key Signature dialog box. Select the key signature you wish to use. Under Transposition Options, select Hold Notes to Original Pitches. From the drop-down menu, choose Enharmonically to respell the notes according to the new key. Choose Chromatically to leave the spelling the same.

To leave all notes at the same staff position and change only the pitches affected by the change of key, choose Hold Notes to Same Staff Lines Modally.

 TIP
If you want to transpose notes without changing the key signature, choose the Mass Edit Tool and select the region of notes you want to transpose. Then, from the Mass Edit menu, choose Transpose. Select an interval and click OK. There will be more information on transposition in Chapter 9.

Changing the Key on a Single Staff Only

If you are working on a bitonal score (one that oversteps traditional key signature usage), you may need to specify a concert key signature change on one staff without affecting the concert key of the other staves. To do this, click the Staff Tool and double-click the staff you want to change. In the Independent Elements section, check Key Signature and click OK. Now use the Key Signature Tool to change the key on the staff you modified with the Staff Tool. Key changes to this staff will not affect the key of other staves, and key changes in other staves will not affect this staff.

Selecting the Default Font for Key Signatures

You may want to change the font of your key signatures to one of the other available Finale fonts or a different music font installed on your computer. To do this

1. From the Options menu, choose Document Options and select Fonts.

2. Click the drop-down menu for Notation and select Key.

3. Click the Set Font button for Notation to open the Font dialog box where you can specify the font, size, and style for your key signatures.

4. Click OK to return to the Document Options dialog box and click the Apply button to apply the change in font.

Since Finale expects the accidental characters to be in one of the Finale music fonts, you may need to re-assign the accidental characters for your key signatures if you are using an external music font. To do this

1. From the Options menu, choose Document Options and select Key Signatures.

2. Click the drop-down menu for Music Characters and choose the type of accidental you want to assign. Then, click the Select button to open the Symbol Selection dialog box.

3. Choose the matching font character and click Select to return to the Document Options dialog box.

4. Choose any other character you need to assign and click the Apply button to apply your new character settings.

Spacing Key Signatures

There are a couple ways to adjust the spacing of key signatures in a document. You may want to increase or decrease the space between the key signature and the barline or the following entry. To do this on a document-wide basis, from the Options menu, choose Document Options and select Key Signatures from the list on the left (see Figure 5.9). Enter a value in the Space Before Key text box to indicate the distance between the barline and the key signature. Enter a value in the Space After Key text box to indicate the distance between the key signature and the following entry.

Figure 5.9

Make document-wide settings for key signature spacing, characters, and appearance in Document Options—Key Signatures

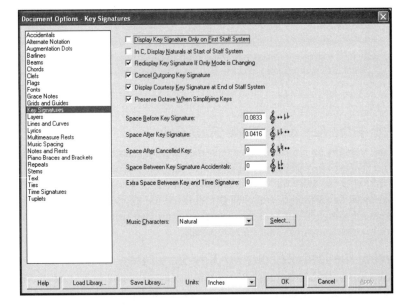

TIP

Use the "Extra Space Between Key and Time Signature" to space key signatures relative to the time signature.

In the Document Options dialog box, you can also change the distance between the sharp or flat characters in a key signature. To do this, enter a new value for Space Between Key Signature Accidentals. Click OK to apply changes and return to the score.

To choose the measurement unit (inches, points, EVPUs, etc.) for any parameter in the Document Options, click the drop-down menu at the bottom of the dialog box, to the right of Units, and make a selection. You can find a description of all the measurement units in Table 1.1 (in Chapter 1).

Showing or Hiding a Key Signature in Staves and Measures

You may want to show the key signature at the beginning of the first measure only. To do this, from the Options menu, choose Document Options. Click the Key Signature category on the left and check Display Key Signature Only on First Staff System. Click OK to apply your settings and return to the score.

To hide all key signatures in a staff, click the Staff Tool and double-click a staff to display the Staff Attributes. Under Items to Display, uncheck Key Signatures. Click OK to return to the score. All key signatures in the specified staff will be hidden. Check this box in the Staff Attributes to show key signatures in the staff. Hidden key signatures apply to the music even though they are not visible.

CAUTION

Hiding the key signature will not automatically make accidentals appear on diatonic notes. You can show these accidentals by using the A key with the Simple or Speedy Entry Tool.

You can also force a key signature to show or hide a key signature at the beginning of any measure with the Measure Tool. Click the Measure Tool and double-click a measure. Click the drop-down menu to the right of Key Signature and choose Always Show to show the key signature in that measure. Choose Always Hide to hide the key signature in that measure. Click OK to return to the score and review your changes.

TIP

To show or hide key signatures or time signatures for a region of measures, select the region with the Measure Tool and double-click the highlighted area. Changes you make in the Measure Attributes will apply to all selected measures.

Showing or Hiding Courtesy Key Signatures

If there is a key change at the beginning of a system, it is customary to place a "courtesy" key signature at the end of the previous system to warn the performer of the upcoming change in key. To show or hide courtesy key signatures, click the Options menu and choose Document Options. Click the Key Signatures category on the left and check or uncheck Display Courtesy Key Signature at End of Staff System. Click OK to apply your settings and return to the score.

To hide a courtesy key signature individually, select the Measure Tool. Double-click the measure prior to the courtesy key signature to open the Measure Attributes dialog box. Check Hide Cautionary Clefs, Key, and Time Signatures and click OK.

Outgoing Key Signatures

While changing key signatures in a score, it is common to indicate changes from the previous key signature to the left of the new key. For instance, in a key change from F major (one flat), to G major (one sharp), you may see a natural to the left of the new key "canceling" the B flat in the key of F major (see Figure 5.10).

Figure 5.10

Canceling the Outgoing Key Signature

To show or hide the canceled key signature by default, from the Options menu, choose Document Options and select Key Signatures from the list on the left. Check Cancel Outgoing Key Signature to show the canceled key signature, or uncheck this box to hide the canceled key signature.

You can also adjust the spacing of the canceled key signature indication in the Program Options by entering a value in the Space After Canceled Key text box.

Nonstandard Key Signatures

In addition to major and minor keys, you can also create your own custom key signatures with any combination of accidentals on any staff position. Though seldom used, this feature does warrant a word or two. To define a nonstandard key signature, double-click a measure to open the Key Signature dialog box. To the right of the preview display, click the drop-down menu and choose Nonstandard. This will open the Nonstandard Key Signature dialog box as shown in Figure 5.11.

There are two types of nonstandard key signatures: linear and nonlinear. Choose the Linear Key Format to define a key signature with a reoccurring sequence of whole and half steps. All linear key signatures will cycle through a "circle of fifths" type of relationship (though your key signature may cycle through sixths, fourths, or another interval). Major and minor key signatures both fall into the linear category, and are already defined as Format 0 (Major) and 1 (minor). While defining a linear key signature, use the scroll bar to the right of the preview display to add sharps, flats, double-sharps, double-flats, etc.

Figure 5.11

Define a custom key signature
in the Nonstandard Key
Signature dialog box

Nonlinear key signatures are not based on a system of related keys. Choose Nonlinear Key Signature to define a key with any number of accidentals in any order. The scroll bar in the preview display will not be available while defining a nonlinear key. You will need to use the options below.

The five buttons at the bottom of the Nonstandard Key Signature dialog box can be used to define linear or nonlinear key signatures (though some parameters will be limited with linear keys). Choose KeyMap to define the number of steps in an octave and the sequence of whole and half steps. Click AOrdAmt to specify where you want to place the accidentals in the staff. Click ClefOrd to assign the octave to place each accidental. Click the ToneCnt button to specify a root for your key signature. Click Attributes for more options, such as assigning special characters to accidentals for quarter-tone key signatures. Whether you are creating a linear or nonlinear key signature, click the Next button to move to the next format or Prev to move back to the previous one.

Time Signatures

Like clefs and key signatures, there are many ways to enter and edit time signatures beyond the options available in the Setup Wizard. Here you will learn how to enter meter changes at any measure, create compound and composite meters, specify beaming patterns, and make other settings related to time signatures on an individual or global basis. Since time signatures and key signatures exhibit many of the same characteristics in Finale, some of these instructions will look familiar.

To prepare for this section, use the same document you have been working with, or open a new Default Document (File > New > Default Document). You should also use the Simple or Speedy Entry Tool to enter a simple melody into the document for the purpose of demonstration. Then, click the Time Signature Tool. I'll assume you have the Time Signature Tool selected unless specified otherwise.

Entering and Changing the Time Signature

Like key signatures, time signatures usually affect all staves in a system, so at any given measure you will only need to make one meter change (I'll cover independent meters later in this section). Since the document you have open is in common time, we'll start by creating a time change to 6/8. With the Time Signature Tool chosen, double-click on measure three. The Time Signature dialog box opens as shown in Figure 5.12.

CHAPTER 5

Figure 5.12

Define a meter change in the
Time Signature dialog box

For Number of Beats, click the left arrow on the scroll bar twice. The preview display now reads 2/4. We will be counting our 6/8 meter in two (beat = dotted quarter) and beaming eighth notes in two groups of three. For Beat Duration, click the right arrow on the scroll bar once. The quarter note in the preview window will update to a dotted quarter and the time signature will change to 6/8. While defining time signatures, always think of the number of beats in the measure and then the rhythmic value (duration) of each beat. Finale will translate the values you enter into the appropriate time signature automatically. Click OK to return to your score and review the change in meter.

In the Time Signature dialog box, specify a region for the time signature change in the Measure Region section. Note that every time you enter the Time Signature dialog box, the setting for Measure Region will reset to Measure _ To Next Time Change, so you may need to make adjustments from this setting as needed.

Shortcuts: Context Menu and Metatools

You can enter time signatures quickly with a context menu. With no measures selected, right/Option-click a measure to see the Time Signature context menu. Choose one of the available time signatures to enter the time change instantly. Time signatures entered this way will apply for all of the music up to the next time change. Right/Option-click a region of measures to change the time signature for that region of measures.

If you intend to enter many time signature changes in a document, you may want to program Time Signature metatools. Hold down the Shift key and press the 1 key to open the Time Signature dialog box. Specify a meter here and click OK to return to the score. Highlight a region of measures and press the 1 key to apply the time change to the selected measures. Program a time signature metatool to any number or letter key on your QWERTY keyboard.

Abbreviated Time Signatures

You may or may not want to abbreviate 4/4 time signatures as 𝄴 and 2/4 time signatures as 𝄵. To change these settings, from the Options menu, choose Document Options and select Time Signatures. Check or uncheck Abbreviate Cut or Common Time. Click the Select button to specify a character you wish to use as an abbreviation in the default time signature font.

Selecting the Default Font for Time Signatures

You may want to change the font of your time signatures to one of the other available Finale fonts or a different music font installed on your computer. To do this

1. From the Options menu, choose Document Options and select Fonts.
2. Click the drop-down menu for Notation and select Time.

3. Click the Set Font button for Notation to open the Font dialog box where you can specify the font, size, and style for your time signatures (regular and abbreviated).

4. Click OK to return to the Document Options dialog box and click the Apply button to apply the change in font.

TIP

Try using the EngraverFontSet or Engraver Time font for an alternative style for your time signatures. For a complete list of characters in all Finale fonts, click the Help menu on Mac (or on Windows, click Help, then User Manual) and select the Engraver, Jazz, or Maestro character map.

Using a Different Time Signature for Display

For a number of reasons, you may need to display a different time signature than the actual one defined in the Time Signature dialog box (pickup measures, measures across systems, etc.). To do this

1. Double-click a measure to open the Time Signature dialog box and specify the beat duration and number of beats. Click the Options button (Mac: More Choices) in the upper right to expand the lower section of the dialog box (see Figure 5.13).

Figure 5.13

Click Options to expand the Time Signature dialog box where you can create a separate time signature for display

2. Set up the time signature as you want it to display in the lower section, then check Use a Different Time Signature for Display.

3. Click OK to return to the score.

The time signature you choose to display will be visible only if it is different than the time signature of the previous measure.

TIP
For information on assigning specific beaming groups for time signatures, see "Beaming Patterns and Time Signatures" in Chapter 10.

Changing the Time Signature on a Single Staff Only

You may need to specify a meter change on one staff without affecting the meter of the other staves. To do this

1. Click the Staff Tool and double-click the staff you want to change.

2. In the Independent Elements section, check Time Signature and click OK.

3. Now use the Time Signature Tool to change the key on the staff you modified with the Staff Tool. Meter changes to this staff will not affect the meter of other staves, and meter changes in other staves will not affect this staff. Finale will continue to line up all barlines regardless of the meters being used. You will find a more in-depth discussion of isorhythmic notation (in which the barlines do not line up) at the end of this chapter.

Spacing Time Signatures

You may want to increase or decrease the space between the time signature and the barline or the following entry. To do this on a document-wide basis

1. From the Options menu, choose Document Options and select Time Signatures from the list on the left (see Figure 5.9).

2. Enter a value in the Space Before Time Signature text box to indicate the distance between the barline and the time signature. Enter a value in the Space After Time Signature text box to indicate the distance between the time signature and the following entry.

3. You can also move any time signature vertically. Click the Options menu and choose Document Options, then select Time Signatures.

4. In the Vertical Adjustment section, specify a value for the bottom and top number in your time signature. To move a 4/4 time signature (in the default font and size) above the staff, enter 100 EVPUs, for example, for both Top Symbol and Bottom Symbol. Then make any fine adjustments. If you are using an abbreviated time signature, you need only modify the Abbreviated Value text box.

Showing or Hiding Time Signatures in Staves or Measures

To hide all time signatures in a staff, click the Staff Tool and double-click a staff to display the Staff Attributes. Under Items to Display uncheck Time Signatures. Click OK to return to the score. All time signatures in the specified staff will be hidden. Recheck this box in the Staff Attributes to show time signatures in the staff.

You can also show or hide a time signature at the beginning of any measure with the Measure Tool. Click the Measure Tool and double-click a measure. Click the drop-down menu to the right of Time Signature and choose Always Show to show the time signature in that measure. Choose Always Hide to hide the time signature in that measure. Click OK to return to the score and review your changes.

Showing or Hiding Courtesy Time Signatures

If there is a time change at the beginning of a system, it is customary to place a "courtesy" time signature at the end of the previous system to warn the performer of the upcoming change in meter. To show or hide courtesy time signatures, click the Options menu and choose Document Options. Click the Time Signatures category on the left and check or uncheck Display Courtesy Time Signature at End of Staff System. Click OK to apply your settings and return to the score.

To hide a courtesy time signature individually, select the Measure Tool. Double-click the measure prior to the courtesy time signature to open the Measure Attributes dialog box. Check Hide Cautionary Clefs, Key, and Time Signatures and click OK.

Multiple Time Signatures

You may want to enter a time signature followed by a second time signature in parentheses, indicating an alternate subdivision as shown in Figure 5.14.

Figure 5.14

Multiple time signatures

To enter multiple time signatures:

1. Double-click a measure to display the Time Signature dialog box.
2. Use the scroll bars to specify the "real" time signature (enough beats to accommodate the notes you want to place in the measure.)
3. Click Options (Mac: More Choices) to display the lower portion of the dialog box.
4. Check Use a Different Time Signature for Display.
5. Click the Composite button in the lower section.

6. Enter the first time signature in the first set of boxes and the second in the second set of boxes (with the top number in the Beat Groups row and the bottom number in the Beat Duration row).

7. Click OK to return to the Time Signature dialog box, then click OK again to return to the score. You should now see the multiple time signatures separated with a + sign.

8. If you want to remove the + sign, from the Options menu, choose Document Options and select Time Signatures. Click the Plus Character button and choose the blank character (#9 on Mac and #32 on Windows). Click Select and OK to return to the score.

9. Now you may want to increase the distance between the two time signatures. To do this, from the Options menu, choose Document Options and select Fonts. For Notation, click the drop-down menu, choose Time Signature Plus Sign, and click the Set Font button. Choose a larger font size, like 96, and click OK. Click OK again to return to the score. If this is too much space, you can go back and adjust the font size of the blank character accordingly.

10. You may want to surround one of the time signatures with parentheses. To do this you'll need to create an expression. Click the Expression Tool. Then, double-click the first measure to open the Expression Selection window.

11. Click Create.

12. In the Text Expression Designer, enter "( )" (with a space).

13. Click the Set Font button. Change the size to 28, and click OK.

14. Click OK, Select, and OK to return to the score.

15. Drag the parentheses into place around the time signature.

Large Time Signatures Placed above the Staff

It is not uncommon to see large time signatures in a score placed between staves as shown in Figure 5.15.

Figure 5.15

Large time signatures

Here is a method for creating large time signatures:

1. From the Document Options menu, choose Document Options and select Fonts.

2. Click the drop-down menu for Notation and choose Time.

3. Click the Set Font button for Notation.

4. In the Set Font dialog box, choose the font EngraverTime, and set the size to 18.

5. Click OK to return to the Document Options.

6. Choose the Time Signature category.

7. At the bottom of the Document Options, click the drop-down menu and choose EVPUs.

8. For Top Symbol, enter 340, and for Bottom Symbol, enter 220.

9. Click OK to apply these settings and return to the score.

The values in these steps assume you are using the default staff spacing and want the time signature to appear above the staff. You will most likely need to adjust the font size for the time signature and/or the vertical offset of the top and bottom symbol. Since these time signatures sometimes apply to more than one staff, you may need to hide time signatures in some staves. Look at the instructions above "Showing or Hiding Time Signatures in Staves or Measures" for details on how to do this.

Pickup Measures within a Score

Often, pickup measures appear somewhere within a score instead of before the first measure (see Figure 5.16). This is typical, for example, in hymnal music.

Figure 5.16

Pickup measures within a score

Here are steps for creating a pickup measure at any point in a document.

1. With the Time Signature Tool selected, double-click the measure you would like to change into a pickup measure.

2. Change the time signature to reflect the beat duration of the pickup. For example, for a quarter note pickup, use 1/4.

3. Click the Options button (Mac: More Choices) to expand the lower portion.

4. Check Use a Different Time Signature for Display.

5. Enter the time signature of the following measure (the measure directly after the pickup).

6. In the Measure Region section, enter the same measure number in both fields (to indicate that measure only).

7. Click OK to return to the score. Notice that you do not see a time signature displayed in the pickup measure. Use the Time Signature Tool again to set the Time Signature in the measure following the pickup.

Now there will be a pickup measure that will space the notes properly as you enter them. This pickup measure will also play back properly.

Isorhythmic Notation

Isorhythmic notation is the practice of using several different time signatures at once. When you do this, each staff will be in a completely independent meter, so barlines for each staff will not line up vertically most of the time (see Figure 5.17).

Figure 5.17

Isorhythmic notation

This is a particularly unconventional notation practice, so getting it to work in Finale is a bit of a rigmarole. Nonetheless, it can be done, and here's how:

1. You will need to set all of your staves to use time signatures independently. Click the Staff Tool, and double-click a staff to open the Staff Attributes. Then, in the Independent Elements section, check Time Signatures. Do this for all staves in the score. To view the attributes for a different staff, select the staff name from the drop-down menu at the top of Staff Attributes and then check Independent Elements for Time Signature. Click OK when you have done so for all staves in your score.

2. Now you will need to create a time signature that will encompass all of the time signatures you wish to use. To do this, you basically need to determine the lowest common denominator for the multiple meters. For example, if you want to use 3/4 in one staff and 2/4 in another, use 6/4—(3 × 2)/4=6/4. This is the shortest measure that will encompass both a 3/4 and 2/4 meter.

3. Click the Time Signature Tool and double-click the first measure in the top staff to open the Time Signature dialog box.

4. Enter the time signature that represents the lowest common denominator (as calculated above), then click the Options button (Mac: More Choices) to expand the lower portion of this dialog box.

5. Check Use a Different Time Signature for Display.

6. In the lower portion, set the time signature you want to display for the staff.

7. Click OK. Then repeat steps 3 through 6 for all staves in the score. Remember, if you will be doing this frequently, set up appropriate metatools for each time signature needed to save yourself the trouble of going to the dialog box every time. You can also save time by using the Time Signature context menu.

8. Now, add additional barlines manually using one of the barline Shape Expressions. Choose the Expression Tool and double-click where you would like to add a barline. The Expression Selection dialog box appears.

9. Ensure Measure Expression is selected and then click the Shape radio button. Notice the barline options in the preview display. Double-click the barline you want to add (8 is a regular barline). The Measure Expression Assignment dialog box appears. Make any desired assignment settings and click OK. The barline appears in the score. It is really just a vertical line defined to match the default staff height, but should work fine for this purpose.

CHAPTER 5

6

SLURS, HAIRPINS, OTHER SMART SHAPES, AND REPEATS

Chapter 3 covered the basics for adding articulation markings and text expressions to a score. There are many other common markings in notation that require curves, brackets, wavy lines, and other shapes. For these, use the Smart Shape Tool. You can use the Smart Shape Tool to enter slurs, hairpins, trill extensions, brackets, bend shapes, glissandi, and other markings. Like Expressions, Smart Shapes are designed to adjust intelligently while you work. As you edit and adjust the layout of your score, each Smart Shape moves with the measure or note it is attached to, and can even adjust automatically to avoid collision with notes, accidentals, and other items. In this chapter you'll learn when to use Smart Shapes and how to enter, edit, and copy them. You'll also learn how to make global changes and create your own custom Smart Shapes.

The end of this chapter will be devoted to Repeats. Repeats are represented by both text and barline figures. You will learn how to easily enter repeat barlines and text repeats, edit their appearance, and get them to play back.

Here's a summary of what you will learn in this chapter:

- ❋ How to work with Smart Shapes, slurs, and hairpins
- ❋ How to enter glissandi, guitar bends, lines, and other Smart Shapes
- ❋ How to define Repeats

Introduction to Smart Shapes

When you click the Smart Shape Tool, you will see the Smart Shape Palette appear (see Figure 6.1).

Use the Smart Shape Palette to choose the shape you'd like to enter. To enter a slur, for example, click the Smart Shape Tool, and then choose the Slur Tool from the Smart Shape Palette. Double-click a note and drag to enter the slur in the score (I'll cover more about entering slurs and other shapes soon). By default, any Smart Shape you enter will appear red in the score (to distinguish them from text blocks, measure expressions, and other items). In addition to the Smart Shape Palette, you will also see the SmartShape menu appear at the top of your screen (see Figure 6.2).

Figure 6.1

Choose a shape from the
Smart Shape Palette for entry
into the score

Figure 6.2

Customize the appearance,
placement, and other attributes
of Smart Shapes by choosing
an item from the SmartShape
menu

Each Smart Shape has its own properties relating to how it can be edited and what it can be attached to (notes, noteheads, or measures). In addition, there are a number of placement and graphical changes you can make from the SmartShape menu at a document-wide level. Throughout this chapter I will refer to this menu to apply some of these changes.

Metatools have been pre-assigned to most Smart Shapes. Whenever the Smart Shape Tool is selected, hold down one of these metatool keys and double-click and drag to enter its corresponding Smart Shape. Table 6.1 displays a list of Smart Shape metatools. Use these at any time as a substitute for choosing one of the tools in the Smart Shape Palette.

Table 6.1

Smart Shape Metatools

Tool	Metatool	Tool	Metatool
Slur	S	Double-Ended Bracket Tool	o
Dashed Curve	V	Dashed Double-Ended Bracket Tool	Z
Decrescendo	>	Bracket Tool	K
Crescendo	<	Line	L
Trill	T	Dashed Line	D
Trill Extension	E	Glissando Tool	G
8va/8vb	8	Guitar Bend	B
15ma/15mb	I	Custom Line	C

NOTE
Human Playback automatically interprets several Smart Shapes during playback, including hairpins, trills, glissandos, and octavos (e.g., 8va). To hear these effects, select a Human Playback style in the Playback Settings dialog box on Windows or Playback Controls on Mac.

General Smart Shape Editing

Before beginning to explore the various Smart Shape types, you should understand some editing techniques common to many Smart Shapes. Whenever the Smart Shape Tool is selected you will see a handle appear on every Smart Shape in the score. I will refer to this handle as the primary handle. Click and drag this handle to move the Smart Shape around. Use the arrow keys to nudge it for fine positioning adjustments. Click and drag over several primary Smart Shape handles to move several of them at once. Press the Delete key to delete all selected Smart Shapes.

Measure, Note, and Notehead-Attached Smart Shapes

Like Expressions, many Smart Shapes can be set to attach to either a measure or a note. Before entering a Smart Shape, from the Smart Shape menu, you can choose Attach to Measures, Attach to Notes, or Attach to Noteheads, depending on the role of the Smart Shape you are about to enter (note that some of these options are limited to certain Smart Shapes). Measure-attached Smart Shapes can be entered anywhere in the score and will attach to the measure closest to the point of entry. They will adjust to their corresponding measure like a measure-attached expression. Note-attached Smart Shapes will adjust according their corresponding notes much like a note-attached expression. Their position is determined by settings in the Smart Shape Placement dialog box (SmartShape > Smart Shape Placement). The Attach to Notehead option is used for the Tab Slide and Glissando Smart Shape. The default setting for Measure/Note/Notehead-Attached is usually adequate for the common usage of each Smart Shape, so you may never need to change this setting. However, making the distinction between these three Smart Shape types is fundamental to the way Smart Shapes are organized in Finale.

Other Techniques

There are some other tricks that apply to all Smart Shapes.

- ❋ Drag-enclose to select several Smart Shapes. You may also select several Smart Shapes by holding down the Shift key and clicking in each handle. Then use the mouse to drag all selected Smart Shapes uniformly, or use the arrow keys to nudge them.

- ❋ Hold down the Shift key while creating or editing a Smart Shape to "constrain" dragging to either vertical or horizontal movement.

- ❋ Hold down the Delete key and drag over as many Smart Shapes as you like to delete them.

- ❋ When a Smart Shape's primary handle is selected, press the Tab key to cycle selection through the editing handles of any Smart Shape. Pressing Esc will select the primary handle again and hide the diamond editing handles. When there are no editing handles showing, the Tab key will cycle through the primary handles of the various shapes in the document.

- ❋ Ctrl/Option-click a primary Smart Shape handle to see its source. (This trick also applies to expressions).

The Smart Shape Context Menu

Any Smart Shape can be edited in the score with a context menu. Right/Control-click any Smart Shape handle to invoke the Smart Shape context menu as seen in Figure 6.3.

Figure 6.3

Quickly edit Smart Shapes in the score with the Smart Shape context menu

This menu can be used to quickly make a number of adjustments to individual Smart Shapes including direction and alignment. The available options in this context menu will depend on the type of Smart Shape (certain options will be grayed out with some smart shapes). Choose Edit from the context menu to show the editing handles on a Smart Shape, or choose Delete from the context menu to delete one. There are also some other options in this context menu that apply to many or all Smart Shapes. To save time, learn to use the context menu frequently while editing Smart Shapes.

Context Menu—Aligning Smart Shapes

You can easily align any number of measure-attached Smart Shapes, such as hairpin crescendo or decrescendos, vertically or horizontally. Click and drag to select several measure-attached Smart Shape handles. Right/Control-click one of the highlighted handles to open the context menu. Choose Align Horizontally to horizontally align all selected Smart Shapes. Click Align Vertically to vertically align all selected Smart Shapes. Then, press the up or down arrow keys, or click one of the highlighted handles to position all of the aligned Smart Shapes at once.

Context Menu—Smart Shapes over System Breaks

Many Smart Shapes can be extended over a system break. When this is done, Finale basically generates a new Smart Shape at the beginning of the second system (and any subsequent system as necessary). If you would like to "flatten" the Smart Shape as it is moved over a system break, from the context menu, choose Make Horizontal Over System Break. This option can also apply to existing Smart Shapes. To allow Smart Shapes to retain their angle across system breaks, choose Maintain Angle Over System Break from the context menu.

Slurs

Slurs can be used to indicate a legato, uninterrupted performance style, or to indicate a musical phrase. To enter a slur, click the Slur Tool in the Smart Shape Palette. Double-click the first note of the slur and drag to the destination note. When you release the mouse button, the slur will adjust automatically to avoid collision of notes and accidentals. As you drag the cursor over subsequent notes, refer to the highlighted note to specify the endpoint of the slur (see Figure 6.4).

Figure 6.4

Specify the slur endpoint by referring to the highlighted note

After you have entered the slur, you will notice a surrounding pentagon with small diamonds at each corner. You can use these diamond editing handles to manually edit the shape of the slur. Click and drag them, or click a handle and use the arrow keys to make fine adjustments. Use these reshaping handles to edit the arc and endpoints

If you want to remove all manual changes you have made to a slur, press the Backspace/Clear key with the handle selected. Or, right/Control-click the slur's handle and choose Remove Manual Slur Adjustments.

Flipping Slurs Over or Under a Staff

After you have entered a slur, you might want to move it to the other side of the staff. To do this, right/Control-click the slur handle to open the context menu. From the Direction submenu, choose Flip. The slur will flip to the other side of the staff. You can also flip a slur easily by pressing Ctrl/Control-F with a slur handle selected. Flipping is available only for note-attached slurs.

Editing the Slur Contour Globally

If you are not satisfied with Finale's default slur contour settings, you can adjust them for an entire document. To do this, from the SmartShape menu, choose Slur Contour. This will open the Slur Contour dialog box as seen in Figure 6.5.

CHAPTER 6

Figure 6.5

Edit the default contour of
slurs in the Slur Contour
dialog box

First, click the drop-down menu and choose from the four available slur lengths. Since no one contour will work for every slur length, Finale divides the contour settings into four different lengths. Choose the length that most closely compares to the slurs you want to change. Then, use the handle in the editable preview window to adjust the default slur contour. Notice the preview window at the bottom will update to display any changes you make. Hold down the Shift key to constrain dragging to vertical or horizontal movement only. If you prefer, enter values in the Height and Inset text boxes for more precise control over slur contour. Click Reset to revert to the default settings for the chosen length. Click OK to apply any changes and return to the score. Contour settings will affect existing slurs in the score.

Editing the Slur Width

You can edit the thickness of slurs in the Smart Shape Options dialog box. With the Smart Shape Tool selected, from the SmartShape menu, choose Smart Slur Options. On the right side of the Smart Slur Options dialog box, use the Thickness Left, Thickness Right, and Tip Width parameters to adjust the thickness of slurs and slur tips.

Editing Default Slur Placement

Finale offers a great deal more flexibility for editing slurs globally. You can change the default placement for any slur based on the surrounding notation. From the SmartShape menu, choose Smart Shape Placement. You will see the Smart Shape Placement dialog box as shown in Figure 6.6.

First, choose the general type of slur from the list on the left. Use the scroll bar to view all the options. Notice the placement of the slur related to the stem settings to determine which type of slur to adjust. In the large, editable preview window, make adjustments to the slur manually. Click the left and right endpoints to adjust the slant and length of the slur. Click the middle of the slur and drag to adjust the vertical placement. You can also enter specific values for the start and end point in the H: (Horizontal) and V: (Vertical) text boxes. Click Reset to revert back to the original default settings. Click OK to return to the score and review your changes.

Changes made in the Smart Shape Placement dialog box will affect any new slurs you create, as well as existing slurs in the score, provided that they have not been adjusted manually.

Figure 6.6

Edit the default placement of slurs, tab slides, glissandi, and guitar bends in the Smart Shape Placement dialog box

S-Slurs

Sometimes slurs need to extend from one staff to another, requiring an "S" shape as shown in Figure 6.7 instead of a simple curve. This type of slur is quite simple to create in Finale. Enter the slur as you normally would, between notes in two adjacent staves (a grand staff for example). Then, drag the endpoints of the slur to the desired location. Drag the editing handles to create the S shape as seen in Figure 6.7.

Figure 6.7

Creating an S-Slur

Raise the endpoint, and then adjust the contour to create an "S" slur

Dashed Curves or Slurs

Dashed curves behave just like slurs. Click the Dashed Curve Tool in the Smart Shape Palette, and then double-click in the score to create a dashed curve/slur. Most settings made in the Smart Slur Options dialog box will apply to dashed slurs as well as regular slurs.

The width of dashed slurs/curves is customizable. Dashed slurs/curves are not tapered, unlike regular slurs, and are basically just curved lines. To change the width of a dashed slur, the dash length, or the space between dashes, use the Smart Shape Options dialog box. From the SmartShape menu, choose Smart Shape Options. In the right side of this dialog box, specify a value for Line Thickness, Dash Length and/or Dash Space. Then, click OK to return to the score. Note that these changes will also apply to Line and Bracket Smart Shapes as well.

Avoiding Collisions with Articulations (TGTools)

If you find that some of your slurs collide with articulation markings, you can use TGTools to tell Finale to automatically reposition the endpoints of slurs to avoid this collision. Here's how:

1. Click the Mass Edit Tool.

2. Select a region of your score containing slurs that collide with articulations, or Ctrl/Command-A to Select All.

3. From the TGTools menu, choose Modify > Slurs.

4. Click the Resolve Collisions tab.

5. Here, you can specify the offset for slurs that collide with articulations. The default values usually work fine.

6. Click Go. Slurs in the selected region adjust to avoid collision with articulations. Depending on the musical passage, you may want to adjust slurs colliding with certain articulations only. Select the Articulation Types tab in the TGTools Slurs dialog box to choose specific articulations to avoid.

 TIP
You can define an articulation to be placed inside a slur by default in the Articulation Designer dialog box. This is especially handy for staccato and tenuto articulations that are typically placed inside slurs.

Engraver Slurs

Finale 2002 introduced a variety of slur improvements, one of which is the ability to avoid collision of slurs with notes, accidentals, and beams automatically. These slurs will even update as you edit notes in the score. Slurs that include this functionality are called engraver slurs, and are used by default in Finale 2002 documents and later. (Finale will not automatically adjust the appearance of slurs in documents converted from Finale versions 2001 or earlier.) As a result of these improvements, there are a number of parameters available that help control the behavior of engraver slurs. From the SmartShape menu, choose Smart Slur Options. On the left side of this box, make adjustments to the way Finale configures engraver slurs.

Any time you edit a slur manually, it will change into a normal slur, meaning, its shape will no longer automatically adjust with the changes you make to your document. Essentially, the slur will be frozen into position and will no longer automatically adjust its shape to avoid collisions. To convert it back to an engraver slur, highlight its handle and press Backspace/Clear.

To set all slurs in a converted document (or selected region) to engraver slurs

1. Click the Mass Edit Tool.

2. Select a region of your score, or Ctrl/Command-A to Select All.

3. From the Mass Edit menu, choose Utilities > Remove Manual Slur Adjustments.

4. Click the Smart Shape Tool.

5. From the SmartShape menu, choose Smart Slur Options.

6. Check Engraver Slurs.

7. Click OK. Slurs in the selected region are now set to adjust to avoid collision with notes, accidentals, and beams.

Hairpins (Crescendos and Decrescendos)

Hairpins in music notation are used to indicate a gradual dynamic contrast. They are also referred to as crescendos and decrescendos, an increase or decrease in dynamics, respectively. In Finale, hairpins generally appear as measure-attached Smart Shapes, and can be entered with either the Crescendo or Decrescendo Tool in the Smart Shape Palette.

With the Crescendo Tool selected (or while holding down the " key), double-click below a staff and drag to the right. Release the mouse button to create the crescendo. You will notice three diamond editing handles on the crescendo in addition to the main handle (if not, double-click the main handle to display the diamond handles). Click and drag the right-most diamond handle to adjust the placement of the end of the hairpin. Click the left-most handle to adjust the placement of the beginning of the hairpin. Move your cursor over the diamond handle on the right side of the hairpin (on the line) to adjust the width of the opening (see Figure 6.8).

Figure 6.8

Use handles to edit the length and opening width of hairpins

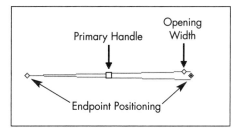

Decrescendos can be entered and edited the same way as crescendos (use the < keystroke for a decrescendo). Press Backspace/Clear to revert a hairpin back to the way it looked when originally entered.

With either hairpin tool selected, you can create both shapes. For example, Click the Crescendo Tool, double-click and drag to the *left*. Instead of a crescendo, you get a decrescendo.

To specify the line thickness and opening width for all hairpins you create, from the SmartShape menu, choose Smart Shape Options. In the Crescendo/Decrescendo section, specify a value for Line Thickness and Opening Width and click OK. All hairpins that have not been edited manually will change to the values you specified. Also, new hairpins will use these values.

TIP

If you want to indicate a crescendo simply as text (e.g., "*Cresc.*"), create a text expression (as described in Chapter 3). To create the text "Cresc." followed by an adjustable dashed horizontal line, create a Custom Smart Shape. You can find information on how to create custom shapes later in this chapter.

Aligning Hairpins

Aligning hairpins horizontally is easy. Drag to select the hairpins you want to align (or Shift-click to select the desired hairpins). Then, right/Control-click one of the selected handles and choose Align Horizontally. They all become aligned with the one you right/Control-clicked.

You may want to align all hairpins horizontally at a certain position above or below the staff. You can do this with the Align/Move Dynamics plug-in. Choose the Mass Edit Tool. Highlight the region of your score containing hairpins (Ctrl/Command-A to Select All). From the Plug-ins menu, choose TGTools > Align/Move Dynamics. You will see the Align/Move Dynamics dialog box. On the right, make sure Hairpins is checked (and uncheck any other items if you do not want them to align). Choose the appropriate option on the left. If you choose Set To Value, enter an offset from the bottom staff line in the Move Vertically text box. Click Apply to align your hairpins.

Hairpins over System Breaks

You may need to create a crescendo or decrescendo over a system break (from the end of one system to the beginning of the next). To do this, simply double-click where you want the hairpin to begin, and drag it down to the next system. When you release the mouse button, there will be a break in the hairpin lines at the beginning of the second system as shown in Figure 6.9.

Figure 6.9

Drag the right editing handle of a hairpin down to extend it across a system break

You can drag a hairpin over as many systems as there are on a page. The width of the opening on each one can be adjusted independently.

Generating Hairpins between Expressions Automatically (TGTools)

If you have already entered dynamic expressions into your score, you can use TGTools to easily extend crescendos or decrescendos between them automatically as long as they are both note-attached or both measure-attached. Here's how:

1. Click the Mass Edit Tool.

2. Select a region of your score containing dynamic expressions you want to extend hairpins between.

3. From the TGTools menu, choose Music > Create Hairpins. The Create Hairpins dialog box appears.

4. Click Go. A hairpin extends between dynamic markings in the selected region. If you do not like the results, press Ctrl-Z to undo. Then try again and specify values for Offset and Opening Width in the Create Hairpins dialog box. You can also choose to add hairpins between specific dynamic expressions in the dialog box.

Other Smart Shapes

There are a number of other Smart Shapes you can use for a variety of other purposes. These include trills, ottavas (8va/8vb), glissandos, bend hats and curves, brackets, lines, and custom shapes. These will all have the note- or measure-attached properties as described earlier in this chapter, as well as many of the same editing capabilities.

Trills and Trill Extensions

Trills can be entered with the Smart Shape Tool as well as the Articulation Tool, although with the Smart Shape Tool you will be able to create an adjustable extension. Click the Trill Tool in the Smart Shape Palette. Then, double-click and drag to the right to create a trill indication with an extension. Use the primary handle to move the whole figure around. Use the left and right handles to adjust the endpoints individually.

TIP

As an alternative to Human Playback, trills, hairpins, and glissandi entered with the Smart Shape Tool can be defined for playback with the Smart Playback plug-in. Click the Mass Edit Tool, highlight a region of the score with a trill, then choose Plug-ins > TGTools > Smart Playback. For more information, see Chapter 14.

The Trill Extension Tool in the Smart Shape Palette can be used to indicate guitar tremolos as well as trill extensions. They can be edited just like regular trill Smart Shapes. To add an accidental at the beginning of a trill figure to indicate the pitch variation, use a Custom Smart Shape. You'll find more information on creating Custom Smart Shapes later in this section.

Ottavas (8va/8vb) and 15va/15vb

To tell the performer to transpose a section of music up or down an octave, an 8va or 8vb symbol is often used (see Figure 6.10). Both of these can be created with the Smart Shape 8va Tool. Simply double-click above a staff to enter an 8va, or below the staff to enter an 8vb. Take note of your mouse cursor because the arrow points to the staff to which the shape will be attached. You can extend the dash line over system breaks, and Finale will place the 8va or 8vb symbol in parentheses automatically at the beginning of each subsequent system. 8va and 8vb figures will always be measure-attached and apply to playback.

Figure 6.10

Click above the staff to enter an 8va; click below the staff to enter an 8vb

Use the 15va Tool the same way as the 8va Tool. This figure is used to indicate a two-octave transposition from the written pitches.

If you are not satisfied with the text attached to default ottava or 15va/vb figures, you can choose your own. To change the attached text, choose Smart Shape Options from the SmartShape menu. This opens the Smart Shape Options dialog box as seen in Figure 6.11.

Figure 6.11

Choose the font, character, style, and other Smart Shape attributes in the Smart Shape Options dialog box

In the Symbols drop-down menu, choose the marking you want to edit. Then, click the Set Font button to choose the font of your new character. Once you have chosen the font, size, and style, click OK. Click the Select button to open the Symbol Selection dialog box. Choose the character you would like to use, and click Select. Click OK to return to the score. Create the figure you edited to review your changes.

Glissandi and Tab Slides

Glissandi are used to indicate a rapid slide through ascending or descending pitches. They appear as wavy lines between adjacent notes (see Figure 6.12). Creating these in Finale is easy. Click the Glissando Tool in the Smart Shape Palette and double-click a note. Finale will automatically extend a glissando to the next note.

Tab slides are generally used in tablature notation to indicate a pitch change by sliding up or down the fretboard of a fretted instrument (see Figure 6.12). Enter these the same as you would a glissando.

Figure 6.12

Double-click to extend a glissando or tab slide to the next note

Both of these Smart Shapes are notehead-attached by default. However, you can create a glissando anywhere in your score (not attached to any notehead). To do this, choose Attach to Measures from the Smart Shape menu, then double-click and drag anywhere in the score.

When a glissando reaches a certain length, you will see the text "Gliss" or "Glissando" attached to the Smart Shape (depending on its length). To enter a glissando without this text, Ctrl/Option-click the Glissando Tool in the Smart Shape Palette to open the Smart Line Style selection dialog box. Choose the regular wavy line (without text) and click Select. Now any glissando you enter will not include the attached text.

The endpoints of glissandos and tab slides can be adjusted relative to the noteheads to which they are attached. To specify placement of these items throughout your document, select the SmartShape menu and choose Smart Shape Placement (see Figure 6.6). From the drop-down menu, choose either Tab Slide or Glissando. For tab slides, specify the type of tab slide from the list box on the left (depending on whether the notes are on staff lines or spaces, ascending or descending). Click the left and right endpoints to adjust the slant and length of glissandi and tab slides. Click the middle of the glissando or tab slide and drag to

CHAPTER 6

adjust the vertical placement. You can also enter specific values for the start and end point in the H: (Horizontal) and V: (Vertical) text boxes. Click Reset to revert back to the original default settings. Click OK to return to the score.

 NOTE
For tab slides, the V: value indicates the offset from the staff line or space of the notehead, depending on the placement type selected on left side this dialog box.

Changes made to tab Slides and glissandi in the Smart Shape Placement dialog box apply to new Smart Shapes and existing Smart Shapes in the score that have not been edited (Finale will not make changes to tab slides or glissandi you have already adjusted manually). You can find more information on Tab Slide Smart Shapes in Chapter 8.

Bend Hats and Guitar Bends

Bend hats and curves are used to indicate a bend in pitch. To enter a bend hat, click the Bend Hat Smart Shape, and double-click a note. Finale will extend the bend hat to the next note automatically (see Figure 6.13). You will see three diamond editing handles attached to the bend hat in addition to the primary handle. Drag the diamond handles on the ends of the bend hat to adjust the placement of the endpoints and drag the handle at the joint to adjust the angle. To create a bend hat that isn't bound to two notes, click the SmartShape menu and choose Attach to Measures. Then double-click and drag anywhere in the score.

Figure 6.13

Use bend hats to indicate a pitch bend

The Guitar Bend Smart Shape was introduced in Finale 2003 and is used primarily for bend and release figures in guitar tablature notation. This is perhaps the smartest Smart Shape due to its ability to analyze the notation and create the appropriate pitch-change text for the existing notes as well as hide unnecessary notes. To enter a guitar bend in a TAB staff, simply choose the Guitar Bend Smart Shape and double-click a fret number to create the guitar bend. Finale will hide the following fret number and indicate the appropriate pitch change in text (see Figure 6.14).

Figure 6.14

Use the Guitar Bend Tool to create bend curves with text automatically generated to indicate the pitch variation

You can customize Finale's handling of Smart Shapes (generated text, font, etc.) with the Guitar Bend Options. From the SmartShape menu, choose Guitar Bend Options. There is a more complete discussion of how to enter and edit guitar bends and how to create guitar tablature in Chapter 8.

Brackets and Lines

There are six remaining Smart Shape Tools for creating brackets and lines. The four Bracket Smart Shapes (bracket, dashed bracket, double-ended bracket, and dashed double-ended bracket) behave almost the same. With one of them selected, double-click and drag to create a horizontal bracket. Use the diamond editing handles to adjust the length and the primary handle to move it around. To create a line, click the Line or Dashed Line Tool, then double-click and drag anywhere in the score. Unlike brackets, lines can be drawn at any slope. Bracket and Line Smart Shapes are always measure-attached.

There are a several ways to customize brackets and lines throughout your document. Change the width, dash length, dash space, and length of bracket hooks in the Smart Shape Options dialog box. From the Smart Shape menu, choose Smart Shape Options. The Smart Shape Options dialog box appears (see Figure 6.11). In the four text boxes on the right, you can specify line thickness, dash length, and dash space. These parameters affect both Bracket and Line Smart Shapes, as well as dashed curves. To change the length of the bracket hooks (the vertical lines on the ends of brackets), enter a new value in the Hook Length text box (of course, the Hook Length setting applies only to brackets). Click OK to review changes in your score.

Custom Smart Shapes

There are a number of other available Smart Shapes that do not exist in the Smart Shape Palette. To see a list of other Smart Shapes, Ctrl/Option-click the Custom Line Tool. You will see the Smart Line Style Selection dialog box as seen in Figure 6.15.

Figure 6.15
Edit or create a smart line in
the Smart Line Style Selection
dialog box

Here, there are a number of other Smart Shape Line styles available for you to choose from. They are basically specialized lines for figures not available in the Smart Shape Palette. To use any of the following, click to highlight it, and then click the Select button. Double-click and drag in the score to create the figure you chose.

❋ **Glissando.** Choose a glissando with or without text. These are the same as regular glissandi.

❋ **Ped. and ❋ (sustain).** These figures are generally used to indicate the beginning and end of a sustained section of piano music. Many Custom Smart Lines, such as this one, do not contain a line at all. This Smart Shape only displays a figure at the beginning and end of an "invisible" line. Also, notice the graphical pedal markings available here.

❋ **Lines with arrowheads.** These are just like regular lines, except with an arrowhead attached.

❋ **Ritardando.** Often, ritardandos are indicated with "rit." followed by a dashed horizontal line.

❋ **Trills.** Choose from a number of trill markings, set to indicate possible pitch variations with accidentals.

❋ **Figures for Guitar Notation.** Choose from a variety of figures for guitar notation, including harmonics (A.H., N.H.), mute indications (P.M.) and picking symbols, hammer-ons, and pull-offs. There will be more information on guitar notation in Chapter 8.

Like regular lines, custom lines are measure-attached. As the name of the tool suggests, you can edit any of the available lines, or create your own from scratch.

Creating Custom Smart Shapes

Create a custom Smart Shape for any type of line you need. Perhaps the most common Smart Shape is the "cresc." marking followed by a horizontal line. Here are steps for creating a crescendo marking followed by a dashed line. Before you begin, from the Options menu, choose Measurement Units and then Inches.

1. Hold down the Ctrl/Option key and click the Custom Line Tool. The Smart Line Style Selection dialog box appears.

2. Click the Create button. You should now see the Smart Line Style dialog box as shown in Figure 6.16.

Figure 6.16

Define the appearance and add text to a smart line in the Smart Line Style dialog box

3. Click the Style drop-down menu and choose Dashed. Notice the updated preview in the lower right. Leave the line thickness and dash settings alone for now.

4. Now, increase the frequency of the dashes. Some find the default dashes a bit too long. For Dash Length, enter .04. For Space, enter .04 (inches). Notice that the preview in the lower right updates after leaving each text box.

5. Check Horizontal if it isn't checked already. You'll want to constrain to horizontal dragging while entering the crescendo markings in the score.

6. Now, add the text. In the text section, at the bottom of this dialog box, click the Edit button for Left Start (since you'll want the text at the beginning of the line). The Edit Text box opens.

7. Type "Cresc."

8. Most often, this type of marking is italicized. Hold down Ctrl/Command and press A to Select All.

9. From the Text menu, choose Style, then Italic. The text becomes italicized.

10. Click OK. You return to the Smart Line Style dialog box.

11. The dashed line should begin after the text. In the upper right, for Start H, check After Text.

12. Click OK and Select to return to the score.

13. Double-click and drag to create the marking anywhere in the score.

You can edit custom lines in the score just as you would a regular line (although this example confined this line to horizontal dragging only). If you want to change the text, line thickness, dash length, etc., Ctrl/Option-click the Smart Line Tool. Your custom Smart Shape will now always appear in the Smart Line Style Selection dialog box. Click it and choose Edit to make any edits to the line.

If there is a custom line similar to the one you would like to create, you can save time by duplicating and then editing the Smart Line. In the Smart Line Style Selection dialog box, click the Smart Line similar to the one you want to create and click the Duplicate button. A duplicate of the Smart Line will appear at the bottom of the list. Click the duplicate Smart Line, and then click the Edit button to make the adjustments.

One additional benefit to Custom Smart Shapes is the ability to rotate text. If you need text to appear vertically, for example, create a Custom Smart Shape line and then create the shape vertically.

Copying Smart Shapes

When you copy music with the Mass Edit Tool, Finale will copy all Smart Shapes along with the notation. You can, however, copy Smart Shapes independently from one area of your score to another. Before following these steps, click the Edit Menu and uncheck Select Partial Measures (if it is checked).

1. Click the Mass Edit Tool.

2. From the Mass Edit menu, choose Copy Measure Items if you want to copy measure-attached Smart Shapes, like hairpins or trills. Choose Copy Entry Items if you want to copy note-attached Smart Shapes, like slurs or glisses. The Measure or Entry Items dialog box appears. If you copy note-attached Smart Shapes (Entry Items), notes in the destination measure will need to have the same rhythmic configuration for the Smart Shapes to copy properly.

3. Put a check in Smart Shapes (Attached to Notes or Attached to Measures).

4. Click OK.

5. Select the region of your score containing the Smart Shapes you want to copy, and drag to the new measures (or Ctrl/Option-Shift-click the first measure in the destination region).

6. The Smart Shapes copy to the new location. If they do not, make sure the Smart Shapes in the region you selected are measure-attached if you chose to Copy Measure Items or note-attached if you chose to Copy Entry Items from the Mass Edit menu.

Automatically Copy Smart Shapes to Rhythmically Identical Passages

You may have a reoccurring motif or ostinato in your score that demands the same set of Smart Shapes at each occurrence throughout the piece. The SmartFind and Paint feature introduced in Chapter 3 also allows you to find and copy Smart Shapes to rhythmically identical passages. To demonstrate this, fill a measure with a combination of eighth and quarter notes on different pitches with the Simple or Speedy Entry Tool. Click the Mass Edit Tool, highlight this measure, and drag-copy it to a different measure. In the Copy Measures dialog box, type "10" and click OK. Now click the Smart Shape Tool and add several Smart Shapes to the original measure. Click the Mass Edit Tool and highlight the measure containing the Smart Shapes. Click the Mass Edit menu and choose Set SmartFind Source. Now click the Mass Edit menu and choose Apply SmartFind and Paint. Click the Find button and the measure containing a passage with an identical rhythm becomes highlighted. Click the Paint button, and the Smart Shapes appear on the notes just as they did in the original measure. This is also a great technique for copying articulations, note expressions, and measure expressions to similar phrases throughout your score.

Defining Repeats

Repeats are a common way to tell the performer to go back and play a section of music once, twice, or several more times. Often, a new ending is specified for each run through the same section of music. In notation, repeat barlines and text are used to indicate these repeated sections. The design for repeats improved significantly in Finale 2005, and they are easier to define than ever. You can now use context menus to define repeated sections that are set up for playback automatically.

Basic Repeat Creation and Editing

Defining basic repeats in Finale is easy. To indicate a single repeated section, or a repeat with a first and second ending, use the Repeat Tool context menus. To create a single repeat with two repeat barlines, one at the beginning, and one at the end

1. Click the Repeat Tool.
2. Highlight the region of your score that will be included in the repeated section (click the first measure, then Shift-click the last measure of the desired region).
3. Right/Control-click the region and choose Create Simple Repeat.

The selected region now begins and ends with a repeat barline and will play back correctly. To create a repeat with a first and second ending is almost as easy:

1. Click the Repeat Tool.
2. Highlight the measure (or measures) you would like to include in the first ending.
3. Right/Control-click the highlighted area and choose Create First and Second Ending (see Figure 6.17).

Figure 6.17
Create a first and second ending easily using a context menu.

4. Now, right/Control-click a measure and choose Create Forward Repeat Bar to add a forward repeat. This first and second repeat will play back correctly. If you do not add a forward repeat prior to the endings, Finale will automatically skip back to the beginning of the score.

NOTE
Feel free to add or delete measures within repeated sections. Finale updates the playback definitions for you automatically.

To see the playback route, from the Repeat Menu, choose Check Repeats. The Check Repeats dialog box appears as shown in Figure 6.18.

Figure 6.18
To see the playback route of your score after adding repeats, use the Check Repeats dialog box.

NOTE
If you have multiple measure regions defined (in the Measure Number dialog box), you will see the region number and then the measure number (e.g., 1:1-10, 2:1-9, etc.).

Deleting Repeats

To delete repeat indications from any region of your score

1. Highlight the region containing the repeat barlines and/or text. Or, highlight just the handles on the repeat text or brackets you want to remove.

2. Press the Delete key

Repeat definitions in the highlighted area of your score are removed along with any playback information.

Assigning Repeat Brackets and Text to Staves

It is common to display the repeat brackets and text on the top staff and not on subsequent staves (in a piano grand staff for example). You can assign these repeat items to appear on one staff and not others (or any number of staves) in the Edit Repeat Assignment and Edit Ending dialog boxes. For example, to display the ending brackets you just created on the top staff only, do the following:

1. Right/Control-click the handle on the number "1." in the first ending bracket and choose Edit Ending. The Edit Ending dialog box appears as shown in Figure 6.19.

Figure 6.19

Assign ending brackets to staves in the Edit Ending dialog box.

2. Under Show On, select Top Staff to display endings on the top staff only. (Note that here you can also choose Staff List and select a staff list to assign the ending brackets to certain staves (or click Edit to modify or create a staff list). See Chapter 7 for a complete description of setting up a staff list.)

3. Click OK to return to the score. The ending bracket appears on the top staff only.

TIP

You can also choose to hide all repeat endings and text for an entire staff. Click the Staff Tool and double-click a staff. Under Items to Display, uncheck Endings and Text Repeats and click OK.

Assigning Multiple Endings

Assigning second, third, fourth, or more endings could not be easier. For this example, we'll create a repeat with three endings.

1. Right/Control-click the first measure of the repeated section and choose Create Forward Repeat Bar.

2. Right/Control-click the desired first ending measure (or selected measure region) and choose Create Ending. The Create Ending dialog box appears. Click OK to add the first ending.

3. Right/Control-click the measure following the first ending and choose Create Ending.

4. Click OK. The second ending appears, and a "2." is placed in the ending bracket automatically.

5. Right/Control-click the measure following the second ending and choose Create Ending.

6. Since this is the third and final ending of our repeat, we'll remove the backward repeat bar. Uncheck Create Backward Repeat Bar and click OK. The third ending appears in the score. Finale adds a "3." in the ending bracket automatically. Add as many endings as you like using the same method, Finale configures playback for you automatically. (From the Repeat menu, choose Check Repeats to review the playback route.)

> **TIP**
> Use the Show On section to assign ending brackets to staves as described in the previous section.

DS al Coda/Fine

It is common for repeats marking to indicate a return back to a sign (D.S. and Segno) and then jump to a Coda. The following instructions can be a continuation of the previous instructions for creating first and second ending repeats. After you have created a repeat definition, use the following steps to enter the D.S., Segno, and Coda. After following these steps, you will be able to create a score containing all of the repeat symbols in the following musical example (see Figure 6.20).

Figure 6.20

First and second ending repeat example with D.S. al Coda

1. Choose the Repeat Tool.
2. Double-click the measure in which you want to place the Segno (sign). The Repeat Selection dialog box appears as shown in Figure 6.21.
3. Double-click the Segno in the Text Repeats list. The Text Repeat Assignment dialog box appears as shown in Figure 6.22.
4. Under Repeat Action, choose Never Jump (Mark). Take note of the Text Repeat ID number assigned to the Segno in the upper-left corner of the dialog. (This is "8" by default.)
5. Click OK.
6. Click and drag the handle of the Segno to reposition it. The Segno sign should be placed at the beginning of the measure to which it is attached. Now, enter its corresponding *D.S. al Coda* indication.

Figure 6.21

Choose from a list of text repeats in the Repeat Selection dialog box

Figure 6.22

Specify the playback properties for text repeats in the Text Repeat Assignment dialog box.

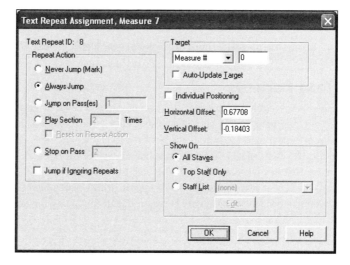

7. Double-click on the measure in which you want the *D.S. al Coda* to appear. The Repeat Selection dialog box appears (see Figure 6.21).

8. Double-click the *D.S. al Coda* in the Text Repeats list. The Text Repeat Assignment dialog box opens.

9. The music does jump from this point back to the Segno, so leave the selection Always Jump. Under Target, click the drop-down menu, choose Text Repeat ID, and then type the number of the repeat that was assigned to the Segno (as you noted in step 4).

10. Click OK.

11. Click and drag the handle of the *D.S. al Coda* to reposition it. The *D.S. al Coda* sign should be placed at the end of the measure to which it is attached. Now, you'll enter the Coda sign.

12. Double-click the first measure of your Coda section. The Repeat Selection dialog box opens.

13. In the Repeat Selection, double-click the Coda sign. The Text Repeat Assignment dialog appears.

14. The Coda sign itself is just a marker, so select Never Jump (Mark) and take note of the Repeat number assigned in the upper-left corner ("7" by default).

15. Click OK. Then, click and drag the handle of the Coda sign to reposition it (to the beginning of this measure). Now you'll enter its corresponding *To Coda* indication.

16. Double-click the measure which will contain the *To Coda* indication. The Repeat Selection dialog box appears.

17. Double-click the *To Coda* **#** in the Text Repeats list. The Text Repeat Assignment dialog box opens.

18. The music does jump from this point to the Coda on the second pass, so for Repeat Action, choose Jump On Pass(es) and type "2." Under Target, click the drop-down menu, choose Text Repeat ID, and then type the number of the repeat that was assigned to the Coda (as you noted in step 14).

19. Click OK. Notice the Coda symbol appearing after the *To Coda* indication.

20. Click and drag the handle of the *To Coda* to reposition it (to the end of the measure). Notice that the **#** has been replaced with the measure number of the Coda, the target measure.

21. To review the playback route, from the Repeat Menu, choose Check Repeats.

Creating Text Repeats

In addition to using the available text repeats, you can create your own or edit the already available ones. Click the Repeat Tool, and then double-click a measure. Click Create to open the Repeat Designer dialog box. Enter the text of your repeat marking here (click Set Font to change the font, size, or style). You can use the **#** character to indicate a customizable measure number or symbol for the text repeat, depending on settings you will make in the Text Repeat Assignment dialog box. Click OK to return to the Repeat Selection dialog box. From now on, the repeat text you created will appear in this dialog box. Like articulations, expressions, and other items, you can transfer text repeats between documents by saving and opening a library.

Playback

You may find that a score containing repeats plays the same section many times (more than intended). If this is the case, it is likely there are repeats in your score that are defined to loop infinitely. To fix this problem, double-check the playback definitions of your repeats. To view or redefine the playback definitions of your repeats, right/Control-click the handle of the repeat and click Edit Repeat Assignment. In the Repeat Assignment dialog box, you can edit the Target Repeat or Measure number as well as the Repeat Action and number of Total Passes.

TIP
Note that there is a limit to the number of times repeats are allowed to loop (to prevent infinite loops). From the Repeat menu, choose Repeat Options. The value entered for Multiple Repeat Passes specifies the greatest number of times a section is allowed to repeat.

After defining the repeats as described earlier, they will play back correctly. However, you may want to specify a performance indication for playback the second time only (for example). You can tell Finale to play back at a specific volume, tempo, or even patch number (sound) for the first, second, or third pass only. To do this

1. Click the Expression Tool.

2. Double-click at the beginning of a repeated section. The Expression Selection dialog box opens.

3. Click Create to open the Text Expression Designer.

4. In the text box, enter a description of the playback definition you are entering ("Play 1st time only," for example).

5. Since you won't want this expression to print, highlight the text, and then, from the Text Menu, choose Style > Hidden.

6. Click the Playback tab.

7. For Type, click the drop-down menu and choose the type of MIDI data you want to modify. In this example, select Key Velocity.

8. For Effect, enter the value of change. For this example, enter 0 (for silence).

9. For Play Only on Pass, enter the number of the pass for which you want this expression to affect playback. In this example, enter "2". The second time these measures are played, the notes will be silent.

10. Click OK, click Select, and then OK to return to the score.

11. You will notice that on the second time through the repeated area, the notes do not sound on this staff. The playback definitions of expressions affect channels. To make sure that this expression affects only the staff you intend, make sure all of your staves are set to their own channel in the Instrument List. You'll also notice this staff will continue to be silent after that point. This is because you need to add another expression that contains a key velocity greater than 0.

12. Double-click a measure after the repeated area or in your second ending. When the Expression Selection appears, click Create. From the Text menu, choose Style > Hidden, and type the desired text. Then click the Playback tab.

13. For type, choose Key Velocity and enter a value greater than 0 and less than 127, such as 64. Note that the dynamic markings in your document are already assigned a key velocity, so you may use a dynamic instead. Click OK, click Select, and then OK to return to the score.

Click the Play button in the playback controls to hear your results. You'll find a more complete discussion of the playback capabilities of the Expression Tool in Chapter 14.

7

CREATING AND WORKING WITH MULTIPLE-STAFF SCORES

So far, this book has emphasized documents with a single staff, or perhaps a piano score with two staves. The aim of this chapter is to get acquainted with procedures applicable to working with scores of two, three, or many staves. To cover material fundamental to working with multiple stave scores, it's time to explore properties of the Staff, Measure, Page Layout, and Expression Tools. You will learn how to position, view, and reorder staves, manage barlines, group staves in brackets, remove empty staves from systems, add expressions to any number of selected staves, and perform a variety of other tricks that apply specifically to multiple stave documents.

Here's a summary of what you will learn in this chapter:

* ❈ How to work with multiple staves
* ❈ How to work with staff groups
* ❈ How to enter expressions in documents with multiple staves
* ❈ How to create and work with optimized scores
* ❈ Other tricks for multiple stave scores

Working with Multiple Staves

A Finale document can contain any number of staves, limited only by the available memory on your machine. Much of the work of beginning a new score can be done automatically by starting with the Setup Wizard or a template. Refer back to Chapter 2 for information on starting a new document. This section focuses on adding and removing staves in any existing document, as well as viewing and editing them most efficiently.

To prepare for this section, open a new Default Document (File > New > Default Document). Then, from the View menu, choose Scroll View. Although staves can be added in Scroll View or Page View, Scroll View is best for demonstrating staff creation and management. You will see a single staff extend across the page. Click the Staff Tool. Unless specified otherwise, assume the Staff Tool is selected for this section.

Adding, Removing, and Positioning Staves

There are a couple ways to add staves to an existing document, with or without the Setup Wizard. To add new, empty staves, with no staff name or other attributes, choose New Staves from the Staff menu. The New Staves dialog box opens as shown in Figure 7.1.

Figure 7.1
Choose the number of staves, and their spacing, in the New Staves dialog box

Type the number of staves you want to add. For now, leave it at 1. Click OK. You return to the score with the new staves at the bottom. Also, in Scroll View, double-click on your document to create a new staff. Then use the staff handle to drag it into position (I'll cover more about staff positioning later in this section). After you have added staves this way, you will need to specify the staff name, clef, transposition, and any other necessary staff attributes (as described in Chapter 2). To do this automatically while you add staves, use the Staff Setup Wizard.

With the Setup Wizard, you will be able to choose the instruments and order of several new staves at once.

1. With the Staff Tool selected, from the Staff menu, choose New Staves (with Setup Wizard). You will see the Choose Parts page of the Setup Wizard (see Figure 2.3).

2. Choose the new instruments and order just as you would in the Document Setup Wizard. For this example, let's add a brass quartet. Choose the Brass category on the left, and then double-click Trumpet in Bb, Horn in F, Trombone, and Tuba. The four instruments appear in the right column.

3. For Score Order, click the drop-down menu and choose Concert Band to put them in a more standard order.

4. Click Finish to return to the score.

The four staves have been added to the score beneath the two undefined staves. Notice the blue bracket to the left. This is called a group bracket, which is used to indicate staves of a similar instrumental group (more about groups soon). Right/Option-Command-click and drag the score so the left edge of the system is in view (from this point on, to move around the score horizontally in Scroll View, always use the scroll bar at the bottom on the screen).

Removing Staves

Now, delete the top two staves.

1. Click the handle on the upper-left corner of the top staff, then from the Staff menu, press Delete. This clears the top staff and shifts the subsequent staves up to take its place.

2. Now, click the handle on the top staff (the remaining undefined staff). Hold down Shift and press the Delete key. This is the shortcut for deleting a staff without repositioning.

3. To delete a staff without changing the positioning of any of the other staves, click the staff handle and select Delete Staves from the Staff menu. To delete many staves, hold down the Shift key and click all of the staff handles on staves you want to delete. Then follow one of the previous methods for deleting the selected staves.

Inserting a Staff between Existing Staves

Let's say you want to insert a second trumpet part above the horn staff in the document you are working on. Click the handle on the horn staff. Then, from the Staff menu, choose New Staves (with Setup Wizard). Choose Brass on the left, and then double-click Trumpet in Bb. Click Finish. The new trumpet staff appears above the horn staff, and all subsequent staves are shifted down.

Positioning Staves

You can move staves manually with the staff handles. Simply click a staff handle (or number of staff handles) and drag to reposition the staves. In the document you have been working on, suppose you want to drag the trombone staff above the horn staff, but leave the spacing the same. Click the handle on the trombone staff and drag it up between the trumpet and horn staves (it will look cramped initially). Then, from the Staff menu, make sure Auto Sort Staves is checked, and then choose Respace Staves. You will see the Respace Staves dialog box as shown in Figure 7.2.

Figure 7.2

Set the distance between staves in the Respace Staves dialog box

For now, just click OK. You return to the score with the original spacing. The trombone staff is now above the horn staff.

You may want to increase or decrease the space between your staves to make more room for music on ledger lines, or to fit additional staves. Let's say you want to bring the staves of the quintet a bit closer together. From the Staff menu, choose Respace Staves to invoke the Respace Staves dialog box (see Figure 7.2). Click Scale To and type "90" in the text box to tell Finale to respace the staves at 90 percent of their original spacing. Click OK to return to the score. Notice the staves respace proportionally bringing them closer together.

To increase the space, follow the same instructions except, in the Respace Staves dialog box, enter a value over 100 in the Scale To text box. If you know a precise value, choose Set To and enter the space between each staff in the corresponding text box as a negative value (the default is -1.111 inches). To change the unit of measurement, from the Options menu, choose Measurement Units.

NOTE

When you choose to scale the spacing percentage in the Resize Staves dialog box, Finale will retain the original proportions of the space between staves. To space the staves evenly, choose Respace Staves from the Staff Menu, and then enter a negative value (in your current measurement unit) in the Set To field. Once your staves are evenly spaced, you may find it more convenient to fine tune your staff spacing by scaling to a percentage.

Resizing Staff Systems

In Page View, if you add many staves to your score, they may end up running beyond the lower page margin. If this is the case, first try respacing the staves so the system takes up less vertical space. If you do this and find that after all staves fit on the page there is not enough space between the staves to fit music and/or expressions and other markings, you will need to resize the systems (reduce them). To do this, first respace the staves so there is an adequate amount of space between them. Click the Resize Tool, and then click an area between two staves in the system. The Resize Staff System dialog box appears as shown in Figure 7.3.

Figure 7.3

Resize systems and/or staff heights in the Resize Staff System dialog box

After And Resize System, enter a new percentage. For example, type "80" in this box to reduce the system to 80 percent of its original size. You will probably want to resize all systems in your score at once. In the Staff System Range section, select System 1 Through End of Piece. Click OK to return to the score and review the system reduction. You may need to experiment with several different system reductions to find the one that fits best on the page.

NOTE

In versions of Finale prior to 2003, the staff height was always fixed at 96 EVPUs, and you will most likely never need to change this value. If you change the staff height in the Resize Staff System dialog box, it will be further adjusted by the system resize percentage. The cumulative system scaling is listed below after Resulting System Scaling.

Working with Barlines

When you edit the appearance of barlines, the changes you make automatically apply to affected measures for all staves in the system. They can also have implications on parts extracted from the score, such as breaking multi-measure rests. To create double, dashed, solid, or other barline styles, first click the Measure Tool, then double-click a measure to open the Measure Attributes dialog box as seen in Figure 7.4.

Figure 7.4

Choose a barline style in the Measure Attributes dialog box

In the top row of barline icons, choose the one you want to use and click OK to return to the score. The new barline appears on all staves in that system at the end of the measure you clicked.

To quickly change barlines, use the Measure Tool context menu. Right/Control-click a measure to open the context menu (barline handles are located on the top staff). Choose the barline style here to edit the barline instantly.

Creating and Editing Barlines

If you can't find the barline style you want to use, create your own. With the Measure Tool selected, double-click a measure to open the Measure Attributes dialog box. In the top row of barline icons, click the rightmost option (the Custom Barline icon), and then click the Select button beside it. The Shape Selection dialog box appears. Click the Create button. The Shape Designer dialog box appears. Use the tools in this window to design your own custom barline (you can find more information on the Shape Designer in Chapter 10). Once you have finished, click OK, Select, and OK to return to the score. Your custom barline now appears on every staff in that measure.

To manage barlines throughout your document, use the Barlines portion of the Document Options. From the Options menu, choose Document Options and select Barlines. The Barline options appear as seen in Figure 7.5.

Here are some common ways to edit barlines using the Document Options. These settings apply to barlines throughout the document:

* Uncheck Display All Barlines to hide all barlines in the score.
* By default there is usually a final barline at the end of the document. To remove this, uncheck Final Barline at End of Piece.

Figure 7.5

Make document-wide settings for barlines in the Barlines category of the Document Options

* Check Display on Single Staves to place a barline on the left edge of each single-staff system. This is particularly useful for lead sheets.

* Use the text boxes to control the thickness of barlines, distance between double barlines, and the length and frequency of dashes on dashed barlines.

Adjusting Measure Width

You can use the Measure Tool to increase or decrease the width of measures. With the Measure Tool selected, click and drag or use the arrow keys to nudge a barline handle horizontally. Notice music in the measure respaces proportionally in all staves as the width of the measure changes. Also note that note-attached items will also respace along with the notes. You can use this method to give a measure more space for chord symbols, lyrics, expressions, and other note-attached items.

NOTE
You may notice two handles on some barlines. The lower one can be used to assign spacing for beats in the measure with a "Beat Chart." You can find more information on beat chart spacing, and other music spacing methods in Chapter 9.

You can also set the width of measures to a specific value.

1. With the Measure Tool selected, highlight a measure or number of measures. Then, double-click the highlighted region to open the Measure Attributes dialog box (see Figure 7.4).

2. For Change Width, enter the amount of space you would like between barlines in the selected measures. You can also add space between barlines by entering a value for Add _ to Width.

3. Click OK to return to the score and review changes. If you don't see a change, your measures may be locked so that they will not reflow across systems (for example, if there are three measures in a system, and you set the measure width for each to .5 inches, Finale needs to be able to reconfigure the number of measures per system to compensate for the extra space. Finale will not adjust the system margins to fit the measure widths you set.).

4. To unlock a system, choose the Mass Edit Tool and highlight the system and adjacent systems. From the Mass Edit menu, choose Unlock Systems. Then go back and change the measure width with the Measure Tool.

TIP
Use the Page Layout Tool to adjust system margins.

Adding Double Barlines at Key Changes Automatically

In conventional notation, you will sometimes find a double barline at every key change. In Finale, instead of using the Measure Attributes to add these double barlines for each key change, you can do it for your whole score automatically with the Automatic Barlines plug-in. To apply these changes to a region of your score, choose the Mass Edit Tool, and select a region of your score (for the whole document, no selection is necessary). From the Plug-ins menu, choose Measures > Automatic Barlines. Double barlines appear at key changes in the region you selected, or throughout the document.

Customizing Staff Viewing: Staff Sets

With large scores, you may not be able to see all staves at the same time while entering or editing your music. Or, to see all your staves, the view percentage needs to be too small to effectively work with them. With Staff Sets, you can specify certain staves for viewing and hide staves you don't need to see.

To demonstrate this, let's add some more staves to our score. First, select the top trumpet staff so that staves will be inserted above this staff. Click the Staff Menu and choose New Staves (with Setup Wizard). In the Setup Wizard, choose the Woodwinds category. Add a Flute, Oboe, Bassoon, Clarinet in Bb, and a Bass Clarinet. For Score Order, click the drop-down menu and choose Concert Band. Click Finish to return to the score. The woodwind parts appear above the brass staves. Now, let's say you are beginning the piece with a flute and tuba duet. Depending on your screen resolution, monitor size, and view percentage, both of these staves may not appear on your screen at the same time (if they do, let's pretend they are spaced too far apart). To isolate the flute and tuba staves for viewing:

1. Move to Scroll View (if you are in Page View). From the View menu, choose Scroll View.

2. With the Staff Tool selected, hold down the Shift key and click the handles of the staves you want to isolate. In this case, the Flute and Tuba staves. If you can't see the Tuba staff, use the scroll bar on the right to move the score vertically.

3. While holding down the Ctrl/Option key, click the View menu.

4. Continue holding down the Ctrl/Option key and choose Program Staff Set > Staff Set 1.

The display now shows the flute and tuba staves only. You can use this view to enter and edit music as you would normally. To see the full score again, from the View menu, choose Select Staff Set > All Staves. You can program up to eight staff sets, each with any number of staves. Select any staff set you program by choosing View > Select Staff Set.

TIP

For even greater control over staff viewing (including the ability to define a view percentage for your staff sets), try the Patterson Staff Sets plug-in. This plug-in is part of the Patterson Plug-in Collection available for download from Robert Patterson's Web site at www.robertgpatterson.com. You can find more information regarding the Staff Sets plug-in in Chapter 15.

Staff Groups

Staves in large scores are often divided into groups of instrumental families (see Figure 7.6). All staves in a group are enclosed by bracket to the left of the score that usually extend through all staves of a group throughout the score.

Figure 7.6
Group brackets

Often, within each group there are also secondary groups, such as the secondary Clarinet group in Figure 7.4. Whenever you use the Setup Wizard to begin a new score, Finale will enter these group indications for you automatically. This is also the case while adding several staves to a score with the Setup Wizard (Staff > New Staves (with Setup Wizard)). In this section, you will learn how to create your own group definitions and edit the ones Finale creates for you.

Start by defining groups for a score from scratch. To prepare for this section, open a new Default Document (File > New > Default Document). Move to Page View (View > Page View). Then, click the Staff Tool and, from the Staff Menu, choose New Staves. Type 3 and click OK. Change your view percentage so all staves are visible (try 50%: View menu > Scale View To > 50%). Also, from the Options menu, choose Measurement Units and make sure Inches is selected.

Adding Groups

To add a group, from the Staff menu, choose Add Group and Bracket. The Group Attributes dialog box appears as shown in Figure 7.7.

Figure 7.7

Define the enclosed staves, group name, and bracket style for a group in the Group Attributes dialog box

From this dialog box, you will be able to create and manage all group definitions. Let's say you need to create a "Strings" group containing the top four staves.

1. In the Group Attributes, click the Edit button for Group Name. The Edit Text dialog box appears. Type the name of the group here. Type "Strings." In the future, you may want to highlight the text and use the Text menu to edit the font size and style of the group name.

2. Click OK to return to the Group Attributes.

3. Click the Edit button for Abbr. Group Name. Type "Str."

4. Click OK to return to the Group Attributes.

5. For Staff:, leave the setting [Staff 1] since the top staff in the score is the top staff of the group.

6. For Through, leave the setting [Staff 4] since it is the bottom staff in the group.

7. For Draw Barlines, leave the setting at Through Staves (this is most common). Use this setting in the future to specify barlines only on staves (for choral music) or Mensurstriche (only between staves) barlines.

8. In the Bracket Options section, choose the style of your bracket. For now, choose the bracket second from the right (the straight bracket with curved hooks).

9. Place a checkmark on Show Group Name.

10. Click OK to return to the score.

You will see a bracket (blue by default) to the left of the four staves, and barlines through them. You should also see the text "Strings" to the left of the group bracket on the first system and "Str." to the left of the second system. The abbreviated group name you define in Group Attributes will appear on the second and all subsequent systems.

Now, let's say you want to add a secondary bracket to the top two staves as if they were both violins.

1. From the Staff menu, choose Add Group and Bracket. The Group Attributes dialog box appears. Notice the number for Group ID: is 2. Whenever you choose Add Group and Bracket from the Staff menu, Finale will begin a new group definition. You can use the arrows here at any time to move between group definitions. Text is often unnecessary for secondary group brackets, so you can leave the Name and Abbr. Name alone.

2. For Staff, leave the setting [Staff 1], since, again, this is the top staff of the group.

3. For Through, click the drop-down menu and choose [Staff 2] since this is the bottom staff in the group.

TIP

Before choosing Add Group and Bracket, you could also highlight the staves you want to include, and the Staff and Through settings will be set up to bracket the highlighted staves automatically.

4. In the Bracket Options section, choose the rightmost bracket (the thin one with perpendicular hooks). This is the most common secondary bracket figure.

5. Finale will always leave the same amount of space between the left edge of the system and the group bracket by default. Since you want this bracket to the left of the existing one, enter a greater value in the Distance from Left Edge of Staff text box. In this case, enter "-0.1666" (inches). You can also adjust the bracket length in this section if necessary, though the defaults should be fine.

6. Click OK to return to the score.

The secondary group bracket appears to the left of the main group bracket. You can use the above methods to enter any number of group and secondary group definitions into a score, specifying the appropriate text, top and bottom staff, bracket style, and positioning for each group.

In the score, drag or nudge text and bracket handles to position them manually. To further edit any group bracket, right/Control-click its handle and choose Edit Group Attributes. The Group Attributes dialog box will open, where you can modify its definition.

To delete a group, as well as the barline settings of the group, click its handle in the score and press the Delete key. You can also right/Control-click a group bracket handle and choose Delete. Hold down the Delete key and drag over any number of group brackets to delete them, but be careful not to delete any actual staves.

Removing Barlines between Staves

You can remove barlines between any two staves, regardless of the group definition. To do this, double-click the lower of two staves connected by barlines. The Staff Attributes dialog box appears. Check Break Barlines Between Staves, and click OK to return to the score. Barlines will no longer connect the two staves. Recheck this box to allow barlines between this and the above staff.

Expressions and Text Repeats in Multiple-Stave Documents

In Chapters 3 and 6, I described the basics for entering expressions and repeats in documents with a single staff. In large scores you can assign an expression or text repeat to appear in all staves or in a single staff, or you can define a Staff List to display the marking on specific staves only. Staff Lists are particularly useful because once you've defined one Staff List you can easily assign any future expressions (or repeats) to the same list of staves.

To prepare for this section, use the same multiple-staff document you have been working with. You could also begin a new document and add three staves. Click the Expression Tool. For this section, assume the Expression Tool is selected unless specified otherwise.

Assigning Measure Expressions

Now, start by assigning an expression to a measure so that it appears on every staff. With the Expression Tool selected, double-click above the first measure of the top staff. The Expression Selection dialog box appears. Double-click an expression, and you will see the Measure Expression Assignment dialog box. In the Show On section, choose All Staves and click OK. You return to the score with the expression above each staff. Click and drag a handle to position the expressions uniformly.

Any measure expression you enter with a metatool will appear on all staves automatically. To tell Finale to use measure expressions while entering with metatools, from the Expression menu, choose Metatools: Measure-Attached.

Assigning Measure Expressions to Specific Staves Using Staff Lists

Now, let's say you want to enter an expression in the top two staves only.

1. Double-click the top staff to open the Expression Selection dialog box.
2. Select the Forte expression (make sure Measure Expression is selected at the bottom of this dialog box) and then click Select. The Measure Expression Assignment dialog box appears.
3. In the Show On section, select Staff List. Then, click on the drop-down menu and choose New Staff List. You will then see the Staff List dialog box as seen in Figure 7.8.
4. Here you'll define the list of staves you want the expression to appear on. For List Name, type "Violin 1 and 2," then click the Add button.
5. These expressions can appear in both the score and parts, so click to place an X under both the Score and Parts column for Staves 1 and 2.

Figure 7.8

Assign an expression to the
score and/or parts in the Staff
List dialog box

6. Click OK to return to the Measure Expression Assignment dialog box and OK again to return to the score. The expression appears on the top two staves. Click a handle and drag to move them into place.

NOTE

The Parts column in the Staff List dialog box refers to expressions in parts extracted from a score. We'll dive into part extraction in Chapter 11.

Now, any time you want to place an expression on staves one and two, you can use the same Staff List. Double-click on the top staff to open the Expression Selection dialog box. Choose the Piano expression and click Select. Now, in the Measure Expression Assignment dialog box, choose Staff List (if it isn't selected already). (The Assignment dialog retains the last setting that was used). The Staff List you just defined is already selected, so click OK to return to the score. The expression now appears on the top two staves.

You can also easily edit the assignment of existing expressions in your score. Simply right/Control-click an expression handle and choose Edit Measure Expression Assignment. Then choose All Staves, This Staff Only, or Staff List to modify the assignment of the expression. Click OK to return to the score.

TIP

To show only the expressions or repeats that you have specifically assigned to appear in the extracted parts in the Staff List, from the Options menu, choose Display Expressions and Repeats for Parts.

Assigning Text Repeats and Repeat Endings to Specific Staves

The steps above also apply to text repeats, such as *To Coda* or *D.S. al Coda,* and to repeat ending brackets. In Chapter 6 you learned how to assign repeat endings and text repeats to a single staff. You can also choose to assign these markings to specific staves using Staff Lists. While defining or editing text repeats or endings, you will see a Show On section in the respective dialog box. Choose Staff List and then either choose a Staff List from the drop-down menu or choose Edit to change or add a Staff List (see instructions in the previous section). You will be able to apply a staff list in the Backward Repeat Bar Assignment, Text Repeat Assignment, Create Ending, and Edit Ending dialog boxes.

Measure Expression Positioning

You have probably noticed that moving any measure expression also moves the corresponding expressions on other staves. To move any measure expression independently, right/Control-click the expression's handle and choose Edit Measure Expression Assignment. Check Allow Individual Positioning and click OK (or check this box while assigning the expression initially). Now, drag or nudge to position each occurrence of the expression individually. If you want to move a number of expressions uniformly, drag-enclose them (or Shift-click each handle), then drag to position all selected expressions.

NOTE

To control positioning independently, right/Control-click a text repeat or repeat ending bracket assigned to more than one staff and select Allow Individual Positioning.

You can also use the H: and V: parameters in the Measure Expression Assignment dialog box to position expressions to a specific distance from the beginning of the measure or top staff line (as described in Chapter 3). Note that if you do this, corresponding expressions in other staves will adjust respectively. In other words, they will remain the same distance apart even if you have checked Allow Individual Positioning.

Copying Measure Expressions

You may want to copy measure-attached expressions to another area of your score, but not the notation. To do this, click the Mass Edit Tool. From the Mass Edit menu, choose Copy Measure Items. Check Measure Expressions and click OK. Then, select the measures (in any staff) containing the measure-attached expressions and drag to the new location (or Ctrl/Option-Shift-click). The expressions will appear in the new measures, and any staff list information is retained (so they appear on the original staves). Edit the Staff Lists on the copied expressions to edit their staff assignment.

NOTE

New to Finale 2005: Any time you copy measure expressions between documents, the Staff List information will be retained or, rather, replicated in the destination document based on the number and configuration of staves. Therefore, copying expressions assigned to Staff Lists across documents is no longer a problem (as it has been in all previous Finale versions).

Optimization

In large scores, it is often unnecessary to show all staves on every system. The empty staves in systems are usually removed to "optimize" the amount of music that fits on a page (see Figure 7.9). In Finale, you can remove these unnecessary staves by optimizing with the Page Layout Tool. In addition to removing empty staves, optimization allows staves in a system to be positioned independently, without affecting the staff positioning in other systems. Also, changes to group definitions in an optimized system will not affect group definitions on any other system. For these, and other reasons (which will be explained in this section), you will want to wait until after you have finished editing the notation of a score before optimizing. Nonetheless, optimization is an important topic to understand in all stages of score preparation.

Figure 7.9

A score before and after optimization. Notice the empty staves are removed and groups adjust accordingly

To prepare for this section, click the Page Layout Tool. Note that any time you click the Page Layout Tool you will automatically be moved to Page View. Optimization, and any page layout changes, affect Page View only, and will not have any effect on the representation of the score in Scroll View. You can continue using the same document you have been working on, or you can begin a new Default Document and add several staves.

Removing Empty Staves in a System

The following demonstration illustrates the concept of optimization.

1. First, open a multi-staff document. From the File Menu, choose New > Document From Template. Double-click Band Templates and then double-click Woodwind Quintet. The Woodwind Quintet template opens.

2. Click the Simple Entry Tool and enter some notes into the top two staves of the first system. Also enter some notes in the fourth staff of the first system. Let's say you want to remove the third staff in the top system from the score

3. Choose the Page Layout Tool.

4. Right/Control-click anywhere within the top system margins and choose Optimize Staff Systems. The Staff System Optimization dialog box appears as shown in Figure 7.10.

Figure 7.10

Choose systems to optimize, or remove optimization, with the Staff System Optimization dialog box

5. Make sure Optimize Staff Systems is selected. For now, leave the rest of the settings alone. Click OK. You return to the score with the third and all other empty staves removed from the top system. You can optimize any number of systems or even the whole document by specifying a system range in the Optimize Staves dialog box.

6. From the View menu, choose Scroll View. Notice all of the staves remain visible.

 CAUTION

If you enter music in Scroll View on a staff that has been removed in Page View as a result of optimization, the staff and notation will remain hidden in the score when you return to Page View. Make sure you have entered all notation into a system before you optimize it to avoid missing music. If you notice notes in Scroll View that do not appear in Page View, re-apply optimization to the appropriate system to add the staff back to the system.

Individual Staff Spacing

Normally, when you use staff handles to position staves vertically, the staff will adjust in every system. In optimized systems you can adjust the vertical staff placement independently. To do this, click the Staff Tool. Notice there are two handles on each staff as shown in Figure 7.11.

Click and drag or use the arrow keys to nudge the lower handle to reposition the staff vertically within that particular system. This will affect only the staff's position within the system. To reposition a staff's placement for all systems, use the upper handles.

Figure 7.11

Spacing staves in systems
independently

Position Staff
in All Systems

Position Staff in
this System Only

Groups in Optimized Systems

Group brackets will always adjust to include the remaining staves in a group after optimizing a system. Any changes you make to these, or any groups in an optimized system will not have any effect on other systems. For example, with the Staff Tool selected, click and drag the group bracket handles on the top system. Notice there are no changes to the group brackets on the second system. Press the Delete key to delete the group bracket. Again, brackets in other systems are not affected. To reset a system to include the original bracket definitions and staff spacing, optimize the system again or remove optimization on the system.

If there is a piano, harp, or other part in your document that requires more than one staff, you can set the group attributes so that all staves for that instrument will always be optimized together (so that Finale will leave both staves visible if there are any notes in either staff in the system). In the Group Attributes for the part, click the drop-down menu for Group Optimization, and choose Only Remove if All Staves Empty.

Removing Optimization

When you remove optimization, all staves return to the system. In addition, staff spacing and group brackets return to their original appearance (i.e., before optimization). Now, remove optimization from the system you have optimized. Right/Control-click the system and choose Optimize Staff Systems. The Staff System dialog box appears. Choose Remove Staff System Optimization and click OK. The system returns to its original appearance before optimization.

Other Tricks for Multiple-Stave Scores

Here are some other tricks you can use while working with large scores.

Selecting Specific Playback Staves

In addition to setting a staff to a general MIDI instrument (as described in Chapter 2), in large scores you may want to mute or select certain staves for playback. To do this, from the Window menu, choose Instrument List. The Instrument List dialog box appears. To the right of the list of staves, there are two columns, P (Play) and S (Solo). By default, there will be a box for each staff under the P column, assigning each staff to play back. Click the square box under the P column for any staff to mute it on playback. Click the S column to choose a specific staff for playback and mute others (a circle will appear in the S column). You can select as many "Solo" staves as you want (so in a score of twenty staves, just click the S column for the two staves you want to play back (for example), instead of removing 18 boxes in the P column).

Viewing Several Regions of Your Score on the Screen

If you are copying music between remote areas of your score, or referencing a different area during entry, you can avoid having to scroll back and forth between sections by using multiple windows. From the Window menu, choose New Window. A new window appears on your screen with the same score visible. Any changes you make to the score in one of these windows will apply to the other as well (these are just two views of the same score). You can scroll to any region of the score independently, or even set one view to Scroll View and the other to Page View. In Figure 7.12, a staff set has been programmed to the top two staves in the left window, and the full score appears in the right.

Figure 7.12

Use multiple windows to see any combination of views for the same score, or to view more than one document at the same time

Also, notice that the windows in Figure 7.12 fit nicely within the active region of the screen. You can set this automatically by choosing Tile Vertically or Tile Horizontally from the View menu. All open windows will resize and arrange themselves horizontally or vertically on your screen. You can use as many windows as you like to view your score on-screen.

CHAPTER 7

Faster Redraw

The more staves and notes you have in a score, the longer it takes Finale to redraw the screen. This can be a nuisance, especially while working in Simple Entry. For faster redraw, try moving to Scroll View, and program staff sets (as described earlier) to eliminate staves from the view that you are not currently working with. The fewer staves there are, the faster Finale redraws. To cut down the number of times Finale redraws the screen, you could also turn off Automatic Music Spacing from the Edit Menu. Note, however, that if you do this, your music will not respace proportionally as it usually does as you enter music. Finale will recalculate the spacing of all entered music once you turn Automatic Music Spacing back on.

You also have control over the specific items on the screen Finale recalculates during each redraw. To eliminate certain items from redraw, from the View menu, choose Redraw Options. The Redraw Options dialog box appears, as shown in Figure 7.13.

Figure 7.13

Specify items to redraw and make other redraw settings in the Redraw Options dialog box

In the Draw section, uncheck items you are not concerned about viewing as you work on the document. If you are using multiple windows to view your score, check Redraw Only the Active Window to eliminate background windows from redrawing.

Adding Cue Notes Automatically

While working on a score with many staves, you may want to add cue notes of existing music in another staff. Add cue notes to any number of staves in your score automatically with the Create Cue Notes plug-in.

1. Select the Mass Edit Tool, and highlight the region of your score containing the original notes.

2. From the Plug-ins menu, choose Scoring and Arranging > Add Cue Notes. The Add Cue Notes dialog box appears as shown in Figure 7.14.

3. From the drop-down menu, choose the layer of the original music. Then, hold down the Ctrl/Option key and click each staff you want to add cue notes to.

4. Type the name of the cue notes (the part/staff name of the original notes).

5. Choose the layer you wish Finale to place the cue notes into and click OK. They will also be reduced to 75 percent of their original size. If you want, you can also change the size of the resulting cue notes in the Add Cue Notes dialog box.

Figure 7.14

Assign cue notes to staves and edit their appearance in the Add Cue Notes dialog box

> **TIP**
> The Add Cue Notes plug-in will be unable to write cue notes over existing notes in the same layer. In the Add Cue Notes window, be sure to choose to write the cue notes into a layer that is not being used.

To scan your entire score and let Finale propose possible cue note locations, and then add them automatically, use the Smart Cue Notes plug-in.

1. From the Plug-ins menu, choose Scoring and Arranging, and then Smart Cue Notes.

2. Here, you can specify the length of cue notes and choose the number of seconds/measures required before a cue note is necessary. You can also choose the layer and percentage of the cue notes you are about to generate.

3. Click Start Search to scan the score. When the plug-in finds a stretch of rests that meet the requirements you have specified, you are prompted to create cue notes (see Figure 7.15).

4. Note that the proposed cue note measures are highlighted. (Drag the dialog box to get a better look at the score.) To specify destination staves, Ctrl/Command-click staves in the Add This Cue to These Staves section.

5. Click Create Cue Notes to generate cue notes from the notes in the highlighted region. Cue notes appear in the score and the plug-in searches for the next applicable region. (Click Continue Search to advance to the next region without creating cue notes).

Global Staff Attributes Plug-In

I have touched on the Global Staff Attributes a few times for specific tasks already. Note that this plug-in is particularly useful while working with large scores. From the Plug-ins menu, choose Scoring and Arranging > Global Staff Attributes to display the Global Staff Attributes plug-in as seen in Figure 7.16.

Figure 7.15

Use the Smart Cue Notes plug-in to find appropriate cue note locations and add them automatically

Figure 7.16

Assign staff attributes to several staves at once by using the Global Staff Attributes plug-in

Here, you see many of the options available in the Staff Attributes dialog box. Apply these attributes to many or all staves of your document at once. In the list of staves, select all staves you want to affect (Ctrl/Command-click to choose non-contiguous staves). Then check the appropriate check box in the Options and Items to Display sections to modify all selected staves.

In the Group Attributes portion of this dialog box, you can apply settings for groups on a global basis as well. Select the group(s) you want to change, and use the check boxes to show/hide brackets on single staves and show/hide group names for the selected groups. Click the Set Font button to select the font, size, and style for staff names or group names. Click Apply to update your score without leaving the Global Staff Attributes, or click OK to apply settings and return to the score.

Generating a Piano Reduction Automatically

Finale can generate a reduction of any number of staves automatically and place the results in a grand staff. To create a piano reduction from any score, from the Plug-ins menu, choose Scoring and Arranging > Piano Reduction. You will see the Piano Reduction plug-in as shown in Figure 7.17.

Figure 7.17
Create a piano reduction for any number of staves with the Piano Reduction plug-in

Hold down the Ctrl/Command key and click the staves you want to reduce. You can also click and drag to select contiguous staves. In the Split Point section, enter the MIDI note number of the lowest note in the treble clef staff. (Middle C is MIDI note 60, for example.) Notes in the original staves lower than this number will go into the bass clef staff. Click OK. A grand staff appears below your score with a reduction of the staves you selected. Note that there will probably be some cleanup necessary.

TIP

Finale will quantize to the smallest note duration while generating a piano reduction. If you want to create independent lines of music in the reduction, try using the Move Layers feature to distinguish voices in your staves before running the Piano Reduction plug-in. With the Mass Edit Tool selected, highlight some music, then choose Mass Edit > Move/Copy Layers. After creating the piano reduction, you may want to move the music back to its original layer on the staves above.

Customizing the Document Setup Wizard

In Chapter 2, you learned how to begin a new score with any number of pre-defined staves by using the Document Setup Wizard. If there are instruments you use regularly that do not exist in the Setup Wizard, you can define your own, then use them at any time while beginning a new document. The information used by the Setup Wizard is stored in the Instrument.txt file located in your Finale/Component Files folder. You can customize any of the available staves in the Setup Wizard or create your own following the steps below (you can leave any parameter out if you do not care to specify a preference).

1. On your computer, navigate to the Finale folder and open the Component Files folder. Double-click on the file named Instrument.txt. The file will open in a text editor (see Figure 7.18).

2. If you are creating a new instrument, begin the entry with [INS: *InstrumentName*] followed by a carriage return. Otherwise, you can edit any existing instrument's existing settings.

Figure 7.18

Customize the instruments available in the Setup Wizard by editing the Instrument.txt file

3. For Name (to the right of the = sign), enter the staff name as you would like it to appear in the score. For accidental symbols, use flat() for a flat, sharp() for a sharp, and natural() for a natural.

4. For Abbr., enter the abbreviated staff name as you would like it to appear in the score. You can use the same symbols mentioned above for accidentals

5. For useKeySigs, type "1" to use key signatures. Type "0" to leave them out (for percussion staves, for example).

6. For Transposition, specify a transposing instrument by typing the number of half-steps up or down from the concert pitch. For example, B-flat trumpet sounds down a whole step, so you would enter enter "-2."

7. For Transclef, type a clef for a transposing instrument. Your options are: treble, bass, alto, treble8vb, percussion, tenor, baritone, bass8vb, frenchviolin, cbaritone, mezzosoprano, soprano, altpercussion, treble8va, bass8va, tabl, or blank.

8. For StaffType, enter the type of staff. Your options are: standard, percussion, single, grand, tab, or organ.

9. For Clef, enter the clef. Your options here are the same as for TransClef.

10. For Patch, type the General MIDI patch number minus 1 (0-127). This controls the playback instrument of the staff. You can find a list of MIDI patches and their corresponding numbers in the appendix of the Finale 2005 User Manual.

11. For PercMap, enter the name of a percussion map (either one you have defined or an existing one). You can also enter a single General MIDI note number. Enclose a percussion map name in quotes if it contains a number.

12. Now, scroll down until you see the [GRP:WW] heading.

13. If you created your own staff, enter the Instrument name (not the staff name) in one of the groups. These groupings represent the category you will find them in while in the Setup Wizard, as well as how they will be grouped together in the score. If you want, you can even create a new group, or edit the existing ones in this section. The "x" tells Finale to include the instrument in the Setup Wizard list.

14. Now, scroll down to the [ORD:] section.

15. If you created your own staff, enter it in the order you want it to appear in the score. Notice there are several different score orders. These correspond to the list for Score Order on page 2 of the Setup Wizard.

16. Save the file (File > Save).

17. Launch Finale and run the Setup Wizard. The instruments you created or edited will appear among the Staff Lists on page 2.

8

ALTERNATE NOTATION, STAFF STYLES, AND GUITAR TABLATURE

In addition to setting up a staff name, clef, and transposition for a part, there are also a number of other ways to configure a staff for specific notation styles. You can set up a staff for slash notation, rhythmic notation, or tablature, or change the number of lines on a staff for percussion notation. All of these notation styles can be applied to an entire staff, or they can also be applied to any portion of a staff using staff styles.

Here's a summary of what you will learn in this chapter:

* How to set up a staff for slash, rhythmic, and other alternate notation
* How to apply alternate notation to part of a staff only: staff styles
* How to create tablature, percussion, and other notation styles
* More on guitar notation and tablature
* How to create a guitar part with TAB

Staff Setup for Slash, Rhythmic, and Other Notation Styles

Any time you want to create notation with slashes, enter one or two bar repeats, or hide the existing music in a staff, apply alternate notation to the staff.

To prepare for this section, open a new Default Document (File > New > Default Document). Click the Staff Tool. In this section, I'll assume you have the Staff Tool selected unless specified otherwise.

Slash and Rhythmic Notation

Slash and rhythmic notation are often used in conjunction with chord symbols to indicate comping, or the background harmonic progression of a piece. This type of notation is particularly common in guitar and piano parts in Jazz ensembles, for example, where rhythm and style take precedence over exact pitches.

In slash notation, there is one slash for each beat of the measure, and chord symbols usually appear above the staff (see Figure 8.1). The precise rhythm is left up to the performer.

Figure 8.1

Apply alternate notation in the
Staff Attributes to create slash
notation

To set up a staff for slash notation with chord symbols:

1. First, use the Simple or Speedy Entry Tool to enter rests into the staff on each beat. Finale needs an entry in the staff for the chord symbols you will be entering. (You could also enter notes as placeholders, which will play back even though they will be replaced with slash notation). If you do not intend to enter chord symbols, skip ahead to step 4. Since we are in common time, enter four quarter rests into the first measure (consult Chapter 3 for information on entering rests in Simple or Speedy Entry).

2. Click the Mass Edit Tool. Select the first measure and drag it to the second. In the Copy Measure dialog box, enter "30" and click OK. Now, all 31 measures of the default document are filled with rests. Of course, in the future you will need to choose the rhythmic value and number of measures specific to the piece you are working on.

3. Click the Chord Tool and enter the chord symbols on any rest you have entered to indicate a harmonic change on a particular beat (see Chapter 4 for more information on entering chord symbols).

4. Click the Staff Tool and double-click the staff. The Staff Attributes dialog box appears.

5. Click the Select button under Alternate Notation. The Alternate Notation dialog box appears as shown in Figure 8.2.

6. Select Slash Notation. In the future, if your piece is in a compound meter, such as 6/8, and you want to add dots to your slashes, check Add Dots to Slashes in Compound Meters. For now, leave this box unchecked.

7. Click OK to return to the Staff Attributes. Notice there is now a check in the Alternate Notation check box.

8. Click OK to return to the score. You should now see slashes throughout your staff. To enter or edit existing chord symbols, you can click on the slashes (since there is a rest hidden under each one).

Figure 8.2

Choose a type of alternate
notation in the Alternate
Notation dialog box

Rhythmic notation is similar to slash notation but more closely resembles regular notes and indicates the specific rhythmic pattern (see Figure 8.3). The slashed notes in rhythmic notation are often used to notate strumming patterns for guitar.

Figure 8.3

Apply alternate notation in the
Staff Attributes to create
rhythmic notation

Before continuing, remove the slash notation you applied. Double-click the staff, and in the Staff Attributes, uncheck Alternate Notation. Click OK to return to the score with the alternate notation removed. Use the Mass Edit Tool to highlight the measures, and use the Backspace/Clear key to remove the rest entries and chord symbols. Now, to set up a staff for rhythmic notation with chord symbols

1. Use the Simple or Speedy Entry Tool to enter notes and rests into the staff in the rhythmic pattern you want. With rhythmic notation, the pitch of any notes you enter will convert to standard slashes. Rests will remain rests (consult Chapter 3 for information on entering notes and rests in Simple or Speedy Entry).

CHAPTER 8

2. Click the Chord Tool and enter any chord symbols (see Chapter 4 for more information on entering chord symbols).

3. Click the Staff Tool and double-click the staff to open the Staff Attributes dialog box.

4. Click the Select button under Alternate Notation to open the Alternate Notation dialog box.

5. Select Rhythmic Notation.

6. By default, Finale will place stems down on rhythmic notation. If you want to change the stem direction, check Stems Up In Rhythmic Notation.

7. Click OK to return to the Staff Attributes and OK again to return to the score. You should now see slashes with stems for each note you entered in the staff and rests wherever you entered a rest.

Since there are underlying notes or rests in the slash and rhythmic notation you applied, you can enter note-attached Smart Shapes or expressions to your slashes as needed. If you only want to apply slash or rhythmic notation to a portion of your staff, apply a staff style (more about staff styles soon).

Managing Playback for Staves with Slash or Rhythmic Notation

You will notice that Finale will play back any underlying notes that exist beneath the alternate notation. You may want to eliminate playback of these notes from rhythmic or slash notation. To do this, from the Window menu, choose Instrument List. Click the drop-down menu to the left of the staff with alternate notation. Under the P (Play) column, click the black box to remove playback from any layer. Do the same for chords or expressions to remove them from playback. Note that this staff is silenced for the entire piece.

Managing Layers in Rhythmic and Slash Notation

If there is more than one layer in the staff to which you want to apply alternate notation, you may want to show the notes in other layers, or items attached to them. For example, you may have a staff that has slash notation throughout, but in a couple of measures you want standard notation in a different layer to appear as well. To do this, double-click a staff and click Select under Alternate Notation. In the Alternate Notation dialog box, choose the layer you want the alternate notation to occupy from the Apply To drop-down menu (any notes in this layer will be overwritten with the alternate notation, but they will still play back). Then, from the check boxes on the right, choose Show Notes in Other Layers and Show Items Attached to Notes in Other Layers to display them. Click OK twice to return to the score.

Blank Notation

Blank notation can be used any time you want to hide a layer of notation. This type of alternate notation is often used to hide notes in a layer that you want to use exclusively for playback. For example, you may have notated a trill in layer one and entered the notes as you want the trill to playback in layer four. Use Blank Notation to hide the notes in layer four.

1. With the Staff Tool selected, double-click the staff to open the Staff Attributes.

2. Click the Select button under Alternate Notation to open the Alternate Notation dialog box.

3. Choose Blank Notation.

4. From the Apply To drop-down menu, choose the layer you want to hide—in this case, layer four.

5. Click OK to return to the Staff Attributes, then OK to return to the score.

Notes in the layer you specified are hidden in the staff, and will play back. To hide notes and eliminate them from playback, use the H key command in Speedy or Simple Entry (see Chapter 3 for details). You can also eliminate playback for any layer of a staff (even one hidden by blank alternate notation) with the instrument list. (See the earlier section, "Managing Playback for Staves with Slash or Rhythmic Notation," for steps to remove a layer from playback.)

NOTE
When you hide notes, they will appear in a lighter color on-screen but will not appear in the printout. To prevent the hidden notes from displaying on-screen at all, from the View menu, uncheck Show Hidden Notes and Rests.

Hide notes with blank notation in any region of a staff, or apply any set of staff attributes to a specific staff region using staff styles.

Applying Staff Attributes to Part of a Staff Only: Staff Styles

The alternate notation types described above, as well as any staff attribute, can be applied to part of a staff using staff styles. A staff style is a collection of staff attributes you can apply to any region of your score. Hide portions of a staff, change the staff transposition, or define any set of attributes for any region using staff styles. You can apply one of Finale's preset staff styles or create your own.

Continuing with the file you've been working with, double-click the staff to open the Staff Attributes, uncheck Alternate Notation, and click OK to return to the score.

Applying a Staff Style

First, you will apply rhythmic notation to a portion of a staff using staff styles. This happens to be one of the styles that already exists in Finale's default Staff Style library. With the Staff Tool selected, highlight a couple measures of a staff or a partial measure. From the Staff menu, choose Apply Staff Style. The Apply Staff Style dialog box appears as shown in Figure 8.4.

Select Rhythmic Notation and click OK. The highlighted region of your staff converts to rhythmic notation. You will also see a blue line above the staff. A (non-printing) blue line will appear above every region of a staff containing a staff style whenever the Staff Tool is selected.

To easily assign a staff style

1. Right/Control-click a highlighted region of your staff and choose the staff style you want to apply from the list. You can also apply any staff style with a metatool.

2. With a region of a staff highlighted, from the Staff menu, choose Apply Staff Style.

3. In the Apply Staff Style dialog box, notice the letter in parentheses to the right of each option. While working with the Staff Tool, you can use any one of these letters to apply the corresponding staff style to the selected region of the staff.

Figure 8.4

Choose a collection of staff attributes (staff style) to apply to a portion of a staff in the Apply Staff Style dialog box

Apply as many staff styles as you like to the same region of a staff. You will see a new blue line appear above the staff for each new staff style you apply. If you find yourself applying several staff styles to the same region, define your own staff style that includes all of the desired attributes. I'll talk about defining your own staff style soon.

TIP

To easily define an instrument transposition for a region of your staff (for example, if the alto sax part in the jazz arrangement switches to flute halfway through), simply highlight the region with the Staff Tool, right/Control-click the highlighted region, and choose the transposition. If you don't see the transposition you are looking for, define your own staff style (see "Defining a New Staff Style" below).

One- and Two-Bar Repeats

One- and two-bar repeats tell the performer to repeat the previous one- or two-bar segment of music (see Figure 8.5). In Finale, one- and two-bar repeats are handled with staff styles.

To enter a one- or two-bar repeat, or a number of consecutive one- or two-bar repeats, highlight a region of the staff. Right/Control-click the highlighted region and choose One-Bar Repeat or Two-Bar Repeat. The staff automatically updates to reflect the selection you made. You can also use the metatool "O" to apply a one-bar repeat or the metatool "T" to apply a two-bar repeat staff style to the selected region of a staff.

The Staff Style Library

There are 21 staff styles in Finale's default file library. You can use these any time you begin a document with the Setup Wizard, the Default Document file, or one of Finale's templates. If the file you are working on does not contain these preset staff styles (such as an older Finale file), you can import them by saving and opening a library. To import the default staff style library, from the File menu, choose Load Library. Navigate

Figure 8.5

Use staff styles to create
one- and two-bar repeats

to your Finale folder and open the Libraries folder. Double-click the file "Staff Styles.lib." Now the default staff styles will appear in the context menu and in the Apply Staff Style dialog box.

Like articulations and expressions, all staff styles in a document can be transferred to another by saving and opening a library.

Removing Staff Styles

To remove the staff style, highlight any region of a staff containing a staff style (refer to the blue lines above the staff) and press Backspace/Clear. You may also right/Control-click the highlighted region to open the staff style context menu and choose Clear Staff Styles. All staff styles are removed from the highlighted region.

Defining a New Staff Style

If the staff attributes you want to apply to a staff do not exist in the default Staff Style library, create your own. To create your own staff style

1. With the Staff Tool selected, from the Staff menu, choose Define Staff Styles. The Staff Styles dialog box appears as shown in Figure 8.6. This dialog box is almost identical to the Staff Attributes.

2. Click the New button in the upper-right corner.

3. Click in the text box to the right of Available Styles and type a name for your staff style.

4. Make sure Display in Context Menu is checked if you want this definition to appear in the staff styles context menu.

5. Make any setting you would like to apply to a region of a staff. Change the number of staff lines, the transposition, the clef, or adjust any other parameter. Gray checks in the check boxes tell Finale to leave the setting alone in the applied region of the staff.

6. Make sure Copyable is checked if you want to be able to copy this staff style via the Mass Edit Tool.

Figure 8.6

Define a custom staff style in the Staff Styles dialog box

7. Click OK to return to the score.

8. Highlight a region of your staff, then right/Control-click the highlighted area to open the staff styles context menu. The staff style you just defined will appear at the bottom. Choose it to apply your staff style to the highlighted region of the staff.

You can also define a new staff style by choosing Define Staff Style from the staff style context menu, or by clicking the Define button in the Apply Staff Style dialog box.

To assign a metatool to any staff style, hold down the Shift key and press any number or letter on the QWERTY keyboard. The Apply Staff Style dialog box appears. Choose the staff style you want to assign to the number or letter you pressed and click OK. Now, highlight a region of measures and press the metatool number or letter to apply the staff style.

Viewing Staff Styles

You have already seen that any staff style applied to a region of your staff is indicated with a blue line. However, there is no indication of which staff style is applied. To tell Finale to include the name of each staff style within this blue line, from the Staff menu, choose Show Staff Style Names. Now, each blue staff style indicator line includes the name of the applied staff style. Zoom in using the Zoom Tool (or the View menu) to see these staff style names more clearly. To remove staff style names from the blue indicator line, uncheck Show Staff Style Names from the Staff menu.

While working with the Staff Tool, if you want to remove the blue indicator lines, from the Staff menu, uncheck Show Staff Styles. Check Show Staff Styles again from the Staff menu to display them.

Tablature, Percussion, and Other Notation Styles

In addition to alternate notation, there are a number of other notation styles you may want to use throughout a staff or in a staff style. Double-click a staff to open the Staff Attributes. Click the drop-down menu to the right of Notation Style. There are four options here: Standard, Percussion, Note Shapes, and Tablature (see Figure 8.7).

Figure 8.7

Choose a notation style for a staff from the Notation Styles drop-down menu of the Staff Attributes

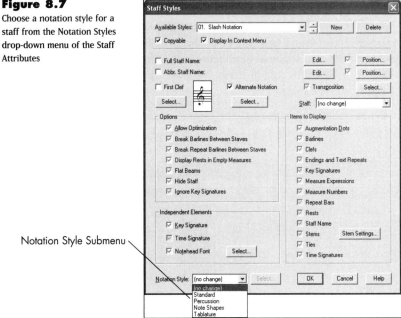

Notation Style Submenu

Most staves in Finale are in the standard notation style, so this option is usually selected by default. If you intend to create percussion, note shape, or tablature notation, choose the corresponding style from this list.

NOTE

When you choose staves for a document with the Setup Wizard, or begin with one of Finale's templates, the notation style for percussion and tablature staves will be set up for you already.

Percussion

If you are notating for a non-pitched percussion instrument, all of the special parameters, including music font, number of staff lines, and the percussion clef can be set in the Staff Attributes dialog box. If you begin by choosing a percussion staff with the Setup Wizard, many or all of the parameters you want might already exist. If you begin with a new Default Document or want to change existing parameters in a percussion staff, use the instructions in this section.

In your score, double-click a staff to open the Staff Attributes dialog box. In most percussion parts, the key signature is absent, and a percussion clef appears at the beginning of each staff line. Under Items to Display, uncheck Key Signatures. Note also that accidentals do not appear in percussion staves. (If you intend to use a pitched percussion instrument for a portion of the staff later on in the same document, you can always apply a staff style later that uses standard notation and includes the key signature and accidentals.) Then, for First Clef, click the Select button. Choose one of the two available percussion clefs and click OK. The clef you chose should appear in the preview window. Again, if you intend to use a pitched instrument for a portion of the staff, you can apply a staff style including a non-percussion clef for any region. Make sure there is no check in the Transposition check box.

Changing the Number of Staff Lines

You may want to change the number of staff lines. Many percussion parts contain staves with only one line. To change the number of lines in the staff, click the drop-down menu for Staff and choose 1-Line with Short Barline. This setting will remove all but the middle staff line from the score. Of course, choose any of the other options depending on the part you are defining.

If you want, you can set up a staff to include any number of staff lines. To do this, from the Staff drop-down menu, choose Other. The Staff Setup dialog box appears as shown in Figure 8.8.

Figure 8.8

Customize the number and placement of staff lines in the Staff Setup dialog box

Click the Custom Staff radio button. Then, click the handles to the left of the staff in the preview window to add or remove staves from the custom staff (as seen in the preview window). Adjust the length of the barlines for the staff in the Settings section. For Top Of Barline, enter the length you want your barlines to extend above the top staff line. For Bottom Of Barline, enter the length you want your barlines to extend below the bottom staff line. Click OK to return to the Staff Attributes.

Specifying a Notehead Font

You can set an independent percussion font for your percussion staff. To do this, in the Independent Elements section of the Staff Attributes, click the Select button for Notehead Font. The Font dialog box appears. To use Finale's standard percussion font, choose Maestro Percussion. You may also want to choose the Tamburo font (an older percussion font), which is also included with Finale. Of course, you can choose any font on your computer from this dialog box if there is an alternative percussion font you want to use. Click OK to return to the Staff Attributes dialog box.

Percussion Maps

In your percussion staff, you also might want to assign certain noteheads to staff positions and configure your staff for playback using the appropriate percussion sounds. Playback of percussion is unique because each staff line or space will play back a unique percussive sound. You can assign noteheads and configure playback for percussion staves by creating a percussion map.

Before moving on, it is important to understand the purpose of percussion maps. When using a MIDI keyboard for entry, a percussion map allows you to assign a staff position for any key (or MIDI note) struck on the keyboard. In a tonal patch, such as Grand Piano (or any tonal instrument sound), each key on a MIDI keyboard represents a unique pitch. When you strike a key, Finale is wired to automatically place a notehead on the correct staff position (according to the clef, transposition, etc.). In a percussion MIDI patch (or when using channel 10 in General MIDI), each key represents a unique percussive instrument. Without a percussion map assigned to a staff, a key struck very low on a MIDI keyboard will display a notehead well below the staff in Finale. With a percussion map applied to the staff, you can assign a specific line or space in the staff for any key, so that a very low key struck on a MIDI keyboard will translate to a notehead on the middle staff line, for example.

When entering into Finale without a MIDI keyboard, percussion maps are important if you want the score to play back properly. Without a percussion map assigned, any note entered on the third space, for example, will sound like a whistle (if you are using General MIDI) because the third space is assigned to MIDI note 72 in Finale. In General MIDI percussion, note number 72 is set to the whistle sound. With a percussion map, you can assign a staff position for any MIDI note, so your score will play back using the desired percussive instrument for each staff line or space.

If you are still in the Staff Attributes, click OK to return to the score. Let's say you want to enter a snare drum part on the middle staff line. To avoid confusion later on, always set up a percussion map before entering notes onto the staff.

1. From the Window menu, choose Instrument List. Under the Instrument Column, click the drop-down menu for your percussion staff and choose Percussion. The channel for the staff should change to 10. Channel 10 is the standard MIDI percussion channel.

TIP

If SmartMusic SoftSynth is selected as your MIDI output device in the MIDI Setup dialog box, you can set a percussion staff to Patch 2 to use Marching Percussion sounds or Patch 49 to use Orchestral Percussion sounds. You can find a list of these sounds in the Appendix of the Finale 2005 User Manual.

2. Close out of the Instrument List.

NOTE

If you are using a MIDI keyboard, setting up a percussion map will be easier. Before moving on, from the MIDI menu, choose MIDI Thru, then Smart, and click OK. Then, click the Speedy Entry Tool and click on the percussion staff. Play a few notes on the keyboard. You should hear percussion sounds. If you hear nothing, make sure you have properly set up your MIDI keyboard with the computer. Also, in the MIDI Setup dialog box (under the MIDI menu), try using the SmartMusic SoftSynth as your MIDI Out device.

3. Click the Staff Tool, and double-click the staff to open the Staff Attributes dialog box.

4. For Notation Style, make sure Percussion is selected and click the Select button. The Percussion Map Selection dialog box appears.

5. Choose General MIDI Entry and Playback and click the Duplicate button. Then click the Edit button. The Percussion Map Designer dialog box appears as shown in Figure 8.9.

Figure 8.9

Assign a staff position, notehead, and playback note in the Percussion Map Designer dialog box

6. In the Map text box, type the name of your custom percussion map. For now, type "Test Percussion Map."

7. Now, find the percussion instrument you want to define. If you are using a MIDI keyboard, click the Listen button in the lower-left corner. The Listen dialog box appears. Press the pitch on your keyboard that sounds like a snare drum (D2).

If you are not using a MIDI keyboard, use the vertical scroll bar to find, then highlight, Snare (Acoustic). It's MIDI playback note 38.

8. Now, choose the staff position in the five-line staff preview window. In this case, the staff position is already set to the third space. The staff position number represents the number of lines and spaces above the first ledger line below the staff (o). The space below the staff is 1, first line, 2, etc.

9. Under Open Notehead, click the Select button to choose a symbol for closed noteheads. Do the same for Closed Noteheads. You can do this to select "X"s or any other character from the font you are using (an open notehead will be used for durations of a half note and larger; closed noteheads will be used for durations of a quarter note and smaller).

10. In the Notes to Use section, check Highlighted Note. If this is not checked, Finale will disregard settings you have just made.

11. Click Done, click Select, and then OK to return to the score.

12. Now, in Simple Entry, enter a note on the middle staff line and it will play back as a snare drum. To enter a note on the middle staff line, press the note on your keyboard that sounds like a Snare Drum (D2) before typing the rhythmic duration. Finale will place the note on the middle staff line.

13. To add more instrument parts to the percussion staff (set up noteheads and playback for a different staff position), double-click the staff to open the Staff Attributes. Click the Select button for Notation Style, select Test Percussion Map (or the name you assigned the map), and click Edit.

TIP

If you're entering percussion notation without using a MIDI keyboard, and if there is more than one MIDI note number assigned to the same staff line, you can cycle through them by using the half-step up or half-step down keystrokes in Simple or Speedy Entry. You might have to do this, for example, if Snare was chosen when creating a document with the Setup Wizard. The side stick and the snare sound are assigned to the same staff line. If you click on the line using Simple Entry, the x notehead of the side stick will appear. Press the + or – key, and the note will change to the snare notehead and sound.

Any percussion map you define can be applied to any portion of the staff using staff styles. To define a percussion map staff style

1. From the Staff menu, choose Define Staff Style.

2. In the Staff Styles dialog box, click the New button and name the new staff style (after Available Styles).

3. Change the Notation Style to Percussion. Here, you can select a percussion clef, choose an independent notehead font, and apply other percussion settings for your staff. To select the percussion map, click the Select button to the right.

4. In the Percussion Map Selection dialog box, choose the desired percussion map and click Select.

5. Click OK to return to the score. Now apply the staff style to use the percussion map for any portion of a staff.

Transfer percussion maps between documents by saving and opening a Percussion Map library. From the File menu, choose Save Library. In the Save Library dialog box, choose Percussion Maps, click OK, and save the library file. Open the destination document, and from the File menu, choose Open Library. Then navigate to the library file you saved and double-click it. The new percussion maps will appear in the Percussion Map Selection dialog box.

CHAPTER 8

You may want to use a percussion map that already exists in your document, or edit one that is similar to what you need in your score to save time. Double-click a staff to open the Staff Attributes, for Notation Style choose Percussion, and then click the Select button to the right to open the Percussion Map Selection dialog box. Notice the available percussion maps. To use one of these, click it so it is highlighted, then click the Edit button to the right. Highlight the instrument you want to use, then make sure to check Highlight Note. Do this for all pitches you want to use. If you want to use all the defined instruments/MIDI notes, click All Named Notes. Make any further desired edits to the percussion map and click Done, Select, and OK to return to the score. The percussion map now applies to the staff.

Note Shapes

Some notation, like chant, sometimes uses note shapes for scale degrees. If you want to use note shapes for every staff in your document, from the Options menu, choose Document Options and then select Note Shapes. Here, you can define shape note notation throughout your document, and even save your note shape settings in a library. To select note shapes for noteheads in a staff and assign them to scale degrees, do the following:

1. With the Staff Tool selected, double-click a staff to open the Staff Attributes dialog box.

2. If you want to use a font for your note shapes other than the default music font, under Independent Elements, click Select. Choose the desired font and click OK.

3. Click the drop-down menu for Notation Style, and choose Note Shapes. The Note Shapes dialog box appears as shown in Figure 8.10.

Figure 8.10

Assign a notehead character for rhythmic values and/or scale degrees in the Note Shapes dialog box

4. Click the drop-down menu for Replace, and choose the notehead type you would like to replace with a shape.

5. Choose the scale degree with the up and down arrows for Noteheads on Scale Degree. Or click and enter a scale degree in this text box manually. Finale will use the key signature of the piece to discern the appropriate note for each scale degree.

6. Click the Select button to choose a shape from the list of characters in your default music font.

TIP
To set the default music font, from the Options menu, choose Set Default Music Font.

7. Repeat steps 2 through 5 for each notehead type and scale degree you want to assign to a shape character.

8. When you have finished assigning note shapes, click OK to return to the Staff Attributes and OK again to return to the score.

9. If you plan on using this notation often, save this file as a template (see Chapter 13 for details).

Now, any notes you add in the staff will use the note shapes you assigned. Check Use Note Shapes, and use the same procedure to assign shape characters to notehead types and scale degrees.

Guitar Notation and Tablature

This brings us to a whole new topic. The tablature notation style is one of many features revised in Finale 2003 as part of program-wide improvement for notation of fretted instruments. In fact, the Automatic Tablature plug-in, which was previously central to tab notation, has been removed entirely from the software in favor of improvements to the Staff, Simple Entry, and Mass Edit Tools. In this section you will learn how to begin a new score for guitar with tablature, and create one from scratch. Also, I'll cover how to enter fret numbers, bends, hammer-ons, pull-offs, and other items specific to tablature notation.

Setting up a Tablature Staff

If you are beginning a new document, and plan to include any fretted instrument (guitar, lute, dulcimer, etc.), use the Document Setup Wizard. From the File menu, choose New, and then Document With Setup Wizard. Page 1 of the Setup Wizard appears. Type the composer, title, and copyright (as necessary), and click Next to move to page 2. Now, in the left column, choose Fretted Instruments. A list of fretted instruments and TAB appears in the second column as shown in Figure 8.11.

Figure 8.11

Choose a fretted instrument and corresponding TAB staff on page 2 of the Setup Wizard

Double-click the fretted instrument you would like to use so it appears in the third column. For now, double-click Guitar. Then double-click its corresponding TAB staff—in this case, Guitar [TAB]. Each type of TAB staff is designed to accommodate string tuning, number of strings, and number of frets for its accompanying fretted instrument. You should now see Guitar and Guitar [TAB] in the third column. Click Next to set up the time and key signature for your piece. Click Next again to choose the tempo, pickup measure, and music font, and then click Finish to generate the score. The notation and TAB staves appear in your new custom document. Now you can enter some tablature notation.

Entering Tablature

There are a number of ways to enter tablature into a TAB staff. You can copy music from a notation standard staff, enter directly into a TAB staff with Simple or Speedy Entry, or use a MIDI guitar for entry into a TAB staff. I'll start by demonstrating the easiest, copying notation directly into a tablature staff from a standard notation staff.

Copying Music to a TAB Staff

I'll assume you have a score with both standard and tablature notation open. If not, go back to the previous section and create a new score with the Setup Wizard containing a notation and tablature staff. For the remainder of this section, I'll refer to the regular five-line staff as the "notation staff" and the tablature staff as the "TAB staff."

1. Select the Simple Entry Tool.

2. Enter the melody seen in Figure 8.12 into the first three measures of the notation staff (you can find information on Simple Entry in Chapter 3).

Figure 8.12

Use the Mass Edit Tool to copy notation to a TAB staff and vice versa

3. Click the Mass Edit Tool.

4. Click the first measure of the notation staff so it is highlighted. Then, hold down the Shift key and click the third measure. Measures one though three of the notation staff should be highlighted.

5. Click within the highlighted area and drag down over the first three measures of the TAB staff. When you see black border around the first three measures of the TAB staff, release the mouse button. The Change Lowest Fret dialog box appears.

6. Click OK. The TAB staff now contains fret numbers that correspond to the above notation.

You can also copy existing tablature into a notation staff. To demonstrate, highlight measure one in the TAB staff. Then drag the highlighted area to measure four of the notation staff. Click OK, and you will see the notes appear in the notation staff.

Now, while copying to a TAB staff, you may want to indicate that the notes should be played higher on the fretboard. For this reason, the Change Lowest Fret dialog box appears (as seen in Figure 8.13) any time you copy from a notation staff into a TAB staff (as you saw in the previous steps).

Figure 8.13

Specify the lowest fret for music copied to a TAB staff in the Change Lowest Fret dialog box.

In this dialog box, you can specify the lowest fret, and Finale will distribute the fret numbers to the appropriate strings. Now use the same document you've been working with to try this.

1. Select the Mass Edit Tool

2. Click to the left of the notation staff to highlight the entire staff.

3. Click within the highlighted area and drag down over the TAB staff (yes, right over the existing music). The Change Lowest Fret dialog box appears.

4. For Specify Lowest Fret, enter "5."

5. Click OK. The tablature now recalculates with fret numbers on new strings, all on fret five or above.

As we saw in this example, you can copy over existing tablature or an empty TAB staff. Finale will recalculate the tablature each time you do this to account for any changes in the notation staff and the value you set in the Change Lowest Fret dialog box.

You can also change the lowest fret of any region of a TAB staff independently. To do this, click the Mass Edit Tool and highlight a region of the TAB staff. Then from the Mass Edit menu, choose Utilities > Lowest Fret. The Change Lowest Fret dialog box opens. Enter the new lowest fret and click OK to modify the highlighted region of the TAB staff.

Entering TAB with Simple Entry

You can also enter fret numbers directly into a TAB staff with the Simple Entry Tool. Click the Simple Entry Tool. Under the Simple menu, make sure Select Fret Numbers on Entry is checked. Select a note duration from the Simple Entry Palette and click in the TAB staff. By default, you will see a "o" appear in the score, and it will be selected. Simply type the fret number using the number keys on your numeric keyboard. Press the up and down arrows to move the fret number up or down a string, and the number will adjust accordingly (to represent the same pitch). Use the left and right arrows to move the selection horizontally between fret numbers. Ctrl/Option-click any fret number to select it.

> **TIP**
> To see a complete list of Simple Entry keystrokes for tablature, or to create your own, from the Simple
> menu, choose Simple Entry Options and click Edit Keyboard Shortcuts. For Mode, choose Simple
> Entry Tablature.

You can also easily enter TAB with the Caret. With the Caret active, use the up and down arrows (or press a number, 1–6, in the QWERTY keyboard) to choose the string. Hold down Ctrl-Alt/Shift and press the duration key in the QWERTY keyboard to specify the duration. Type the fret number on the number pad. You can continue entering on the same string and duration by typing with the number pad. To add an additional fret number above or below the one you just entered, hold down Alt/Option and press the string number on the QWERTY keyboard. An "o" appears on the string. Now, before releasing the Alt/Option key, type the fret number on the number pad.

> **TIP**
> While entering fret numbers into a TAB staff, Finale will warn you if a fret number is beyond the range
> of a string by turning it orange. If it is below the range of the string, you will also see a "–" (minus
> sign) preceding the fret number. If a fret number is orange, try moving it to a different string, changing
> the string tuning, changing the default lowest fret of the staff, or the number of frets in the staff. You
> can find information on how to do all of this later in this chapter.

Entering TAB with a MIDI Guitar

Chapter 4 covered the basics for entering music into Finale with a MIDI guitar. You can enter into a TAB staff just as you would a standard notation staff by using the HyperScribe Tool. When you do this, Finale can even record the correct string you play and place fret numbers on the appropriate TAB line. Finale can distinguish between strings because each string is set to a different MIDI channel. Your guitar-to-MIDI interface will send the MIDI data to Finale on specified channels. You can coordinate the MIDI string channels assigned on your guitar to MIDI interface with Finale by editing the MIDI Channels For Tablature dialog box (see Figure 8.14).

First, check the guitar-to-MIDI interface device to see which channel is assigned to each string. Consult the MIDI interface's instruction manual for information on how to assign and view the string channels. Then, assign the corresponding channel for each string in the MIDI Channels For Tablature dialog box (located under the MIDI menu). Now, Finale will be able to translate your performance properly into a TAB staff.

Adding Tablature Markings

Beyond fret numbers, there are several other figures standard in tablature notation. These include bends, releases, tremolos, hammer-ons, hammer-offs, and tab slides.

Entering Bends and Releases

In tablature, bends are usually indicated with a curved line pointing up and text indicating the pitch variation from the original note. A bend can be followed up by a release, telling the performer to "bend back down" to the original pitch. You can see an example of a bend and release in Figure 8.15.

Figure 8.14

Coordinate MIDI notes to strings in the MIDI Channels For Tabulature dialog box

Figure 8.15

Easily create a bend and release with the Guitar Bend Tool

Creating these in Finale is easy with the Guitar Bend Smart Shape:

1. First enter three fret numbers on a string, "5," "6," then "5" again (as in the "Before" example in Figure 8.15). Then click the Smart Shape Tool.

2. In the Smart Shape Palette, choose the Guitar Bend Tool.

3. Double-click the first "5" you entered (then press Ctrl/Command-D to redraw). Notice Finale creates the bend, adds the "?" text, and hides the second fret number. Any time you create a new guitar bend, Finale will add text corresponding to the pitch variation of the fret numbers (whole step=1, minor third= 1-?, etc.).

4. Now, double-click on the hidden fret number and redraw the screen (it should be on the same TAB line directly under the ? text). Finale creates a release for you automatically, and parenthesizes the destination fret number.

To create a quarter bend, Ctrl/Option-double-click on any fret number.

You can also generate bends and releases automatically by copying any music from a standard notation staff into a TAB staff that contains a Bend Hat Smart Shape. Finale automatically takes into account the pitch variation.

Use the primary handle to reposition the entire Guitar Bend, or use the small diamond arrows to reposition the end points. You can set the default placement for your bends in the Smart Shape Placement dialog box. From the SmartShape menu, choose Smart Shape Placement. From the drop-down menu on the upper left, choose Guitar Bend. You will see a list of three options for default placement of guitar bends (see Figure 8.16).

Figure 8.16

Edit the default placement of Guitar Bend Smart Shapes in the Smart Shape Placement dialog box

Drag the figure in the preview window to reposition the default appearance of bends, releases, and quarter bends. Changes here will apply to all new guitar bends you enter as well as all existing guitar bends that have not been repositioned manually.

In addition to placement, you can also manipulate other default characteristics of the Guitar Bend Smart Shapes with the Guitar Bend Options. From the SmartShape menu, choose Guitar Bend Options. The Guitar Bend Options dialog box appears as shown in Figure 8.17.

Here, choose Finale's default behavior while entering guitar bends. You can tell Finale to place release bend numbers in parentheses, hide the "Bend-to" number, and automatically generate text. You saw Finale do all of these things in the above example. They are all turned on by default. Changes here apply to all guitar bends in the score as well as newly created ones. Sometimes the text "Full" is used to indicate a bend of a whole step instead of the number "1." Check Replace "1" with "Full" to use "Full" for any guitar bend of a whole step. Then, click the Set Font button if you want to modify its font, size, or style. Also, set the font, size, and style for whole numbers and fractions by clicking the corresponding Set Font button at the bottom of this dialog box. Click OK to return to the score and review any settings you made.

Figure 8.17

Make settings for default text, parentheses, and other attributes of guitar bends in the Guitar Bend Options dialog box.

Tremolos and Tab Slides

Like guitar bends, tremolos and tab slides can be entered as Smart Shapes. Tab slides tell the performer to slide to a note without leaving the string. Tremolos are used to tell the performer to add vibrato to the pitch. You can see an example of a tremolo and tab slide in Figure 8.18.

Figure 8.18

Create tab slides with the Tab Slide Tool and tremolos with the Trill Extension Tool

Simply double-click a note or fret number with the Tab Slide Tool selected to extend a tab slide to the next note or fret number. When you copy regular notation that contains tab slides into a tablature staff, the tab slides copy with it. In the tablature staff, tab slides will always begin near the bottom of the first fret number and slant upwards to end near the top of the second fret number (since tab slides will always appear between fret numbers on the same TAB line).

To enter a tremolo above a staff, use the Glissando Smart Shape. Click the Glissando Tool in the Smart Shape Palette. From the SmartShape menu, choose Attach to Measures. Now, Ctrl/Option-click the Glissando Tool. The Smart Line Style Selection dialog box appears. Choose the wavy line without text and click Select. Now, hold down the Shift key (to constrain dragging), and click and drag above the staff to create the tremolo.

CHAPTER 8

Entering Hammer-Ons and Pull-Offs

Hammer-ons tell the performer of a fretted instrument to temporarily "capo" a string with one finger, and use another for the next fret number. A pull-off tells the performer to release the top fret position to sound the lower of the two pitches. You can see an example of a hammer-on and pull-off in Figure 8.19.

Figure 8.19

Add hammer-ons and pull-offs with the Custom Line Tool

To enter a basic hammer-on or pull-off requires a regular Smart Shape Slur. Click the Slur Tool in the Smart Shape Palette. From the SmartShape menu, select Attach to Notes. Then, double-click a fret number to extend the slur to the next fret number. You now have a basic hammer-on or pull-off figure. To add accompanying text for hammer-ons ("H") or pull-offs ("P"), as shown in Figure 8.19, use one of Finale's preset custom shapes. To do this

1. Ctrl/Option-click the Custom Line Tool to open the Smart Line Style Selection dialog box
2. Scroll down and click to highlight the "H" or "P" custom line. These are basically hidden Smart Shape lines with attached text.
3. Click Select to return to the score.
4. Double-click on the first of two fret numbers and drag to the right until the "H" or "P" appears in the desired location.

TIP

You can also add several guitar markings with Smart Shape metatools. Hold down the H key, and then click and drag to add a hammer-on. Use the O key for a pull-off. Use the A key for an "A.H." or the N key for an "N.H."

Entering Picking Figures

It's common to see picking indicators in tablature that tell the performer which direction to pluck the string or strings (see Figure 8.20).

Figure 8.20

Use articulation to specify picking

For these, use articulations. Click the Articulation Tool, and then double-click a fret number. The Articulation Selection dialog box appears. Choose either the up pick marking (#19) or the down pick marking (#20) and click Select. You return to the score with the marking above the staff directly above the fret number you clicked. For more information regarding adding articulations, see Chapter 3.

Editing TAB Staves

There are a number of ways to modify existing tablature staves in a document. You can add stems and beams to fret numbers in a staff, change the default lowest fret for a specific fretted instrument, change the string tuning, or even customize the pitch variation between frets for diatonic fretted instruments, such as a dulcimer.

To make general settings for any TAB staff, click the Staff Tool, and double-click the TAB staff to open the Staff Attributes dialog box. Click the Select button next to Notation Style to open the Tablature Staff Attributes as seen in Figure 8.21.

Here, click the Instrument drop-down menu to choose from a number of pre-defined fretted instruments. Each one contains a different string tuning. Choose the instrument you are writing for here so fret numbers will display properly. You can also create your own custom instrument (we'll explain how to do that soon).

The Default Lowest Fret and Capo Position settings dictate the lowest fret number you want to allow in the TAB staff you are working with. In the Fret Numbers section, you can change the font and vertical placement of your fret numbers. If you want to use Finale's default TAB settings in its Staff Attributes, make sure On "OK," Reset Staff Attributes To Tablature Defaults is checked before clicking OK. If this box is checked, when you click OK, all of the settings in the Staff Attributes (number of staff lines, staff line spacing, items to display, etc.) will reset so your TAB staff will appear as it would after creating it with the Setup Wizard.

Figure 8.21

Set up a TAB staff for use with any fretted instrument in the Tablature Staff Attributes dialog box

If you have changed settings in the Staff Attributes and do not want these settings to be reset, leave this box unchecked and click OK. If you have changed any settings in your Tablature Staff Attributes that affect the number of strings in your TAB staff, then you must check On "OK," Reset Staff's Attributes To Tablature Defaults to see the changes in your document (as the number of lines on the staff is directly linked to Staff Attributes.) This includes selecting a different instrument that contains a different number of strings in the Tablature Staff Attributes or editing the number of strings of the current instrument by clicking Edit Instrument.

Adding Stems and Beams

To tell Finale to add stems and beams to fret numbers in a tablature staff, do the following:

1. Click the Staff Tool.

2. Double-click the TAB staff to open the Staff Attributes.

3. In the Items to Display section, click the Stem Settings button to the right of Stems. The Staff Stem Settings dialog box appears as shown in Figure 8.22.

4. Here, specify how you want your stems to appear in the score. Choose the stem direction, placement, and whether or not to show beams. If you want to use Finale's default TAB stem settings, you can leave these parameters as they are.

5. Click OK to return to the Staff Attributes.

6. Click OK to return to the score. Stems and beams appear in the TAB staff, reflecting the settings in the Staff Stem Settings dialog box.

Creating a Custom Fretted Instrument Definition for Your TAB Staff

If you're using an instrument in your score that requires a special number of strings or string tuning, you can define your own fretted instrument. To do this

1. Click the Staff Tool.

2. Double-click the TAB staff to open the Staff Attributes.

Figure 8.22

Customize stems for a specific staff in the Staff Stem Settings dialog box

3. Click the Select button next to Notation Style to open the Tablature Staff Attributes.

4. Click the Edit Instrument button in the upper right to open the Fretboard Instrument Definition dialog box as seen in Figure 8.23.

Figure 8.23

Specify tuning, number of strings, and number of frets for a fretted instrument in the Fretboard Instrument Definition dialog box

5. Click the New button to begin a new instrument definition. Then, click in the Instrument text box to enter a name for your custom instrument.

6. Enter the number of strings on your fretted instrument in the Number of Strings text box.

7. Enter the number of frets on your fretted instrument in the Number of Frets text box.

8. Now, specify the pitches for each open string as MIDI notes. If you are using a MIDI keyboard (or other external MIDI device), simply click in the text box for a string, click the Listen button, and then play the open string pitch. Repeat for each string on your instrument. If you do not have a MIDI keyboard, click in each text box and enter the MIDI note number that corresponds to each open string (60 = middle C). Click the Play All button to hear the pitches you've assigned.

9. If you are creating an instrument with a non-chromatic fretboard (a dulcimer, for example), click the Define button to open the Diatonic Instrument Definition dialog box as seen in Figure 8.24. If you are not creating an instrument with a diatonic fretboard, skip to step 12.

Figure 8.24

Specify fret tuning for a non-chromatic fretboard in the Diatonic Instrument Definition dialog box

10. Enter the pitch variation between each fret here. Enter "1" for a half-step, "2" for a whole step, "3" for a minor third, etc. For example, if you want a note played on the first fret to sound a whole step higher than the open string, enter "2" as the first number. Separate each entry with a comma.

11. Click OK to return to the Fretted Instrument Definition dialog box.

12. Click OK. In the Tablature Staff Attributes box, be sure to check On "OK," Reset Staff's Attributes to Tablature Defaults. Click OK twice to return to your score. Your TAB staff now contains the number of strings you specified. Any music you copy to the TAB staff will accurately reflect the string tuning, fret tuning, and number of frets for the instrument you defined.

Creating a Guitar Part with TAB

Now use the skills you have learned in this chapter (and previous chapters) to create a guitar part with TAB, chord symbols, and custom fretboard diagrams.

Finale comes with some nice guitar templates. Use one of these to start with. From the File menu, choose New > Document from Template. In the Finale/Guitar/Templates folder, double-click the Tablature Templates folder to open it. Then double-click the file "House Style 3." A new document appears containing a standard and TAB staff. In the future, if you are creating a score for another fretted instrument, use the Document Setup Wizard to choose from a variety of fretted instruments with other string tunings.

Now, use the following steps to create a short guitar score with TAB. After following these steps, your document should look like Figure 8.25.

Figure 8.25

Guitar notation example with TAB

1. First, add the title and composer. From the File menu, choose File Info. The File Info dialog box appears. For Title, enter "Guitar Example." Then, for composer, enter "Arr. by" followed by your name. Click OK to return to the score.

2. This piece is in the key of A major, so you'll need to change the key. Click the Key Signature Tool and double-click the first measure. The Key Signature dialog box appears. To the right of the preview display, click the up arrow three times so the key of A (with three sharps) is displayed. Then, click OK to return to the score.

3. Now, enter the notation into the standard (top) staff using any of the available entry methods. Use the Smart Shape Tool to enter the slurs and TAB slides. If you own a MIDI guitar, you could also use HyperScribe to enter the music into the standard or TAB staff (see "Entering TAB with a MIDI Guitar" above). When you get to measure nine, use the TAB Slide Smart Shape to add the TAB slides on beat four.

4. After you have entered the notation, click the Mass Edit Tool. Click to the left of the standard (top) staff so the entire staff is highlighted. Now, click and drag in the highlighted area and drag down into the TAB staff. Release the mouse button. The Change Lowest Fret dialog box appears. Click OK. Fret numbers for each note now appear in the TAB staff.

5. In this template, you may want to move the fret numbers down a bit so they are more centered on the line. To do this, click the Staff Tool, and then double-click the TAB staff. In the Staff Attributes, click the Select button at the bottom (to the right of Tablature). The Tablature Staff Attributes dialog box appears. In the Fret Numbers section, for Vertical Offset, enter "-0.05" inches. Then click OK twice to return to the score.

6. Click the Mass Edit Tool and press Ctrl/Command-A to Select All. Then from the Mass Edit menu, choose Fit Music. Type "4" and click OK. Now there are four measures per system. To delete the extra measures, click measure seventeen so it is highlighted, hold down the Shift key and press the right arrow button, and then press the Delete key.

7. Click the Simple Entry Tool. Notice the third beat of measure three contains fret numbers on the B and E strings. Ctrl/Command-click and drag these down a string. Notice the numbers update accordingly. Also, do this to modify the fret numbers in measure seven, ten, thirteen, and fifteen so they appear as shown in Figure 8.25 (and/or in your example printout).

8. Click the Smart Shape Tool. To enter the "Let Ring" indications, Ctrl/Option-click the Custom Line Tool in the Smart Shape Palette. The Smart Line Style Selection dialog box appears. Scroll down and click to highlight the "Let Ring" smart line. Click Select. Now, double-click and drag in the score to enter the Let Ring indications.

9. Now, enter the hammer-ons and pull-offs. Click the Smart Shape Tool, and then click the Slur Tool in the Smart Shape Palette. In measure four, beat three and four, notice the slurs didn't carry over from the standard staff. Double-click the lower "2" on the third beat. The slur is now actually overlapping the slur above. Click the handle on the slur attached to the top "2" on the third beat. Then, press and hold the down arrow key to nudge it over the lower fret numbers. Do the same for the fret numbers on the fourth beat. To place the letter "H" above the slur, hold down the H key, click the left side of the slur, and drag to the right. Click the first note of the hammer-on and drag the second. Notice the H appears above and between the two fret numbers. Now, you need to enter pull-offs in measures eight and twelve. Click the Slur Tool again and double-click the fret number on the "and of two" in measures eight and twelve. Now, to add the P, hold down the O key, click the fret number on the "and of two" in measure eight and drag to the next fret number. Do the same in measure twelve.

10. Now, enter the chord symbols (as described in Chapter 4). Then, to show fretboard diagrams, from the Chord menu, choose Show Fretboards. When you get to measure three, notice the fretboard diagrams shown in Figure 8.25 are slightly different. To add the thumb indication on the low E string, create a custom fretboard diagram. With the Chord Tool selected, right/Control-click the chord symbol handle and choose Edit Chord Definition. In the Fretboard section, click Select, and then click Create. The Fretboard Editor appears. Click the T tool, and then click the second fret E string to place the T on the fretboard diagram. Then click OK, Select and OK to return to the score. Now, the second fretboard diagram in measure three is quite different than the default fretboard. Right/Control-click the second chord symbol handle in measure three and choose Edit Chord Definition. In the Fretboard section, click Select, and then click Create. Now, use the available tools to create the new fretboard (as shown in Figure 8.26). This chord will need to be fingered higher on the fretboard, so in the Fretboard Number section, check Show, and then for Number, enter "4." The Fretboard Editor dialog box should now look like Figure 8.26. Click OK, Select, and OK to return to the score. Your custom fretboard now appears above the staff. Use the same method to create custom fretboards as necessary for the remaining measures (you won't have to create the same fretboard twice for the same chord, just choose the one already created in the Fretboard Selection dialog box by clicking Select in the Fretboard section of the Chord Definition dialog box).

11. Now, you may notice the chord symbols overlap, particularly in measure fifteen. To resolve this, from the Options menu, choose Document Options, and then select Music Spacing. Under Avoid Collision Of, check Chords and click OK. Your music adjusts to avoid collision of chord symbols. (To apply music spacing manually, choose the Mass Edit Tool, highlight the region, and press 4).

Figure 8.26

Use the Fretboard Editor to
quickly edit fretboard diagrams
in your score

12. Now, click the Page Layout Tool. From the Page Layout menu, choose Space Systems Evenly
and click OK. Make any other changes to the layout as necessary.

If you like, play back the piece for review. If you want to disable chord playback, click the Chord Tool, and
then, from the Chord menu, uncheck Enable Chord Playback. You can use the general method above at any
time while creating a guitar part with TAB. If a guitar part you are writing requires slash or rhythmic
notation, look previously in this chapter under "Staff Setup for Slash, Rhythmic, and Other Notation Styles"
for more information.

9
EDITING YOUR MUSIC

One of the great advantages of creating music notation with a computer is the ability to make large-scale changes to an existing score. If, after finishing a score, you find that one of your articulations or note-expressions is the wrong character, font, size, or style, you can change every one in seconds in a score of any size (using the Mass Edit Tool). Or, perhaps you need to change all G sharps in a certain motif of a score to A flats. Again, it can be done in seconds (with the Note Mover Tool). The number of possible changes you might need to make to specific regions, or to the whole score, is endless. In this chapter, you will learn the most common ways to change existing notation in a score of any size.

Here's a summary of what you will learn in this chapter:

* ❋ How to copy and clear music
* ❋ How to change music *en mass* (transpose, edit entry items, move pitches, etc.)
* ❋ How to space your music
* ❋ How to change and manage fonts

Copying and Clearing Music

As covered briefly in Chapter 2, you can copy music from a selected region of your score to any other region with the Mass Edit Tool. As basic as this concept seems, there are a variety of ways to copy music depending on what you want to move (everything, just notes, just expressions, etc.), and where you want to move it (across staves, across documents, across programs). You may also need to perform more advanced operations like search-and-replace for specific pitches, or find similar rhythmic passages to apply articulations and expressions consistently. In this section I'll cover a variety of ways to move and change music with the Mass Edit and Note Mover Tools.

The first step to copying will always include selecting a region. For information on selecting measures and partial measures, see "Selecting Regions" in Chapter 2.

Methods of Copying

Chapter 2 already discussed the basics for cutting, copying, replacing, and inserting music. This might be a good time to go back and to review these basics before moving on, as the topics in this chapter expound on these concepts. Here, you'll use the same methods described previously to select measures/partial measures and copy music (drag-copy, Ctrl/Option-Shift-click copy, etc.). You'll learn how these methods also apply to copying specific items from any selected region and copying across documents.

To prepare for the following instructions, open a new Default Document (File > New > Default Document).

Copying Single Layers

You can isolate any layer for copying by showing the active layer only. First, choose the layer you want to copy from the Layer selection buttons/pop-up menu in the lower-left corner of the screen. Then, from the Options menu, choose Show Active Layer Only. Now copy the music as you would normally. Only the layer that displays will be copied. Also, music in other layers in the destination measures will not be affected.

> **TIP**
> Move music from one layer to another with the Mass Edit Tool. Choose the Mass Edit Tool, highlight a region of music and, then, from the Mass Edit menu, choose Move/Copy layers. Note that this method will not combine music into one layer. If there is music in the destination layer, it will be replaced.

Selecting Specific Items to Copy

By default, when you copy music within a document, Finale copies everything (notes, expressions, articulations, Smart Shapes, etc.). You can isolate any entry item or measure-attached item for copying. To copy measure-attached items, do the following:

1. Click the Mass Edit Tool.

2. From the Mass Edit menu, choose Copy Measure Items. The Measure Items dialog box appears as shown in Figure 9.1.

Figure 9.1

Specify measure-attached items to copy in the Measure Items dialog box

Measure Items

- ☐ Continuous Data
- ☐ Graphics (Assigned to Measures)
- ☐ Key Signatures
- ☐ Measure Number Enclosures
- ☐ Measure Positioning...
- ☐ Measure Widths...
- ☐ Ossia Measures (Assigned to Measures)
- ☐ Repeats
- ☐ Measure Expressions
- ☐ Smart Shapes (Assigned to Measures)
- ☐ Split Points
- ☐ Staff Styles
- ☐ Tempo Changes
- ☐ Text Blocks (Assigned to Measures)
- ☐ Time Signatures

[All]   [None]

[OK]   [Cancel]   [Help]

3. Check each item you want to copy from the selected region. Click All if you want to copy all measure items.

4. Click OK.

5. Highlight a region of your score containing the measure items you want to copy. Make sure to highlight a region of music that contains all of the measure-attached items you wish to copy.

6. Ctrl/Option-Shift-Click the first measure of the destination region (or drag-copy to the destination region). All of the measure-attached items appear in the new location.

Now, click the Mass Edit menu. Notice Copy Measure Items is still checked. You can continue to copy the measure items you selected (in the Measure Items dialog box) for other areas of your score. When you want to go back to copying everything, choose Copy Everything from the Mass Edit menu.

In addition to copying measure-attached items, you can also isolate entry and note-attached items for copying (notes, note-attached expressions, lyrics, chords etc.). To do this

1. Click the Mass Edit Tool.

2. From the Mass Edit menu, choose Copy Entry Items. The Entry Items dialog box appears as shown in Figure 9.2.

Figure 9.2

Specify note or entry-attached items to copy in the Entry Items dialog box

3. Check each item you want to copy from the selected region. Click All if you want to copy all entry items.

4. Click OK.

5. Highlight a region of your score containing the entry items you want to copy. Make sure to highlight the notes to which the entries are attached for all note-attached items you wish to copy.

6. Ctrl/Option-Shift-click the first measure of the destination region (or drag-copy to the destination region). All of the note-attached items, with a note on the corresponding beat, appear in the new location.

When copying note-attached items, keep in mind that each will require a note on the same beat in the destination measure. If a there is no corresponding note, the note-attached item will be left out of the destination region. Like copying measure items, you will need to choose Copy Everything from the Mass Edit menu to copy all items in a region.

TIP
You can select a combination of note-attached and measure- attached items by selecting items in both the Entry Items and Measure Items dialog boxes.

Copying between Documents

You can copy notation between documents just as you would within the same document. First, open both the source and destination document. Then, from the Window menu, choose Tile Horizontally (or Tile Vertically) so you can see both documents simultaneously on your screen. Now, drag-copy to move music between documents.

Aside from drag-copying music between documents, you can use the commands under the Edit menu. After selecting a region with the Mass Edit Tool and choosing Copy from the Edit menu (or Ctrl/Cmd-C), there are two ways Finale can transfer this information to the destination document: by replacing the existing entries or by inserting a new measure containing the copied material.

❋ Replacing existing entries only transfers note entries and note-attached items. This option is called Replace Entries under the Edit menu, or is otherwise invoked by the traditional Ctrl/Cmd-V (for paste) command. While using Replace Entries to copy music between documents, Finale will leave measure items (such as measure expressions and key signatures) out of the destination region. Note that new measures are not added, but the highlighted destination region is overwritten with the copied material.

❋ Inserting the copied material into a new measure (or measures) transfers everything Replace Entries does, as well as measure expressions and key and time signatures. After highlighting a region of music and selecting Copy from the Edit menu (or Ctrl/Cmd-C), highlight a measure in the destination document and, from the Edit menu, choose Insert. Inserting to another document transfers the most amount of material from the destination region. The disadvantage of this method is that staff lists for measure expressions are not transferred.

TIP
If you want to view documents on the entire screen while copying, switch between documents by choosing the file name at the bottom of the Window menu.

Copying Music to a Clip File

There may be a region of music you want to save and archive for use later, in a different or future document perhaps. To do this, save a clip file. With the Mass Edit Tool selected, highlight a region of your score. Then, hold down the Ctrl/Option key, click the Edit menu and choose Copy or Cut to Clip File. The Save Clipboard File dialog box appears. Name the clip file, choose a location, and click Save. Then, when you want to use the clip file, open the destination document and highlight the desired region with the Mass Edit Tool. Hold down the Ctrl/Option key, click the Edit menu, and choose Replace or Insert from Clip File. The Paste (Mac: Open) dialog box appears where you can choose a clip file you have saved. Select the desired clip file and choose Open to place the music from the clip file into the selected region.

Clearing Items

You can clear any type of musical item from a selected region of your score. With the Mass Edit Tool selected, highlight a region of your score. Then, from the Mass Edit menu, choose Clear Items. The Clear Items dialog box appears as shown in Figure 9.3.

Figure 9.3
Specify measure or entry items to clear in the Clear Items dialog box

In this dialog box, choose Only Selected Items. Then, click the check box for Measures to open the Measure Items dialog box (Figure 9.1), or click the check box for Entries to open the Entry Items dialog box (Figure 9.2). Choose the type of items you want to clear from the Measure or Entry Items dialog box, and then click OK to return to the Clear Items dialog box. At this point, either click the other check box (Measures or Entries) to specify more items to clear or click OK to return to the score. The items you specified are cleared from the highlighted region.

Changing Music

Anything you enter in Finale can be changed, moved, or deleted. This section focuses on the many ways to edit existing notes, expressions, chords, tuplets, and other items for any region of your score or for the whole document. Unlike editing items individually, which usually requires the tool used to create the item, the following techniques require the use of either the Note Mover or Mass Edit Tool only.

Changing Notes: Search and Replace

There may be a reoccurring passage of music in a score, or even a short motif, that you want to edit for every occurrence. You can change the pitch or enharmonic spelling of individual notes in a reoccurring musical passage with the Note Mover Tool's Search and Replace function. To do this

1. Choose the Note Mover Tool (on Windows, first click the Window menu and choose Advanced Tools; then, choose the Note Mover Tool from the Advanced Tools Palette).

2. Click a measure containing an arrangement of notes that you want to change for another, or all other occurrences in the score. You will see a handle on every note as shown in Figure 9.4.

3. Drag over a region of handles to choose the notes in your source region. If you want to select non-consecutive notes, hold down the Shift key and click the handle on each note you want to include.

4. From the Note Mover menu, choose Search and Replace. The Search and Replace dialog box appears as shown in Figure 9.5.

Figure 9.4

Selecting a region for search and replace

Figure 9.5

Customize your search in the Search and Replace dialog box

5. Here, choose In All Octaves if you want Finale to search for the selected notes in every octave of your score. Choose In Selected Octave Only to isolate the search to the octave of the selected notes. Check Match Durations if you only want Finale to search for the selected arrangement of notes in their rhythm only.

6. Click OK. The Alteration for Slot dialog box appears.

7. Each "slot" is a selected note. The first selected note is slot 1, the second, slot 2, etc. Move to the slot of a selected note you want to change by clicking Next. If you want to change the enharmonic of the slot, select Enharmonic. If you want to change the pitch, select Transposition. If you select Transposition, the Transposition dialog box appears. Choose an interval to transpose the note in the specified slot. If you wish to apply the same transposition to each selected note, set your transposition first and then click Set All. Click OK.

8. Once you have finished specifying the changes, click OK to return to the score. You will now see a new menu at the top of the screen—the Search menu.

9. From the Search menu, choose Find. Finale will look for a matching arrangement of notes and will highlight their handles.

10. From the Search menu, choose Replace Then Find to apply the changes you specified to the region and automatically select the next occurrence. To find and replace all occurrences at once, from the Search menu choose Replace All.

Changing Entry Items *En Mass*

In addition to changing notes with the Note Mover Tool, Finale can also modify the appearance of several other items in any region of the score with the Mass Edit Tool.

Swapping Articulations and Expressions

You can swap a note-attached expression or articulation for another in any selected region of your score with the Mass Edit menu's Change Articulation Assignments and Change Note Expression Assignments features. If you would like to swap an expression or articulation, first make sure the new figure exists in the Expression Selection or Articulation dialog box (you can find information on creating and editing expressions and articulations in Chapter 3). Use the following steps to change articulations in a selected region of your score:

1. Click the Mass Edit Tool, and select a region of your score containing articulations you want to change.

2. From the Mass Edit menu, choose Change > Articulation Assignments. The Change Articulation Assignments dialog box appears as shown in Figure 9.6.

Figure 9.6
Swap articulations with the Change Articulation Assignments dialog box

3. Select Position Selected Articulation. If you want to change all articulations in the selected region to the same one, leave Position All Articulations chosen and move to step 6.

4. Click the Select button to the right of Position Selected Articulation. The Articulation Selection dialog box appears.

5. Choose the existing articulation that you would like to change from the list and click Select. You return to the Change Articulation Assignment dialog box and the number of the articulation you selected appears in the top text box.

6. Check Change All Articulations (or Selected Articulation).

7. Click the Select button next to "to Articulation." The Articulation Selection dialog box appears.

8. Choose the new articulation from the list and click Select. You return to the Change Articulation Assignment dialog box, and the number of the articulation you selected appears in the middle text box.

9. For H and V, enter a value if you wish to adjust the default positioning of the new articulations. Or, click the drop-down menu and choose Add to Current Position to make adjustments from where they are currently positioned.

10. Click OK to return to the score and review your changes. The articulations you specified (or all articulations) change and reposition accordingly.

To change a specific note-attached expression assignment, or all note expressions in a region, follow the same steps but choose Change Note-Attached Expressions from the Mass Edit > Change menu.

Editing Chords

Like articulations and note expressions, every chord symbol in a selected region can be changed at once. You can edit their transposition, playback, and visual definition. To do this

1. Click the Mass Edit Tool and select a region of your score containing chord symbols you want to change.

2. From the Mass Edit menu, choose Change > Chord Assignments. The Change Chord Assignments dialog box appears as shown in Figure 9.7.

Figure 9.7

Change the visual definition, playback, or transposition of an existing chord symbol in the Change Chord Assignments dialog box

3. Here, choose how you want to change the selected chord symbols (any check boxes in gray mean the settings will be unaltered). In the Show section, choose chord components to show or hide. In the Play section, assign components of the chords for playback. Click the Transpose button to open the Transpose dialog box where you can choose a new transposition for the selected chord symbols. Transposition will apply to fretboard diagrams as well as chord symbols.

NOTE

When you change the key of a piece using the Key Signature Tool, all chord symbols will also transpose accordingly. Use the Change Chord Assignments dialog box only to transpose chord symbols independently from the key signature.

4. When you have finished specifying changes, click OK to return to the score. All chords and fretboards in the selected region change according to the settings you made.

To make global changes to the appearance of accidental characters on chord symbols, from the Options menu, choose Document Options, and then select Chords. In the Chords portion of the Document Options, you can set the baseline (vertical placement) and change font characters for accidentals in chord symbols. Note that any changes you make in Document Options apply only to the document you are working on.

Ties and Tuplets

The placement and visual definition of ties and tuplets can be altered in a selected region like expressions, articulations, and chords. With a region of the score selected, choose Mass Edit > Change > Ties to change ties, or Mass Edit > Change > Tuplets to change tuplets. However, you will most likely want these items to remain consistent throughout an entire document. To edit the placement, visual definition, and other attributes of ties and tuplets throughout a document, from the Options menu, choose Document Options. In the Document Options dialog box, choose the Ties or Tuplets category to make global changes to ties and tuplets.

Changes applied in the Document Options dialog box apply only to future tuplets you add to the score. To modify existing tuplets, select the Mass Edit Tool, highlight the region containing the tuplets you want to change and, from the Mass Edit Menu, choose Change > Tuplets. Make desired settings here and click OK.

TIP

Tuplets were improved in Finale 2005 and now slope according to the angle of notes and beams. They also avoid notes and stems automatically. These are called "Enhanced Tuplets" and apply only to tuplets added in Finale 2005. If you want to update tuplets in a document converted from an old Finale version, use the Mass Edit > Change Tuplets command described above. (Refer to the Finale 2005 default tuplet settings, in the default file, to convert old tuplets so they appear exactly the same as native 2005 tuplets.)

TIP

To alter tie and tuplet definitions and placement for a region of music, try the Patterson Tuplet Mover and Tie Mover plug-ins.

CHAPTER 9

Changing Note Durations and Appearance

With the Mass Edit Tool, you can easily change the note duration, notehead character, and note size for any selected region of music. Like the previous features, these can be found in the Mass Edit > Change submenu.

Changing Note Durations

You have a great deal of control over the duration of notes in a selected region. You may need to change note durations if you decide to change the time signature (doubling note durations while changing from common time to cut time, for example). To modify the duration of notes in any region, use the following steps

1. Click the Mass Edit Tool and select a region of your score containing notes you want to change. If you want to change note durations in a specific layer, choose the layer and, then, from the Options menu, choose Show Active Layer Only.

2. From the Mass Edit menu, choose Change > Note Durations. The Change Note Durations dialog box appears as shown in Figure 9.8.

Figure 9.8

Edit the duration of a region of notes according to settings in the Change Note Durations dialog box

3. To change all note durations, ensure Change All Note Durations By is selected. Then click the drop-down menu and choose the new percentage (200 percent doubles the note values, 50 percent reduces durations by half, etc.). If there is a specific note duration within the selected region you want to change, choose Change Selected Note Duration. In the From row, click the duration of the note you want to change (use the dot on the right to indicate a dotted note). In the To row, click the new duration you want to assign.

4. Check Rebar Music if you want the resulting notes to flow into different measures as dictated by the time signature. If this box is not checked, Finale will leave the resulting notes in their original measures (likely creating overfilled or incomplete measures).

5. Click OK to return to the score and review changes to note durations.

When you use these steps, all notes and rests in the selected region change except default whole rests. If you would like to include default whole rests while changing note durations with this method, use the Change To Real Whole Rests plug-in. With the Mass Edit Tool, highlight the region of your score you want to change. Then, from the Plug-ins menu, choose Note, Beam and Rest Editing > Change to Real Whole Rests. Now rests in the selected region are "real" and will be affected by note duration changes with the Mass Edit Tool.

Changing Notehead Characters

You can change the notehead character in any selected region of your score. However, for the most flexibility, there are a few preliminary steps to ensure that you can set noteheads to characters in any font, which is not supported by the Change Noteheads feature directly.

NOTE
If you are creating percussion notation, use the Percussion Map Designer to assign notehead characters to staff lines (see Chapter 8).

If the character of the notehead you want to use is in your existing Notehead font, use the Change Noteheads plug-in in the Notes, Beams and Rests submenu of the Plug-ins menu. The following steps display the true power of Finale.

To change noteheads in any region to characters in any font

1. First, find the font containing the character you want to use. From the Help menu, choose a font character set (Windows: Help > User Manual > Character Map) to see each character in the Finale Music Fonts. Note the keystroke required for the character you want to use ("Q," "Alt-0130", etc.). If you're using a third-party music font, locate the keystroke for the desired character in that font. After you have found it, move back to Finale. If the character exists in the document's default music font (Maestro by default), skip ahead to step 8. You can see your current default music font by choosing Set Default Music Font from the Options menu.

2. Click the Staff Tool.

3. From the Staff menu, choose Define Staff Styles. The Staff Styles dialog box appears.

4. Click New, and after Available Styles, type "Notehead Font," and then the name of the font containing the character you want to use (for future reference).

5. In the Independent Elements section, click the Select button and choose the font containing the character you want to use. Click OK to return to the Staff Styles dialog box. Then, click OK to return to the score.

6. Highlight the region containing the noteheads you want to change.

7. Right/Control-click the highlighted region and choose the "Notehead Font _ (*font name*)" staff style you just created. The staff style (with the independent notehead font setting) is applied and marked with blue bars.

8. Click the Mass Edit Tool and highlight the measures containing the noteheads you want to change (if they are not highlighted already). If you want to change noteheads in a specific layer, choose the layer, and then from the View menu, choose Show Active Layer Only.

9. From the Mass Edit menu, choose Change > Noteheads. The Change Noteheads dialog box appears as shown in Figure 9.9.

10. In the Find section, choose All Noteheads if you want to change all noteheads in the region. If you want to change noteheads you have already changed, choose All Custom Noteheads. Choose Selected Notehead if there is a specific notehead character in the highlighted region that you want to change.

Figure 9.9

Change noteheads for a region of your score according to settings in the Change Noteheads dialog box

11. In the Change To section, click Selected Notehead, and then click in the text box to see a blinking cursor. Type the keystroke of the character (as seen in its Font Character Map). You can also click the Select button to open the Symbol Selection dialog box containing a list of fonts in the current default music font. If your character is not in the default music font, your choices in this box do not reflect how the character will appear in the score (since you applied an independent notehead font to the region).

12. Click OK to return to the score and review the new notehead characters.

TIP

To apply a staff style to a region containing a partial measure, from the Edit menu, choose Select Partial Measures.

Changing the Note Size

You may want to change the size of notes in a region (to create cue notes, for example). Before using this method for cue notes, however, be sure to try the Add Cue Notes and Smart Cue Notes plug-ins under the Plug-ins menu > Scoring and Arranging. To change the size of notes, and their corresponding stems and beams:

1. Click the Mass Edit Tool, and select a region of your score containing notes you want to resize. If you want to change note size in a specific layer, choose the layer, and then from the View menu, choose Show Active Layer Only.

2. From the Mass Edit menu, choose Change > Note Size. The Change Note Size dialog box appears as shown in Figure 9.10

3. Enter a new percentage for notes in the selected region (200% doubles the note size, 50% reduces the size by half, etc.).

4. Click OK to return to the score. All visible notes in the selected region are resized.

Figure 9.10

Change the size for a region of notes according to settings in the Change Note Size dialog box

 TIP

You can also change the size of notes individually by clicking them with the Resize Tool. Notice that when you click on the stem you get the Resize Note dialog, and when you click directly on the notehead, you get the Resize Notehead dialog box.

Transposing

We have already seen how to transpose music by changing the key signature (in Chapters 2 and 5). You may, however, need to transpose music without changing the key. To transpose notes diatonically or chromatically in any region of your score within the key, do this:

1. Click the Mass Edit Tool, and select a region of your score containing music you want to transpose.

2. From the Mass Edit menu, choose Transpose. The Transposition dialog box appears as shown in Figure 9.11

Figure 9.11

Specify an interval to transpose a selected region in the Transposition dialog box

3. For Transpose, choose the direction you want to transpose the music (Up or Down). Then choose Chromatically to transpose any number of half-steps, or choose Diatonically to transpose within the key.

4. Click the drop-down menu for Interval and choose an interval to transpose the notes. The options you have here depend on the Diatonic/Chromatic setting above.

5. In the text box for Plus _ Octaves, enter the octave displacement. "1" = up one octave, "-1" = down one octave, etc.

6. Choose Preserve Original Notes if you want to leave the existing notes in the score and make copies of them at the specified transposition. For example, this works well for quickly creating octave doubling in a staff or doubling at the third, etc.

7. Click OK to return to the score. Music in the selected region is now transposed to the interval you specified.

To quickly transpose your music, assign transposition metatools. With the Mass Edit Tool selected, hold down the Shift key and press the 6, 7, 8, or 9 key on the QWERTY keyboard. The Transposition dialog box appears. Define a transposition and click OK. Now, highlight a region of music and press the number key you assigned to transpose it.

TIP

Try assigning metatools for four transposition settings: up a whole step, up a half step, down a whole step, and down a half step. Then, you can use the number keys you assign to increment to the desired transposition (for example, press the 6 key four times to transpose up a fourth).

If you want to transpose the music for an instrument doubling, remember to use a staff style that will display the new key signature, play back correctly, and affect only the region to which the style is applied. If you want to transpose music by semitones, try the Canonic Utilities plug-in under Plug-ins > Scoring and Arranging.

Music Spacing

By default, Finale is configured to do most music spacing for you. You may have noticed notes shifting after you enter them. This is Finale's attempt to space music proportionally during entry. If you are not satisfied with the default spacing, or want to make manual adjustments on your own, Finale offers you plenty of power to do so. Manipulating the automatic music spacing settings, stretching measures by moving barlines, or moving notes around individually are just a few ways to adjust the spacing of your music in Finale. In this section you'll learn how to use several of Finale's most effective music spacing methods.

Music spacing is largely affected by the width of systems, so for the following instruction, it is best to be working in Page View (remember there is one continuous system in Scroll View). From the View menu, choose Page View.

Automatic Music Spacing and Music Spacing Libraries

Automatic Music Spacing is turned on by default, so it is likely you have put it to use without even knowing it. It affects the spacing of your music after entering notes with any of the available entry methods. It can automatically adjust the space between notes and the width of measures. It can also make fine adjustments to your music to avoid collisions. Automatic Music Spacing can be turned on or off from the Edit menu.

TIP

Highlight a region of measures with the Mass Edit Tool and press the 4 key to easily apply Note Spacing to the region.

You can modify the parameters Finale uses for spacing in the Music Spacing category of the Document Options dialog box (see Figure 9.12). From the Options menu, choose Document Options, and then select Music Spacing from the list on the left.

Figure 9.12

Make changes to document-wide settings for music spacing in the Music Spacing portion of the Document Options dialog box

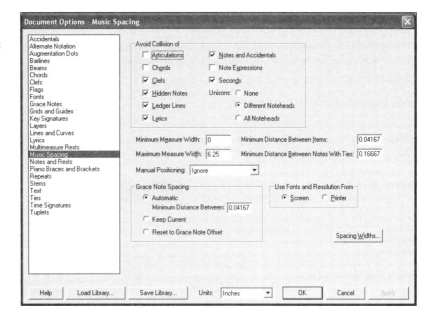

In this dialog box, you can make adjustments to Finale's default music spacing settings. Here, tell Finale to avoid collision of certain items, choose a minimum and maximum measure width and specify the minimum and maximum space between notes. You can also tell Finale to ignore, clear, or incorporate spacing of notes you have positioned manually by choosing one of these items from the Manual Positioning drop-down menu. For example, if you have manually positioned some notes and later you decide that you want to space your music using Finale's defaults, select Clear for Manual Positioning and then apply Note Spacing to your document. You can then set Manual Position back to Ignore so that future manual adjustments you make will be retained unless you specify otherwise.

You can have further control over Finale's automatic spacing by modifying the spacing widths. Click the Spacing Widths button to specify a number of EDUs allotted to each rhythmic duration. The process of adjusting spacing widths manually and reviewing the score can be quite time consuming and tedious. Instead, choose from a number of preset spacing width configurations by loading one of Finale's available Music Spacing libraries. (The Fibonacci Spacing library is already loaded into Finale's default documents.)

Click the Load Library button in the Document Options dialog box (or, from the File menu, choose Open Library or Load Library). The Open Library dialog box appears. Double-click the Music Spacing folder. Now, double-click one of the available music spacing libraries to open it (then click OK to return to the score if necessary). Now, Finale will use the spacing widths defined by the library you opened. One of the five music spacing libraries should meet your needs. If not, configure custom music spacing settings in the Spacing Widths dialog box, and save your own music spacing library to use with any document. After customizing the spacing widths, click the Save Library button in the Document Options to save a Music Spacing library.

CHAPTER 9

Updating the Layout

By default, Finale updates the page format and number of measures per system during entry, while adding measures or making other changes that have an effect on the page layout (in Page View only). You may have seen measures jumping between systems while entering music. This is a result of Automatic Update Layout, Finale's attempt to create evenly spaced measures within systems. Updating the layout also brings together other elements of the page format, such as the number of systems per page while resizing systems, staves, or pages. Press Ctrl-U on Windows or Cmd-U on Mac (or choose Update Layout from the Edit menu) to update the layout at any time.

Locking Measures Per System

To tell Finale how to handle the number of measures per systems while updating the layout, use the Update Layout Options. From the Options menu, choose Update Layout Options. The Update Layout Options dialog box appears as shown in Figure 9.13.

Figure 9.13

Tell Finale how to reconfigure systems and pages while updating the layout in the Update Layout Options dialog box

From the Options menu, choose Update Layout Options, and, from the drop-down menu, make sure Across Systems (Maintain System Locks) is selected. This is Finale's default setting and perhaps the most flexible setting. Click OK to return to the score. From the View menu, make sure Show Page Layout Icons is checked so that any system locks will be visible. To lock a system or systems, click the Mass Edit Tool, and then highlight measures in the systems you want to lock. From the Mass Edit menu, choose Lock Systems. You will notice a padlock icon to the right of the selected systems. This icon indicates that the number of measures in the system are locked and will not be changed while updating the layout. To remove system locks, highlight a region and choose Unlock Systems from the Mass Edit menu.

You may have noticed that any change you make in the measure layout results in the appearance of lock icons. While moving measures between systems manually, or using the Fit Music command to fit a number of measures to systems (described in Chapter 2 under "Moving Measures Across Systems"), Finale locks changed systems automatically. To demonstrate this, clear system locks from a page with the Mass Edit Tool (select the region and press the U key). Then, click the last measure of a system, and press the down arrow to move it to the next system. Notice a lock appears to the right of both changed systems. Systems also become locked any time you change the number of measures with the Fit Music command (under the Mass Edit or Page Layout menus).

Systems Per Page

While updating the layout, you will usually want Finale to move systems across pages automatically (to update for resizing other page format changes). However, you can tell Finale to leave the same number of systems on a page in the Update Layout Options dialog box. From the Options menu, choose Update Layout Options. The Update Layout Options dialog box appears (see figure 9.13). Here, uncheck Reflow Systems Across Pages and click OK. Now Finale will leave the same systems on each page while updating the layout. Move them manually with the Page Layout Tool (as described in chapter 2). There will be more information on page layout in Chapter 11.

Spacing with the Mass Edit Tool

You may want to apply spacing changes to a certain region of the score without affecting any other region. You can apply music spacing to any desired region with the Mass Edit Tool. First, turn off Automatic Music Spacing under the Edit menu. Then, click the Mass Edit Tool and highlight a region of measures containing music you want to respace. From the Mass Edit Menu, choose Music Spacing, then Apply Note, Beat, or Time Signature Spacing. Or, instead of choosing the menu item, simply press the 3 key to apply Beat Spacing to a region, or press the 4 key to apply Note Spacing to a region.

Beat Spacing will space each beat according to the table of widths and will space notes between beats linearly (quarter note gets twice the space of an eighth note, and so on). Note Spacing provides more precision by using the spacing widths table for each note. (Note Spacing is also used for Automatic Music Spacing.) Time Signature Spacing will use linear spacing throughout the measure. For example, a half note would get twice as much space as a quarter note. This is how your music looks directly after entering it into the score with Automatic Music Spacing off.

Spacing Notes Individually

You can use the Speedy Entry Tool or the Special Tools to space notes individually. Click the Speedy Entry Tool and click a measure containing notes to open the Speedy frame. Now, simply click and drag notes in the active layer to move them horizontally. To use the Special Tools for spacing, first click the Special Tools Tool (on Windows, from the Window menu, choose Advanced Tools Palette, then click the Special Tools Tool). You will see the Special Tools Palette appear on the screen. From this palette, choose the Note Position Tool. Then click in a measure to see positioning handles appear above the measure. Click and drag these handles to move the corresponding notes left or right in the measure.

To incorporate your manual note spacing into all future music spacing applied to the region, from the Options menu, choose Document Options, then select Music Spacing. Click the drop-down menu for Manual Positioning and choose Incorporate. Or, choose Ignore to tell Finale to reapply your manual positioning after spacing the music. You can also choose Clear to remove manual spacing adjustments while spacing.

The Beat Chart and Spacing with the Measure Tool

Chapter 7 showed how to increase or decrease the width of measures by dragging barlines with the Measure Tool. When dragging the barlines, the entries in the measures will respace proportionally. There are some other music spacing techniques possible with the Measure Tool.

Occasionally, you may want to respace all notes on a certain beat for all staves in a measure. You can manually adjust the placement of each beat using the Measure Tool's Beat Chart. To space your music using a Beat Chart, do this:

1. Click the Measure Tool and highlight a region of measures containing notes.

2. Double-click the highlighted area to open the Measure Attributes dialog box.

3. Click the drop-down menu for Position Notes, and choose Using Beat-Chart Spacing. This step is not necessary if Note Spacing (or Automatic Music Spacing) has already been applied to the region.

4. Click OK to return to the score. You will now see two handles on each barline in the selected region.

5. Click the bottom barline handle. The Beat Chart appears above the top staff in the system as shown in Figure 9.14.

Figure 9.14

Specify the placement of beats for a measure in all staves of a system with the Beat Chart

Beat Chart

6. Drag the bottom handle to position all notes on the beat in all staves of the system.

7. For more information about the placement of each beat, double-click the top handle in the Beat Chart to open the Beat Chart dialog box as shown in Figure 9.15. The Elapsed Duration indicates the number of EDUs from the beginning of the measure. The remaining values use the measurement unit selected under the Options menu (Options > Measurement Units). You can use these values to space measure-attached items in your score relative to the placement of the note.

8. Click OK to return to the score. Click anywhere in the score to hide the Beat Chart.

Figure 9.15

Specify the precise placement of beats using the Beat Chart dialog box

{
TIP
You can use measure spacing handles (added in Finale 2005) to manually adjust the space before and after music in each measure. From the Measure Menu, choose Show Measure Spacing Handles. Now, two handles appear on the bottom staff line in each measure. Drag these handles to adjust the spacing.

Positioning Notes Evenly in a Measure

With the Measure Tool, you can also tell Finale to position notes evenly in a measure regardless of the time signature, measure width, or number of notes in the measure. This is sometimes used for chant notation where a measure takes up an entire staff system or a long cadenza in a solo. Also, use this method when you want to space a measure containing too many beats relative to the time signature—for example, in a cadenza passage.

Click the Measure Tool and double-click a measure to open the Measure Attributes dialog box. In the Options section, check Position Notes Evenly Across Measure. Click OK to return to the score. Notes in the measure are now positioned evenly. Any notes you add to this measure will also be positioned evenly.

Setting a Measure to Begin a Staff System

If you know you want a specific measure to always begin a new staff system, you can mark the measure with the Measure Tool. With the Measure Tool selected, double-click a measure to open the Measure Attributes dialog box. In the Options section, check Begin a New Staff System. Click OK to return to the score. Now, the measure will always mark the beginning of a new system. Notice the resulting arrow icon in the left margin as a reminder to you.

CHAPTER 9

Changing and Managing Fonts

Just about everything you enter into a score—music, text expressions, articulations, and other items—are font characters. Just as you can change the font, size, or style of your letters in a word-processing program, you can do the same for most items in a score. All font settings are document-specific, so they are saved along with each document. You can see the fonts currently selected in an open document by looking in the Document Options. From the Options menu, choose Document Options and select Fonts from the list on the left. The Font options appear as shown in Figure 9.16.

Figure 9.16
Set the default font for any item in the Fonts portion of the Document Options dialog box

Here you can choose any font on your system for each option under the four drop-down menus. The fonts on your system include the Finale music fonts that were added when you installed Finale. (You can find a list of the Finale fonts and their characters under the Help menu—on Windows, choose Help > User Manual.) Let's say you want to set the font of your lyric verses to Arial. First, click the drop-down menu for Lyrics and choose Verses. Then click the Set Font button to the right. The Font dialog box opens as shown in Figure 9.17.

Use the scroll bar on the left to move up the list, and click Arial to select it. Notice that you can change the point size and style of a font just as you would in a word-processing program. When you have set up your font, click OK to return to the Document Options dialog box.

Notice that there is an asterisk (*) next to many of the items listed under the four drop-down menus. The asterisk tells you that any change to the font in the Document Options will apply only to new items added to the score and will not apply to existing items. If you want to change the font of one of the asterisked fonts, try using the Change Fonts plug-in under Plug-ins > Miscellaneous (more about how to do this soon).

Changing Your Music Font

Finale makes changing the default music font easy. From the Options menu, choose Set Default Music Font to open the Font dialog box where you can choose a new music font. The Finale music fonts include Maestro, Maestro Percussion, Maestro Wide, Jazz, Jazz Perc, and Engraver fonts.

Figure 9.17

Specify the font, size, and style for an item in the Font dialog box

{ **TIP**
If you want to use Finale's Jazz font for a new document, use the Setup Wizard (File > New > Document With Setup Wizard). On page 4, for Default Music Font, choose Jazz. You will see the music in the preview window change to the Jazz font.

Remember, you can see a list of all of Finale's fonts and their characters under the Help menu (on Windows, choose User Manual from the Help menu). Remember that Finale also gives you the ability to change different elements of music, as mentioned above. The Default Music font changes all of these elements at once.

Swapping and Checking Fonts

You can change all characters in a certain font to another font by using Finale's Font Swapping utility. From the Options menu, choose Data Check, then Swap One Font For Another. The Swap One Font For Another dialog box appears as shown in Figure 9.18.

Here, click the Set Font button next to Search For This Font to open the Font dialog box. Select the font you want to change and click OK. Now, click the Set Font button next to Replace With This Font. The Font dialog box appears again. Select the new font, size, and style for your font and click OK. Click OK to return to your score and review the appearance of items in the new font. Keep in mind that changing the font this way will apply to all items in the selected font in this file. Consult the Fonts category of the Document Options (as described above) to see all items that use any given font.

CHAPTER 9

Figure 9.18

The Swap One Font For
Another dialog box

The Change Fonts Plug-In

You can change the font for some existing items in the score with the Change Fonts plug-in. From the Plug-ins menu, choose Miscellaneous > Change Fonts. The Change Fonts dialog box appears as shown in Figure 9.19.

Figure 9.19

Change the font for existing
staff names, group names,
text blocks, and lyrics in the
Change Fonts dialog box

Click the Change button for any of the available items to open the Font dialog box where you can set a new font for the item. If Finale does not detect any existing entries for one of these categories, the selection will not be available. Change the font for any of the desired items in this dialog box and click OK to return to the score.

Checking Document Fonts against System Fonts

Finale remembers the fonts you use in any document after saving. When you open a file, Finale finds each font used in the document on your computer and displays it. If Finale cannot find a font on your computer that it needs to properly display one or more elements, you may end up seeing incorrect-looking music or markings in your score. This can happen when you use a third-party music font, or any uncommon font, and open the file on a different computer that does not have the font installed. To check a document to ensure that all fonts used in the document exist on the computer, and to substitute missing fonts, use the Check Document Fonts Against System Fonts utility. From the Options menu, choose Data Check and choose Check Document Fonts Against System Fonts. If Finale finds any fonts in your document that do not exist on your computer, the Font dialog box appears as shown in Figure 9.20.

Figure 9.20
Checking document fonts
against system fonts

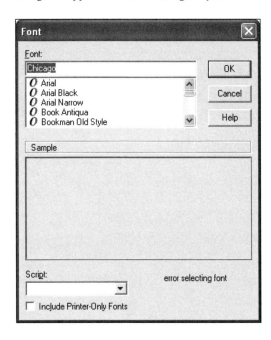

Here, choose a substitute for any missing fonts that Finale finds. For example, if you are using Windows, you may see the Times font appear in this dialog box. This is a font standard on Macintosh, but not on Windows. Choose a new font (like Times New Roman—similar to Times) just as you would normally, and click OK to tell Finale to display the next missing font, or return to the score (if there are no more missing fonts).

Everything Looks Funny: Reinstalling Your Finale Music Fonts

If all music in a document looks completely messed up—for example, you see funny symbols or letters instead of notes and clefs—you probably just need to reinstall your Finale music fonts. You may have uninstalled a previous version of Finale, thus removing your music fonts. The easiest way to fix this is to simply reinstall fonts from the original Finale installation CD using a Typical (Macintosh: Easy) install when prompted to do so. You can also download the fonts from Coda's Web site, www.finalemusic.com. Search their site for the Finale Font Pack download. Follow instructions on the site for installing these fonts.

10

FINE TUNING: THE DETAILS

In Chapter 9, you learned large-scale editing procedures that are often applied during score creation. In this chapter, I'll cover additional editing techniques that allow you to have greater control over the appearance of individual items. The following instructions apply primarily to fine-tuning the appearance of markings and notation rather than creating, editing, and moving pitches and rhythms. Here, I'll focus on details that can make any score look neat, clean, and professional. Many prefer to use the techniques described below after all markings and notation have been entered into a score, though the method you adopt for using any editing technique will depend on the project you are working on and your own work style. In this chapter, I'll describe how to align and position a variety of items on the page, as well as make global and individual changes to beams, stems, accidentals, dots, and ties.

Here's a summary of what you will learn in this chapter:

- ✺ Techniques for alignment and positioning
- ✺ How to edit beams
- ✺ How to edit stems
- ✺ How to edit notes and noteheads
- ✺ How to edit accidentals
- ✺ How to edit dots and ties

Alignment and Positioning Techniques

After creating a page of music, you may want to specify precise placement for text, chords, graphics, or other marking in your score relative to the page edge and/or each other. Here, I'll show you how to easily position items using a ruler, grid, or guide as a reference.

Since we are only concerned with adjusting the placement of items as they will appear after printing, move to Page View (View > Page View). Remember, only in Page View can you see the score as it will appear in the printout.

NOTE

Use the following alignment and positioning techniques in Page View to place various markings before finalizing your page layout. See Chapter 11 for more information on laying out your staff, system, and page margins for printing.

The Selection Tool

Introduced in Finale 2001 and improved several times since, the Selection Tool has made general positioning a breeze for most items. With this tool, you can select almost anything on the page and drag it into position without having to switch tools. Simply click the Selection Tool, click an item, and drag it around. See Figure 10.1 for a description of items you can move and delete with the Selection Tool.

Figure 10.1

Position items easily with the Selection Tool

After you click an item, it will be surrounded with a rectangle. Then, you can either click and drag or use the arrow keys to nudge the item into place. Press the Delete key to delete the item. Double-click any item with the Selection Tool to select the item's corresponding tool for further editing. Use the Selection Tool in conjunction with the following positioning techniques to specify precise placement of just about any item in your score.

In addition to dragging and deleting items, you can also invoke context menus for many items with the Selection Tool and make edits without leaving the Selection Tool. For example, with the Selection Tool chosen, right/Control-click a measure expression. The measure expression context menu appears. Choose Edit Measure Text Expression Definition to open the Text Expression Designer. Enter some new text for the expression and click OK. You return to the score with the Selection Tool still selected. While editing existing scores, make a habit of using the Selection Tool as much as possible to avoid the hassle of switching tools frequently.

NOTE
Press the Esc key at any time to select the Selection Tool. (If a note is selected in Simple Entry, press Esc twice.)

Rulers and Margins

By default, in Page View, page edges and staves are the only visual references when positioning text and other items. For greater control over the exact placement of an item as it will appear on the printed page, use rulers. From the View menu, choose Show Rulers. You will now see two rulers appear, one across the top of the screen and one on the left side (see Figure 10.2).

Figure 10.2

Use rulers and margins for precision placement

Rulers

Margins

As you click and drag any item, you will notice dashed lines extending vertically and horizontally. Use these lines to position items in your score relative to the distance from the top and left page edge. To specify inches, centimeters, EVPUs, or another measurement unit to display on the rulers, from the Options menu, choose Measurement Units, and then select the desired unit of measurement.

> **TIP**
>
> For more precision, try zooming in. Press Ctrl/Command-= to zoom in or Ctrl/Command—(minus) to zoom out. Right/Command-Option-click and drag to move the viewable region of the page. As you change the view percentage and viewable area of the page, the rulers will adjust accordingly.

If you would like to position items relative to the system or page margins, from the View menu, choose Show Margins. Now, the system and page margins appear in a light gray line (see Figure 10.2). With Show Margins selected, you can also see two vertical lines—one marks the midpoint of the page, and the other marks the midpoint of the page margins. There are two horizontal lines marking the page and page margin midpoint as well. You can hide rulers and margins by unchecking Show Rulers or Show Margins under the View menu.

Grids and Guides

Like rulers and margins, grids and guides can also be used as a reference to position a variety of items in your score. Grids and guides are both basically horizontal and vertical reference lines that extend through the page at specified points along the vertical or horizontal axis. A key advantage to both grids and guides is the ability to snap items to them.

Positioning with Grids

Instead of manually dragging or nudging expressions, text, Smart Shapes, and other items into place, Finale contains a powerful utility for snapping items to a grid automatically. To do this, click the View menu and choose Show Grid. There is now a grid covering your page (with a quarter inch between each line by default). Each intersection of the grid displays as a + on your page. To tell Finale to snap specific items to the closest intersection, click the View menu and choose Grid/Guide Options. Document Options—Grids and Guides displays as shown in Figure 10.3.

Figure 10.3

Make document-wide settings for grids and guides in the Grids and Guides category of the Document Options

In the Grid Line Settings section, click the Items To Snap To Grid button. The Items to Snap To Grid dialog box appears. Here, check any items you want to position in the score using the grid and click OK. Then, check Snap To Grid and click OK to return to the score. Now, any time you drag one of items checked in the Items To Snap To Grid dialog box, it will snap to the nearest intersection. See Figure 10.4 for an example of a score with the grid visible.

Figure 10.4

Viewing the grid

To increase or decrease the distance between each grid intersection, click the View menu, choose Grid/Guide Options, and specify a value in the Grid Line Every field. In this section, you can also choose to display fewer grid lines and, using the Grid Line Style drop-down menu, change the grid line style from crosshairs to dots, dashes, or a solid line.

Positioning with Guides

A guide is basically a vertical or horizontal line that that you can add as a reference point. To create a guide, right/Control-click a ruler to open the context menu and choose New Guide (or you can also double-click in the ruler to create a Guide). The New Horizontal/Vertical Guide dialog box appears as shown in Figure 10.5

Figure 10.5

Specify the guide location in the New Horizontal/Vertical Guide dialog box

Here, specify the distance you want to position the guide from the top or left edge of the page and click OK. Notice the triangle appear on the ruler with a dashed line extending through the score. Click and drag the triangle to reposition the guide if needed.

Like the grid, you can also snap items to this guide:

1. From the View menu, choose Grid/Guide Options.

2. In the Grid Line Settings section, click Items To Snap To Guide to open the Items To Snap To Guide dialog box.

3. Make sure the items you want to position using the guide are checked, and click OK to return to the Grid/Guide options.

5. Check Snap To Guides. For Gravity Zone Size, enter the region to either side of the guide you want the Snap To setting to affect. For example, enter 1 inch if you want any item moved within an inch of the guide to snap to it.

6. Click OK to return to the score. Now, use guides to align markings vertically or horizontally. You can use grids and guides simultaneously or independently.

To see the "gravity zone" of your guides (the region in which an object will snap to the guide), Right/Ctrl-click on an existing guide in the ruler and choose Show Gravity Zone (see Figure 10.6).

TIP

Remember, you can align expressions vertically above or below the score using the expression positioning triangles. Refer to Chapter 3 for details.

Figure 10.6
Specified items will snap to
a guide if they are dragged
within the gravity zone.

Positioning Rests

By default, Finale places rests according to standard notation conventions. In measures with a single layer, rest placement generally lies in the middle of the staff (the precise placement depends on the rest's duration). As long as you are using one of Finale's music fonts, placement of rests should look fine. However, if you are using a third-party music font, the rest characters may be offset. Or, you may be creating notation that calls for rests in a document to be repositioned vertically. You can change the default placement of rests in the Document Options dialog box. From the Options menu, choose Document Options and select Notes and Rests. The Notes and Rests options appear as shown in Figure 10.7.

Figure 10.7
Make document-wide settings
for rests in the Notes and
Rests category of Document
Options

Document Options - Notes and Rests

Accidentals
Alternate Notation
Augmentation Dots
Barlines
Beams
Chords
Clefs
Flags
Fonts
Grace Notes
Grids and Guides
Key Signatures
Layers
Lines and Curves
Lyrics
Multimeasure Rests
Music Spacing
Notes and Rests
Piano Braces and Brackets
Repeats
Stems
Text
Ties
Time Signatures
Tuplets

☐ Use Note Shapes

Replace: Double Whole   Noteheads on Scale Degree: 1

With This Symbol: W   Select...

Vertical Rest Positioning

Eighth: 0   Spacing Before Music: 0.0833
16th: 0   Spacing After Music: 0
32nd: 0   Gutter for Accidentals: 0
64th: -0.08333   Gutter for Ties: 0
128th: -0.16667

☐ Scale Manual Positioning of Notes
☐ Display Cross-Staff Notes in Original Staff

Notehead Characters: Quarter/Eighth   Select...
Rest Characters: 128th   Select...

Help   Load Library...   Save Library...   Units: Inches   OK   Cancel   Apply

In the Vertical Rest Positioning section, set the offset for any rest duration of an eighth or less from the middle staff line. Click OK to apply changes and return to the score.

In measures with more than one layer, Finale automatically offsets rests higher or lower in the staff to distinguish between multiple voices. These are called "Floating Rests." For example, enter a quarter rest in layer 1, and then in the same measure, enter a quarter rest in layer 2. Notice that as you enter the rest in layer 2, the rest in layer 1 jumps up, and the rest in layer 2 appears lower in the staff. You can tell Finale how to treat the placement of rests while working in multiple layers in the Layer options. From the Options menu, choose Document Options and select Layers. The Layer options appear as shown in Figure 10.8.

Figure 10.8

Make document-wide settings for layers in the Layers category of Document Options

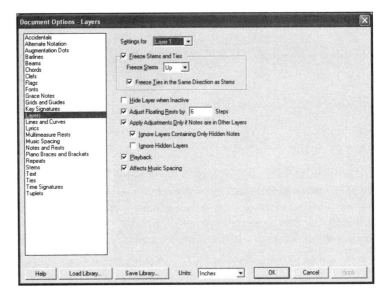

From the drop-down menu at the top, choose the layer of the rests you want to change. Then, enter the offset in steps for Adjust Floating Rests by _ Steps (a step is a line or space in the staff). The default value is 6 for layer 1 and –6 for layer 2, so floating rests appear centered on the first ledger line above the staff for layer 1 and below the staff for layer 2. Uncheck this option to tell Finale to use the positioning for rests as specified in Document Options > Rests for all rests in the selected layer.

If you want to use the vertical rest positioning specified in the Layer options even when there are no notes in other layers, uncheck Apply Adjustments Only if Notes Are in Other Layers. With this box unchecked, all rests in the layer will position themselves according to the floating rest setting. Click OK to return to the score and review your settings. Changes made will apply to all existing music and all new music added to the document.

Editing Beams

By default, Finale beams together all notes in a beat (with the exception of eighth notes in common time, which can be beamed in groups of four). You can find general beaming settings for a document in the Document Options dialog box. From the Options menu, choose Document Options and select Beams. The Beam options appear as shown in Figure 10.9

Figure 10.9

Make document-wide settings for beams in the Beams category of Document Options

Use these options to adjust the default appearance of beams throughout your document. Here you can tell Finale to use Flat beams (under the Beaming Style drop-down menu), beam over rests, modify the maximum slope of beams, and make other document-wide adjustments. Settings here dictate largely how your beaming will look immediately after entering the notation. Here are some common ways to edit beams throughout your document in the Document Option's Beam settings:

❋ By default, Finale beams groups of four eighth notes together in common time. In other words, it breaks eighth note beams only on beat three. To break eighth note beams on every beat in common time (to always beam eighth notes in groups of two), uncheck Beam Four Eighth Notes Together in Common Time.

❋ Note the section containing five check boxes and a preview example. This short musical example updates to display the appearance of beams based on the combination of check boxes selected. For example, check Allow Rests to Float and Extend Beams Over Rests. Notice the figure updates as you check or uncheck these options. Use this preview as a guide to customize the default appearance of beams for your document.

❋ In the lower portion, enter values to specify beam thickness, broken beam length, secondary beam separation, and max slope for beams. To change the measurement unit to use for these settings (inches, centimeters, etc), click the drop-down menu for Units at the bottom of this dialog box.

Besides settings for treatment of eighth note beams in common time, the beam settings in the Document Options do not apply to the default beam grouping. To specify default beam groups to use as you enter music into the score, use the Time Signature Tool.

Beaming Patterns and Time Signatures

Beaming patterns are stored in time signatures. When you specify a time signature, Finale will apply a beaming pattern for the music based on the duration of the main beat. For example, in 6/8 time, with a dotted quarter note as the main beat, Finale will automatically beam six eighth notes in two groups of three as seen in Figure 10.10.

Figure 10.10

Beaming for a 6/8 time signature

You can specify a custom beaming pattern for any time signature manually, and even apply a new beaming pattern without changing the time signature. To demonstrate this, here are steps for creating a custom beaming pattern for a 7/8 measure. In this example, you will create a beaming pattern with eighth notes in groups of two and three. Start fresh with a new Default Document (File > New > Default Document).

1. With the Time Signature Tool selected, double-click a measure to display the Time Signature dialog box.

2. Click the Composite button at the top to open the Composite Key Signature dialog box. This is where you will specify the beats/beaming pattern.

3. After Beat Duration, enter the rhythmic value that represents the smallest subdivision of notes you will be beaming. In this case, enter 8. This value will usually be the same as the bottom number in your key signature.

4. Now, after Beat Groups, in the *first* box, specify the number of notes in each group. In this case you'll enter 3 + 2 + 2 (see Figure 10.11). Notice the preview display indicates the beamed groups.

5. Click OK. You will now see the composite time signature in the preview display, though you will probably just want to display 7/8 in the score.

6. Click the Options (Mac: More Choices) button to expand the lower section.

7. Adjust the Number of Beats and Beat Duration in the lower section of the Time Signature dialog to indicate a time signature of 7/8. For Number of Beats, click the right arrow until 7 appears as the top number in the preview display. For Beat Duration, click the left arrow until 8 appears as the bottom number in the preview display, indicating a key signature of 7/8.

Figure 10.11

In the Composite Time Signature dialog box, you can specify the beat duration and beaming for any time signature.

8. Check Use a Different Time Signature for Display. By checking this box, you tell Finale to use the time signature in the lower section for display, but the actual time signature and beaming pattern that will be used is in the upper display of the Time Signature dialog.

9. Click OK to return to the score.

10. Enter eighth notes into the staff with the Simple or Speedy Entry Tool. You will see the notes beamed to the pattern specified in the Composite Time Signature dialog box.

Rebeaming a Selected Region

At any time, you can reset the beaming for a region of music back to the settings specified in the time signature and Document Options. To do this

1. Click the Mass Edit Tool and highlight a region of your score.

2. From the Mass Edit menu, choose Rebeam > Rebeam Music. Beaming in the selected region reverts back to the region's time signature settings and updates the region to your settings in Document Options > Beams (see Figure 10.9).

Most often you would use this feature if you wanted to return to the default beaming after having manually edited beams with Simple or Speedy Entry. For more control over the beaming of a selected region, you can rebeam to a time signature with the Mass Edit Tool as well.

Rebeaming to Time Signature

Above, you learned how to adjust beaming patterns for a time signature. You can also apply beaming settings for any region of your score without changing the time signature, or even going into the Time Signature Tool. To do this, click the Mass Edit Tool and select a region of music. From the Mass Edit menu, choose Rebeam > Rebeam to Time Signature. The Rebeam to Time Signature dialog box appears as shown in Figure 10.12.

Here, edit the beat groups for the region as you would by changing the time signature. Click the Composite button to open the Composite Time Signature dialog box (see Figure 10.11) where you can specify beaming groups for each beat (as described in the steps above under "Beaming Patterns and Time Signatures").

Figure 10.12
Edit beamed groups in the
Rebeam to Time Signature
dialog box

Rebeaming to Lyrics

In some vocal music, beams appear only over melismas (when more than one note is sung for a syllable). In Finale, you can rebeam music to lyrics automatically to fit this paradigm. Click the Mass Edit Tool and select a region of a score with lyrics and notes of an eighth note (or shorter) duration. From the Mass Edit menu, choose Rebeam > Rebeam to Lyrics. The Rebeam to Lyrics dialog box appears as shown in Figure 10.13.

Figure 10.13
Specify a lyric to rebeam to in
the Rebeam to Lyrics dialog
box

Here, after Break Beams at Each Syllable In, click the drop-down menu and specify the type of lyric you want Finale to take into account while beaming to syllables. If you have only one line of lyrics, choose All Lyrics here. From the lower drop-down menu, choose a specific verse, section, or chorus to beam to. If you want Finale to break beams over melismas that carry over a beat, check Also Break Beams at Each Beat in the Time Signature. Click OK to apply lyric beaming to the selected region. See Figure 10.14 for an example of music before and after running Rebeam to Lyrics.

Figure 10.14
Beaming before and after
applying Rebeam to Lyrics

Editing Beams Individually

Finale lets you edit the appearance of individual beams in several ways. You can add or remove beams between notes with the Simple or Speedy Entry Tool, or modify the appearance of beams using several tools in the Special Tools Palette.

Use the Simple Entry Tool or Speedy Entry Tool to add or remove a beam between any two notes. To add or remove beams in Simple Entry

1. Click the Simple Entry Tool.

2. Ctrl/Option-click the second of two eighth notes (or any two notes of lesser value than a quarter note).

3. Press the / key on the QWERTY keyboard to break or join a beam from the previous note.

To add or remove beaming in Speedy Entry

1. Click the Speedy Entry Tool.

2. Move the cursor over the second of two notes of an eighth duration or smaller.

3. Press the / (or B) key to break or join a beam from the previous note.

In Simple Entry, press Alt/Option-/ to flatten an angled beam. In Speedy Entry, press the M key. To revert to the default beaming, in Simple Entry, press Shift-/. To view all Simple Entry and Speedy Entry commands, from the Simple (or Speedy) Menu, choose Simple (or Speedy) Edit Commands.

TIP

To flatten all beams in a region, use the Flat Beams plug-in. Select a region of measures with the Mass Edit Tool, then from the Plug-ins menu, choose Note, Beam and Rest Editing > Flat Beams. Choose Flat Beams (Remove) to remove flat beams in a region.

Changing the Beam Angle

You can edit the angle of any beam individually with the Beam Angle Tool.

1. Click the Special Tools Tool to display the Special Tools Palette (on Windows, click the Window menu and choose Advanced Tools Palette, then select the Special Tools Tool from the Advanced Tools Palette).

2. Click the Beam Angle Tool in the Special Tools Palette.

3. Click a measure to display a handle on the end of each beam in the measure.

4. Click the right handle to adjust the angle of the beam and the left handle to adjust the vertical placement of the beam (see Figure 10.15).

Figure 10.15

Adjusting beams with the
Beam Angle Tool

Adjust Beam Angle —

Adjust Beam Height —

Feathered Beaming

Editing beams with the Beam Angle Tool will adjust all beams in the group (eighth, sixteenth, etc.) evenly. You can also adjust the height and angle of secondary beams individually, to create feathered beaming for example (see Figure 10.16). To create feathered beaming:

1. Enter a string of consecutive 32nd notes (or notes of any duration that are connected with multiple beams).

2. Click the Special Tools Tool to display the Special Tools Palette (on Windows, click the Window menu and choose Advanced Tools Palette, then select the Special Tools Tool from the Advanced Tools Palette).

3. Click the Secondary Beam Angle Tool in the Special Tools Palette.

4. Click the measure containing the 32nd notes so there is a handle on each end of all secondary beams.

5. Drag the left handle to position the placement of the start point for each secondary beam, and drag the right handle to adjust the angle and endpoint for each secondary beam as you would with the Beam Angle Tool. Using these positioning handles, you can create feathered beaming in both directions as shown in Figure 10.16. Use the up and down arrow keys to nudge handles for fine adjustments.

6. Now, if you want to adjust the angle of all beams, click the Beam Angle Tool and adjust the left handle to change the height, and the right handle to adjust the angle of all beams in the group evenly. This way, you can slant the primary beam as well, as shown in Figure 10.17.

Figure 10.16

Feathered beaming

Figure 10.17

Feathered beaming adjusted
with the Beam Angle Tool

Extending Beams

In addition to adjusting the beam angle, you can also change the length of any beam.

1. Click the Beam Extension Tool in the Special Tools Palette.

2. Click a measure containing beamed notes. You will see a handle appear on each end of primary beams.

3. Click and drag or use the arrow keys to nudge the start or endpoint of the beam.

4. If you want to extend a secondary beam, double-click one of the handles to open the Beam Extension Selection dialog box as shown in Figure 10.18.

Figure 10.18

Select the beams you want to extend in the Beam Extension Selection dialog box

Beam Extension Selection

Extend Selected Beams

☑ 8th   ☐ 256th   OK
☐ 16th   ☐ 512th   Cancel
☐ 32nd   ☐ 1024th
☐ 64th   ☐ 2048th   Help
☐ 128th   ☐ 4096th

5. Here, check the beam type you want to extend (8th = primary beam, 16th = first secondary beam, 32nd = second secondary beam, etc.). Then click OK.

6. Drag a handle to adjust the beams you selected in the Beam Extension Selection dialog box. You might use this technique to beam over rests individually.

7. If you find yourself making many changes to your score with the Beam Extension Tool, try adjusting the default beaming settings in the Document Options (from the Options menu, choose Document Options > Beams—see Figure 10.9).

Flipping Broken Beams Across Stems

Broken beams can appear when a beamed group contains different rhythmic durations. Any broken beam can be flipped to the other side of the stem with the Broken Beam Tool. To see this, enter a dotted eighth note followed by a sixteenth note and then another eighth note in a measure. Beam the second eighth note to the previous sixteenth with the Simple Entry Tool. Your measure should look like the top example in Figure 10.19.

Figure 10.19

Flipping broken beams across stems

Click the Broken Beam Tool in the Special Tools Palette. Then, click the measure. You will see a handle appear above and below the broken beam. Click the bottom handle to flip the broken beam across the stem as shown in Figure 10.19.

Breaking Through Secondary Beams

Sometimes secondary beams are broken within beamed groups, as shown in Figure 10.20.

Figure 10.20

Breaking through
secondary beams

To break secondary beams, click the Secondary Beam Break Tool in the Special Tools Palette. Click a measure containing secondary beams. You will see a handle appear above each note. Double-click the handle on the second of two notes (you will be editing the beams to the left of the note you double-click). The Secondary Beam Break Selection dialog box appears as shown in Figure 10.21.

Figure 10.21

Specify the beams you want to
break in the Secondary Beam
Break Selection dialog box

Here, check the beams you want to break. To break all beams up to the primary beam (as shown in Figure 10.19), choose Break Though, and check all boxes in the Beam Durations section. Click OK to return to the score. All secondary beams to the left of the note disappear.

You can also specify individual beams to break. Follow the same instructions as described above, but in the Secondary Beam Break Selection dialog box, choose Break Only. Then, in the Beam Durations section, check all beams you want to break.

Beaming Over Barlines

Sometimes beams extend across barlines into the next measure as shown in Figure 10.22.

Figure 10.22

Beaming across barlines

Up until Finale 2004, beaming across barlines was an arduous task. Now, Patterson's Beam Over Barlines plug-in makes this easy. To extend a beam across a barline

1. Enter the notes on either side of the barline as you would normally.

2. Choose the Mass Edit Tool.

3. Highlight the region you want to beam over barlines. This plug-in will connect the full beamed group before and after each barline.

4. From the Plug-ins menu, choose Note, Beam, and Rest Editing > Patterson Plug-ins Lite > Beam Over Barlines.

5. Beams extend over barlines automatically. You will see hidden notes (that will not print) to the right of the barline. These are "placeholder notes" to maintain correct spacing.

> **TIP**
> The beamed notes to the right of the barline are actually a part of the previous measure. To edit these notes, select a note in the previous measure in Simple Entry and press the right arrow until the selection moves across the barline.

To remove these beams, highlight the region with the Mass Edit Tool and, from the Plug-ins menu, choose Note, Beam, and Rest Editing > Patterson Plug-ins Lite > Beam Over Barlines (Remove).

Patterson Beams Plug-In

The Patterson Beams plug-in can make adjustments to beam angles, widths, and stems automatically to produce a publisher-specific look to beaming for a region of measures or for the entire score. To use this plug-in

1. From the Options menu, choose Document Options and select Beams.

2. Check Allow Primary Beam Within a Space, uncheck Extend Beams Over Rests and set the Max Slope to 6 EVPUs.

3. Click OK to return to the score.

4. Highlight a region of the score with the Mass Edit Tool (or, if you want to apply the plug-in to the entire score, no selection in necessary).

5. From the Plug-ins menu, choose Note, Beam, and Rest Editing > Patterson Plug-Ins Lite > Patterson Beams. The Patterson Beams dialog box appears as shown in Figure 10.23.

Figure 10.23

Use the Patterson Beams plug-in to specify the appearance of beams for a region or for your entire document

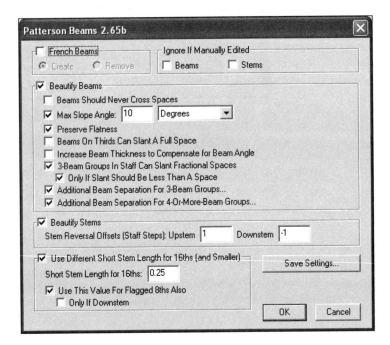

6. Here, you can choose from a variety of options for beam and stem adjustment. Robert Patterson, the third-party plug-in developer responsible for the Patterson Beams plug-in, explains each parameter in the Patterson Beams dialog box at his Web site, www.robertgpatterson.com. Also, refer to this Web site for specific settings you can use that meet professional publishing standards. Click the About Patterson Beams button for a link to this Web site.

7. After making your settings, click OK to return to the score and review your results. Note that the Patterson Beams plug-in makes static adjustments based on note position, measure width, and page layout. It is recommend that you make these adjustments when your score is nearing completion.

Editing Stems

As you enter notes, Finale determines stem direction and length based on a number of factors. The default settings are based on standard notation practice. Stems on notes below the middle staff line go up; stems on notes on or above the middle staff line go down; stems on notes above and below the staff always extend to the middle staff line. You can adjust several default stem settings in the Document Options dialog box. From the Options menu, choose Document Options > Stems. The Stem options appear as shown in Figure 10.24.

CHAPTER 10

Figure 10.24

Make document-wide settings for stems in the Stems category of Document Options

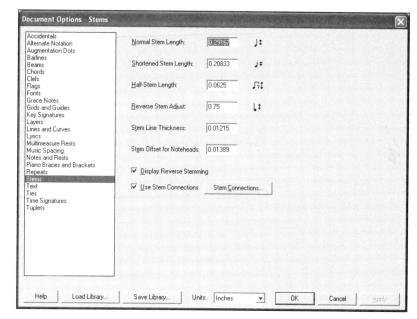

Use these options to adjust the default appearance of stems throughout your document. Change the default stem length, flipped stem length, or even modify the placement of stems relative to notes by selecting Stem Connections (more about stem connections later). In addition to the Stem Options, you can also modify the default direction of stems in measures with multiple layers in the Layer Options.

Without leaving the Document Options, click the Layers category on the left. The Layer Options appear (see Figure 10.8). In the Layer options, you can set the default stem direction for each layer. From the drop-down menu at the top, choose the layer you want to change. Check Freeze Stems and Ties, and then choose the default direction from the Freeze Stems drop-down menu. This setting also affects the default direction of ties. Click OK to apply all settings you have made in the Document Options dialog box and return to the score.

Stem Connections

You can modify Finale's default placement of stems relative to any notehead character for any document. Setting up stem connections may be necessary if you are using custom noteheads or noteheads in a third-party music font. To edit stem connections for a notehead character, use the Stem Connection Editor.

1. From the Options menu, choose Document Options > Stems. Then, click the Stem Connections button. The Stem Connections dialog box appears as shown in Figure 10.25.

Figure 10.25

All custom stem connections are visible in the Stem Connections dialog box

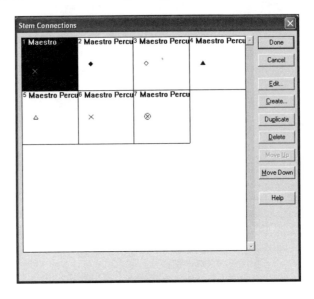

2. Here you see a list of custom noteheads that require specialized stem connections. In the upper left of each selection you will see the name of the font for each notehead character. You will not see the default noteheads here because they use default stem connection settings (and need no adjustments, though they can be edited).

3. To edit any of the existing stem connections, click one of the notehead characters and then click the Edit button. To create a stem connection for a character not available in the Stem Connections dialog box, click Create.

4. After choosing either Edit or Create, the Stem Connection Editor dialog box appears as shown in Figure 10.26.

Figure 10.26

Edit the placement of a stem for a specific notehead character in the Stem Connection Editor dialog box

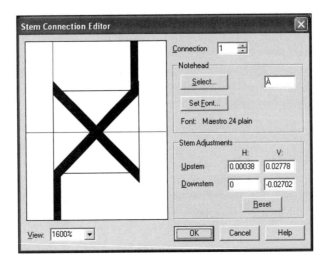

5. Here, make adjustments to the placement of the stem relative to the notehead. If you clicked Create, use the Set Font button to open the Font dialog box where you can choose the font for a notehead.

6. Click the Select button to open the Symbol Selection dialog box where you can choose a specific character. Use the following tricks to adjust the stem connection to the selected character in the Stem Connection Editor dialog box:

   ❊ Click and drag the stems to move them around manually. Hold down the Shift key to constrain dragging vertically or horizontally. Notice the values change in the Stem Adjustments section as you move the stem. You can also enter specific values for the stem connections placement offset from the default placement in the Stem Adjustments section.

   ❊ Use the View drop-down menu to adjust the view percentage to zoom in for fine adjustments, or zoom out to see the complete figure.

   ❊ Right/Option-Command-click and drag in the preview window to move the visible area.

   ❊ To change the character of the notehead, click the Select button in the Notehead section. The Symbol Selection dialog box appears where you can choose a new character.

   ❊ To change the font of the existing character, click the Set Font button in the Notehead section. The Font dialog box appears where you can choose a new font, size, and style for the notehead.

   ❊ Click Reset in the Stem Adjustments section to remove stem adjustments and return stems to the default placement.

   ❊ Use the up and down arrows for Connection (at the top) to move between notehead characters as they appear in the Stem Connections dialog box.

7. Once you have finished editing your stem connection, click OK to return to the Stem Connections dialog box.

8. Click OK to return to the Document Options, and click OK again to return to the score. Stems on notehead characters you edited will appear according to your settings in the Stem Connection Editor.

Editing Stems for a Selected Region

There are a number of ways to edit stem direction, placement, and visual definition for a selected region of your score. You can easily freeze stems up or down with the Mass Edit Tool. To do this, click the Mass Edit Tool and highlight a region of measures. From the Mass Edit menu, choose Utilities > Freeze Stems Up or Freeze Stems down.

TIP

To apply the Freeze Stem utility or any Mass Edit function to a specific layer, choose Show Active Layer Only from the Options menu. Then, select the layer you want to edit. Now, changes with the Mass Edit Tool will apply only to the visible layer.

Defining Stem Settings for Individual Staves

Starting with Finale 2003, you can edit stem placement, direction, and the visual definition for individual staves in the Staff Attributes. Click the Staff Tool and double-click a staff to open the Staff Attributes dialog box. In the Items to Display section, click the Stem Settings button to open the Staff Stem Settings dialog box (see Figure 8.22). Here are some ways to edit stems for a staff in the Staff Stem Settings dialog box:

* In the Stem Direction section, define a default stem direction for notes in the staff. Note that if there is more than one layer in a measure, the stem direction settings will revert to those specified in Document Options > Layers.

* Uncheck Show Beams to remove all beams from a staff.

* Click the Units drop-down menu to change measurement units (Inches, EVPUs, Centimeters, etc.) for values in this dialog box.

* To place stems directly above the staff or below the staff (as commonly used in TAB notation), check Use Vertical Offset for Notehead End of Stems. Then, choose Offset from Staff and enter 25 EVPUs for Up Stem and −25 EVPUs for Down Stem. Check Use Vertical Offset for Beam End of Stems (Offset from Staff) and, then, in the section beneath, set Up Stem to 115 EVPUs and Down Stem to −115 EVPUs. You can also make these settings automatically. To do so, in the Tablature Staff Attributes, check On "OK," Reset Staff's Attributes to Tablature Defaults. Then, in the Tablature Staff Attributes, under Items to Display, check Stems. See Chapter 8 for more details on TAB notation.

Once you have finished making stem settings, click OK to return to the Staff Attributes, and click OK again to return to the score. Stems throughout the staff change to reflect settings you configured in the Staff Stem Settings dialog box.

Since the Staff Stem Settings are a staff attribute, you can create a new staff style and apply stem settings to any region of your score. From the Staff menu, choose Define Staff Styles. Click New at the top and enter a name in the Available Styles text box. Click the Stem Settings button and make your custom settings. Click OK twice to return to the score. Now, highlight a region of your score, right/Control click the highlighted area, and choose the staff style you created. See Chapter 8 for more information on staff styles.

Midline Stem Direction Plug-In

Usually, the stem direction is down for notes on the middle staff line. However, if the previous note's stem is up it is common to flip this stem for a cleaner look. With this plug-in, you can tell Finale to flip the stem on notes on the middle staff line based on the stem direction of the previous and following notes (see Figure 10.27). Click the Mass Edit Tool and highlight a region of music. From the Plug-ins menu, choose Note, Beam and Rest Editing > Midline Stem Direction.

Changing the Default Midline Stem Direction

You can set the stem reversal (point in the staff where stems flip automatically) in the Staff Setup dialog box.

1. With the Staff Tool selected, double-click a staff to open the Staff Attributes.

2. Click the drop-down menu for Staff, and choose Other. The Staff Setup dialog box appears (see Figure 8.8).

Figure 10.27

Use the Midline Stem Direction
plug-in to edit the midline stem
direction based on surrounding
notes

3. In the Stem Reversal text box, enter the position, in steps, from the top staff line you want Finale to flip stems down (the default setting is −4, so notes on the middle line and above flip down by default). Enter −3 if you want all stems on the middle line to flip up automatically and all notes on the third space and above to flip down.

4. Click OK twice to return to the score with the new stem reversal applied. Apply these settings to all desired staves, or create a staff style to apply them to any selected region.

Editing Stems Individually

Finale lets you edit stems individually in many ways. You can flip stem direction for any note with the Simple or Speedy Entry Tool, or you can modify the length and appearance of stems using several tools in the Special Tools Palette.

Use the Simple Entry Tool or Speedy Entry Tool to flip stems. Click the Simple Entry Tool, and then Ctrl/Option-click a note. Press the L key to flip the stem (you may have to press it twice). To flip the stem back, simply press the L key again. To edit the stem direction in Speedy Entry, click the Speedy Entry Tool and click a measure to open the Speedy frame. Move the cursor over an entry and press the L key to flip the stem direction.

While in Simple Entry, hold down the Shift key and press L to tell Finale to use the default stem direction for the specified note. Use Ctrl-L in Speedy Entry.

You can also change the stem direction for a number of individual notes quickly with the Stem Direction Tool. Click the Special Tools Tool to display the Special Tools Palette (on Windows, click the Window menu and choose Advanced Tools Palette, then select the Special Tools Tool from the Advanced Tools Palette). Click the Stem Direction Tool in the Special Tools Palette. Now, click a measure to see a handle above and below each note in the active layer. Click the top handle to flip a stem up or the bottom handle to flip a stem down.

Changing the Stem Length and Horizontal Positioning

You can change the length and horizontal positioning of any stem with the Stem Length Tool. Click the Stem Length Tool in the Special Tools Palette, and then click a measure containing notes. You will see a handle above and below all the notes in the active layer. Now, click and drag the handle to increase or decrease the length of the stem. You can also move the stem left or right relative to the note. Use the arrow keys to nudge a selected handle to make fine adjustments. Hold down the Shift key to constrain to horizontal or vertical dragging.

Changing the Appearance and Hiding a Stem

You can change the appearance or hide a stem with the Custom Stem Tool. Click the Custom Stem Tool in the Special Tools Palette, and then click a measure to display a handle on each stem. Double-click a stem to open the Shape Selection dialog box where you can choose from a library of shapes to use for the stem. To create your own shape, or replace the stem with a blank entry to hide it, click the Create button to open the Shape Designer. Here, use the various tools to design your own stem shape. If you want to hide the stem, leave this window blank. Click OK and Select to return to the score with your new settings applied.

Editing Notes and Noteheads

There are many ways to edit notes and noteheads individually without using the basic editing functionality of the Simple or Speedy Entry Tool. Here are special ways to edit a variety of properties of individual notes using the Edit Frame dialog box and the Special Tools.

The Edit Frame Dialog Box

This is a seldom-used dialog box that allows you to view and change the raw data stored with every note. Here, you can tell Finale to remove an individual note from playback, or ignore a note during music spacing and make other changes. You will probably never need to use this dialog box, but it's good to know it exists. To get there, click the Speedy Entry Tool. Then, click outside a staff to ensure that the Speedy Frame is not active. Then Ctrl/Option-click a measure containing at least one note.

Figure 10.28

Use the Edit Frame dialog box to make fine changes to notes individually or to change their properties

The frame number (in the upper left) tells you the number of the frame you are editing. The frame number is ordered not by measure number, but the order in which the frame/measure was added. The First Entry and Last Entry numbers indicate the range of notes that exist in the measure. Like frames, entries are numbered sequentially (in the order they were added). The Current Entry number is the entry you are currently editing. Use the options in the upper section to edit the entry. If the entry contains more than one note (a chord), you can specify settings for individual notes in the chord by editing the lower section.

 NOTE
The Edit Frame dialog box will display notes in the current active layer only.

Here are some ways to edit notes using the Edit Frame dialog box:

✽ Uncheck Playback to remove a note or entry from playback. Do this when you are using notes in another layer (hidden with a staff style, for example) for playback of trills, tremolos, or other figures.

✽ If you want to hide a note but still want to play it back, check both Ignore and Playback (pressing the O or H key in Simple or Speedy Entry both hides and mutes the entry).

✽ If you want an entry to be ignored while Finale reconfigures the music spacing, uncheck Spacing.

✽ If you have entered a tuplet in voice two overlapped by a tuplet in voice one, you will notice unwanted spacing in voice one. To correct spacing in this specific situation, check V2 Tup Para.

Editing Noteheads and Note Positioning with the Special Tools

There are three Special Tools devoted to editing notes individually. You can use the Note Position Tool to reposition a note horizontally, the Notehead Position Tool to position a notehead, or the Note Shape Tool to change the character of a notehead individually.

To Reposition Notes Horizontally

1. Click the Special Tools Tool.

2. From the Special Tools Palette, choose the Note Position Tool.

3. Specify the layer containing the notes you want to reposition (choose the layer as you would normally).

4. Click the measure containing the notes. Handles appear above the staff for each note in the measure.

5. Click and drag (or use the arrow keys to nudge) a handle to reposition its corresponding note horizontally.

NOTE
You can also reposition individual notes horizontally by dragging them in the Speedy Frame.

To Reposition Noteheads Horizontally

1. Click the Special Tools Tool.
2. From the Special Tools Palette, choose the Notehead Position Tool.
3. Specify the layer containing the notes you want to reposition (choose the layer as you would normally).
4. Click the measure containing the notes. Handles appear by each notehead in the measure (in the active layer).
5. Click and drag (or use the arrow keys to nudge) a handle to reposition the noteheads horizontally.

To Change Notehead Characters Individually or Remove a Notehead

1. Click the Special Tools Tool.
2. From the Special Tools Palette, choose the Note Shape Tool.
3. Specify the layer containing the notes you want to reposition (choose the layer as you would normally).
4. Click the measure containing the notes. Handles appear by each notehead in the measure (in the active layer).
5. Double-click a handle to open the Symbol Selection window where you can choose from the characters available in the current music font.
6. Double-click a character to use it for the selected note. If you want to remove the notehead, choose the blank character (# 32 in the Maestro font).

After choosing the new notehead, you may need to move it so it appears correctly next to the stem. To define a stem connection for any notehead character, use the Stem Connections dialog box (from the Options menu, choose Document Options and select Stems, and then click Stem Connections—see "Stem Connections" above for details).

Editing Accidentals

I have already described how to enter accidentals with the Simple and Speedy Entry Tool. You can make a variety of changes to the positioning and appearance of accidentals for your entire document or for individual entries. You can change the default character or positioning for accidentals throughout your document in the Document Options dialog box. From the Options menu, choose Document Options and select Accidentals. The Accidentals options appear as shown in Figure 10.29.

Figure 10.29

Make document-wide settings
for accidentals in the
Accidentals category of
Document Options

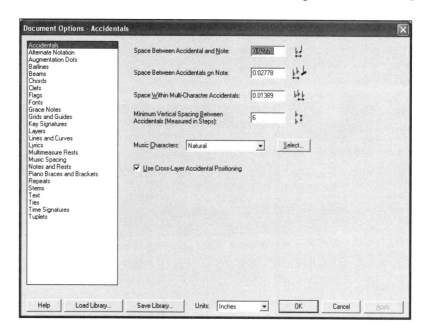

Use these options to adjust the positioning and character of accidentals throughout your document.

❋ Enter new values in the four available text boxes for positioning of accidentals relative to notes and to each other. Click the drop-down menu for Units to change the unit of measurement.

❋ Here, you can change the character of any accidental. Click the Music Characters drop-down menu and select the character you want to change. Then, click the Select button to the right to open the Symbol Selection dialog box where you can choose a new character for the accidental. Click Select to return to the Document Options.

If you would like to select a different font for your accidentals, click the Fonts category in the Document Options dialog box to display the font options. Click the drop-down menu for Notation and choose Accidentals. Then, click the Set Font button to the right to open the Font dialog box where you can choose a new font, size, and style for your accidentals.

Changing the Default Enharmonic Spelling

You can adjust the default spelling for pitches in the score that lie outside the key by using settings under the Options menu. These settings generally apply to music entered with a MIDI keyboard. If you want Finale to tend to use sharps while representing pitches in your score, from the Options menu, choose Favor Sharps. Choose Favor Flats if you want Finale to tend to use flats to represent pitches. Choose Use Spelling Tables to tell Finale to use a custom definition for enharmonic spelling as specified in the spelling tables.

Editing the Major and Minor Key Spelling Table

Use this table to define the automatic spelling of non-diatonic pitches in major and minor keys. From the Options menu, choose Enharmonic Spelling > Edit Major and Minor Key Spellings. The Edit Major and Minor Key Spellings dialog box appears as shown in Figure 10.30.

Figure 10.30

Edit the spelling of non-diatonic pitches in the Edit Major and Minor Key Spellings dialog box

In this dialog box, choose whether to use a raised or lowered note to represent pitches between whole steps in a major or minor diatonic scale. In the key of C, for example, step 1 = C, step 2 = D, step 3 = E, etc. For example, in the key of C, to display the D flats instead of C sharps, choose b2 under the 1 column. Finale will use the settings you specify in the Major or Minor spelling table, depending on the mode (major or minor) of the key specified in the Key Signature dialog box.

If you are using a nonstandard key that is modal or chromatic, you may want to assign a spelling for each pitch in the chromatic scale. To do this, from the Options menu, choose Enharmonic Spelling > Edit Modal or Chromatic Key Spellings. The Edit Modal or Chromatic Spellings dialog box appears as shown in Figure 10.31.

Figure 10.31

Edit the spelling of non-diatonic pitches for modal or chromatic key signatures in the Edit Modal or Chromatic Spellings dialog box

Here, choose the enharmonic spelling for each pitch of the chromatic scale. Click OK to return to the score. Notes entered with a MIDI keyboard will reflect the settings you specified in the spelling tables (be sure Use Spelling Tables is checked in the Enharmonic Spelling submenu of the Options menu if you want to use them).

Checking Accidentals

Occasionally, there may be an accidental visible at the conclusion of a tie that should be hidden. To check for and remove extraneous accidentals, run the Check Accidentals utility. Click the Mass Edit Tool and select a region of the score (Ctrl/Command-A to Select All). From the Mass Edit menu, choose Utilities > Check Accidentals. Extra accidentals in the selected region are removed.

Positioning Accidentals Individually

You can manipulate the positioning of each accidental in your score individually with the Special Tools. Click the Special Tools Tool to display the Special Tools Palette (on Windows, click the Window menu and choose Advanced Tools Palette > Special Tools Tool). Click the Accidental Mover Tool in the Special Tools Palette. Now, click a measure containing notes with accidentals. You will see a handle on each accidental. Click and drag, or use the arrow keys to nudge accidentals horizontally.

If you are creating early music notation that requires Musica Ficta markings, click the Accidental Positioning Tool, right/Control-click an accidental handle, and choose Edit. Set the size of the accidental (usually 75%) and place a checkmark on "Allow Vertical Positioning." Click OK and return to the score. Click this accidental's handle and drag it up above the notehead.

> **TIP**
> Use the Canonic Utilities plug-in (under the Plug-ins menu) to show accidentals on all notes. A handy
> tool for atonal music.

Editing Augmentation Dots and Ties

Like beams and stems, augmentation dots and ties can be positioned for an entire document or individually. To edit the default positioning and visual definition of augmentation dots, from the Options menu, choose Document Options and select Augmentation Dots. The Augmentation Dot options appear as shown in Figure 10.32.

Use these options to adjust the positioning and character of augmentation dots throughout your document.

* Enter new values in the four available text boxes for positioning of augmentation dots relative to notes and to each other. Click the drop-down menu for Units to change the unit of measurement.

* To change the character of augmentation dots, click the Select button to open the Symbol Selection dialog box where you can choose a new character for your augmentation dots.

If you would like to select an augmentation dot character in a different font, click the Fonts category in the Document Options dialog box to display the font options. Click the drop-down menu for Notation and choose Augmentation Dot. Then, click the Set Font button to the right to open the Font dialog box where you can choose a new font, size, and style for your augmentation dots.

To edit the default positioning and visual definition of ties, from the Options menu, choose Document Options and select Ties. The Tie options appear as shown in Figure 10.33.

Figure 10.32

Make document-wide settings for augmentation dots in the Augmentation Dots category of Document Options

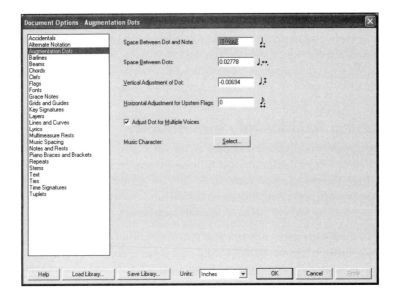

Figure 10.33

Make document-wide settings for ties in the Ties category of Document Options

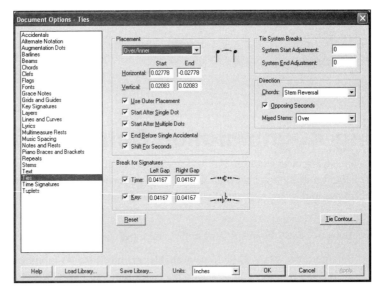

Use these options to define the default visual definition of ties:

❋ In the Placement section, click the drop-down menu and choose the type of tie you want to edit (depending on note placement). Look to the preview display on the right to see the selected tie style.

❋ Use the Horizontal and Vertical text boxes to enter a start and stop point for ties of the selected style. Click the drop-down menu for Units to change the unit of measurement.

❋ In the Break for Signatures section, specify the treatment of ties over meter and key changes. Use the text boxes to indicate the amount of space before and after the tie break.

❋ Click the Reset button to revert all settings in this box back to the defaults.

❋ Click the Tie Contour button to open the Tie Contour dialog box where you can specify the precise shape of ties throughout your document.

Editing Dots

You can edit augmentation dots individually with the Dot Tool. Click the Special Tools Tool to display the Special Tools Palette (on Windows, click the Window menu and choose Advanced Tools Palette > Special Tools Tool). Click the Dot Tool in the Special Tools Palette. Then, click a measure containing notes with dots. A handle appears next to each dot in the measure. Click a handle and drag, or use the arrow keys to nudge augmentation dots. Hold down the Shift key to constrain dragging vertically or horizontally. Use the Zoom Tool to zoom in on the measure for precision editing.

Adding and Editing Ties

Use the Simple Entry Tool or Speedy Entry Tool to add or remove a tie between any two notes of the same pitch. To add or remove ties in Simple Entry, click the Simple Entry Tool, and then Ctrl/Option-click a note to select it. Press the T key to extend a tie to the next note or remove an existing tie or use the / key on the num pad. Hold down the Shift key and press T or Ctrl-/ to extend or remove a tie to the previous note. Finale will automatically remove extra accidentals. To add or remove a tie in Speedy Entry, click the Speedy Entry Tool and click a measure to invoke the Speedy Frame. Then, move the cursor over a note and press the T key or the = key to extend a tie to the next note or remove an existing tie. Hold down the Shift key and press T or use Ctrl-= to extend or remove a tie to the previous note.

You can edit the shape of ties individually with the Tie Tool. Click the Tie Tool in the Special Tools Palette. Then, click a measure containing notes with ties. Three handles appear on each tie in the measure. Click a handle and drag, or use the arrow keys to nudge these handles to adjust the start point, end point, and contour (see Figure 10.34). Hold down the Shift key to constrain dragging vertically or horizontally.

Figure 10.34

Use the handles to edit ties with the Tie Tool

To ensure that all ties in your document will play back correctly and appear over system breaks, run the Check Ties Utility. Choose the Mass Edit Tool and press Ctrl/Command-A to Select All. From the Mass Edit Menu, choose Utilities > Check Ties.

TIP
Use the Patterson Move Ties plug-in to regionally edit the shape of ties. This is a powerful tool to mix tie appearance between Use Outer Placement and Avoid Staff Lines. Many publishers allow context to dictate the appearance of ties, and this plug-in makes the task quick and easy.

11

MEASURE NUMBERS, GRAPHICS, PART EXTRACTION, AND PRINTING

Chapter 10 covered a variety of ways to position and fine-tune elements of a score in the later stages of a project. Now, this chapter will focus on techniques for finalizing the score for printing. You will learn how to edit measure numbers and define measure number regions, add graphics, finalize system/page layout, extract parts from a multiple-staff score, and print the score and parts. You will find that a number of techniques discussed in Chapter 10, such as alignment and positioning, come into play throughout the final stages of score development. Some of the following topics expand on concepts introduced in earlier chapters, such as page layout and printing.

Here's a summary of what you will learn in this chapter:

* How to edit measure numbers
* How to work with graphics
* How to extract parts
* Techniques for printing

Measure Numbers

Measure numbers are an important element to any score. They can be added and manipulated with the Measure Tool. By default, Finale places a measure number at the beginning of each system, though you can edit their frequency, positioning, and appearance individually or for any region of your score. You can begin numbering at any measure, or even create several measure number regions to number multiple movements within the same file independently.

To prepare for this section, open a new Default Document. From the File menu, choose New > Default Document. You will see a measure number at the beginning of each system.

TIP

To add rehearsal letters, use expressions. See Chapter 3 for information on creating expressions.

Editing Measure Numbers in the Score

You can make a number of adjustments to measure numbers individually in the score. Click the Measure Tool to display handles on all measure numbers. Use the following techniques to make basic changes to measure numbers:

* Click and drag to adjust the positioning of a measure number manually. Hold down the Shift key to constrain to horizontal and vertical dragging.

* Select a measure number handle and press Backspace/Clear to return a measure number to its original placement.

* Select a measure number handle and press Delete to remove a measure number.

* Right/Command-click a measure number handle to open the Measure Number context menu where you can restore the default position, delete the measure number, or edit its enclosure.

* Double-click a measure number handle to edit its enclosure or add an enclosure.

When you double-click a measure number, the Enclosure Designer dialog box appears as shown in Figure 11.1.

Figure 11.1

Create or edit a measure number enclosure in the Enclosure Designer dialog box

In the Enclosure Designer dialog box, click the Shape drop-down menu to choose an enclosure shape. Check Opaque to tell Finale to hide any item behind the enclosure in the score. Click and drag the handles in the preview window to resize or move the enclosure. Click OK to return to the score. The enclosure now surrounds the measure number you selected.

You can also use the Measure menu to edit and manage measure numbers in the score.

* Select one or more measure number handles, and choose Measure > Measure Numbers > Add Enclosures to open the Enclosure Designer where you can define an enclosure for all selected measure numbers.

❋ To show measure numbers for every measure in a selected region of your score, highlight the region of measures and choose Measure > Measure Numbers > Show Numbers. Measure numbers appear above all selected measures.

❋ Select one or more measure number handles, and choose Measure > Measure Numbers > Hide Numbers to clear the selected measure numbers.

❋ Select one or more measure number handles, and choose Measure > Measure Numbers > Restore Defaults to revert back to default settings for measure numbers as specified in the Measure Number dialog box (explained below).

Creating and Editing Measure Number Regions

The default settings for measure numbers are stored in the Measure Number dialog box. From the Measure menu, choose Measure Numbers > Edit Regions. The Measure Number dialog box appears as shown in Figure 11.2.

Figure 11.2

Edit the frequency, font, size, style, and positioning, and create measure number regions in the Measure Number dialog box

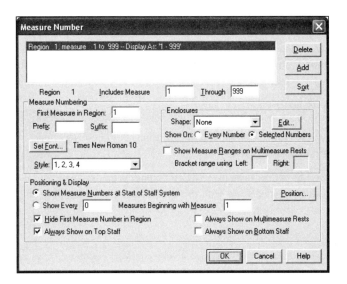

In this dialog box, make global changes to the appearance and positioning of measure numbers. All measure numbers in your score are organized by measure region. Notice the existing default entry at the top of this box, "Region 1, measure 1 to 999—Display As: '1-999'." This entry tells Finale to number measures 1-999 as 1-999.

The pre-defined measure number region includes 999 measures beginning with the first measure of your document. This means each measure in the score is numbered consecutively for up to 999 measures. If each measure of your score consists of a valid musical measure, without interruption, the default measure number region will serve your purposes fine (for the first 999 measures). However, the actual measures in your score may not always serve the purpose of a "real" measure. Your numbering may need to skip a hidden measure used as a placeholder, or begin from measure one within the document for a second movement, for example. Resolve any such measure numbering problems by creating a new measure number region.

For the following example, let's say measure 11 is hidden with the "hide staff" staff style and should not be included in the measure numbering. "Real" measures are those as they exist in the Finale document and "defined" measures are those you assign deliberately.

1. Click the Measure Tool.

2. From the Measure Menu, choose Measure Numbers > Edit Regions. The Measure Number dialog box appears (see Figure 11.2).

3. Define the measures for the existing (first) region, in this case 1–10. Just below the region display window, for Includes Measures, enter the first and last "real" measure, "1" in the first box and "10" in the second.

4. In the Measure Numbering section, for First Number in Region, enter "1," since the first region begins at the first measure of the document..

5. For this demonstration, in the positioning and Display section, choose (and enter) Show Every "1" Measures Beginning with Measure "1."

6. Click the Add button. A new region appears in the region display window. It is selected by default.

7. Now, define the measures for the new region, in this case 12–999 (the second region will extend to the end of the score). Just below the region display window, for Includes Measures, enter the first and last "real" measure of the second region. We want to skip measure 11, so enter "12" in the first box and "999" in the second.

8. In the Measure Numbering section, for First Number in Region, enter "11."

9. Click OK. Notice that all measures are numbered consecutively, with an extra measure between numbers 10 and 11.

Use the above method to define as many measure number regions as you like. You can also easily assign measure number regions in your score with the Easy Measure Numbers plug-in (described below).

TIP
To tell Finale to display actual measure numbers instead of defined measure numbers (beginning from the first "real" measure), from the Options menu, choose Program Options, and select View. Choose Display Actual Measure Numbers and click OK. Now, from the View menu, choose Scroll View. The measure indicator at the bottom left of the screen now displays the "real" measure number.

Edit each measure region independently in the Measure Number dialog box. Simply click the desired region in the region display window, and then apply settings for the region using the available options. You can edit each region without leaving the Measure Number dialog box. Here are some common ways to edit measure numbers for a region:

❋ To set the font, size, and style for measure numbers in a region, click the Set Font button in the Measure Numbering section. The Font dialog box appears where you can choose the font, size, and style.

❋ If you would like to use a numbering convention other than standard measure numbers, such as letters, click the Style drop-down menu to choose a different format for your measure numbering.

❋ To show measure numbers only at the beginning of each system, in the Positioning and Display section, choose Show Measure Numbers at Start of Staff System.

❋ Check Always Show on Top Staff or check Always Show on Bottom Staff to show measure numbers on the top or bottom staff, regardless of measure number settings in the Staff Attributes. These settings can be particularly useful if you plan to optimize the score or extract parts.

❋ To display measure number ranges for multimeasure rests, check Show Measure Ranges on Mulitmeasure Rests. In the Left and Right text boxes, enter the character to use (brackets, parentheses, etc.) to enclose the number ranges (see Figure 11.3). Assigning measure regions for multimeasure rests will apply to multimeasure rests both in the existing score and in any extracted parts.

Figure 11.3

Measure regions on multimeasure rests

❋ To position measure numbers for a measure region, click the Position button in the Display and Positioning section. The Position Measure Number dialog box appears as shown in Figure 11.4. Click and drag the measure number in the preview window to specify the measure positioning, or enter specific values in the H: and V: text boxes.

Figure 11.4

Use the Position Measure Number dialog box to position measure numbers for a measure number region

Easy Measure Numbers Plug-In

In addition to assigning measure regions in the Measure Number dialog box, you can also use the Easy Measure Numbers plug-in. Use this plug-in to apply regions to selected measures in the score. To prepare for the following instructions, delete existing measure number regions in your scratch document. With the Measure Tool selected, click the Measure menu and choose Measure Numbers > Edit Regions to open the

Measure Number dialog box. Now, click the Delete button several times until all regions have been removed. Click OK to return to the score. Now, you'll use the Easy Measure Numbers plug-in to create two measure number regions in your score.

1. Click the Mass Edit Tool.

2. Highlight measures one through ten.

3. From the Plug-ins menu, choose Measures > Easy Measure Numbers. The Easy Measure Numbers dialog box appears as shown in Figure 11.5.

Figure 11.5

Use the Easy Measure Numbers dialog box to easily assign measure number regions

4. Type the first measure number in the selected region, in this case "1."

5. Click OK. Measures one through ten are now defined as a measure number region. Now, let's say you want to skip a measure before you resume numbering.

6. Click the twelfth measure so it is highlighted.

7. Hold down the Shift key and press the right arrow key to select all remaining measures.

8. From the Plug-ins menu, choose Measure Numbers > Easy Measure Numbers. The Easy Measure Numbers dialog box appears.

9. Type "11" and click OK. Now, the remaining measures are numbered in a second measure number region.

To view or edit measure number regions created with the Easy Measure Numbers plug-in, open in the Measure Number dialog box. Click the Measure Tool, and choose Measure > Measure Numbers > Edit Regions. Notice the regions you defined using the plug-in appear in the measure region display window.

Show or Hide Measure Numbers on a Staff

You can show or hide measure numbers for a specific staff in the Staff Attributes. Click the Staff Tool and double-click a staff to open the Staff Attributes dialog box. In the Items to Display section, uncheck Measure Numbers. Click OK to return to the score.

NOTE

Settings in the Measure Number dialog box override the Display Measure Number setting you assign in the Staff Attributes. If editing the Staff Attributes does not change the appearance of measure numbers on the staff, edit the corresponding measure region in the Measure Number dialog box. From the Measure menu, choose Measure Numbers > Edit Regions. Uncheck the "Always Show" check boxes under Positioning and Display.

Clear Measure Number Positioning

You can clear manual measure number positioning for any selected region of your score with the Clear Measure Number Positioning plug-in. Click the Mass Edit Tool and highlight a region of your score. From the Plug-ins menu, choose Measures > Clear Measure # Positioning. Measure numbers in the selected region return to their default placement.

Number Repeated Measures

If you have several consecutive measures that are identical, you may want to number them (independently from the measure numbering) to aid the performer. To do this, click the Mass Edit Tool and highlight a region of identical measures. From the Plug-ins menu, choose Measures > Number Repeated Measures. The repeated measures are now numbered consecutively. They are entered as measure expressions, so you can edit or delete them with the Expression Tool.

Working with Graphics

Graphics are commonly used in Finale documents for figures in your score outside of music notation, such as a logo. You'll want to use a separate graphics program to prepare an image to place into a Finale document. You also may need to save a page or excerpt of music from a Finale document as a graphic to import into a file in another program. On Windows, Finale can open or save graphics in TIF or EPS format. On Macintosh, Finale can open or save graphics in TIFF, EPS, or PICT format. Use the Graphics Tool to import or export a graphic.

To prepare for this section, open a new Default Document (File > New > Default Document). Then, click the Graphics Tool. On Windows, first choose Advanced Tools Palette from the Window menu, and then click the Graphics Tool.

NOTE

Due to OS limitations, Finale does not support EPS export in Windows 2000/XP. As a workaround, if you own Acrobat Distiller, you can print to a PDF, and then open the file in a graphics editor that supports EPS export, such as Adobe Illustrator, to convert the file to an EPS image. On Mac, EPS was not supported in the original release of Finale 2004. (If you have Finale 2004 for Mac, update to 2004C to export EPS graphics. Finale 2005 for Mac does support EPS export.)

Exporting a Graphic

You can export a portion of a page or an entire page from Finale as a graphic file. To export a graphic, you will always need to be in Page View (View > Page View). To export a rectangular section of a page, with the Graphics Tool selected, double-click and drag to enclose the desired region. When you release the mouse button, a dashed rectangle should remain. Then, from the Graphics menu, choose Export Selection. To export an entire page, or several pages, first move to Page View (View menu > Page View). Then, click the Graphics menu and choose Export Pages. After choosing Export Selection or Export Pages from the Graphics menu, the Export Pages/Selection dialog box appears as shown in Figure 11.6.

Figure 11.6
Choose properties for an
exported graphic in the
Export Pages/Export Selection
dialog box

From the Type drop-down menu, choose the format of the graphic you want to export. Here is a brief description of each of the available graphics formats:

✳ The TIFF (Tagged-Image File Format) format is very versatile. TIFF files can be exchanged between just about any program that supports graphics. They can also be transferred from Macintosh to Windows and vise versa. Placed TIFF files will appear in a Finale document, and print as they display on screen.

✳ Graphics in EPS (Encapsulated PostScript) format will generally produce cleaner results than graphics in TIFF format. If you need professional looking graphics in the printout, EPS is the way to go. However, you will need a PostScript printer to print or create any EPS graphic. EPS files placed into a Finale document will not display on-screen, only in the printout (though you may see a crude TIFF preview of the graphic on screen).

✳ The PICT file format (available only on Mac)is generally used to transfer between Macintosh applications. Like TIFF files, graphics in PICT format print as they appear on-screen.

After you have chosen the file type, specify the pages you want to export. If you are exporting the entire document, each page will be saved as a separate graphic file. Choose Generate Names From to tell Finale to name each graphic with the file name of the Finale document followed by a number (increasing by one for each successive page). If you are exporting a single page, choose Prompt for Each Name if you wish to name the file yourself.

If you are exporting an EPS graphic, choose Include TIFF Preview if you want a preview of the graphic to display on-screen before printing. Choose Embed Fonts if you plan to move the file to a computer that does not have fonts used in the graphic. If you are exporting a TIFF or PICT file, click the drop-down menu for Resolution to choose a resolution for the graphic. 72 dpi is screen resolution; choose a higher resolution to export a sharper graphic file. Most inkjet printers print at 600 dpi or higher.

Click OK. Finale generates the graphics, or, if Prompt for Each Name is selected, the Open window appears. Choose a name and location for the file and click OK to save the graphic.

Importing a Graphic

On Windows, you can place TIFF, WMF, and EPS graphics into a Finale document. On Macintosh, you can place TIFF, PICT, or EPS graphics into a Finale document. To import a graphic, with the Graphics Tool selected, double-click in the score. The Place Graphic/Open File window appears. On Windows, click the drop-down menu for Files of Type and choose the format of the file you want to import. Navigate to the file and double-click to open it. You return to the score with the graphic placed in the document.

Editing Placed Graphics

You can edit a graphic in the score in many ways. Double-click a graphic's handle to activate six black editing handles around the graphic. Click and drag the graphic (not on the handles) to reposition it manually on the page. To stretch the graphic, click and drag one of the editing handles. Double-click the graphic again to open the Graphic Attributes dialog box (see Figure 11.7) where you can make specific settings for positioning and appearance.

Figure 11.7

Position and scale graphics in the Graphic Attributes dialog box

Here are some common ways to edit graphics in the Graphic Attributes dialog box:

❋ In the Attach To section, choose Page to place the graphic at a set location on the page. Changes to system and page margins will have no effect on the placement of the graphic. It will remain static relative to the page edge or page margin (depending on the setting in the Alignment and Positioning section). With this option selected, all items in the Alignment and Positioning section become active. Indicate specific horizontal and vertical placement for your graphic in this section.

❋ In the Attach To section, choose Measure to attach the graphic to a specific measure. Do this if you want the graphic to always reposition with a measure respectively. Specify the measure and staff in the text boxes to the right of this option.

❋ Scale the graphic by changing the percentage in the Scale Section. 100% always equals the original size of the graphic. Check Fixed Percent if you want the graphic to remain the same size regardless of page resizing with the Resize Tool.

After you have finished editing the graphic, click OK to return to the score and review your changes.

Graphics are not embedded in Finale documents. Instead, Finale references graphics by using the path you specify when you initially place the graphic or the folder of the Finale file. This means that if you move the Finale file or graphic to a different folder, the association will be lost and the graphic will not appear in the document (just the file name of the missing graphic). Use the Check Graphics menu item in the Graphics menu to see where Finale is expecting to find the graphics (See Figure 11.8).

Figure 11.8
Use the Check Graphics dialog box to view or change the path for referenced graphics

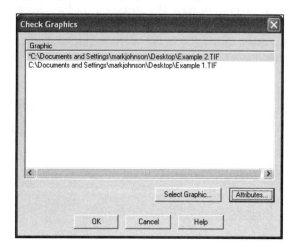

Missing graphics are marked with an * (asterisk). If you know where the graphic has been moved, or want to choose a new graphic, click Select Graphic to specify a new path.

TIP
To avoid missing graphics, store each graphic file in the same folder as its host Finale file. Then, if you ever move the Finale document, be sure to also move the associated graphic with the Finale file. Finale will always find a graphic if it exists in the same folder as the Finale document.

Entering a Graphic as an Expression

In addition to placing graphics directly into the score, you can store and enter graphics as expressions. You might want to do this if you would like to enter the same graphic at various locations in the score. To do this

1. Click the Expression Tool.
2. Double-click the score to open the Expression Selection dialog box.
3. Choose the Shape radio button in the lower-right corner of the Expression Selection dialog box.
4. Click the Create button. Then, click Select and Create to open the Shape Designer.
5. In the Shape Designer, click the Graphics Tool (it looks just like the Graphics Tool in the Main/Advanced Tool Palette).
6. Double-click in the Shape Designer window. The Place Graphic/Open File window appears.
7. Navigate to the file you want to import and double-click it. The graphic appears in the Shape Designer window.

8. Use the other editing tools in the Shape Designer to make any further graphical edits to the image (if needed). For example, use the Selection Tool to move or scale the graphic.

9. Click OK, Select, OK to return to the Expression Selection dialog box. Notice the graphic now exists among the available options.

10. Click Select to open the Note/Measure Expression Assignment dialog box.

11. Edit the expression assignment as you would with any expression (see Chapter 3 for details).

12. Click OK to return to the score. The graphic now appears where you originally clicked and is attached to the designated measure/note as an expression.

Now, any time you want to use the graphic in the document, double-click a measure with the Expression Tool, choose Shape, and select the expression you created. If you would like to be able to edit the graphic independently in the score, click Duplicate in the Expression Selection dialog box to create a duplicate of the graphic expression (or simply use a metatool to enter the shape expression, which creates a duplicate automatically). You can treat this expression just as you would any other shape expression.

Page Layout

Chapter 2 covered the basics for editing the page layout. You learned how to edit system margins, the distance between systems, and page margins. These basic layout concepts are important throughout the score production process and can be quite adequate for smaller projects. However, there are several other options that can save you time while preparing the layout of a score. By devoting a little extra time for page layout after completing the entry process, you can produce a consistent, professional-looking score.

TIP

If you're worried about mangling the layout of your score beyond repair, save a backup copy of the Finale document. In fact, you may want to save a separate version of your score specifically for the purpose of experimentation, especially if you are less familiar with this aspect of the program.

Editing the Overall Page Format for Your Score or Extracted Parts

To decrease the amount of manual editing necessary in a score, you may want to define the overall page format, and then go back and make additional page layout changes. You may also want to redefine the format of a document before entering any music if you know how the overall page format should look outright. To define the overall format for a score (system margins, page margins, and spacing), use the Page Format for Score dialog box. From the Options menu, choose Page Format > Score to open the Page Format for Score dialog box.

The exact same options are available for predefining the layout of parts extracted from the full score. From the Options menu, choose Page Format > Parts to open the Page Format for Parts dialog box where you can edit the format of extracted parts before extraction (I'll cover part extraction soon). The Page Format for Score and Page Format for Parts dialog boxes appear as shown in Figure 11.9 (these two dialog boxes are identical in structure).

Figure 11.9

Use the Page Format for Score or Parts dialog box to reformat the layout for your score or future extracted parts

To establish consistent spacing, system margins, and page margins, redefine the layout for the score or parts in the Page Format for Score or Parts dialog box.

> **TIP**
>
> If you intend to redefine the format for your score (using one of the Redefine Pages options under the Page Layout menu), note that all optimization and other adjustments made with the Page Layout Tool will be lost. Apply optimization after updating the page format, and then make any final manual adjustments with the Page Layout Tool to completely rework the layout.

❋ Select the measurement unit you would like to use from the drop-down menu in the lower-right corner of this dialog box. See Table 1.1 for equivalent values for each measurement unit.

❋ At the top, in the Page Size section, choose the page size of the Finale document (any new page that is generated gets its dimensions here). Click the drop-down menu for a list of available choices. After setting up the page size, you will then need to select the actual size of the printed page in the Page Setup dialog box (File > Page Setup). If you want to print one "Finale" page on one "physical" page, enter the same page size in both the Page Format for Score (or Page Size) and Page Setup dialog boxes.

❋ For System Scaling, you can reduce or enlarge all systems in the document and their contents. Note that the values for Staff Height and Scale System are cumulative, so adjustments to either of these parameters will affect the overall system scaling. Finale calculates this value for you and displays it to the right of Resulting System Scaling.

❋ Enter a page reduction for all items on the page in the Scale Page To text box. The page reduction can also be adjusted with the Resize Tool.

* In the Staff System Margins section, enter specific value to control the system margins for the entire document. Here, you can also set the space between each system. Usually, the first system is indented to allow more space for the full staff name. You can define the top and left margin for the first staff system in the section to the right. First check First Staff System Margins, then enter the top and left margin for the first staff system in the section below this check box.

* Under Left Page Margins, enter the space between page margins and the edge of the page. If you want to define separate page margins for odd numbered pages, check Facing Pages, and then enter the margin values in the Right Page Margins section.

Once you have finished making changes to the Page Format for Score/Parts dialog box, click OK to return to the score. If you made settings for the layout of your current score, you will need to redefine the pages for these settings to take effect. To apply these changes, click the Page Layout Tool, and then from the Page Layout menu, choose Redefine Pages > All Pages. Then click OK. Any settings you made in the Page Format for Parts dialog box will apply to parts after they have been extracted.

Optimizing Large Scores

Whether or not you have redefined your pages as described above, you will probably want to optimize your entire score before the final printout. Optimizing is the process of removing empty staves from each system, often referred to as a French Score style. You will want to do this before making further adjustments to system margins and spacing. By removing empty staves within systems, optimization will usually change the size of systems, so it's best to do this task before tweaking your final system layout. Make sure that you have completed entering all of the music before optimizing the entire score. To optimize, first click the Page Layout Tool. From the Page Layout menu, choose Optimize Staff Systems. The Staff System Optimization dialog box appears (see Figure 7.10). In the Change section, choose Whole Document, and then click OK. You return to the score with all systems optimized. Now you are ready to continue editing the layout.

You can also optimize systems in your score independently. Right/Control-click a system and choose Optimize Staff Systems to open the Staff System Optimization dialog box, where you can apply optimization to the system you clicked (or a range of systems).

NOTE
Remember to always finalize the measure layout before optimizing.

Cutaway Scores

Sometimes empty measures within systems are hidden from the score, as shown in Figure 11.10. This method of score formatting is known as a cutaway score.

Figure 11.10

Use the Hide Staff staff style to create cutaway scores

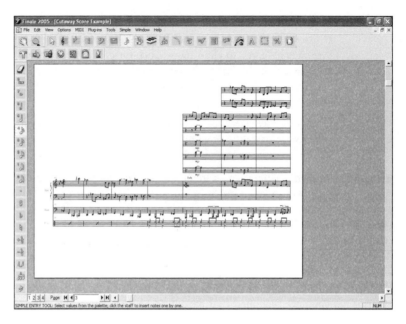

First, optimize the score to remove empty staves from systems. Then, use the Hide Staff staff style to hide any number of remaining measures from a score as needed. To do this

1. Click the Staff Tool.

2. Highlight the measure or measures you want to hide.

3. Right/Control-click the highlighted area and choose Hide Staff from the staff style context menu (or press H). The measure(s) disappear, and the staff style is marked with a horizontal blue line.

4. Repeat these steps for all occasions where a measure needs to be hidden within a staff system.

Customizing Systems and Pages

In Chapter 2 you learned how to manually adjust system margins individually. You can also adjust margins for several systems at once. The following methods are particularly useful while editing the layout for extracted parts or scores with more than one system on a page.

To quickly edit many or all system margins at once, and view results immediately, select a region of systems (to select more than one region, drag-enclose system handles or hold down the Shift key and click a handle on each desired system). Then, from the Page Layout menu, choose Edit System Margins. The Edit System Margins dialog box appears as shown in Figure 11.11.

In the Edit System Margins dialog box, check the box that corresponds to the margin or margins you want to edit (left, right, top, bottom). Then specify the new system margin value in the appropriate text box. Check Distance Between Systems, and enter a value to specify the distance between systems. In the Change section, specify a system range. (You can type 2 through 0, for example, to indicate systems 2 through the end of the score.) Click Apply to see results without leaving the dialog box. Also, pressing the Enter or Return key is the

Figure 11.11

Use the Edit System Margins
dialog box to edit margins of a
selected region of systems

same as clicking Apply. Whenever the Edit System Margins dialog box is open, you can click a system to see the values for that system. Enter new values in this box and click Apply as many times as you like before clicking Close to dismiss the dialog box.

 TIP
To select several staff systems at any time, from the Page Layout menu, choose Systems > Select Staff System Range. Also remember that you can always select the system range in the Edit System Margins dialog box.

You can also edit page margins for a selected region of pages. From the Page Layout menu, choose Page Margins > Edit Page Margins. The Edit Page Margins dialog box appears as shown in Figure 11.12.

Figure 11.12

Edit page margins for a region
of pages in the Edit Page
Margins dialog box

Check the box that corresponds to the margin or margins you want to edit (left, right, top, bottom), and then enter a value to specify the space between the page edge and page margin. Specify the margins to edit in the Change section. Click Apply to update the page. Enter new values in this box and click apply as many times as you like before clicking Close to remove the dialog box. This dialog box can be open at the same time as the Edit Page Margins dialog box if desired.

Systems Per Page

As of Finale 2003, you can specify a certain number of systems to place on each page. To do this

1. Click the Page Layout Tool.

2. From the Page Layout menu, choose Space Systems Evenly. The Space Systems Evenly dialog box appears as shown in Figure 11.13.

Figure 11.13

Specify the number of systems per page in the Space Systems Evenly dialog box

3. In the Space Systems Evenly On section, choose the page or pages you want to change.

4. In the Distribute Systems section, choose Place _ Systems on Each Page.

5. Click OK. Finale will place the number of systems you specified on the chosen pages provided there is room on the page. The systems will be spaced evenly as well. If there is not room on the page or if your music looks scrunched, try reducing the system scaling with the Resize Tool.

Page Turns

To format a part for optimal page turns automatically, use the Smart Page Turns plug-in. This plug-in adds page breaks and adjusts the measure spacing to avoid difficult page turns. From the Plug-ins menu, choose Scoring and Arranging > Smart Page Turns. Here, you can specify the timing, choose whether the rests should appear at the end or beginning of the page, and even add warnings for quick page turns (e.g., "V.S."). If you need to format parts for a large ensemble, this plug-in can save you a lot of time. Experiment with the settings in this dialog box on one part until you have found the best settings, and then use the same settings for additional parts from the same score. (Note that the best settings will vary depending on the tempo, instrument type, and other factors).

You can also set a system to always appear at the beginning of a page by assigning a page break. To assign a page break

1. Click the Page Layout Tool. All system and page margins appear in the score.

2. From the View menu, make sure Show Page Layout Icons is checked.

3. For the system you want to assign to the beginning of the page, right/Control-click the upper-left handle to display the Page Layout context menu.

4. Choose Insert Page Break. The context menu disappears and a yellow box appears to the left of the measure. Now, this system will always appear at the top of a page. Note that this system is still subject to moving between pages based on other page layout changes.

Splitting Measures across Systems

It is not uncommon to see a measure split across a system break. In other words, the first portion of a measure appears at the end of one system and the second portion at the beginning of the next, as shown in Figure 11.14.

Figure 11.14

Notice measure six extends across the system break

You could create two shorter measures by defining "invisible" meter changes with the Time Signature Tool (there's a QuickStart Video about it under the Help Menu), but this will throw off your measure numbering. To split a measure across a system break without disturbing the measure numbering, use the Measure Tool.

1. Make sure all notes have been entered in the measure you want to split. Also, for these steps, use the Mass Edit Tool to move the measure to the end of a system. You'll be moving the second half of this measure to the next system.

2. Click the Measure Tool, then double-click the measure you want to split. The Measure Attributes dialog box appears.

3. In the Options section, check Allow Horizontal Split Points.

4. Click OK to return to the score.

5. Notice there are now three handles at the right edge of the measure/system. Click the lowest handle to display a rectangle above the measure.

6. Double-click within this rectangle to specify the split point (see Figure 11.15). You will see a handle appear in the rectangle. Drag the handle to adjust the position of the split point.

Figure 11.15

Double-click within the split point rectangle to establish a split point in the measure

7. Click the Mass Edit Tool.

8. Click the measure so it is highlighted.

9. Press the down arrow to move the right portion of the measure to the next system.

Extracting Parts

After you have finalized the notation and layout, you are ready to generate parts. Finale's ability to generate parts from a score is perhaps the biggest time-saver over creating sheet music by hand. When you extract parts, you basically tell Finale to separate out each staff, or group of staves, and place them into new Finale documents. Finale will automatically include the title, composer, and staff name in each generated part, and also consolidates empty measures into multimeasure rests. You can customize the page format and music spacing for your parts before extraction to minimize the amount of editing necessary for each part.

Before part extraction, you will want to review your score to ensure that each staff contains all the markings you want to include in your extracted parts:

❊ From the Options menu, choose Display Expressions and Repeats for Parts. Review the score for any missing expressions, or expressions defined to staff lists incorrectly. Check the tempo marking and rehearsal letters to ensure that they appear on all staves (for more information on setting expressions and repeats to display on the score or parts, see Chapter 7).

❊ If you have excluded the appearance of repeat brackets or measure numbers for certain staves using the Staff Tool, you will want to turn those back on for part extraction. From the Plug-ins menu, choose Global Staff Attributes. Check Endings and Text Repeats (so there is a solid check in the check box), and then click OK to place the repeat brackets and text back into all staves.

❊ On Windows, Finale saves the extracted parts to the same location as the score file. On Mac, Finale saves the extracted parts to the Music folder designated in the Program Options dialog box. From the Options menu, choose Program Options and select the Folders category. After Music, see the path Finale will use while saving extracted parts. Click the Browse button to change the Music folder to specify a new folder for your extracted parts.

After you have made final preparations, use the following steps to extract parts from a score. To demonstrate part extraction, open any multiple-staff score, or create a new document with the Setup Wizard (File > New > Document with Setup Wizard) and add several staves.

1. From the File menu, choose Extract Parts. The Extract Parts dialog box appears as shown in Figure 11.16. In the Extract Parts dialog box, you can define the default appearance for all extracted parts. You could extract parts using all of the default settings and then edit each part individually as needed, or you can customize these parameters for more consistency (and less editing) in each extracted part.

2. Under the Staves field, select the staves you want to extract. All staves are selected by default, so if you want to extract all staves, you can leave this field as is. Ctrl/Command-click staves to deselect or select them individually. Hold down the Shift key and click to select several consecutive staves.

3. Under the Groups field, you can specify any group in your score for extraction. Select them just as you would staves. For more information on groups, see Chapter 7.

Figure 11.16

Configure the page format, music spacing, and multimeasure rest settings for extracted parts in the Extract Parts dialog box

4. In the Music Layout section, define the measure layout and music spacing. If you like, set the number of measures per system and type of music spacing here. Click the Music Spacing button to open the Music Spacing options where you can make specific adjustments to spacing in the resulting parts. See Chapter 9 for information on Music Spacing.

5. Click the Page Format button to open the Page Format dialog box where you can set the page size, system scaling, and margins (see Figure 11.9). Edit the page format for all extracted parts here (as described earlier in this chapter). To test your page format settings, try extracting a single part from the score. Go back and revise your page format settings and extract again, and overwrite the previously extracted file. Do this until the part looks good, and then use the settings you have established when you generate all the parts.

6. Click the Multimeasure Rests button to open the rests portion of the Document Options dialog box where you can make settings for rests in the extracted parts. Here, choose the number of measures to allow before creating a multimeasure rest, width between barlines of multimeasure rests, and other options. Click OK to return to the Extract Parts dialog box.

7. Click the Options button to open the Page Options dialog box as shown in Figure 11.17.

   Here, select items to remove from the extracted parts, including certain text blocks, staff names, and group names. Also, select the font, size and positioning for the part name. Finale will place the staff/instrument name in the upper-left corner of the page as it would appear on a standard part. Click OK to return to the Extract Parts dialog box.

8. In the File Names section of the Extract Parts dialog box, choose Generate Names From if you want to use one of the available naming conventions for your extracted parts. If you let Finale generate your part names, you must use at least one, preferably two, of the naming conventions. They are listed below the text box (for example, type "%f%s.MUS" to tell Finale to name each new file with the score file name followed by the staff or group name). Choose Prompt For Each Name to name each extracted part yourself during the extraction process.

Figure 11.17

Remove text from extracted
parts and position the
instrument name in the
Page Options dialog box

{ **CAUTION**
If you get the warning message, "This file already exists. Replace Existing File?", and you have chosen
Prompt For Each Name in the Extract Parts dialog box, be absolutely sure that you name each part
with a unique file name to avoid overwriting your score.

9. Check Open Extracted Part to tell Finale to open each part immediately after extraction.

10. Click OK to begin part extraction. Finale will generate new files for each chosen staff and/or group. This may take a while with larger scores.

If you get the error message, "Cannot Rename Part," there is a staff name using an illegal character (such as a slash (/), back slash (\), or comma (,). Try changing the naming convention in the Extract Parts dialog box to avoid using staff names in the file name (try "%i"—the staff or group number—instead of "%s"). Then extract again.

If you get the error message, "the generated part name is too long," go back and shorten the file name, or use a naming convention that will produce shorter file names.

If Open Extracted Part was chosen in the Extract Parts dialog box, every part will open in a new window. You can easily move to any extracted part by choosing its file name from the bottom of the Window menu. If you find yourself making many of the same layout changes to each part, it may be worth your while to go back to the score, make more adjustments to the Page Format for Parts, and extract parts again.

Editing Extracted Parts

You will usually have to manually edit some aspect of the layout of each extracted part. Use the basic page layout instructions from Chapter 2 to make manual system and page adjustments. Use layout techniques described earlier in this chapter to define the number of systems per page, page turns, and measures split across system breaks. Use the Selection Tool to move various elements (text blocks, expressions) into place.

Be sure to retain consistency between the score and extracted parts. If you make any adjustments to the music in the extracted part, return to the score and make the same changes. View the score and part at the same time while making these adjustments. With just the score and one part open, from the Window menu, choose Tile Vertically or Tile Horizontally to place the score and part side by side or one above the other.

TIP

Plug-ins can greatly reduce the amount of time you spend editing extracted parts. If your score contains multi-part staves, you can divide them into two or more parts with the TGTools Process Extracted Parts plug-in (Plug-ins > TGTools > Process Extracted Parts). This plug-in will even look for text such as "Div." and "a2" to determine the resulting parts. See Chapter 15, or the TGTools User Manual PDF, for details. If you used the Patterson Beams plug-in on the score, you probably want to run it again on each part to ensure that beam angles are consistent with your style.

Special Part Extraction

While working on the score, you can use Special Part Extraction to display a single staff in Page View for printing. To select a single part for display while working in the score:

1. In the score, move to Scroll View (View menu > Scroll View).

2. Click the Staff Tool.

3. Click the staff handle of the staff you want to display. Or, hold down the Shift key and click all staves you want to display.

4. From the Edit menu, choose Special Part Extraction. The Multimeasure Rest dialog box appears.

5. Make any desired settings for the appearance of multimeasure rests and click OK.

6. Move to Page View (View menu > Page View). The selected staff or staves become isolated on the page.

To view your full score, from the Edit menu, uncheck Special Part Extraction.

Printing Techniques

The final step to almost any project is generating the physical sheet music from your Finale document. In Chapter 2, you learned the basics for printing a document by configuring the Page Size and Page Setup dialog boxes. Here are a couple methods you can use to customize the page format, placing two-up on a single page, or printing half of a score on two pages if a printer doesn't support a large enough page size.

Printing Two-Up

You can easily place two pages of your Finale document in portrait orientation on a letter page in landscape orientation (see Figure 11.18).

CHAPTER 11

Figure 11.18
Two-up printing

To do this

1. From the File menu, choose Page Setup. The Page Setup dialog box appears.

2. Set the size to Letter (or any preferred page size) and the orientation to Landscape. On Macintosh, be sure to keep the Scale percentage at 100%.

3. Click OK.

4. From the File menu, choose Print. On Mac, click the General pop-up menu and choose Finale 2005 (or your version of Finale). The Finale print options appear.

5. Check 2-up, then choose the page range.

6. Check Ignore Printer Margins for N-up printing if you want to extend the music as close as possible to the page edges.

7. Click Print to print the document. Two documents appear side by side on the page.

TIP
To view more than one page in Finale, from the View menu, choose Show Multiple Pages.

Fitting a Score on Two Pages: Tile Pages

If your score is too large to fit on a paper size supported by your printer, you can, for example, print two 8.5 × 11 inch pages tiled so the full score appears on the two pages stacked horizontally. This way the score appears as if it were printed on tabloid size paper (11 × 17 inch). To print a score on tiled pages

1. First, set the page size to Tabloid. Click the Page Layout Tool and, from the Page Layout menu, choose Page Size. From the Page Size drop-down menu, choose Tabloid (11 × 17). Then click OK.

2. Use the Page Layout Tool to customize the layout of systems to properly fit on this page size. You may want to use the Resize Tool to resize the page, or the Staff Tool to change the distance between staves.

3. From the File menu, choose Page Setup. The Page Setup dialog box appears.

4. Set the orientation to landscape, the page size to 8.5 × 11, and click OK.

5. From the File menu, choose Print. On Mac, click the "General" popup menu and choose Finale 2005 (or your version of Finale). The Finale print options appear.

6. Check Tiled Pages.

7. If you want the pages to overlap slightly, enter the margin of overlap in the Tile Overlap text box. Specify the overlap in the unit of measurement you have selected in the Measurement Units submenu of the Options Menu. About 1/4 inch usually works well.

8. Choose the page range and print the document. Half of each system will appear on each 8.5 × 11 inch page. Stack the pages horizontally to view a full page of the score.

Batch Printing and Booklets

You can easily print in booklet format or print several documents at once (batch print) using the FinaleScript plug-in. From the Plug-ins menu, choose Miscellaneous > FinaleScript Palette. In the FinaleScript Palette, open the "Print Booklet" and "Batch Print" scripts for instructions. You can also batch print with the full version of TGTools. From the TGTools menu, choose Print Multiple Files. See the TGTools User Manual for more information. The JW Booklet plug-in can also be used to print in booklet format.

 TIP
There is a good description of how to batch print and print booklets in the Finale 2005 User Manual—see "Booklets" and "Batch Printing" in Chapter 38, "Printing."

CHAPTER 11

12

TRICKS FOR SPECIFIC PROJECTS AND COMPOSING WITH FINALE

In the last 11 chapters you have learned the fundamentals for efficiently producing a score, from starting a new document to the final printout. You have seen numerous features that save you time and give you ultimate control over the details of your notation. Still, we have only scratched the surface of Finale's capabilities. In this chapter, you will learn a variety of techniques for notation of specific instruments, such as cross staff notation for a piano score, figured bass, and other common notation types.

Some of Finale's most impressive features are particularly useful to arrangers and composers. If you plan to arrange with Finale, you will learn how to use valuable orchestration utilities. Explode a single staff of music into many, or easily compress any size score into a grand staff for a piano reduction. If you plan to compose with Finale, you can use the Composer Assistant, Auto Harmonizer, and other plug-ins to aid in the creative process.

Here's a summary of what you will learn in this chapter:

* Tricks for specific projects
* How to use Finale's Orchestration Tools
* How to use Finale's Creative Tools

Tricks for Specific Projects

It would be impossible to cover the endless number of notational styles possible in Finale. I have already discussed percussion notation (in Chapter 7) and tablature (in Chapter 8), though there are a number of other common types of music notation made easy with Finale. These include cross staff notation for piano, figured bass, chant, and notation for handbells and harp.

Cross Staff Notation and Tricks for Piano Scores

Cross staff notation is a common occurrence in piano music. It is a way of beaming notes placed across the right- and left-hand staff in a piano score, often with stems up and down on the same beam (see Figure 12.1).

Figure 12.1

Cross staff notation

Prior to Finale 2004, creating this type of notation was difficult. Now, the TGTools Cross Staff plug-in included with Finale makes this easy. To create cross staff notation

1. In a grand staff, enter all notes into one staff. For this example the notes are entered in the top staff (see Figure 12.2).

Figure 12.2

To create cross staff notation, first enter the notes into the same staff

2. Choose the Mass Edit Tool.

3. Select the region containing the notes you want to move to the other staff.

4. From the Plug-ins menu, choose TGTools, and then Cross Staff. The Cross Staff dialog box appears as shown in Figure 12.3.

5. In the Cross Staff dialog box, for Split Point, enter the lowest pitch you want to appear in the top staff (C4 = Middle C). For Pitches, choose whether you want to move the selected notes to the previous staff (above) or next staff (below).

6. Click Apply. The specified notes move across the staff. The stems and beams adjust for you automatically (see Figure 12.4).

7. Now, you can simply highlight a region of measures with the Mass Edit Tool and press Alt/Option-down arrow (or Alt/Option-up arrow) to move notes to the next or previous staff based on the settings you have already specified.

Figure 12.3

Specify the lowest note you
want to appear in the top staff
and other settings for cross
staff notes in the Cross Staff
dialog box

Cross Staff 3.00

tg Options

You can also invoke this tool using the hotkeys Alt-Up/Down, with the last used dialog settings in effect. Please note that it can only move complete entries (notes/chords) to an adjacent staff. If you would like to split chords, please use Finale's Note Mover Tool instead.

Fill empty destination measures with invisible whole rests: ☑

Remove existing cross-staff data: ☑

Single Notes : ☑   Octaves : ☑   Chords : ☑

Apply to one entry out of: 1

Start with which entry number of selection: 1

Split Point: C4

Pitches
○ All   ◉ Below   ○ Above

Cross Notes To Which Staff
○ Previous   ◉ Next

Apply   Close   TGTools...

Figure 12.4

After clicking Apply, notes
move across the staff
automatically

> **NOTE**
> After using the plug-in to create cross staff notation, notes moved to the other staff are still technically a part of their original staff. To edit them, use the Simple Entry Tool to select a note in the original staff and use the left and right arrow keys to move selection to the cross staff notes.

For complete control, you can also create cross staff notation the "old fashioned" way using the Note Mover and Special Tools (Reverse Stem Tool, Beam Angle Tool, etc.). See the Finale 2005 User Manual for details. But always try the plug-in before even thinking of using the Note Mover/Special Tools method (the plug-in almost always does the trick).

Here are some other tips that will come in handy while working with piano scores.

❋ To begin a new piano document, use the Setup Wizard (File > New > Document With Setup Wizard). Then, on page 2, choose the Keyboards category and select Piano (or another keyboard instrument). You can also easily add a grand staff to your document with the Setup Wizard. Choose the Staff Tool and then, from the Staff Menu, choose New Staves (with Setup Wizard).

CHAPTER 12

❋ To add a pedal marking to your score (as shown in Figure 12.5), use the Custom Line Tool. Click the Smart Shape Tool, then Ctrl/Option-click the Custom Line Tool in the Smart Shape Palette (the Smart Line Style Selection dialog box appears). Choose the Pedal Custom Line and click Select. Now, simply double-click and drag to add the pedal marking.

Figure 12.5

Use the Custom Line Tool to create pedal markings

❋ You can add an 8va or 8vb marking with the Smart Shape Tool as well. With the Smart Shape Tool selected, choose the 8va/8vb Tool in the Smart Shape Palette. Double-click above the staff and drag to enter an 8va. Double-click below the staff and drag to create an 8vb (notice your cursor points to the staff the Smart Shape will be attached to). These indications will also apply to playback (with or without Human Playback enabled).

❋ Use the Articulation Tool to enter fingerings. With the Articulation Tool selected, hold down the fingering number and click an entry to add it to the score (the number keys 1 through 5 are preset fingering metatools).

Figured Bass

Figured bass (or basso continuo) originated in the baroque period as a method for notating accompaniment. It is basically a system of shorthand written beneath the bass part that indicates the chord to be played above it (see Figure 12.6).

Figure 12.6

Use the Chord Tool to enter figured bass

In Finale, figured bass can be entered with the Chord Tool by using Finale's Figured Bass chord library.

1. From the File menu, choose Load Library. The Load Library window appears.

2. Navigate to the Finale/Libraries folder (if you aren't there already) and double-click the Chord Suffixes folder.

3. Double-click the library file "Figured Bass." You return to the score.

4. Click the Chord Tool.

5. From the Chord menu, choose Manual Input.

6. Click a note in the score on which you want to add a figured bass symbol. The Chord Suffix Selection dialog box appears.

7. Click Show Advanced to display the lower portion of this dialog box (if it's not visible already).

8. Click the Select button in the Numeric Definition section. The Chord Suffix Selection dialog box appears.

9. Scroll down to the bottom to find the figured bass symbol you want to use and click to select it. You return to the Chord Definition dialog box.

10. In the Show section, uncheck Root.

11. Click OK to enter the symbol into the score.

12. Use the positioning arrows to the left to position the figured bass symbols just as you would chord symbols.

Using the Chord Tool is just one way to enter figured bass in Finale. You could also use the Lyrics Tool. If you do this, use different verses to stack symbols on top of each other. Use the Edit Lyrics dialog box to choose the font to use for the figured bass characters.

TIP

There are several figured bass fonts available, most notably FinalFiguredBass by Ansgar Krause. You can find it at www.ansgarkrause.de/finalfonts.htm. Use this font as a single verse of lyrics for your figures.

Chant

There are a number of common techniques for producing chant in Finale. Generally, you will want to make some global adjustments first, like removing the time signature and barlines. To prepare a document for chant notation

1. From the File menu, choose New > Default Document. A new default document opens.

2. Choose the Mass Edit Tool, and then press Ctrl/Command-A to select all.

3. From the Mass Edit menu, choose Fit Music. The Fit Music dialog box appears.

4. For Lock Layout With _ Measure(s) per System, enter "1."

5. Click OK. There is now a single measure in every system. It is impossible to "eliminate" measures in Finale, so you can place a single measure on each system to give the appearance of a measureless document.

6. Choose the Measure Tool, and then press Ctrl/Command-A to select all.

7. From the Measure menu, choose Edit Measure Attributes. The Measure Attributes dialog box appears.

8. In the Measure Attributes, if you want to eliminate the barline at the end of each system, choose Invisible from the row of icons next to Barline. For Time Signature, choose Always Hide. In the Options section, check Position Notes Evenly Across Measure.

9. Click OK. You return to the score. Now, tell Finale to accommodate many notes in each measure/system with the Time Signature Tool.

10. Choose the Time Signature Tool and double-click the first system. The Time Signature dialog box appears.

11. After Number Of Beats, click the right arrow to select the number of beats you want to place in the first measure/system. For example, if you want 24 quarter notes in the first system, create a time signature of 24/4.

12. Click OK. You return to the score.

Now you have created what appears to be music without measures. If you intend to create chant notation in the future, save this document as a template to use later (and avoid having to repeat the previous steps). To do this, from the File menu, choose Save As (then, on Windows, for Save As Type, choose Coda Template File). Save the file to your Templates folder for use later.

Notes entered in the score will be spaced evenly across the system. You will probably want to turn off Fill with Rests under the Simple menu > Simple Entry Options and in the Speedy menu > Speedy Options.

Here are some other helpful tips to use as you enter chant notation:

❊ To remove stems from all notes in a staff, click the Staff Tool and double-click the chant staff. In the Items to Display section, uncheck Stems. Click OK. You return to the score with all stems removed from the selected staff.

❊ To position notes manually, choose the Measure Tool, and click a system containing notes. Now, click the lower handle on the right side of a staff to display the beat chart above the measure. Use the lower handle to position any note horizontally.

❊ As you enter lyrics into chant notation, you may want to enter more than one syllable under a note. To do this, use a "hard space." Type the first syllable, then type a hard space (Windows: Alt-0160 on the numeric pad; Mac: Option-Spacebar). Then type the second syllable and so on.

❊ If you want to use tick barlines for chant, without setting one measure per system, choose the Measure Tool and highlight a region of your score (or press Ctrl/Command-A to Select All). Then, double-click the highlighted area to open the Measure Attributes dialog box. In the Barline row, choose Tick and click OK.

❊ Use the Note Shapes notation style to select shapes for pitches and/or note durations. With the Staff Tool selected, double-click a staff to open the Staff Attributes. Click the drop-down menu for Notation Style and choose Note Shapes. The Note Shapes dialog box appears. Choose the shapes you want to use and click OK to return to the score. For more information on the Note Shapes notation style, see Chapter 8.

NOTE
If you are interested in creating medieval notation, such as Franconian or Gregorian notation, try Klemm Music Technology's Medieval plug-in. You can find a free demo on their Web site at www.klemm-music.de/medieval.

Mensurstriche Notation

Due to the absence of pulse in chant and other early notation, some reproductions of this music include barlines between staves rather than through them to offer a general sense of meter. This practice is known as mensurstriche notation. In Finale, mensurstriche barlines can be specified with the Staff Tool.

To create mensurstriche notation with barlines between staves

1. Begin with any document containing more than one staff.
2. Choose the Staff Tool.
3. Select any number of desired staves.
4. From the Staff menu, choose Add Group and Bracket. The Group Attributes dialog box appears.
5. Click the drop-down menu for Draw barlines and select Between Staves (mensurstriche).
6. Make any other settings you would like to apply to the group and click OK. You return to the score with barlines extending between staves, and not through them.

Handbells

If you are creating a score for handbells, use Finale's Handbells template. From the File menu, choose New > Document From Template. Double-click the Church Templates folder, and then double-click the file "Handbells" to open it. The score opens with two bells used charts in the first system (see Figure 12.7).

Figure 12.7

Use the Handbells template to begin a new score for handbells

You can choose from two available bells used charts, one with regular noteheads, and one with diamonds. To delete the extra bells used chart, click the Page Layout Tool, and then right/Control-click the system you want to remove and choose Delete System. The selected system disappears. Note that this particular template will look different if you are using a version older than Finale 2003.

CHAPTER 12

Now, you may need to remove some of the bells in the bells used chart. To edit the bells used chart

1. Click the Simple Entry Tool.

2. From the Simple menu, choose Simple Entry Options. Uncheck Fill With Rests at End of Measure, and click OK.

3. Ctrl/Option-click a note you want to remove to select it, and then press the Delete key to delete it. Leave any extra parentheses in for now.

4. Use the right and left arrow keys to select any other notes you want to remove and use the Delete key to delete them as well.

5. Once all extra notes have been removed, click the Articulation Tool.

6. Select the handles of the articulations you want to delete and press the Delete key.

7. Click the Text Tool and double-click the handle on the Octaves and Bells Used text block to edit it. Or, select the handle and press the Delete key to delete it. Also, delete the informational text block between the staves of the bell used chart.

8. To edit or delete the Optional bracket, click the Smart Shape Tool. Click the primary handle to activate the smaller editing handles which you can use to adjust the length and angle of the line. Press the Delete key to delete it.

After you have edited the bell used chart, enter the notation into the following staves normally. The measures numbering begins in the measure after the bell used chart. The Handbells template contains a number of special symbols in the Articulation Selection dialog box specifically designed for handbell notation (such as "LV," "SK," "+," and several others). Also, use available expressions in the Expression Selection dialog box for other indications ("Mallets," "vib.," etc.). In the Expression Selection dialog box, duplicate existing expressions and edit them to retain consistency when adding new expressions to the library.

Tremolos

Tremolo markings indicate a rapid succession of notes, usually on two different pitches (see Figure 12.8). The speed at which tremolos can be added drastically improved with the introduction of the Easy Tremolos plug-in in Finale 2002.

Figure 12.8
Easily create tremolos such as these with the Easy Tremolos plug-in

To create a tremolo

1. Enter the two notes so they equal the full duration of the tremolo. For example, for a half-note tremolo, enter two quarter notes (one after the other in the same layer).

2. Choose the Mass Edit Tool.

3. Highlight the measure containing the notes you would like to convert to a tremolo. If you need to select part of a measure, from the Edit menu, choose Select Partial Measures, and then highlight the desired region.

4. From the plug-ins menu, choose TGTools > Easy Tremolos. The Easy Tremolos dialog box appears as shown in Figure 12.9.

Figure 12.9

Use the Easy Tremolos dialog box to specify the visual appearance of the resulting tremolo

5. In the text box, enter the total number of beams. If you check Include Playback Notes, Finale will enter hidden notes in layer four for playback. (Note that if you do not choose to add playback notes, Human Playback will play back the tremolo using its interpretation, depending on the style chosen).

6. Click Apply. The notes in the selected region convert to tremolo markings.

Feel free to adjust settings in the Easy Tremolos dialog box and apply them to the same selected region. The figure will update accordingly.

TIP

If you add or delete notes in the same measure as a tremolo created with the Easy Tremolos plug-in, beaming may be lost on the tremolo. If this happens, simply run the plug-in on the region again to restore beaming.

Harmonics

Harmonics are notes manipulated to sound at a higher partial (in the harmonic series) of the fundamental pitch, and are most common in string notation. They are usually notated with a regular note on the fundamental pitch, and the secondary note above on the same stem (see Figure 12.10). These have become far easier to create with the introduction of the Easy Harmonics plug-in in Finale 2002. This plug-in is designed to generate string harmonics from an interval of a third or fourth.

Figure 12.10

Use the Easy Harmonics plug-in
to easily create harmonics

To create a harmonic

1. Enter the fundamental pitch and the interval required for the desired harmonic on the same beat and in the same layer. Enter an interval of either a perfect fourth, major third, or minor third (intervals of a fourth will sound two octaves higher, an interval of a major third will sound two octaves and a major third higher, and an interval of a minor third will sound two octaves and a fifth higher than the fundamental).

2. Choose the Mass Edit Tool.

3. Highlight the measure containing the notes. If you need to select part of a measure, from the Edit menu, choose Select Partial Measures and then highlight the desired region.

4. From the plug-ins menu, choose TGTools > Easy Harmonics. The Easy Harmonics dialog box appears as shown in Figure 12.11.

Figure 12.11

Use the Easy Harmonics dialog
box to specify the interval to
look for

5. Select the interval of the notes you want to convert to harmonics.

6. Click Apply. The notes in the selected region convert to harmonics. Play back the region to hear the resulting harmonic pitch. (The harmonic will play as notated with or without Human Playback.)

Cadenzas

Cadenzas are solo passages with no barlines, and are usually notated with smaller than normal noteheads. There are several ways to create a cadenza passage in Finale. The most widely agreed upon method is to alter the time signature of a single measure (preserving the music spacing), enter the notes, and then use the Mass Edit Tool to reduce the note size.

To create a cadenza

1. Click the Time Signature Tool, and then double-click the measure you want to enter the cadenza into. The Time Signature dialog box appears.

2. Change the time signature to accommodate the number of notes you want to enter in the cadenza passage. For example, if your cadenza is 48 eighth notes, define a time signature of 48/8. (Here, you could also use a time signature with a larger beam grouping like 24/4 or 12/2 so that not every single eighth note is flagged).

3. Click the Options/More Choices button to expand the dialog box.

4. Check Use a Different Time Signature for Display.

5. Set the time signature at the bottom to whatever you want to use for the display. For example, if the time signature for the measure previous to the cadenza is 3/4, define 3/4 here so there is no time change indicated on the cadenza measure.

6. In the Measure Region section, choose Measure _ Through _ and enter the measure number for the cadenza in both entry fields (to define this time change for the cadenza measure only).

7. Click OK to return to the score.

8. Enter the notation into the measure.

9. Click the Mass Edit Tool, and then click the cadenza measure to highlight it.

10. From the Mass Edit menu, choose Change > Note Size. Enter 75 and click OK.

Orchestration Tools

Whether you are composing a piece from scratch or copying from an existing handwritten score, Finale can be used as an excellent orchestration tool. Play an excerpt of music into one staff and explode it into many, or reduce large scores into a grand, or single, staff. You can even check for notes outside of an instrument's range, or tell Finale to search for occurrences of parallel motion in your score. Use the following techniques to save time while orchestrating.

Explode Music

While creating a score with several staves, you may want to enter many chord voicings into a single staff at once and then separate each voice into its own staff. To do this, use the Mass Edit Tool's Explode Music utility. This utility basically takes each note from chords entered in a single staff and delegates them into new staves or existing staves in the score. The result is an independent line of music in each staff consisting of a note from each original chord (see Figure 12.12).

Here is a quick demonstration showing how to explode chords in one staff into independent voices on several staves.

1. Open a new default document (File > New > Default Document).

2. Enter some four-note chords into the first few measures (in a single layer). If you are using a MIDI keyboard, Simple Entry, Speedy Entry, and HyperScribe can all be used with a MIDI keyboard to quickly enter the chords.

3. Choose the Mass Edit Tool.

4. Click just to the left of the staff to highlight the entire staff.

5. From the Mass Edit menu, choose Utilities > Explode Music. The Explode Music dialog box appears as shown in Figure 12.13.

Figure 12.12

Explode each note of a chord into its own staff with the Explode Music utility

Figure 12.13

Choose the number of new staves to create and where to put the extra notes while exploding music in the Explode Music dialog box

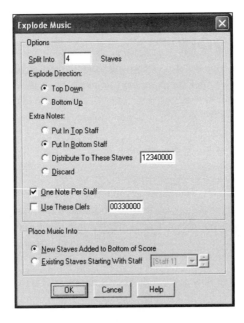

6. You will want to create four new staves, so for Split Into, enter "4" (if it isn't there already). For Place Music Into, select New Staves Added to Bottom of Score.

7. Click OK. Finale adds four new staves to the score, with each voice in its own staff.

Now, make any additional edits to the new staves. Use the Staff Tool to edit their transposition, staff name, or clef in the Staff Attributes (see Chapter 2). You can use the Explode Music utility to explode music into up to eight staves.

Here are some ways to customize the results generated by exploding music while in the Explode Music dialog box:

* If some of your chords contain extra notes, in other words, if some chords have more notes than the number of staves you're exploding to, you can tell Finale on which staff to place the extra notes. If you want Finale to put the extra notes into the bottom staff, in the Extra Notes section, select Put In Bottom Staff. If you want Finale to group the extra notes in the first staff, choose Put In Top Staff.

* If a chord contains fewer notes than the number of staves, you can use the Top Down and Bottom Up functions to add notes from the top staff down or from the bottom staff up. For example, if you explode to four staves with Top Down chosen, a three-note chord will be dispersed among the top three staves and a rest will appear the fourth staff. With Bottom Up chosen, the rest would appear in the top staff and the three notes would be distributed among the bottom three staves.

* Assign a clef to each new staff in the Use These Clefs text box. Each number represents the clef for each successive staff created. Use 0 for treble clef, 1 for alto clef, 2 for tenor clef, 3 for bass clef, and 4 for vocal tenor clef (assuming you haven't changed the default clef definitions).

* If there are more notes in a chord than the number of staves you create, there will be extra notes to manage. You can choose to discard or select a staff for these notes using the Extra Notes radio buttons. Enter the order of staves to place each successive extra note into in the Distribute To These Staves text box.

* If your score already contains the staves you want to explode to, choose them from the Existing Staves Starting With Staff drop-down menu.

TIP
To isolate a specific layer for explosion, from the Options menu, choose Show Active Layer Only, and then choose the layer you want to explode.

Implode Music

You can also squeeze music from many staves into one with the Mass Edit Tool's Implode Music utility. This utility takes notes from a region of selected staves and stacks them within a single staff as shown in Figure 12.14.

To implode notes from many staves into one

1. Start with any document containing several staves, and a single line of music on two or more staves.

2. Choose the Mass Edit Tool.

3. Highlight the region of measures you want to consolidate into a single staff.

4. From the Mass Edit menu, choose Utilities > Implode Music. The Implode Music dialog box appears as shown in Figure 12.15.

Figure 12.14

Use the Implode Music Utility to consolidate notes in many staves into a single staff

Figure 12.15

Choose a destination for the notes you want to implode and edit their quantization in the Implode Music dialog box

5. Here, choose whether you want to place the resulting notes in the top staff of the selected region or into a new staff added to the bottom of the score. Click the Quant Settings button to open the Quantization Settings dialog box (see Figure 4.3) where you can choose the smallest note value and other parameters for your results. See Chapter 4 for more information on Quantization.

6. Click OK. You return to the score. All notes from the selected region now appear in one staff.

The Piano Reduction Plug-In

The Implode Music utility works well for consolidating regions of the score into a single staff, but if you want to generate a complete piano part for all or certain staves of a score, use the Piano Reduction plug-in. This plug-in will take notes, articulations, and note expressions from selected staves and place them into a grand staff (see Figure 12.16).

Figure 12.16

Generate a piano reduction automatically with the Piano Reduction plug-in

Original

Piano Reduction Plug-in Results

To generate a piano reduction automatically with the Piano Reduction plug-in

1. Start with any document containing several staves with music.

2. From the Plug-ins menu, choose Piano Reduction. The Piano Reduction dialog box appears as shown in Figure 12.17.

Figure 12.17

Select staves to include and a split point for your piano reduction in the Piano Reduction dialog box

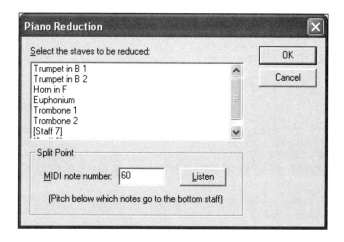

3. Here, highlight the staves you want to include in your reduction. Hold down the Shift key and click to select consecutive staves. Hold down the Ctrl/Command key and click to select non-consecutive staves. For Split Point, choose the lowest note you want to include on the right-hand staff of your piano reduction (60 = middle C).

4. Click OK. It may take a while for Finale to generate the reduction. When it's done, your reduction appears in a new grand staff added to the bottom of your score.

You will most likely need to edit the results of the generated piano reduction. Finale will sometimes need to shorten a note if it finds a shorter one on the same beat of a different staff. When this happens, try entering the note in a different layer.

The Check Range Plug-In

While orchestrating, arranging, or composing, you may want to check over a region of your work to ensure all notes are within a playable range for the instrument. You can check for notes out of range, change them, or delete them with the Check Range plug-in.

To check a region of your score for notes out of range for an instrument, do the following:

1. To check range for the whole score, move to step 2. To check range for a staff or staves, click the Mass Edit Tool, and then click to the left of the staff (Shift-click to the left of additional staves you want to check to select them).

2. From the Plug-ins menu, choose Scoring and Arranging > Check Range. The Check Range dialog box appears as shown in Figure 12.18.

Figure 12.18

Check your score for notes out of an instrument's range with the Check Range plug-in

3. Look after Staff Name at the top to see the staff you are currently checking. In the Instrument section, choose the instrument you are using for the current staff. Notice the High Note and Low Note fields update as you move between instruments. For Range Class, choose the skill level for the instrument range. You can also adjust the high and low pitches by using the up and down arrows, or by entering your own pitch manually.

4. Click Check. If Finale finds any notes out of range, the Note Out of Range dialog box appears as shown in Figure 12.19.

Figure 12.19

Erase or change out-of-range
notes in the Note Out of
Range dialog box

5. Click Erase Note to remove the note from the score. Click Change Note to change the
note to the pitch specified in the Change To field. Click Stop to return to the score.

If you are using an external MIDI device, like a MIDI keyboard, click the Listen button while checking the
range (in either of the range checking dialog boxes) to specify the pitch by simply playing a note on your
external MIDI device.

TIP

To transpose any selected region of music, choose the Mass Edit Tool, highlight the region, then from
the Mass Edit menu, choose Transpose.

Find Parallel Motion

If you are composing or arranging a score and need to observe classical rules of voice leading, try running
the Find Parallel Motion plug-in to find all occurrences of parallel motion in your score.

To check for parallel fifths or octaves

1. Choose the Mass Edit Tool.

2. Select a region of your score you want to check for parallel motion, or press Ctrl/Command-A
to Select All.

3. From the Plug-ins menu, choose Scoring and Arranging > Find Parallel Motion. The Find
Parallel Motion dialog box appears as shown in Figure 12.20.

4. Click Find. Finale will search for parallel fifths and octaves in all staves, layers, and voices.
Finale reports the measure, beat, layer, and staff in the two rows at the bottom of this dialog
box.

5. Click Find again to move to the next occurrence, or click Cancel to return to the score.

CHAPTER 12

Figure 12.20
Use the Find Parallel Motion
plug-in to find occurrences of
parallel fifths and octaves in
your score

> **TIP**
> If you're using this plug-in to quickly analyze a score for parallelism in a music theory homework
> assignment, be sure to learn the rules of parallel motion in traditional voice leading in case Finale
> isn't available in an upcoming exam.

Creative Tools

Many composers and arrangers prefer to use Finale throughout the process of writing an original score.
Among the advantages of composing with Finale are the numerous plug-ins and other features designed to
offer ideas and spark creativity. There are ten Composer's Assistant plug-ins available that are specifically
designed to help generate musical ideas. These tools won't write a piece for you, but they will analyze
existing music and offer suggestions for chords, rhythms, and voicing. If you are looking to generate
harmony for a melodic passage, Finale can offer a large number of suggestions for up to six parts with the
Band-in-a-Box Auto Harmonizer plug-in. You can even create an entire jazz accompaniment for any melody
with the MiBAC Jazz Rhythm Section Generator plug-in. Finally, if you are composing serial music, or a
related genre, you can easily rearrange notes by inversion or retrograde with the Canonic Utilities. Use any
of the following utilities to generate thousands of musical possibilities to choose from while creating a score.

Composer's Assistant Plug-Ins

The ten Composer's Assistant plug-ins use principles of music theory to generate possibilities for modulation,
voicing, and rhythm. In general, you will enter a series of notes or chords, run one of the plug-ins on the
desired region, and Finale will place results in a new staff or staves added to the bottom of the score. After
running one of these plug-ins, use the Mass Edit Tool to copy chosen results into your score (see Chapters 2
and 9 for more information on the Mass Edit Tool). After running these plug-ins, use the playback controls
to play back the results for review.

In this section, you will learn how to effectively use each of the ten Composer's Assistant plug-ins.
To prepare for the following instructions, open a new default document (File > New > Default Document).
After each example, use the Mass Edit Tool to clear all entries and use the Staff Tool to delete the extra
staves. Or, you can also open a new default document for each example. Though many of the following
examples begin with notes in the first measure, you can run any of these plug-ins at any measure of your
score. Make sure to always enter notes in layer one, voice one.

Chord Morphing

The Chord Morphing plug-in basically takes two chords and offers suggestions for intermediate chords you can use to modulate between them. You can choose from three methods of morphing to vary your results. Here, we'll use the Chord Morphing plug-in to find suggestions for modulating between two higher tertian (big) chords.

1. Enter two chords into the first measure of your score in layer one as shown in Figure 12.21.

Figure 12.21

Find possible ways to modulate between chords such as this one with the Composer's Assistant Chord Morphing plug-in.

2. Click the Mass Edit Tool, and then highlight the first measure.

3. From the Plug-ins menu, choose Scoring and Arranging > Composer's Assistant > Chord Morphing. The Chord Morphing dialog box appears as shown in Figure 12.22.

Figure 12.22

Choose from three possible morphing methods in the Chord Morphing dialog box

4. Here, choose the type of morphing method you want to use. Each type processes removal, mutation, and addition of notes in a different order. Each type will offer slightly different results. Choose A to tell Finale to mutate, remove, and then add notes. Choose B to tell Finale to remove, mutate, and then add the notes. Choose C to tell Finale to remove, add, and then mutate.

5. Click OK. Finale adds a staff to your score containing the generated chords. Each one appears as a whole note in duration (see Figure 12.23). There is a marking entered above each original chord as a note expression. Now, you can use the Mass Edit Tool to edit the duration of the notes and add copy to your score, or undo your changes (Ctrl/Command-Z) and try one of the remaining two morphing methods.

CHAPTER 12

Figure 12.23

Chord Morphing results
with type B

Chord Morphing

Chord Realization

The Chord Realization plug-in can be a very useful tool if you are creating an SATB (Soprano, Alto, Tenor, Bass) arrangement. It takes a chord entered in a single staff and generates four-part realizations on that chord in root position, first and second inversion. You can then choose from a variety of suggestions for four-part voicing. In the following example, we'll use the Chord Realization plug-in to generate voicing options for chords.

1. Enter the chords from Figure 12.21 again into the first measure of a scratch document.

2. Click the Mass Edit Tool, and then highlight the first measure.

3. From the Plug-ins menu, choose Scoring and Arranging > Composer's Assistant > Chord Realization. The Chord Realization dialog box appears as shown in Figure 12.24.

Figure 12.24

Use the Chord Realization plug-in to generate voicing options for a chord

4. For Tonality, choose the key of the piece. Finale will transpose your results into any (major) key you specify. Also, specify the root scale degree of the chord by choosing from the Degree drop-down menu. In this dialog box, you can also specify the range for each part, limit the number of generated inversions, and number of staves produced (two or four).

5. Click OK. Finale adds two staves to your score containing the generated realization. Each one appears a whole note in duration (see Figure 12.25). Now, you can use the Mass Edit Tool to edit the duration of the notes and add copy to your score, or undo your changes (Ctrl/Command-Z).

Figure 12.25

Chord Realization results using settings in Figure 12.24 and the entries from Figure 12.21

Chord Reordering

The Chord Reordering plug-in simply reorders the sequence of chords randomly or by number of common notes. Voicing and staff positions remain the same. To reorder chords using the Chord Reordering plug-in

1. Enter several chords into a staff.
2. Click the Mass Edit Tool, and then highlight the region containing the chords.
3. From the Plug-ins menu, choose Scoring and Arranging > Composer's Assistant > Chord Reordering. The Chord Reordering dialog box appears as shown in Figure 12.26.

Figure 12.26

Reorder chords randomly or by number of common notes with the Chord Reordering plug-in

4. Choose Find Best Solution to tell Finale to order the chords based on the number of common notes. Finale will rearrange the chords with the maximum number of similar notes between adjacent chords. This can result in a smooth, yet somewhat unspectacular, harmonic progression. To specify the first chord in the reordered region, enter the sequential number of the chord after Find Best Solution Beginning with Chord Number_. Select Find Random solution to tell Finale to reorder the chords randomly.
5. Click OK. Finale adds a staff to your score containing the reordered chords.

Chord Splitting

While orchestrating large chords, it is a common practice to separate consonant pitches from the chord into subsets and give each subset to a particular instrumental section. In large ensembles, this technique can give the chord a smoother sound. The Chord Splitting plug-in extracts consonant notes from a chord (based on the harmonics of an implied fundamental pitch) and places them together in measures of a new staff below the score. Each of these "subsets" of the original chord can be then used in a unique instrumental section to achieve a blended overall sound. To generate subsets from a large chord

1. Enter a large chord into the first measure of a scratch document.

2. Click the Mass Edit Tool, and then highlight the first measure.

3. From the Plug-ins menu, choose Scoring and Arranging > Composer's Assistant > Chord Splitting. The Chord Splitting dialog box appears as shown in Figure 12.27.

Figure 12.27

Use the Chord Splitting plug-in to extract harmonic pitches from a chord to delegate to an instrumental section of your score

4. Finale will separate pitches from the chord in groups of one to three notes. At the top of this box, click the drop-down arrow and choose the number of times you want Finale to split the chord. Enter a higher number for larger chords. Also, check Add the Virtual Fundamental if you want to add the virtual fundamental into the results (more about the virtual fundamental later).

5. Click OK. Finale creates a new staff for each split chord. Look to the staff with the most even number notes in each measure for the best results. Then, you can copy these suggestions to instrumental sections with the Mass Edit Tool.

Common Tone Transposition

Finale can offer several chord ideas by generating a list of chords that share at least one common pitch with the original. To tell Finale to create several new chords containing at least one common tone

1. Enter a chord into the first measure of a scratch document.

2. Click the Mass Edit Tool, and then highlight the first measure.

3. From the Plug-ins menu, choose Composer's Assistant > Common Tone Transposition. The Common Tone Transposition dialog box appears as shown in Figure 12.28.

4. Choose a highest and lowest MIDI pitch for the generated chords.

Figure 12.28

Generate a list of chords containing at least one common tone with the Common Tone Transposition plug-in

5. Click OK. Finale creates a new staff and places a list of chord ideas as whole notes in each measure, each with at least one note in common with the original chord.

Frequency Modulation Chord Generator

This plug-in is used to generate increasingly complex chords from two pitches. Finale uses the method of frequency modulation, popular in keyboard synthesizers, to do this. To create a list of chords with the Frequency Modulation Chord Generator

1. Enter two notes on different pitches in the first measure of a scratch document.

2. Click the Mass Edit Tool, and then highlight the first measure.

3. From the Plug-ins menu, choose Scoring and Arranging > Composer's Assistant > Frequency Modulation Chord Generator. The Frequency Modulation Chord Generator dialog box appears as shown in Figure 12.29.

Figure 12.29

Use the Frequency Modulation Chord Generator to create chord ideas rich in texture and complexity

4. Since the results may exceed a useful range, choose a highest and lowest pitch for your results in the Specify Range section. You can then specify the number of results and number of notes in each chord in the Modulation Index section. The number of resulting chords will equal one greater than the Highest modulation index minus the Lowest.

5. Click OK. Finale creates a new staff, including a list of chord ideas as whole notes in each measure. After using the Frequency Modulation Chord Generator, try using the Chord Morphing plug-in to generate additional chord ideas or the Chord Splitting plug-in to separate each chord into harmonic subsets.

Melodic Morphing

Use the Melodic Morphing plug-in to generate a transition between two melodies. To do this

1. Begin a scratch document with two empty staves.

2. Enter a simple melody in the top staff and one in the bottom.

3. Click the Mass Edit Tool, and then highlight the measures in both staves.

4. From the Plug-ins menu, choose Scoring and Arranging > Composer's Assistant > Melodic Morphing. The Melodic Morphing dialog box appears as shown in Figure 12.30.

Figure 12.30

Generate a transition between two melodies with the Melodic Morphing plug-in

5. The results of this plug-in will begin with the first original melody, followed by the plug-in's transition, and will end with the second original melody. The length of Finale's generated transition depends on the value you enter in the Number of Morphing Steps field. Enter a high number for a subtle transition or a lower number for a more sudden transition.

6. Click OK. Finale creates a new staff including the first original melody, transition, and second original melody. Finale disregards rhythm while morphing the melodies (its output is steady 16th notes), so you will have to edit the note durations manually with the Simple or Speedy Entry Tool.

TIP

After running the Melodic Morphing plug-in, you will probably see a number of repeated 16th notes. To merge all repeated notes into single notes of larger durations, use the Tie Common Notes plug-in, and then retranscribe the region with the Mass Edit Tool (Mass Edit menu > Retranscribe). Note that retranscribing looks at your Quantization settings when deciding on notated rhythms.

Rhythm Generator

You can quickly create a percussion part for your score using the Rhythm Generator plug-in. With this plug-in, you can define beat patterns for notes entered into up to six new staves at the bottom of your score. To create a rhythm section with the Rhythm Generator plug-in

1. From the Plug-ins menu, choose Scoring and Arranging > Composer's Assistant > Rhythm Generator (no selection is necessary). The Rhythm Generator dialog box appears as shown in Figure 12.31.

Figure 12.31

Generate a complex rhythm section easily with the Rhythm Generator plug-in

	Rhythm Generator								
								Created by OpenMusic	

Voice		Sieve 1	Offset	Sieve 2	Offset	Sieve 3	Offset	Invert	Random %	Instrument
1	☑	8	0	Off	0	Off	0	☐	0	Bass drum
2	☑	8	7	Off	0	Off	0	☐	20	Bass drum
3	☑	8	4	Off	0	Off	0	☐	0	Snare Drum
4	☑	8	0	Off	0	Off	0	☑	0	Closed High Hat
5	☐	Off	0	Off	0	Off	0	☐	0	Closed High Hat
6	☑	2	1	Off	0	5	0	☐	60	Claves

Number of Measures: 10   ☐ Group Resulting Staves

More Info...   Reset   OK   Cancel

2. Each row in this dialog box represents a new staff that you can add to your score. Check the box on the left for each new staff you want to add to your rhythm section. Define up to three rhythmic patterns from the Sieve drop-down menus for each staff. Each measure is separated into 16th notes. Choose 1 from a Sieve drop-down menu to enter straight 16th notes. Choose 2 for a sieve to enter a note on every other 16th note pulse. Choose 3 for a sieve to enter a note on every third 16th note pulse, and so on. You can specify up to three rhythmic patterns (sieves) for each staff. Under the Instrument column, choose a MIDI instrument for each staff you define.

TIP

After specifying an instrument for a staff in the Rhythm Generator plug-in, you will need to assign the same instrument to the staff in the Instrument List (see Chapter 2).

3. Click OK. Finale creates the new staves with the specified rhythms and adds them to the bottom of the score. Use the Staff Attributes to change the clef of these staves to a percussion clef and make other percussion-specific changes (staff lines, notation style, etc.).

TIP

Apply a percussion map to staves created with the Rhythm Generator plug-in to assign a staff position for each part. See Chapter 8 for information on creating percussion maps.

Tie Common Notes

This plug-in is straightforward enough. It looks for consecutive notes on the same pitch and ties them together automatically. To tie all consecutive common notes

1. Click the Mass Edit Tool, and then highlight a region of measures containing consecutive notes on the same pitch.

2. From the Plug-ins menu, choose Scoring and Arranging > Composer's Assistant >
Tie Common Notes. The Tie Common Notes dialog box appears.

3. Click OK. Finale creates ties between the common notes.

After using the Tie Common Notes plug-in, convert tied notes into single notes of a larger duration with the Mass Edit Tool's Retranscribe feature. Select the region with the Mass Edit Tool, and then, from the Mass Edit menu, choose Retranscribe.

Virtual Fundamental Generator

Any collection of pitches you enter as a chord will best fit the partials in the harmonic series of a particular fundamental pitch. The Virtual Fundamental Generator plug-in analyzes pitches in a chord, generates the most appropriate fundamental pitch, and places it in a new staff added to the bottom of the score. This pitch is basically an "implied root" of the chord. To generate a virtual fundamental for a chord

1. Enter one or more chords into the staff of a scratch document.

2. Click the Mass Edit Tool, and then highlight the first measure.

3. From the Plug-ins menu, choose Scoring and Arranging > Composer's Assistant > Virtual Fundamental Generator. The Virtual Fundamental Generator dialog box appears as shown in Figure 12.32.

Figure 12.32

Create the virtual fundamental (or "implied root") for a chord with the Virtual Fundamental Generator plug-in

4. Since the virtual fundamental may be well below the usable range, specify the lowest pitch (as a MIDI note number) in the Specify Lowest Pitch field. If the virtual fundamental is below the note you specify, Finale will raise it an octave (or more if necessary) as long as Allow Octave Displacement is checked. If Allow Octave Displacement is not checked, and the virtual fundamental is lower than the specified lowest pitch, the plug-in will return nothing for that chord.

5. Click OK. Finale creates a new staff including a virtual fundamental for each chord in the highlighted region.

Band-in-a-Box Auto Harmonizing

As questionable as it sounds, Finale can actually create a viable harmonic solution for up to six parts from any given melody. By choosing from an extensive collection of harmonization options, you can usually find one that works well. In practice, it is best to use the Auto Harmonizing plug-in for a basic harmonic outline, and then edit the voice leading, spelling, and texture to your own taste. Use the following instructions to easily create a four-part saxophone arrangement from a simple melody.

1. Start by creating a new document. From the File menu, choose New > Document with Setup Wizard. Click Next to move to page 2. Here, choose the Woodwinds category and add a Soprano, Alto, Tenor, and Baritone saxophone. Click Next, Next, and Finish to create the new document with four saxophones.

2. Enter a simple melody with chord symbols like the example in Figure 12.33.

Figure 12.33

To prepare for running the Band-in-a-Box Auto Harmonizing plug-in, enter a melody with chord symbols

3. Choose the Mass Edit Tool and click the left of the top staff to highlight the entire staff.

4. From the Plug-ins menu, choose Scoring and Arranging > Band-in-a-Box Auto Harmonizing. The Band-in-a-Box Auto Harmonizing dialog box appears as shown in Figure 12.34.

Figure 12.34

Choose the type of harmonization you want to apply and where you want to place the generated notes in the Band-in-a-Box Auto Harmonizing dialog box

5. Here, choose the number of parts and the type of harmonization. For this example, I used four parts and the Super Brass type of harmonization. In the Place New Voices Into section, choose the staves you want Finale to place the harmonization into. For this example, I chose the Three Existing Staves Starting With the Alto Sax staff.

6. Click OK. Finale generates the harmonization and places the resulting notes into the subsequent staves (see Figure 12.35).

Figure 12.35

Band-in-a-Box Auto
Harmonizing results

After auto harmonizing, you may need to edit the enharmonic spelling of certain notes. Also, use the Simple Entry Tool to change any pitches to customize the harmonization to get the sound you're looking for. Press Ctrl/Command-Z to undo the harmonization and try one of the other harmonizing options available in the Band-in-a-Box Auto Harmonizing dialog box.

> **TIP**
> To give your score a handwritten look (like the score in Figures 12.33 and 12.35, for example), choose the Jazz Font option on page 4 of the Document Setup Wizard.

The MiBAC Jazz Rhythm Generator Plug-In

If you are creating a jazz chart, try using the MiBAC Jazz Rhythm Generator plug-in to create a piano, bass, and drum accompaniment for any melody. You can even choose from four accompaniment styles: Ballad, Swing, Beebop, or Bassa Nova. To create a rhythm section for any melody

1. You can start by simply using the Staff Tool to delete the lower three staves from the previous section. Or, start a new default document (File > New > Default Document) and enter a melody with chord symbols. Before running this plug-in, your staff should look something like the example in Figure 12.36.

2. Choose the Mass Edit Tool and click the left of the staff to highlight the entire staff.

3. From the Plug-ins menu, choose Scoring and Arranging > MiBAC Jazz Rhythm Generator. The MiBAC Jazz Rhythm Section Generator dialog box appears as shown in Figure 12.37.

Figure 12.36

To prepare for running the MiBAC Jazz Rhythm Generator plug-in, enter a melody with chord symbols

Figure 12.37

Choose the style and staves, and customize the appearance of items in the generated staves in the MiBAC Jazz Rhythm Section Generator dialog box

4. Here, click the Style drop-down menu and choose a style for your accompaniment. For this example, use Ballad. In the Generate section, choose the staves you want to place chord symbols on. You will probably want to choose the Percussion Map setting for the generated drum part. In the Place Music Into section, for this example, choose New Staves Added to Bottom of Score. In the future, you may want to use this section to tell Finale to place the results into existing staves in your score.

5. Click the Options button to open the Scale Volume dialog box where you can adjust the balance of your accompaniment. Click OK to return to the MiBAC dialog box.

6. Click OK. Finale generates the accompaniment in a piano, bass, and drum staff added to the bottom of the score (see Figure 12.38).

Figure 12.38

MiBAC Jazz Rhythm Section
Generator results

Like the Band-in-a-Box Auto Harmonizing plug-in, you may need to adjust the enharmonic spelling and notation of your results as you see fit. See Chapter 4 for information on adding chords, and see Chapter 8 for information on defining a percussion map to a staff.

Inversions, Retrogrades, and More: The Canonic Utilities

The Canonic Utilities plug-in is particularly useful if you are composing serial music. Invert or retrograde a portion of music easily with this plug-in. You can also add or remove accidentals and transpose the region while performing these tasks. To invert (flip the music upside-down), or retrograde (flip the music end-to-end), or both, do the following:

1. Open a new default document (File > New > Default Document).

2. Enter a series of notes into the first few measures like those shown in Figure 12.39, for example.

3. Choose the Mass Edit Tool and highlight the region containing the notes you want to manipulate.

4. From the Plug-ins menu, choose Canonic Utilities. The Canonic Utilities dialog box appears as shown in Figure 12.40.

5. Here, choose the type of inversion from the drop-down menu at the top. For this example, select Diatonic Mirror Inversion. Click the Retrograde check box if you would also like to retrograde the selection (as in this example). You can also make additional settings for mirror inversions, transposition, and retrogrades by clicking the corresponding buttons on the right. Click Verify Retrograde to check the selection for invalid entries. You will not be able to retrograde music containing slurs, note expressions, or mirrored measures.

6. Click OK. Finale calculates the inversion and/or retrograde and adjusts the notes accordingly (see Figure 12.41).

You can also use the Canonic Utilities plug-in to show or hide accidentals on all notes, or to remove all ties.

Figure 12.39

Invert or retrograde any passage such as this one with the Canonic Utilities plug-in

Figure 12.40

Choose the type of inversion or retrograde you want to apply to the selected region and select a transposition in the Canonic Utilities dialog box

Figure 12.41

Canonic Utilities results with both diatonic mirror inversion and retrograde applied

13

CUSTOMIZING FINALE, SCANNING, AND TRICKS FOR MUSIC EDUCATORS

From its conception, Finale has been designed to give you nearly unlimited control over the workings of the program. If there is something about the way Finale works that you don't like, you can probably customize it. For example, you can tell Finale to always open a new lead sheet on startup, or nudge four pixels instead of one. You can even remove tools you don't use from certain palettes to save space or modify Finale's overall appearance.

Scanning-in music notation software is a popular feature. Some purchase Finale for the sole purpose of transferring sheet music to a digital format. In this chapter, you will learn how to use Finale to produce the industry's best results while converting scanned files without having to purchase an entirely separate scanning program. You will also learn techniques for cleaning up files after conversion.

If you're a music educator, you can use one of Finale's education templates to create examples, worksheets, and quizzes. You can also create customized technique-building exercises for any sized ensemble in minutes with the Exercise Wizard.

Here's a summary of what you will learn in this chapter:

- ❉ How to create custom documents
- ❉ How to customize Finale
- ❉ How to work with scanned files
- ❉ Tricks for music educators

Creating Custom Documents

Avoid the redundancy of adding the same libraries and making the same document settings for each new project. Do this by modifying the default file or creating your own Finale templates.

Customizing the Default Document

As you have seen, whenever you open a new default document (File > New > Default Document), Finale creates a single-staff, thirty-one-measure document. This document is Finale's standard template, called the

Maestro Font Default. It contains default libraries for articulations, expressions, chord suffixes and other items, as well as default settings for all items in the Document Options dialog box (Options > Document Options). If you want to use your own custom articulations, expressions, or document settings for the majority of your projects, add these elements to the Maestro Font Default file.

To customize the Maestro Font Default file

1. From the File menu, choose New > Default Document. A new untitled default document appears.

2. Now, load any libraries you intend to use often (File > Load Library). Then, you can look in the appropriate selection window (articulation, expression, etc.) and delete any of the items you do not intend to use.

3. Program all metatools you want to include. Remember, metatools are always saved with the document.

4. If there is a particular layout you have in mind for the majority of your new documents, adjust the Page Format for Score. From the Options menu, choose Page Format > Score to open the Page Format for Score dialog box where you can make these layout settings. After changing the Page Format for Score dialog options, redefine your pages (Page Layout Tool > Page Layout > Redefine pages > All Pages).

5. If you have a particular music font you want to use for the majority of your documents, choose a new music font. From the Options menu, choose Set Default Music Font to open the Font dialog box where you can make this setting. If you have a particular text font you wish to use with lyrics, text blocks, staff names, or text expressions, go to the Options menu, choose Document options, and then choose Fonts. Make the necessary changes. Click OK to return to the score when you're finished.

6. If you want to change the default settings for any other notational items (font, beaming, noteheads, stem connections, repeats, ties, etc.), define these in the Document Options dialog box. From the Options menu, choose Document Options to open the Document Options dialog box. Choose the category on the left, make settings on the active page, click Apply to apply your settings, and then do the same for any other category you want to edit. Click OK when you are finished to return to the score. If these settings already exist in another document, save and open the Document Options library to transfer all document settings to this document.

7. Remove any items you never plan to use, such as articulations, shapes, expressions, or custom Smart Shapes. This will help to reduce the size of your document and prevent any potential problems. To further clean the file, choose Remove Deleted Items from the Data Check submenu of the Options menu.

8. After you have made all adjustments to your document, from the File menu, choose Save As. The Save As window appears.

9. On Windows, from the Save As Type drop-down menu, choose Coda Template File [*.FTM] (Mac users, skip ahead to step 8).

10. Name the file "Maestro Font Default" (on Windows, this should also have the extension .FTM). On Mac, make sure that the .MUS extension does not appear after the "Maestro Font Default" file name.

11. Save the file to your Finale/Component Files folder (or, in versions previous to Finale 2003, save to the Finale folder).

12. Click Save. A warning should appear that the file exists; would you like to replace it? Confirm Yes, you want to replace it.

13. Now, open a new default document. The libraries, page format, and document settings you specified now exist in this or any future new default document.

Resetting or Transporting All Document Settings

You just learned how to specify a collection of document settings for future new files by modifying the Maestro Font Default file. You may want to apply a collection of document options to an existing file or reset all document options to revert back to the default settings.

Reverting All Document Options to the Default Settings

1. From the File menu, choose Load Library. The Load Library window appears.

2. Navigate to the Finale/Libraries folder.

3. Double-click the Document Options library. Or, choose a customized Document Options library you have saved. Finale's Document Options revert to default settings (or, your own customized default settings).

Some items will not change after loading the Document Options library. Certain changes to the document options apply only to future items entered in the score, and not existing items. For example, open the Document Options dialog box (Options > Document Options). Click the Fonts category. Notice the items marked with an asterisk (*). Changes to these will not apply after you return to the score. To change these items, use the Swap One Font for Another feature (Options > Data Check), the Change Fonts plug-in (Plug-ins > Miscellaneous > Change Fonts), or Change Chord Suffix Fonts (select the Chord Tool, then, from the Chord menu, choose Change Chord Suffix Fonts). To change the font of existing lyrics in your score, click on the Lyrics Tool and from the Lyrics menu, choose Edit Lyrics.

Moving Document Options from One Document to Another

Use the FinaleScipt plug-in to transport all document options as well as page format information from one document to another, or from one document to many. This technique is especially useful if you want to apply a "house style" to a collection of files.

1. Open the document containing the settings you want to apply to additional documents.

2. Open the destination document(s), and then bring the document containing the desired settings to the front, so it is the "active" document (not necessary if you're batch processing the entire folder).

3. From the Plug-ins menu, choose Miscellaneous, and then FinaleScript Palette. The FinaleScript Palette appears as shown in Figure 13.1.

4. Scroll down and select Import House Style. You can double-click this script to see the contents.

5. To apply settings from the current document to the contents of a folder (in other words, "batch process" all files in a folder), click the second icon from the right in the FinaleScript Palette, choose the desired folder, and click OK.

Figure 13.1

Use the New page of the Program Options dialog box to specify a default file and the default view for all documents you open, including new documents

6. Click the green Play button. FinaleScript applies the document settings from the active document to all other open documents (or files in the specified folder).

7. Click the blinking Report icon to review your results.

You can also use the FinaleScript plug-in to transport any number of specific document options between documents. Double-click the Command Reminder script or see the appendix of the User Manual for a list of all FinaleScript commands.

TIP

FinaleScript is perhaps Finale's most versatile and powerful plug-in. You can automate many repetitive tasks by creating your own scripts using hundreds of available commands. Basically, it's an easy way to create your own plug-ins.

Creating Your Own Templates

As you have seen, Finale contains a variety of template files that you can use as a starting point for working on a specific type of project (File > New > Document from Template). When you open a template file, Finale opens a copy of the template as an untitled document, so you won't have to worry about overwriting it. To create your own custom template

1. Open any file. You might want to begin with a new default document, a new document with the Setup Wizard, or an existing template file.

2. Edit or load any desired libraries, edit the Page Format for Score, or make any other document-specific settings (such as the ones suggested above for customizing the Maestro Font Default).

3. From the File menu, choose Save As. The Save As window appears.

4. Navigate to the Finale/Templates folder (if you want to store this template along with the other Finale templates, though any location will work fine).

5. On Windows, from the Save As Type drop-down menu, choose Finale Template File [*.FTM]. On Macintosh, a template is a regular Finale Notation file.

6. Give your template file a unique name. You should now see your file name followed by the .FTM extension on Windows or a .MUS extension on Mac. On Mac, you must enter a new name before saving. If the document is saved with the original template name, the template will be replaced with the current file.

7. Click Save.

8. Now, any time you want to use this template, from the File menu, choose New > Document From Template. Then double-click the file you created. A copy of the file will open as a new untitled document.

Customizing Finale

In addition to the basic program options described in Chapter 2, there are a number of other ways to customize the way Finale works both from within the Program Options dialog box and by using other tools Finale provides.

Customizing Finale via Program Options

Use the Program Options dialog box to customize a variety of default program settings that you have probably been using without even knowing it. For example, you can tell Finale to open all new files in Scroll View at any view percentage, use a different startup action (instead of starting the Launch window every time), or use the arrow keys to nudge five pixels instead of one. As of Finale 2005, these, and many other program settings, are conveniently located in the Program Options dialog box.

Options for Opening New Documents

The New page of the Program Options dialog box allows you to customize settings for new or newly opened documents. From the Options menu, choose Program Options and select New from the list on the left. The New page of the Program Options dialog box appears as shown in Figure 13.2.

Figure 13.2

Use the New page of the Program Options dialog box to specify a default file and the default view for all documents you open, including new documents

CHAPTER 13

Here are some ways to specify the way Finale treats new documents from the New page of the Program Options dialog box:

* In the Default Document text box, specify any template file to use for your default document in place of the Maestro Font Default file. For example, you can specify that Finale always use the Jazz Font Default file as the default document. On Windows, click the Browse button to open a Windows Explorer window where you can navigate to the desired file. This is the file Finale will use when you open a new default document (File > New > Default Document). On Mac, just type the name of the file you want to use as your Default file. The file, however, must be located in the Finale folder in the Component Files folder. If you leave the Default Document text field within the Program Options blank on Mac, Finale will automatically use the Maestro Font Default document.

* For Default New Operation, specify the result of opening a file using the Ctrl/Command-N keyboard shortcut by choosing Setup Wizard or Default Document.

* By default, every time you start Finale, you see the Launch window. You may want to tell Finale to open the Document Setup Wizard, a new default file, template, or other file during startup instead. If this is the case, from the Startup Action drop-down menu, choose what you want Finale to do when you first start the program.. If you choose New Document from Template, at startup you will be prompted to choose a file from the Templates folder (as specified in the Templates field on the Folders page). If you choose Open Document, at startup you will be prompted to choose a file from your Music folder (as specified on the Music field of the Folders page).

* In the New Document Windows section, choose the view percentage and view (Page or Scroll View) to use for all documents you open or create.

The Open page of the Program Options dialog box allows you to customize the way Finale treats new and existing documents while opening them. Click the Open category in the Program Options dialog box to display the Open options. Here you can tell Finale to automatically convert text (upper ASCII characters) while opening files cross-platform and make settings for opening documents created in earlier versions. You will probably want to leave these default settings alone. If you are using Windows, however, enter a value for Number Of Recent Files In File Menu to specify the number of recently opened files to make readily available at the bottom of the File menu.

TIP
For information on using Finale's AutoSave and Backup features on the Save page of the Program Options dialog box, see Chapter 1.

View Options

Use the View page of the Program Options dialog box to customize the appearance of certain items. In the Program Options dialog box, choose the View category from the list on the left. The View page appears as shown in Figure 13.3.

Figure 13.3

Make settings for the
appearance of certain items in
the View page of the Program
Options dialog box

Here are some ways to edit Finale's appearance in the View page of the Program Options dialog box:

❊ Uncheck Show Tools Menu to remove the Tools menu from the list of menus atop your screen. You might want to do this if you always select tools from palettes and are just plain sick and tired of looking at that darned Tools menu.

❊ Check Show All Messages to tell Finale to show all dialog boxes for which you have already checked Do Not Show Again.

❊ On Windows, check Save Windows States While Exiting Finale to tell Finale to save your palette configuration for the next Finale session. If you check this, make sure to also check Load Windows States When Starting Finale to load the previous palette configuration. This option is not available on Mac, but the palette and window placement is saved automatically as a preference when you quit the program on Mac.

❊ For Pitch Representation, you can tell Finale to display pitches as MIDI Note Numbers (C = 60) or Pitches (C = C4). This representation of pitch crops up in a variety pf places. For example, choose the HyperScribe Tool, and then from the HyperScribe menu, choose Record Mode > Split Into Two Staves. The split point representation (60 or C4, by default) will depend on this setting.

❊ If you are defining measure number regions, you may want to tell Finale to display the actual measure numbers beginning from the "real" measure one. To do this, after Measure Numbers, choose Display Actual Measure Numbers. Choose Display Defined Measure Numbers to go back to displaying measure regions as defined in the Measure Number dialog box.

Undo Options, Dragging, and Nudging

You can adjust Finale's default Undo settings as well as settings for dragging and nudging in the Edit page of the Program Options dialog box. Choose the Edit category from the list on the left of the Program Options dialog box to see the Edit page as shown in Figure 13.4.

Figure 13.4

Customize Finale's Undo Settings and settings for dragging and nudging on the Edit page of the Program Options dialog box

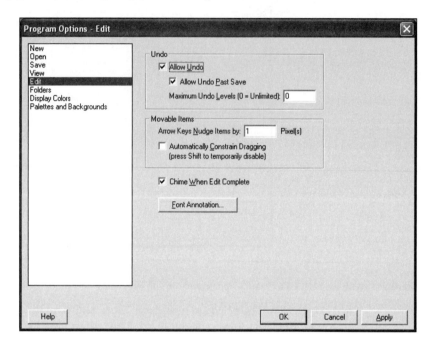

Here are some ways to edit Finale's treatment of Undo, dragging, and nudging in the Edit page of the Program Options:

* Finale records just about everything you do in your open file(s) in case you want it undone (Ctrl/Command-Z). Make sure Allow Undo is checked. You will probably want to keep the default settings, so you can undo any unwanted changes while working on the score. Also, make sure Allow Undo Past Save is checked to tell Finale to keep a record of your work so you can undo changes even after you have saved. To redo an Undo, press Ctrl/Command-Y. Note that Undos will not work after you close and reopen the file.

* Finale can record an unlimited number of edits as you work on your score in case you want to undo them later. To tell Finale to do this, for Maximum Number of Undo Levels, enter "0."

* In the Movable Items section, specify the number of pixels to nudge an item each time you press an arrow key.

* Check Automatically Constrain Dragging to tell Finale to always constrain to horizontal or vertical dragging (then press Shift to drag normally at any time).

* Finale will chime to notify you when it is finished processing a major operation. Uncheck Chime When Edit Complete to disable this feature.

Customizing Placement of Finale Files on Your Computer

I have touched on the Folders page of the Program Options a few times already. This page of the Program Options can be used to manage the placement of files used by Finale, or those you create. Choose Folders in the Program Options dialog box from the list on the left to display the Folders page as shown in Figure 13.5.

Figure 13.5

Designate a folder for files used by Finale and those you create on the Folders page of the Program Options dialog box

Use this page as a reference if you're looking for a specific file type used by Finale on your system. Or, select a folder to use for any of these file types by clicking the Browse button and choosing a path. On Mac, to specify a folder, click the check box or the Select button. For example, if you select the Finale 2005/Templates/Band Templates folder for Templates, Finale will open this folder when you choose New Document from Template under the File menu.

TIP
For a description of the Finale file types, see Chapter 1.

Customizing Finale's Display Colors

You can customize the color associated with any item, or turn off all display colors, in the Display Colors page of the Program Options dialog box. Choose Display Colors from the list on the left. You can also open this page from the View menu (View > Select Display Colors). The Display Colors options appear as shown in Figure 13.6.

Figure 13.6

Specify a color for any item, or turn off display colors altogether on the Display Colors page of the Program Options dialog box

Click the item you want to customize to open the Color dialog box where you can choose a new color for the item. Check Layer Colors Apply to All Layer Items if you want all articulations, note expressions, or other note-attached items to match the color of the layer to which they are attached. Uncheck Use Score Colors to tell Finale to use only black and white for display in the score.

TIP

To print the display colors on a color printer as they appear on-screen, check Print Display Colors in the Print dialog box.

Customizing Finale's General Appearance

Finale's graphic interface was overhauled in Finale 2003. Changes include all new tool palettes and backgrounds. These improvements are purely cosmetic and were designed to give Finale a more desirable appearance. You can change the style to use for both palettes and backgrounds, and make other palette settings, in the Palettes and Backgrounds page of the Program Options dialog box. Choose Palettes and Backgrounds from the list on the left to display the Palettes and Backgrounds page as shown in Figure 13.7. Here, you can customize the general appearance of Finale.

Here are some ways to customize the graphic style of tool palettes and the background on the Palettes and Backgrounds page of the Program Options dialog box:

 ❋ Click the Style drop-down menu to choose from the several available palette styles. Choose Traditional if you want to revert back to the palettes as they existed in Finale 2002 or prior (you can save some screen real estate this way).

Figure 13.7

Choose a style for your palettes and backgrounds on the Palettes and Backgrounds page of the Program Options dialog box

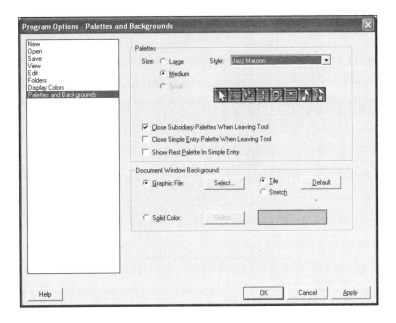

❋ Check Close Subsidiary Palettes When Leaving Tool if you want Finale to automatically remove palettes not associated with the selected tool. For example, with this option checked, Finale will display only the Smart Shape Palette when the Smart Shape Tool is selected. The following two check boxes allow you to make specific palette settings for the Simple Entry Tool Palettes.

❋ In the Document Window Background section, you can set a color or graphic file to appear behind the page while working with Finale in Page View. Click the Select button to open one of Finale's background graphics, or navigate to your own graphics file to set it as the background. On Windows, you can set any bitmap graphic as your background. On Mac, you can set any PICT graphic as your background.

❋ Choose Solid Color and click the Select button to the right to open the Color dialog box where you can select a solid color for your background.

Customizing the Tool Palettes

If there are some tools you do not use at all, you may want to hide them from the tool palette to save space on your screen. You can do this with the Main Tool Palette, any of the secondary palettes, or the menu toolbars. Since this functionality is closely tied to the operating system, it works differently on Macintosh than on Windows.

TIP
To display any tool palette, select it from the Window menu.

To customize your tool palettes on Windows

1. From the View menu, choose Customize Tool Palettes and then choose the palette you want to modify. The Customize Toolbar dialog box appears as shown in Figure 13.8.

Figure 13.8

Remove items from any palette using the Customize Toolbar dialog box

2. Choose any of the icons on the right and click the Remove button to remove it from the palette. After removing a palette icon, select it from the list on the left and click Add to place it back into the palette.

3. Select a palette icon on the left and click the Move Up or Move Down button to change the order of the palette icons. Click Reset at any time to restore the palette back to the default settings.

4. Click Close to return to the score. The modified palette appears on your screen. To change another palette, select it from the Customize Palette submenu of the View menu.

To customize your tool palettes on Macintosh

1. While holding down the Shift key, click and drag a tool icon in the Main Tool Palette to move it to any location in the palette. You can do this with any Finale tool palette, but your changes to the Main Tool Palette can be retained from session to session if you program a Tool Set. Changes to the tool reordering on subsidiary palettes are lost when you quit Finale.

2. You can also save the Main Tool Palette configuration to use at any time. Shift-click and drag the tool icons to the desired configuration. Then, hold down the Option key and, from the View menu, choose Program Tool Set > Tool Set 1. Then, to choose this palette configuration at any time, from the View menu, choose Set Tool Set > Tool Set 1. You can program up to three tool sets. Choose Master Tool Set from the Select Tool Set submenu to use Finale's default palette settings

3. If you intend to resize the palette to hide certain icons, move the ones you want to keep to the left side of the palette. Click one of the icons you want to remain visible before resizing the palette. This way, Finale won't change the arrangement of icons as you resize.

4. Click and drag the resize box at the lower-right corner of the palette to change the size and number of visible tools (see Figure 13.9).

Figure 13.9

Use the resize box on the lower right of any tool palette to change its shape and the number of visible tools

Resize Box

Menu Shortcuts (Windows only)

On Windows, you can map any menu selection to a keystroke using the TGTools Menu Shortcuts plug-in. This way, you can quickly access the dialog boxes you use often or easily activate and deactivate parameters.

To program a keystroke to any menu item

1. From the Plug-ins menu, choose TGTools > Menu Shortcuts. The Menu Shortcuts dialog box appears as shown in Figure 13.10.

Figure 13.10

Use the Menu Shortcuts dialog box to program keystrokes to any menu item for easy access

2. Check Enable Keyboard Shortcuts. For this example, program two menu shortcuts: one to toggle the Display in Concert Pitch setting, and one to open the Global Staff Attributes dialog box.

3. Click the Add button to open the Key Assignment dialog box where you can specify the key and menu item for your menu shortcut (see Figure 13.11).

Figure 13.11

Choose the keystroke and menu item for your menu shortcut in the Key Assignment dialog box

4. Click the Key drop-down menu and choose the keystroke you want to use. For this example, choose the F4 key (in the future, you can select a modifier for any keystroke by checking Ctrl, Alt, or Shift on the right for more options).

5. Under Select Menu Command, choose the menu from the first drop-down menu and the submenus in the following drop-down menus. You may need to use all four tiers for some menu items. For this example, choose Options from the top drop-down menu and Display in Concert Pitch from the second.

6. Click OK to return to the Menu Shortcuts dialog box.

7. Now, let's add another menu shortcut that opens a dialog box. Click the Add button again to open the Key Assignments dialog box.

8. Now, click the Key drop-down menu and choose the F3 key.

9. Under Select Menu Command, choose Plug-ins from the top drop-down menu, Scoring and Arranging from the second drop-down menu, and Global Staff Attributes from the third.

10. Click OK twice to return to the score.

11. Now, to demonstrate these menu shortcuts at work, from the File menu, choose New > Document With Setup Wizard. Move to page 2 and add any transposing instrument (Horn in F, for example). Then click Next, Next, and Finish to open the new score. You might also want to enter some notes.

12. Press the F4 key. Your score displays in concert pitch. Press the F4 key again to display the score in its transposed form. Now, pressing the F4 key does the same thing as choosing Display in Concert Pitch from the Options menu.

13. Press the F3 key. The Global Staff Attributes appears. Now pressing the F3 key does the same thing as choosing Global Staff Attributes from the Plug-ins menu.

Program as many keyboard shortcuts as you like in order to creatively improve efficiency while working on any project. For example, try assigning the F keys to Simple Entry Note durations (Simple menu > Simple Edit Commands) so you can use keystrokes for note durations with Select Notes on Entry activated under the Simple menu. The shortcuts you program will be available whenever you use Finale. To turn off Menu Shortcuts, uncheck Enable Keyboard Shortcuts in the Menu Shortcuts dialog box.

TIP

For more options for keyboard shortcuts on Windows or Macintosh, you might investigate Quickeys. Visit www.quickeys.com for more info.

Working with Scanned Files

Scanning in Finale has improved drastically since its introduction to the File menu (MIDIScan) in Finale 2001. In the past, this particular feature was a technical-support nightmare as scanning technology overall really wasn't ready for prime-time score recognition. Though there are still a number of limitations and problems with translating a scanned page of sheet music into Finale, you can produce far better results with SmartScore Lite, included in Finale 2005, than in previous versions. In this section, you will learn tricks for getting the best possible results while translating a page (or pages) of sheet music into a Finale document.

CAUTION

TWAIN support is not included in the original release of Finale 2005 for Macintosh. If you are using the original Macintosh version, visit www.finalemusic.com to check for a free, downloadable Finale 2005 update.

Scanning Sheet Music

To use Finale's scanning features you will need a scanner and compatible scanning software. Most flatbed scanners will do the trick. Do not try to use a hand scanner while scanning music intended for Finale. For best results, the goal is to create the cleanest possible black and white graphic image of the page. In Finale 2005, TWAIN support was introduced. This means you can now acquire sheet music directly from your scanner. When you do this, Finale attempts to configure your scanning software to optimal settings automatically. Before you scan, note the following:

* The original document should be 16 staves or less.
* Do not expect quality results while translating handwritten scores, or poor-quality printed manuscripts. The cleaner the piece looks on the page, the better Finale will be able to translate it.
* Before scanning, the page should be aligned square with the plate of the scanner.

To acquire sheet music and translate it to a Finale file, do the following. (If you want to translate TIFF graphics that have already been scanned, skip to the next section).

1. Place the first page of sheet music on the bed of the scanner.

2. In Finale, from the File Menu, choose Scanning: SmartScore Lite, and then Acquire. At this point, Finale launches your scanning software and optimizes it for Finale import. If you see the message, "Cannot Communicate with Scanner" or have more than one scanner installed and want to choose a different one, first ensure that the desired scanning software is installed properly. Then, from the File menu, choose Scanning: SmartScore Lite, and then select Twain Source. Choose the desired scanner and click OK.

3. Scan the first page.

4. When the scan is complete, Finale asks you if you want to scan another page. If you do, click Yes, place the next page of music in your scanner, and scan the next page. Keep doing this until you have scanned all pages of the score. After you have scanned all pages, when you are prompted to scan another page, click No.

5. Click Add Files to List. Here you see the files you just acquired from you scanner. (From here, you can also navigate to a folder containing existing scanned files.) Ctrl/Command-click to select the files you want to translate. When you have chosen the desired files, click Open. The files you selected now appear listed in the middle of the SmartScore Lite dialog box as shown in Figure 13.12. Click a file name to see a preview of the file in the preview window on the left.

Figure 13.12

Prepare for scanning recognition in the SmartScore Lite dialog box

6. SmartScore Lite will translate each scanned image as a new page of the same Finale document if you have added several files to the list. Rearrange the file/page order by clicking the Move Up and Move Down buttons on the right to reposition the selected file.

7. Click Begin Recognition. Finale translates each file and opens the resulting document.

The raw results you get immediately after translation will depend on the image quality and complexity of the original sheet music. You may find somewhat of a mess after translating a staff with many voices and complex rhythms. Use the Simple or Speedy Entry Tool to edit any basic notation errors after translation (see Chapters 2 and 3 for information on editing with Simple and Speedy Entry). Here are some tricks for editing scanned files opened with SmartScore Lite:

❋ After translation, all staves will be set for independent key signatures. To turn independent key signatures off, click the Staff Tool, double-click the staff, and then, under Independent Elements, uncheck Key Signature. Now any key changes you make will apply to all staves as they would normally.

❋ If you have scanned a score containing a transposing instrument's part, configure the staff transposition in the Staff Attributes dialog box. Then, use the Mass Edit Tool to transpose the notes back to their original positions accordingly.

❋ Use the Document Options dialog box (Options > Document Options) to change anything from clefs to time signatures to beaming on a document-wide basis.

❋ Use the Selection Tool to reposition items throughout the score as necessary.

❋ Use the Edit Page Margins and Edit System Margins dialog boxes to update system and page margins, or, drag them around manually (see Chapter 11). Note that the page margins are positioned directly over the page edge, so you will probably want to adjust them. If you want to edit the overall layout of your score, use the Page Format for Score dialog box (Options > Page Format > Score). Then, redefine pages (Page Layout > Redefine Pages > All Pages).

❋ To improve the layout, you might want to start a new document with the Document Setup Wizard, and the use the Mass Edit Tool to copy the music from the scanned document file to the new document.

❋ You may find a variety of other changes necessary, for which you can find help throughout this book. If your results are poor (due to file complexity or image quality of the original score), evaluate the time necessary to fix the scanned score compared to entering the music from scratch with the Speedy Entry Tool or any of the other entry methods.

Scanning TIFF Files for Finale Import Manually

Finale is not capable of automatically setting up all scanning software. If SmartScore Lite is unable to recognize files you have scanned using the Acquire feature, try scanning the sheet music manually and then import the files from within the SmartScore Lite dialog box. Following are some guidelines to follow while scanning the sheet music. Consult your scanning program's user manual if you have trouble making any of these settings.

❋ SmartScore Lite accepts TIFF and bitmap files. Always scan in black and white or line art (not color or grayscale). This also might be the FAX setting depending on your scanning software (1 bit per pixel, in any case). Some scanners save TIFF files specific to their product line. If you find your scanning software is producing non-standard TIFF files, try using a black-and-white bitmap file instead. Open the image in another graphics program and then save it in standard (black and white) TIFF or bitmap format.

❋ Set the resolution of your scan to 300 or 350 dpi.

❋ Save your scan as an uncompressed TIFF file (without LZW compression).

Scan each page and save it to a convenient place on your computer. Save each page as a separate file. You might try using a naming convention that relates to the page number (e.g., mypiece1.tif, mypiece2.tif, etc.).

After you have scanned and saved the music, open Finale. From the File menu, choose Scanning: SmartScore Lite, and then TIFF Import. Now, follow the steps in the previous section, beginning with step 5.

{ **NOTE**
SmartScore may have problems recognizing TIFF graphics saved directly from your computer (a screenshot taken from another notation program for example). The SmartScore Lite scanning recognition software expects to see fine inconsistencies in lines and shapes that occur while scanning a printed page. Try printing the document, then scanning the printout to prepare a TIFF graphic for Finale.

Using SharpEye Scanning with Finale (Windows Only)

If you are interested in another scanning option, try using SharpEye scanning software to convert a scanned image into XML format, which can then be imported into Finale with the Dolet MusicXML Import plug-in. Some report that this method produces very accurate results. In addition, this method retains lyrics from the original sheet music, which is not supported in the scanning options included with Finale.

First, if you do not own SharpEye, download and install the SharpEye demo from their Web site at www.visiv.co.uk/dload.htm (you can find instructions for how to do this on the site). Close all programs running on your computer and double-click the installer. When installation is finished, you are ready to continue. You will be able to use the SharpEye demo for 30 days without restriction. After that, you will need to register the software to use it.

To import scanned sheet music into Finale using SharpEye

1. Scan your sheet music and save each page as an uncompressed, black-and-white TIFF or bitmap file. If you have any trouble scanning the file and saving the image, see the instruction manual that came with your scanner and/or scanning software.

2. Open SharpEye (Start > Programs > Visiv > SharpEye).

3. If your sheet music contains more than one page, from the Read menu, choose Batch Process. The Setup Batch window appears. If you want to open a single page, from the File menu, choose Open Image, navigate to the image file and double-click to open it. Then, from the Read menu, choose Read to convert the file to SharpEye format. When conversion is finished, skip ahead to step 9.

4. Click Add Files. Now, navigate to the folder containing your scanned images. Drag or Ctrl-click to highlight the ones you want.

5. Click Open. The selected files now appear in the Setup Batch window.

6. Click the Browse button, and choose a location for the processed files. For now, choose your desktop and click OK.

7. Click Start Batch. SharpEye starts converting the images into SharpEye files. This may take some time, depending on the size and complexity of the scanned images.

8. When conversion is complete, navigate to the desktop. Double-click the first page so it opens in SharpEye. Then, go back to your desktop and double-click the second page. Choose Append to add it to the end of the SharpEye score. Do this for each remaining page.

9. Now you can do some basic editing to optimize the file for Finale import. Many errors can be corrected in either SharpEye or Finale, but it is important to check that the time signatures, key signatures, and clefs are correct before exporting from SharpEye (to ensure that rhythmic durations and pitches translate properly).

10. After you have edited the score, from the File menu, choose MusicXML > Save. Name the file, and save it to your desktop.

11. Open Finale and click the Default Document button in the Launch Window if it appears. Or, from the File menu, choose New > Default Document.

12. From the Plug-ins menu, choose MusicXML Import.

13. Click the Browse button, navigate to the desktop, and double-click the MusicXML file you saved from SharpEye.

14. Click OK. The MusicXML file opens into a Finale document.

Tricks for Music Educators

Finale can make an excellent addition to a music educator's toolbox. Use Finale to create examples, quizzes, worksheets, or even custom exercises for warm-ups for your ensemble. Whether you are a music theory instructor or a band director, in this section you will learn how to effectively benefit from some of Finale's educational features.

Finale's Educational Templates

Finale 2005 offers several templates designed specifically for use in music-oriented classes for worksheets or quizzes. To use one of these, from the File menu, choose New > Document From Template. Then, open the Education Templates folder. Here, you will find seven educational templates.

Two- and Four-Measure Examples

Finale's two- and four-measure templates can be used to create musical examples with descriptions or questions for music theory tests or quizzes (see Figure 13.13).

These documents are specialized in many ways. Courtesy key, clef, and time changes have been turned off, so you won't see extra material at the end of your examples if you decide to change one of these items. The final barline has been removed, the page layout altered, and other minor modifications have been made. The "2 Measure Examples" file offers some suggestions for managing these files in an existing text block. To delete this text block, use the Text (or Selection) Tool. Here are some suggestions for creating musical examples or questions:

* There are two staves per system in both of these documents. Some staves in the two-measure example document have been hidden with a staff style. To hide or show any region of measures, click the Staff Tool. Blue lines appear above all hidden staves. To display the staff, drag-enclose the blue line to highlight the hidden measures (they overlap the subsequent system). Then, press Backspace/Clear to clear staff styles. Now, the two systems overlap.

Click the Page Layout Tool, and then from the Page Layout menu, check Avoid Margin Collision. Click and drag the overlapping system slightly to snap the systems to a more acceptable layout, then make fine adjustments accordingly.

✷ To insert a measure in an example, select the Measure Tool. Click a measure to highlight it, then, from the Measure menu, choose Insert. Finale will insert a measure to the left of the highlighted one. To move a measure from system to system, highlight it with the Mass Edit Tool and press the up or down arrow buttons on your keyboard. To add a measure to the end of your document, double-click the Measure Tool (pages added will appear in the same format as the first page by default).

✷ For the two-measure document, use the Page Layout Tool to increase the overall width of the example. Click the Page Layout Tool, then click one of the system handles on the left. Press Ctrl/Command-A to select them all. Now, all of the left system margins will move in uniform.

✷ Use the Text Tool to edit any of the title information or the questions (double-click the handle to view the editing frame).

✷ Use Staff Styles to change in selected measures the clef, transposition, number of staff lines, or any other staff attribute (see Chapters 7 and 8).

Figure 13.13

Use Finale's two- and four-measure example templates for music theory examples or questions

You can also use the Full System, No Barlines template to create musical examples or questions (see Figure 13.14).

{ **TIP**
E-mail your students a worksheet or musical example. They can open and make basic changes with Finale NotePad, Finale's free notation software available for download at www.makemusic.com.

Figure 13.14

Use the Full System, No
Barlines template to create
dictation and other types of
examples that do not require
a meter

Kodály/Solfège Templates

Finale offers two templates designed for teaching rhythm and sight singing in the Kodály method. With these templates, create stick notation and easily place solfège indications beneath the staff with preset articulation metatools. Following is an example created with the Kodály 1 template.

Figure 13.15

Use Finale's two Kodály
templates to create solfège
and stick notation for
instruction in the Kodály
method

To create a score like the example in Figure 13.15

1. From the File menu, choose New > Document from Template. Then open the Education Templates folder and double-click the file "Kodály 1."

2. Use the Time Signature Tool to change the meter of the document; use the Key Signature Tool to change the key. In this template, the key change will not be visible in the score.

3. You can specify a moveable do by choosing a moveable do clef. Click the Staff Tool and double-click the lower staff. In the Staff Attributes dialog box, click the Select button to the right of the clef display. Choose a moveable do clef from this list to coordinate with the key signature you chose.

4. Click OK to return to the score.

5. Enter your notation into the lower staff.

6. Click the Mass Edit Tool, and then click the left of the lower staff so it is highlighted.

7. Click and drag the highlighted region into the top (hidden) staff. Your notes convert to stems and beams to indicate rhythm. The solid noteheads will disappear, such as quarter notes or smaller. Only half notes and whole notes will still have noteheads.

8. Click to the left of the top staff so it is highlighted.

9. From the Plug-ins menu, choose Note Beam and Rest Editing > Single Pitch.

10. Enter "G4" and click OK. All of your stems and beams are aligned in the top staff.

11. Click the Articulation Tool.

12. Now, move your cursor under the first stem in the top staff (so a small note appears on the cursor). On your QWERTY keyboard, hold down the first letter of the solfège syllable (D=Do, R=Re, etc.) and click. The letter appears below the stem. Repeat this for all other stems in the top staff.

13. If you would like to hide barlines, click the Staff Tool, double-click the staff, uncheck Barlines, and click OK. To hide an individual barline, click the Measure Tool, double-click the measure, and in the Measure Attributes, Barline row, choose Invisible, and click OK.

14. If you want the noteheads on the solfège staff to appear as shapes, apply the Note Shapes Staff Style. Click the Staff Tool and double-click to highlight the lower staff. Right/Ctrl-click the staff and select Note Shapes from the context menu.

Manuscript Paper

You can print a page of manuscript paper from Finale containing staff lines only. To do this, open the Blank Manuscript template. From the File menu, choose New > Document from Template. Then, open the Education Templates folder and double-click the file "Blank Manuscript." A page appears with blank staves and some text. Use the Text Tool (or Selection Tool) to delete any unwanted text. Use the Page Layout Tool to adjust the system spacing. Then print this document to produce a sheet of blank manuscript paper. Rename and save this file as a template for future use.

The Exercise Wizard

If you are a music educator responsible for directing an instrumental ensemble, use Finale as a professional tool for enhancing your students' warm-up routine with customized technique-building exercises. The

Exercise Wizard was added in Finale 2002 and has become a popular tool among educators for enhancing their rehearsal sessions. Create scales, arpeggios, and twisters with custom articulations, in any key, transposed for any instrument. Best of all, this can be done in minutes (you can usually create a customized lesson faster than you can print the parts). You can see an example of a part generated by the Exercise Wizard in Figure 13.16.

Figure 13.16

Create customized lessons, such as this one, orchestrated for any ensemble with any number of performers

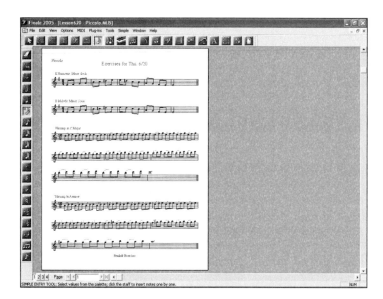

A lesson can contain several different exercises occurring sequentially on the page. You can print or save the lesson for a single part or any combination of instruments (with any number of copies of a part for multiple persons in a section). Here, you will learn how to easily create, save, and print custom lessons.

There are two types of files you can produce with the Exercise Wizard:

* The first is a Lesson file (.LSN). This is basically a text file containing all of the settings you have made in an Exercise Wizard session. You can open a lesson file to launch the Exercise Wizard automatically and edit a collection of settings you have already made.

* The second type of file is the actual notation file (.MUS). Instead of printing directly from the Exercise Wizard, you can save a standard Finale file for each instrumental part to be viewed on-screen or stored and printed at a later time.

Exercise Wizard—Page 1

From the File menu, choose New > Exercise Wizard. Page 1 of the Exercise Wizard appears as shown in Figure 13.17.

First, click the Set Font button and choose a font for the lesson title. Then enter the lesson title in the text box (this title will appear at the top of the printed page). From the Page Size drop-down menu, choose a page size for your exercises. Then, click the Next button to move to page 2.

CHAPTER 13

Figure 13.17

Specify a title and the page size for your exercises on page 1 of the Exercise Wizard

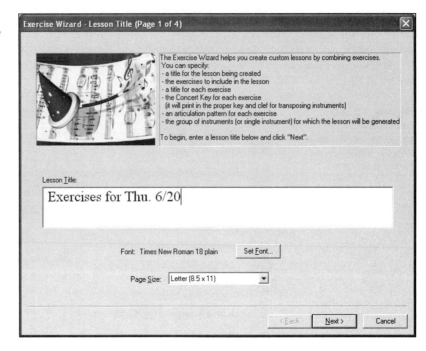

Exercise Wizard—Page 2

On page 2, choose from hundreds of available exercises (see Figure 13.18).

Figure 13.18

Choose the type of exercises you want to include on page 2 of the Exercise Wizard

Click the plus sign (+) to the left of any category to view and choose from items in the subcategories. First choose the melodic structure, then scale type, interval, and note duration. The actual exercises will appear as a number (1–5571). Click a number to see an example of the exercise in the preview window on the lower right. Double-click the exercise number (or click Add) to add the exercise to the lesson. Add as many exercises as you like. Select one of the exercises you have added, and use the up and down arrows to the right of the list to change the order of the exercises as you want them to appear on the page. When you have finished adding and arranging your exercises, click Next to move to page 3.

Exercise Wizard—Page 3

Here you can enter an exercise title, concert key, and articulation pattern for each exercise (see Figure 13.19).

Figure 13.19

On page 3 of the Exercise Wizard, specify a title, concert key, and articulation pattern for each exercise.

First, click the exercise you want to edit from the list at the top. Then, after Exercise Title, type a title for the selected exercise (the title will appear above the first measure of each exercise as shown in Figure 13.14). In the Apply Concert Key section, use the up and down arrows in the scroll bar to modify the concert key. Under Apply Articulations, select an articulation pattern for the exercise. Click Next to move on to page 4.

Exercise Wizard—Page 4

On page 4 of the Exercise Wizard, choose the instruments you want to include in your lesson and number of instruments for each part and range (see Figure 13.20).

First, in the Select an Ensemble section, choose the instrumental ensemble that most closely matches the one you are instructing. Notice the instruments in the list on the right update to your selection. This is the master list of instruments for which you will be generating parts.

Use the following methods to edit the instruments in your ensemble:

❋ Click to select an instrument you want to remove from the list on the right, and click the Remove button to clear it from the list.

❋ To add an instrument, choose the instrument type from the list on the far left, then double-click the desired instrument from the second column. Notice that the instrument appears in your ensemble list on the right.

❋ To add or remove the number of copies per part, click one of the instruments in your ensemble to select it. Then, click the up and down arrows for Number of Copies. Notice the number to the right of the instrument changes to reflect the number of copies for that part.

Figure 13.20

On page 4 of the Exercise Wizard, create an ensemble, then print or save your lesson

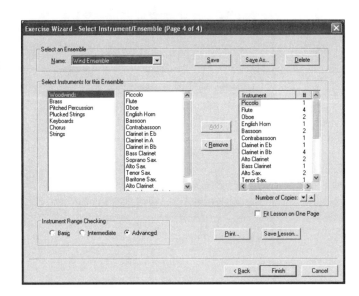

After you have created an ensemble, you might want to save it for the next time you create a custom set of exercises. To do this, in the Select an Ensemble section, click Save As. The Save Ensemble dialog box appears. Type a new name for your ensemble and click OK. Now, next time you create a lesson, this ensemble will be available from the Name drop-down menu.

Under Instrument Range Checking, choose a skill level for your ensemble. If the range of an exercise is too high or too low, Finale will transpose it an octave so all notes fit within a playable range for the selected skill level.

Check Fit Lesson on One Page to tell Finale to manipulate the page layout to fit the lesson on a single page. Finale will make adjustments up to a certain point but will still create more than one page if the layout becomes unreasonable.

Click Print to open the Print dialog box where you can immediately send the lesson to the printer. Finale will place the exercises in the order specified on each page and will also print the number of parts chosen for each instrument. Click Save Lesson to open the Save Lesson As dialog box where you can save the current configuration of settings for future use (choose Lesson File), or save the lesson files as standard Finale files to your computer (choose Notation File). Choose Both to save the lesson configuration and Finale files.

Click Finish to exit the Exercise Wizard. If you have made changes to the current lesson, Finale will ask you if you want to save the lesson before returning to the score.

> **NOTE**
>
> When you are ready to come back and edit a lesson you have already created, from the File menu, choose Open. Select Lesson File as the format. When you open a lesson file (.LSN), Finale will automatically launch the Exercise Wizard where you can make changes to the lesson.

14
PLAYBACK AND THE MIDI TOOL

If you are someone who upgrades each year, you were probably shocked and amazed to experience playback in Finale 2004. This version was a revolution in many ways, and improved playback was perhaps the sweetest frosting on the cake; and it's even better in Finale 2005. First of all, with native Sound Font support, you no longer need a fancy sound card or synthesizer to play back using realistic sounding MIDI instruments. Finale's new SmartMusic SoftSynth provides professional-quality General MIDI sounds forged from live audio samples. If you have always used your computer speakers for playback, your piano score is now performed on a full sized Steinway in a recital hall rather than a tinny electronic spinet. And by performed, I mean processed by a sophisticated Human Playback engine that interprets all musical markings, reads text, and even understands stylistic conventions to generate a simulation of a live human performance.

In this section you will first learn how to manage Human Playback to generate a realistic performance of your score with minimal effort. Then, you'll learn how to use Finale's playback features to spot-check any beat on the fly, play back from any measure, or even isolate specific staves or layers for playback. Finally, you'll learn how to dig in and edit the MIDI data yourself, and even combine Human Playback's interpretation of the score with your own. You'll learn how to manipulate MIDI data for a single note or any selected region with the MIDI Tool, and define a variety of playback effects manually using expressions including volume, pitch bends, tempo, and MIDI controller data.

Here's a summary of what you will learn in this chapter:

* How to use Human Playback
* General playback techniques
* How to use the Instrument List
* How to define playback with expressions
* How to use the MIDI Tool
* How to define other markings for playback

How to Use Human Playback

Using Human Playback (also called HP) isn't difficult. In fact, if you haven't changed any HP settings, all of your new files will play back using the Standard HP style. Here's how it works: When you click the Play button, Human Playback basically analyzes the entire score and adds its own MIDI data temporarily. This

MIDI data is based on articulations, dynamics, and any other marking a performer would respond to during the performance. Although many of Finale's default articulations and expressions have included a default playback effect for years (such as key velocity), HP applies many types of MIDI controllers simultaneously to generate a realistic performance. After the performance, this temporary MIDI data is deleted. Of course, a live performer wouldn't sit down and play a new piece for the first time without evaluating the style of the music. (A Romantic piano concerto is performed differently than a Baroque one.) Because of this, HP allows you to specify the style of your piece. For example, if your Jazz Band score requires a swing feel, simply choose the Jazz HP style, and the swing effect is applied automatically.

To specify the Human Playback style, do the following:

1. If you do not see the Playback Controls, from the Window menu, choose Playback Controls. Windows users, click the speaker icon to open the Playback Settings dialog box. Macintosh users, click the expand arrow on the Playback Controls to show the Advanced options.

2. For Human Playback style, click the drop-down menu and choose the desired style. See Figure 14.1. (Note that you can also turn off HP by choosing None from this list. Or, choose Custom to define your own style, which I'll talk about soon).

Figure 14.1

Choose a Human Playback style, create a new style, or turn off HP in the Playback Settings (Windows)/Playback Controls (Mac) dialog box.

3. Windows users, click OK. Macintosh users, click the expand arrow to minimize the Playback Controls (if desired).

Now, click the Play button in the Playback Controls to review playback. The document plays back using HP's interpretation. HP temporarily removes all MIDI data in the score and replaces it with its own. All existing MIDI data is restored when playback ends.

TIP

When you open a file that was created and saved in a version of Finale prior to 2004, HP is set to None automatically (to respect the same playback you would have experienced in the older Finale version). If you want to use Human Playback for all files converted from earlier versions, from the Options Menu, choose Program Options and select Open. Check Set Human Playback to Standard for Finale Notation Files Created Prior to Finale 2004, then click OK.

If you hear shuddering during playback with HP active, assign each staff to its own unique channel in the Instrument List. To do this

1. From the Window Menu, choose Instrument List. Note any duplicate channels under the Chan. column, and also note channels that are not already used (1–16, with 10 reserved for percussion).

2. To change the channel of a staff, you need to define a new instrument. To do this, click the drop-down menu for the staff under the Instrument column and choose New Instrument. Name the instrument (e.g., "Trumpet 2"), enter a unique channel between 1 and 16, and then click the General MIDI drop-down menu and choose the desired instrument sound.

3. Click OK. Do the same for other staves set to duplicate channels. You'll learn more about the Instrument List later in this chapter.

TIP

HP has a repertoire of words it understands. For example, you can add an expression that contains the text "stretto," and HP will increase the tempo accordingly. For a list of text that HP understands, see "HP Dictionary" in the Appendix of the Finale 2005 User Manual.

It's important to remember that assigning a Human Playback style in the Playback Settings/Playback Controls is like handing your score over to a performer. None of the MIDI data you have added yourself will be used, and the entire score will play back using Human Playback's interpretation. If you want to hear your own manually defined MIDI data for playback (as will be described later in this chapter), you have two options: You can either set Human Playback to None in the Playback Settings/Playback Controls so no HP is applied, or you can specify types of MIDI data HP should use or incorporate in the Human Playback Preferences dialog box (see "Human Playback Preferences" later in this chapter).

If you want to apply Human Playback to specific regions of your score (described next), you need to set the Human Playback style to None in the Playback Settings/Playback Controls.

Applying Human Playback to a Region

When you assign a Human Playback style in the Playback Settings/Playback Controls, you resign to using the same HP style for the entire piece. If you want to apply HP to a specific region of your score, or use more than one HP style in the same score, you can do so with the Apply Human Playback plug-in (introduced in Finale 2005). Rather than temporarily adding MIDI data to your score, the Apply Human Playback plug-in actually adds the HP MIDI data to the selected region.

To apply Human Playback to a region

1. If you do not see the Playback Controls, from the Window menu, choose Playback Controls. Windows users, click the speaker icon to open the Playback Settings dialog box. Macintosh users, click the expand arrow on the Playback Controls to show the advanced options

CHAPTER 14

2. For Human Playback Style, click the drop-down menu and choose None. Since this plug-in actually adds MIDI data to your score, HP needs to be set to None. (Remember, if you choose an HP style in the Playback Settings/Playback Controls, all existing MIDI data is ignored in favor of HP's interpretation during playback). Windows users, click OK. Mac users can minimize the Playback Controls.

3. Choose the Mass Edit Tool.

4. Select a region of measures.

5. From the Plug-ins menu, choose New Plug-ins for Finale 2005, and then Apply Human Playback. The Apply Human Playback dialog box appears as shown in Figure 14.2.

Figure 14.2

Specify a Human Playback style and assign other HP settings in the Apply Human Playback dialog box

6. Here, you can choose an HP style. Select Apply Specific Elements to specify which items you want HP to incorporate or ignore. Select Clear MIDI Data to specify types of existing MIDI data to clear from the selected region.

NOTE

To apply a Jazz style with swing, choose the Jazz style from the list at the top. Choose Apply Specific Elements and click Select. Click the Swing drop-down menu and choose a swing setting. Click OK.

7. Click Apply to apply these settings to the selected region.

8. Click the Play button in the Playback Controls to review playback.

Now, you can follow the same steps to apply HP to other regions of your score. For some playback effects, like tremolos and trills, HP adds hidden notes to your score, so you may see a clutter of gray notes among your original notation. These apply to playback but will not print. (To hide these completely, from the View menu, uncheck Show Hidden Notes and Rests). The MIDI data that the Apply HP plug-in adds to your score can be edited with the MIDI Tool, like any MIDI data you add yourself. You will learn how to create and edit MIDI data manually later in this chapter.

Creating a Custom Human Playback Style

To make fine adjustments to existing HP styles

1. Windows users, click the speaker icon in the Playback Controls to open the Playback Settings dialog box. Macintosh users, click the expand arrow on the Playback Controls to display the Advanced options.

2. From the Human Playback Style drop-down menu, choose Custom. The Human Playback Custom Style dialog box appears as shown in Figure 14.3.

Figure 14.3

Modify an existing Human Playback style in the Human Playback Custom Style dialog box

3. From the Human Playback Style drop-down menu, choose the style that most closely resembles the piece. When you do this, you see the dialog update to the settings for that style. (Note that changing the settings will not affect the existing style in any way.)

4. Use the options and sliders here to modify the resulting playback effect. Here is a quick description of some of the less-obvious parameters:

    ❋ **Rhythmic Feel**. This slider controls the amount of rhythmic variance allowed from the designated time signature and tempo. Moving this slider to the right allows HP more freedom to make subtle stylistic adjustments to the rhythm (without making any changes to the global tempo).

❀ **Rhythm Accents**. This slider controls the amount of dynamic accentuation that is allowed. Move the slider to the right to instruct HP to exaggerate dynamic changes it applies.

❀ **Interpret section**. Here, check items you want HP to recognize in its interpretation.

❀ **Mood slider**. This is the most nebulous parameter in HP. It affects many other HP settings, and no one really knows precisely how (except maybe Mr. Piechaud, who designed HP). Moving the slider to the right increases general chaos, or randomness, during playback.

❀ **Automatic Expression**. This option adds expressivo to held notes for sustaining instruments, and smoothes attacks and releases for soft notes. The degree to which Automatic Expression is applied depends on the Mood slider.

❀ **Detection of Solo Instrument**. If you have a solo instrument in you score, or any solo sections, this box should be checked. HP finds solos in your score (sections marked with the text "solo"), and brings them out automatically.

❀ **Match Harmonic Cadences**. This feature keeps track of the harmonic progression and automatically slows the tempo slightly for cadences.

5. Click OK to return to the Playback Settings/Playback Controls. Notice "Custom..." now appears for Human Playback Style. You can choose Custom from this drop-down menu again to edit your custom style.

6. Windows users, click OK. Macintosh users, click the expand arrow to minimize the Playback Controls (if desired).

7. Click the Play button in the Playback Controls to review playback.

TIP
To apply this custom style to a selected region, in the Apply Human Playback dialog box, under Apply a Defined Style, choose File's Custom Style.

Human Playback Preferences

You can apply additional settings to HP's interpretation, like the number of notes per second in trills, or length of Fermatas in the Human Playback Preferences dialog box (see Figure 14.4). You can also use this dialog box to combine existing MIDI data with Human Playback's interpretation, which is one of the big improvements made to HP in Finale 2005. *Important*: There are two HP Preferences dialog boxes that house the same parameters: one will apply to standard HP (defined in the Playback Settings/Playback Controls) for the entire document; the other will apply to HP applied with the Apply Human Playback plug-in.

To edit HP Preferences for standard HP (defined in the Playback Settings/Playback Controls)

1. Windows users, click the speaker icon in the Playback Controls to open the Playback Settings dialog box. Macintosh users, click the expand arrow on the Playback Controls to display the Advanced options.

2. Click HP Preferences. The Human Playback Preferences dialog box appears as shown in Figure 14.4. (Changes you make here apply to regular HP and do not apply to HP data added to a region with the Apply Human Playback plug-in).

To edit HP Preferences for HP data added to regions of your score with the Apply Human Playback plug-in

1. In the Playback Settings/Playback Controls, set Human Playback Style to None.

2. From the Plug-ins menu, choose New Plug-ins for Finale 2005, and then Apply Human Playback. The Apply Human Playback dialog box appears.

3. Click Preferences. The Apply Human Playback Preferences dialog box appears (which looks the same as the Human Playback Preferences dialog shown in Figure 14.4, except for the word "Apply" in the title bar). Changes you make here apply to all regions of your score for which HP is applied with the Apply Human Playback plug-in, and do not apply to HP defined in the Playback Settings/Playback Controls.

Figure 14.4

Define global settings for HP in the Human Playback Preferences dialog box

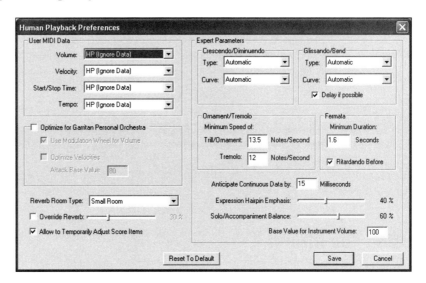

Later in this chapter, you'll learn how to add MIDI data to your score manually. If there is a type of playback effect you can't seem to get right using one of HP's options, you can apply the effect manually using the MIDI Tool, and then tell HP to use your manually defined MIDI data, or even incorporate it into HP's interpretation. This can also come in handy if you are using a score that already contains manually defined MIDI data that you want to use in combination with HP. Look at the four drop-down menus in the upper-left corner of the Human Playback Preferences dialog box (Figure 14.4). These are the four types of MIDI data you can meld with HP. Following is a list of the effects and how you can add them (select the MIDI Tool to display the MIDI menu):

❋ **Volume**. HP uses this type of MIDI data for crescendos, diminuendos, and other dynamic effects for sustaining instruments (winds, strings, voice, etc.). Add this data using the Edit Continuous Data option under the MIDI Tool menu.

❋ **Velocity**. (Also called Key Velocity.) HP uses this type of MIDI data for crescendos, diminuendos, and other dynamic effects for non-sustaining instruments (piano, harp, etc.). This type of MIDI data affects the attack volume only. Add this data using the Edit Key Velocity option under the MIDI Tool menu.

❄ **Start/Stop Time**. HP uses this type of MIDI data to create subtle changes to the duration of notes, and to, for example, overlap notes slightly for slurred passages. Add this data using the Edit Note Durations option under the MIDI Tool menu.

❄ **Tempo**. HP uses this type of MIDI data for tempo changes (*rit.* or *acc.*) and other effects to interpret fermatas, breath marks, and other slight tempo variations. You can add tempo changes manually with the Tempo Tool or by assigning expressions defined for a tempo change.

Each one of these types of MIDI data offers the same three options described below:

❄ **HP (Ignore Data)**. Choose this option to ignore existing MIDI data in the score and use Human Playback's interpretation exclusively.

❄ **HP (Incorporate Data)**. Choose this option to tell HP to recognize existing MIDI data of this type so that it influences HP's interpretation.

❄ **No HP Effect**. Choose this option to tell HP to use the MIDI data that exists in the score. If you choose this option for Velocity, for example, key velocity MIDI data you have applied yourself will be used instead of HP's interpretation. (HP is still free to apply key velocity to regions of the score where the key velocity is not defined already.)

NOTE

The Garritan Personal Orchestra (or GPO), is a professional-quality sound sample library that can be used alongside Finale for extremely realistic playback. If you are using GPO for MIDI Out, check Optimize for Garritan Personal Orchestra in the Human Playback Preferences dialog box. See www.garritan.com for more details on GPO.

Using SoundFonts

A SoundFont is a collection of instrument sounds (WAV files) that can be loaded by a soundcard or software program and triggered by MIDI controllers. You can use SoundFonts as your MIDI output device in Finale. In fact, the SmartMusic SoftSynth SoundFont is loaded for you by default when you first launch Finale. This is a General MIDI SoundFont, the same used in MakeMusic!'s intelligent accompaniment software, SmartMusic. To use this SoundFont on Windows, from the MIDI menu, choose MIDI Setup. Then, ensure SmartMusic SoftSynth is selected for your MIDI Out device. To use this SoundFont on Mac, from the MIDI menu, choose Internal Speaker Playback, and then make sure SmartMusic SoftSynth Playback is checked.

You can use any SoundFont in ".sf2" format. To choose a different SoundFont on Windows, in the MIDI Setup dialog box, click SoftSynth Settings. Then click Select to find and load another SoundFont. Click OK twice to return to the score. On Mac, select a different sound font by going to MIDI > Internal Speaker Playback > SmartMusic SoftSynth Playback Settings.

General Playback Techniques

Now that you've learned how to manage Finale's Human Playback capabilities, let's move on to techniques you can use to review your score in progress. You have a great deal of control over the region of playback

TIP

To use the SmartMusic SoundFont's percussion sounds, set the staff to Channel 10 in the Instrument List (from the Window menu, choose Instrument List). In addition to standard General MIDI percussion, the SmartMusic SoftSynth also contains marching percussion and orchestral percussion sounds. To use the marching percussion, set the patch to "2." For orchestral percussion use patch "49" (for the desired percussion staff in the Instrument List). You can find a list of marching and orchestral percussion sounds in the appendix of the Finale 2005 User Manual. Refer to the Instrument List section later in this chapter for more information on how to use the Instrument List.

while working on a score. You can play back an entire document from the beginning (as you've already seen), easily start playback at any measure, or drag your mouse over a region to deliberately listen for specific chords (scrubbing playback). For any of these methods, you can isolate any number of staves and/or layers using the Instrument List, or even specify a staff or the full score for playback on the spot while scrubbing. In this section, you will learn how to make the most of Finale's playback versatility to spot-check a score in progress, or generate a quality MIDI performance.

Playback Controls

You can use the Playback Controls to manage the basics for playing back your score. If you do not see the Playback Controls on your screen, from the Window menu, choose Playback Controls. They appear on your screen as shown in Figure 14.5.

Figure 14.5

Start, pause, stop, record, or specify the measure to start playback with the Playback Controls

To use the Playback Controls

* Click the Play button to begin playback at the measure specified in the counter box. Playback will start at measure 1 by default. To use the counter on Windows, click the Playback Settings icon (the speaker) on the right side of the Playback Controls. Then, under Always Start At, choose Current Counter Setting and click OK. On Macintosh, click the expand arrow on the Playback Controls to display the Advanced options. After Play From, choose the lower radio button. Now, on Mac or Win, enter a measure number in the counter box to specify a start point for playback.

* Click the square Stop button to stop playback.

❋ Click the Pause button (two vertical bars) to pause playback. Then use the Fast Forward (right arrow) and Rewind (left arrow) buttons to advance to a specific measure. Click the Play button again to resume playback.

❋ Click the single bar on the left to move to the beginning of the piece for playback. Click the single bar on the right to move to the end of the piece.

❋ You can click the Record button to automatically select the HyperScribe Tool and begin recording into the first measure of the staff specified for recording in the Instrument List. While recording into your score, you won't need to use the Record button. Instead, just the select HyperScribe Tool and click the measure you want to record into (see Chapter 4 for more information on HyperScribe).

❋ You can choose a tempo for playback in the Playback Controls. On Windows, click the duration icon (quarter note with arrows). On Macintosh, click the arrow on the left side of the Playback Controls to expand the settings. Click the note duration icon you want to use for the main beat. Then, enter the number of beats per minute in the text box to the right. Note that tempo markings defined for playback in your score will override this setting.

You can make a number of other settings for playback in the Playback Settings dialog box (Windows) or the expanded Playback Controls (Mac). On Mac, click the arrow on the left to expand the Playback Controls; on Windows, click the Playback Settings (speaker) icon as shown in Figure 14.5. You will now see additional playback settings as shown in Figure 14.6. Use these settings to adjust the start point for playback, change the base key velocity, or set swing playback.

Figure 14.6

Use the Playback Settings(Windows)/expanded Playback Controls(Mac) to make a variety of settings for playback

Windows

Macintosh

Here are some common ways to manage playback with these settings:

❋ For Play Mode, you can choose between three types of playback: Non-Scrolling, Non-Scrolling (Pre-Scan Music), and Scrolling. You will probably want to choose Scrolling. With this setting, Finale always scans the music for changes, and then plays back with a scrolling bar. To save time, you could choose Non-Scrolling. With this setting, Finale does not scan the music before playback. Choose Non-Scrolling (Pre-Scan Music) to tell Finale to scan for changes and play back without a scrolling bar. To hear a Human Playback style chosen in the Playback Settings/Playback Controls, you must choose either Scrolling or Non-Scrolling (Pre-Scan Music). (HP applied to regions with the plug-in does not require a Pre-Scan for every playback session.)

✸ In the Always Start At (Mac: Play From) section, choose Leftmost Measure to tell Finale to always begin playback at the leftmost measure displayed on your screen when clicking the Play button in the Playback Controls.

✸ The Base Key Velocity is basically the default dynamic level. This can be set anywhere from 0 (silent) to 127 (loudest). This is set at 64 by default to give you the optimal amount of contrast as you enter dynamic expressions and MIDI data that adjust the key velocity throughout the piece. This option applies to playback with or without HP enabled.

✸ If HP is set to None, you can easily set swing playback here. Choose the type of swing playback you want from the Swing Values (Mac: Swing) option. Click the arrow to choose Light, Standard, Heavy, or Dotted Eighth, Sixteenth from the menu to set swing playback. This setting applies to the entire document. To remove swing from playback, click the same option and choose None from the menu.

Defining Regions for Faster Playback

Though the Playback Controls can be adequate for general playback, if you really want more speed while reviewing a score in progress, you may want to begin playback at a specific measure on the page, or play back a specific staff of your score. Following are ways to quickly isolate specific regions for playback.

Spacebar-Click Playback

Here are ways to easily specify a particular measure for playback using the spacebar-click method. After starting playback with the following methods, click anywhere in the score to stop playback.

NOTE
Human Playback defined in the Playback Settings/Playback Controls is not applied when using the spacebar-click method to start playback.

✸ Press the spacebar (on Macintosh, the Playback Controls must be open), to begin playback at the measure specified in the counter box.

✸ To play back starting at any visible measure, hold down the spacebar and click the desired measure (with the Playback Controls closed on Mac).

✸ To play back the contents of a single staff starting at any visible measure, Shift-spacebar-click the staff in the desired measure.

✸ If you are using a staff set, spacebar-click on a staff to play back the visible staves.

✸ If you are using a staff set, spacebar-click between two staves to play back all visible and hidden staves (see Chapter 7 for more information on creating staff sets in Scroll View).

✸ To begin playback starting with measure one, spacebar-click to the left of the staff

Scrubbing Playback

Listen to notes in your score as you drag by using the Scrubbing Playback feature. (This is called Audio Spot-Checking in the Finale manual.) This is the fastest way to play back a small portion of your score for review.

* Ctrl-spacebar (Mac: Option-spacebar) and drag (without clicking the mouse button) over a region of music to hear music in all staves. (On Mac, make sure to press Option before Spacebar to scrub).

* Shift-Ctrl-spacebar (Mac: Option-Shift-spacebar) and drag over a staff to hear music in that staff only. (On Mac, make sure to press Option before spacebar to scrub).

Recorded versus Notated Playback

If you recorded a performance into Finale with HyperScribe, and Human Playback is set to None in the Playback Settings/Playback Controls, Finale plays the score back as you performed it, including all of the subtleties that go along with your recorded performance. This performance data includes key velocities, note durations, start times for each note, and continuous data you have specified in the Record Continuous Data dialog box. You can tell Finale to play back a score as recorded, or precisely as it appears in the notation in the Playback Options dialog box. From the Options menu, choose Playback Options. The Playback Options dialog box appears as shown in Figure 14.7.

Figure 14.7

Tell Finale to play back a score as recorded or as notated in the Playback Options dialog box

To tell Finale to play the score as notated (without the nuances of your recorded performance), in the Options section, uncheck the Play Recorded Key Velocities and Play Recorded Note Durations check boxes. Uncheck Play Recorded Continuous Data if you want playback to ignore continuous data as well. Then click OK to return to the score and play back the document to review your changes. Or, simply choose a Human Playback Style in the Playback Settings/Playback Controls to use HP's interpretation instead.

NOTE
To specify type of Continuous MIDI data you want to record in a HyperScribe session, from the HyperScribe Menu, choose Record Continuous Data. Refer back to Chapter 4 for details.

Using the Instrument List

In Chapter 2, you learned how to assign a General MIDI instrument to a staff for playback. There are a variety of other ways to customize playback by editing the Instrument List. You can tell Finale to mute certain staves, or even layers within a staff. To demonstrate this, open a score with several staves. Or, begin a new document with the Setup Wizard (New > Document with Setup Wizard). Move to page 2 and add several different instruments. Click Next, Next, and Finish to open the document. Now, use the following steps to explore the options available in the Instrument list. Note that you can play back at any time, even with the Instrument List open.

1. From the Window menu, choose Instrument List. Then, make sure View by Staves is selected in the lower-left corner.

2. Notice the column labeled "P." This is the Play column. To remove a staff from playback, click its box under the P column to clear it. Now, during playback, the staff will remain silent.

3. Designate a solo staff under the "S" column. To designate a solo staff (and mute all other staves), click its box under the S column. Now, only the solo staff will play during playback. Feel free to choose as many solo staves as you like. Finale will play all staves set to solo.

4. Now, click the arrow to the left of a staff name to expand and display more options for that staff. You now see options for layers, expressions, and chords as shown in Figure 14.8. Use the P and S columns to mute or solo any layer within a staff. You can also mute or solo the staff's expressions and chord symbols here. Note that even when you solo a layer, expressions, or chords in a staff, all other staves and their elements become muted.

CHAPTER 14

Figure 14.8

Mute or solo layers, expressions, and chord symbols in the Instrument List

5. Click the Play All button or Solo All button to set every staff to play or solo. Click the Play None or No Solos button to remove all play or solo settings.

Creating Non-General MIDI Instruments

If you are using an external MIDI device, you can use any sound from that device by defining a new instrument in the Instrument List. To create a non-General MIDI instrument for playback

1. From the Window menu, choose Instrument List (if it isn't visible already). Then, make sure View by Staves is selected in the lower-left corner.

2. Under the Instrument column, click the drop-down menu for an instrument and choose New Instrument (at the top of the list). The Instrument Definition dialog box appears as shown in Figure 14.9.

Figure 14.9

Define a non-General MIDI instrument in the Instrument Definition dialog box

3. In the Instrument Name text box, enter the name of the instrument as it appears on your external MIDI device (for reference in the future).

4. In the Channel text box, enter a channel not yet used by any other instruments assigned to staves in the current document.

5. For Patch, choose Bank Select 0, Bank Select 32, Program Change.

6. Under Bank Select 0, enter the primary bank number for the desired instrument. Consult the user manual for your external MIDI device to find this number. Look for one of the bank numbers labeled MSB (Most Significant Byte).

7. Under Bank Select 32, enter the secondary bank number. For the bank you want to use, this will be the LSB (Least Significant Byte) number. If the bank does not have another associated bank number, you can leave this text box empty.

8. Under Program Change, enter the instrument's number. Because some MIDI devices begin numbering at 0 instead of 1, you will need to enter the number of the instrument plus 1 to get the correct sound. (If you want to access instrument number 11 on your keyboard, for example, enter 12 in the Program Change box.)

9. Click OK, and then play back the document for review. Finale will send the playback data to the external MIDI device for the instrument selected.

Instrument Libraries

After you have created a number of instruments, you can save them in a library to be used in any other document. This is especially useful if you have created a number of non-General MIDI instruments for a particular external MIDI device. You can save and load an instrument library just like any other library.

NOTE

Make sure the external MIDI device you want to use for playback is properly installed on your computer and chosen as your output device in Finale's MIDI Setup dialog box. (When using two or more MIDI devices, the base channel may be set higher (such as 17) in the MIDI Setup dialog box, but the device will still respond to instrument channels 1–16 until the device is configured to match Finale's MIDI Setup dialog.) If you are using a software synthesizer, choose the driver for the synthesizer in the MIDI Setup dialog box. Follow the same steps as above for defining non-General MIDI sounds on a software synth.

From the File menu, choose Save Library. Choose Instruments and click OK. Name the library and save it to your Finale/Libraries folder (or another convenient location). Then, to load the library in any document, from the File menu, choose Load Library. Navigate to the Finale/Libraries folder (or wherever you saved the library) and double-click the library file to open it. Now, all of the instruments in the library will appear in the Instruments drop-down menu in the Instrument List. Note that after loading an instrument library into a document, you will still have to select the instruments for each staff in the Instrument List.

Defining Playback with Expressions

Human Playback is capable of interpreting dynamic markings, tempo changes and other markings that apply to playback automatically. For example, enter an expression with the text "rit." and HP knows it is supposed to slow the tempo. Add an expression with the text "cresc." and HP will gradually increase the dynamic level. If you decide to set HP to None and define playback for your score manually, or if you have set the Human Playback preferences to use or incorporate existing MIDI data, expressions can be a good way to define these playback effects. Also, in some cases, such as changing the playback instrument mid-score, expressions are well suited to define the playback effect.

You can define a variety of playback effects in your score with expressions including dynamics, tempo, and the playback instrument. You can apply a playback effect to your score without displaying an expression marking. You can edit the playback effect of any existing expression or define your own playback effect. In this section, you will learn a variety of ways to edit the MIDI performance of your score using the Expression Tool.

NOTE

For specific information on creating, assigning, and editing expressions, see Chapter 3.

Dynamics

As a general rule, use HP (or the Apply Human Playback plug-in) to incorporate dynamics during playback. And then if, for example, a forte section isn't coming through, you might think about using a fortissimo instead. Believe it or not, HP can be used this way to discover the appropriate balance for your ensemble.

However, to apply a dynamic level manually, you can assign a specific key velocity to an expression. Here's how:

1. Click the Expression Tool.

2. Double-click above a measure to open the Expression Selection dialog box.

3. Click to select an existing expression and click the Edit button. Or, to create your own new expression, click the Create button. The Text Expression Designer dialog box appears.

4. Edit the text box as necessary. Then, click the Playback tab.

5. For Type, choose Key Velocity.

6. For Effect, enter the new key velocity, 0–127 (0 =silent, 127 = loudest). (See Figure 14.10.)

Figure 14.10

Use the Playback tab in the Text Expression Designer dialog box to specify a playback effect for the expression.

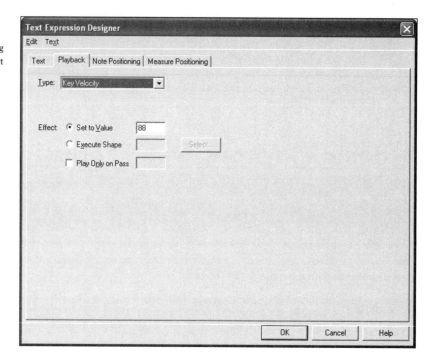

7. Click OK, Select, and OK to return to the score. Play back the region for review. Finale will use this key velocity for the staff until it reaches another key velocity change.

NOTE

Remember, to hear your manually defined playback effects, either set Human Playback to None in the Playback Settings/Playback Controls, or choose Incorporate or No HP Effect for that type of MIDI data (in the example above, choose Velocity in the Human Playback Preferences dialog box.

Setting a Tempo

You may want to enter text indicating the tempo and also define it for playback (Allegro, for example). To do this

1. Click the Expression Tool.

2. Double-click above a measure to open the Expression Selection dialog box.

3. Click to select an existing expression and click the Edit button. Or, to create your own new expression, click the Create button. The Text Expression Designer dialog box appears.

4. Edit the text box as necessary. Then, click the Playback tab.

5. For Type, choose Tempo.

6. Click the drop-down menu to the right and choose the main beat.

7. For Set to Value, enter the number of beats per minute.

8. Click OK, Select, and OK to return to the score. Now, your score will adjust the playback upon reaching this expression. Create another tempo expression if you want to change back to the original or a different tempo.

Changing a Staff's Playback Instrument Mid-Score

Parts sometimes call for an instrumentalist to switch instruments during the piece. If this is the case, you may want to apply this instrument change to playback of your Finale document. The following steps apply with or without Human Playback active. To change the playback instrument for a staff at any point by adding an expression defined to change the MIDI instrument, do this:

1. Click the Expression Tool.

2. Double-click above a measure. The Expression Selection dialog box appears.

3. Click Create. The Text Expression Designer dialog box appears.

4. In the text box, enter text that tells the performer to switch instruments ("to saxophone," for example).

5. Click the Playback tab.

6. For Type, choose Patch. Several new parameters appear.

7. Choose the new instrument just as you would in the Instrument Definition dialog box. If you want to specify a General MIDI instrument, simply click the drop-down menu for GM and select the instrument. To define a non-General MIDI instrument, enter the appropriate Bank Select and Program Change numbers below (see the section above, "Creating Non-General MIDI Instruments," for details on how to do this).

8. Click OK, Select, and OK to return to the score. Finale will now change to the specified instrument during playback upon reaching the added expression.

NOTE

After you have changed the playback instrument, use a Staff Style to update the staff transposition accordingly. See Chapter 8 for more information on applying a Staff Style.

Using the MIDI Tool

The remainder of this chapter describes advanced techniques for defining playback effects manually. If you are satisfied with Human Playback's results, and do not care to manipulate MIDI playback data manually, skip ahead to Chapter 15.

The MIDI Tool is a powerful way to manipulate playback in Finale. Set, scale, add, change percent, or randomize the key velocity and duration of notes for any selected region, or number of selected notes. Or, apply continuous data to a region. Use the MIDI Tool window for a visual display of the MIDI data as you fine-tune changes to the playback. I won't cover every feature of the MIDI Tool, but the following instructions include concepts you can use as a foundation for exploring the thousands of possibilities for creating a custom MIDI performance.

CAUTION
IMPORTANT! To hear your manually defined playback effects, either set Human Playback to None in the Playback Settings/Playback Controls or choose Incorporate or No HP Effect for that type of MIDI data in the Human Playback Preferences dialog box. A Human Playback style selected in the Playback Settings/Playback Controls overrides all manually defined MIDI data by default. To learn how to incorporate MIDI data you define with the MIDI Tool with Human Playback's interpretation, refer back to "Human Playback Preferences" earlier in this chapter.

Key Velocity, Note Durations, and Continuous Data

The MIDI Tool's framework is split into three sections: Key Velocity (how hard a key is struck as if it were played on a MIDI keyboard), Note Durations, and Continuous Data. Click the MIDI Tool, and then choose the MIDI menu. Whenever you are using the MIDI Tool, you can choose which type of MIDI data you want to edit from the three items at the top of this menu. Key Velocity and Note Durations are somewhat self-explanatory. Continuous data encompasses everything from pitch bends and patch changes to more than one hundred types of MIDI controller data, including sustain, panning, volume, and many others. You can manipulate Key Velocity, Note Durations, and Continuous Data in several ways as shown lower in the MIDI menu (Set to, Scale, Add, Percent Alter, etc.).

Here are general steps you can take to edit MIDI data for a region of your score.

Key Velocity (Crescendo Example)

For this example, you'll scale the key velocity over two measures of eighth notes to create a crescendo effect. To prepare for these steps, open a new default document and add eighth notes into the first two measures.

1. Click the MIDI Tool.
2. Drag-select the first two measures so they are highlighted.
3. From the MIDI Tool menu, make sure Key Velocities is selected.
4. From the MIDI Tool menu, choose Scale. The Scale dialog box appears as shown in Figure 14.11.

Figure 14.11

Specify the opening and closing values for MIDI data applied to a selected region in the (Key Velocity) Scale dialog box

5. In the first text box, enter the key velocity for the first note in the region. Try 64. In the second text box, enter the value for the final note in the region. Try 120. These values can be anywhere from 0 to 127. In this case 0 is silent, 127 is very loud.

6. Click OK.

Play back the region. Notice the crescendo effect. You just told Finale to evenly scale the key velocities for the selected region. Now, if you want to set all notes in the selected region to the same key velocity, from the MIDI Tool menu, choose Set To. To change by percent, choose Percent Alter (note that using Percent Alter after the previous example will retain the crescendo). Use any of the available menu items in the second menu section to manipulate the key velocity of the selected region as you wish.

TIP

To remove all MIDI playback data from a region, select the region with the MIDI Tool and press Backspace/Clear. (Since Human Playback applies its own MIDI data temporarily each time you start playback, you will always hear the Human Playback performance if a Human Playback style is selected in the Playback Settings/Playback Controls.)

Note Durations (Start Time Example)

You can alter the start and stop times for any region of notes with the MIDI Tool as well. For this example, enter two measures of quarter notes into your scratch document. Let's say you want notes in the second of these measures to anticipate the beat by a sixteenth note. To do this with the MIDI Tool

1. Click the MIDI Tool.

2. Drag-select the second of the two measures of quarter notes.

3. From the MIDI Tool menu, choose Note Durations.

4. From the MIDI Tool menu, choose Add. The Add dialog box appears as shown in Figure 14.12.

5. Enter −256 in the text box. This setting is in EDUs. There are 1024 EDUs in a quarter note, so 256 EDUs equals a sixteenth. It's negative because you want the notes to play prior to their original placement. Any time you edit note durations in the MIDI Tool by entering a value, you will be using EDUs.

6. Click OK.

Figure 14.12

Edit the start or stop times for a region of notes in the Note Durations > Add dialog box

Play back the region. Notice the second measure of quarter notes anticipates the beat by a sixteenth note. You can use the same basic procedure to change the start time, stop time, or overall duration of notes for a selected region.

Continuous Data (Continuous Crescendo Example)

Continuous Data is somewhat different than Key Velocity and Note Duration data. Continuous Data applies not only to the MIDI Note On and Note Off signals, but also to the entire duration of sustained pitches. For example, to enforce a crescendo or pitch bend on a single sustained pitch, you would need to apply Continuous Data to the region.

To prepare for the following steps, start a new document with the Setup Wizard. Click Next to move to page 2. Choose any sustaining instrument (like Trumpet in C). Click Next, Next, and Finish to open the document. Enter a whole note in the first measure. Use the following steps to apply a crescendo to the whole note.

1. Click the MIDI Tool.

2. Click measure one to select it.

3. From the MIDI Tool menu, choose Continuous Data. The View Continuous Data dialog box appears as shown in Figure 14.13.

Figure 14.13

Choose the type of continuous data you want to apply to your score in the View Continuous Data dialog box

4. From the Controller drop-down menu, choose Controller 7, Volume.

5. Click OK.

6. Click to highlight the first measure.

7. From the MIDI Tool menu, choose Scale. The Scale dialog box appears.

8. Scale continuous data from 40 to 120 in increments of 1.

9. Click OK.

Play back the region and notice the change in volume. To see a graphical representation of this continuous data, double-click the measure to open the MIDI Tool Window.

The MIDI Tool (Split) Window

Instead of editing your MIDI data directly in the score, you can use a separate window to view and edit MIDI data on a graph. When you double-click any measure with the MIDI Tool selected, the MIDI Tool window will appear. This window takes up the top half of the screen on Windows, and opens as a moveable window on Macintosh (See Figure 14.14).

Figure 14.14

View MIDI data applied to a region of your score, or edit MIDI data in the MIDI Tool window

The shaded (Mac) or black (Windows) area indicates continuous data applied to the measures. You can use the MIDI Tool window to view or edit Key Velocities, Note Durations, or Continuous Data.

Macintosh: Editing MIDI Data in the MIDI Window

In your scratch document, enter four quarter notes into a measure. Then, choose the MIDI Tool and double-click the measure containing the four quarter notes to open the MIDI Tool window. To edit the MIDI data for this region, first choose the type of MIDI data from the icons on the left (see Figure 14.14), or choose from the MIDI menu. If you choose Continuous Data, choose the type of continuous data from the View Continuous Data dialog box and click OK. Then, click and drag in the MIDI display portion (upper right) to select the region you want to edit as shown in Figure 14.15. The selected region will be highlighted in blue.

Figure 14.15

Click and drag in the MIDI display portion of the MIDI Tool window to select the region you want to edit

If you want to highlight more than one non-consecutive region in the graph area, Shift-click and drag. If you are editing Key Velocities or Note Durations, you can also highlight the handles to select individual notes in the measure display portion at the bottom (Shift-click to select non-consecutive notes). Now, from the MIDI Tool menu, choose the type of modification (Set to, Scale, Add, etc.). Enter the desired value and click OK. The MIDI display portion of the MIDI Tool window updates to display your changes.

To navigate in the MIDI Tool window:

✻ Use the arrows to the left of the measure display portion to navigate to the desired measure or staff. Click the left arrow to move back a measure, the right arrow to move forward a measure, the up arrow to move up a staff, and the down arrow to move down a staff. Notice the Staff and Measure indicator above the arrows indicates the exact measure you are currently viewing.

✻ Click the layer select pop-up menu in the lower left to choose the layer you want to edit.

✻ From the MIDI Tool menu, choose Show Selected Notes to isolate the selected notes in the MIDI display portion of the MIDI Tool window.

To play back the region without leaving the MIDI Tool window, from the MIDI Tool menu, choose Play. Click anywhere to stop.

Windows: Editing MIDI Data in the MIDI Split Window

In your scratch document, enter four quarter notes into a measure. Move to Scroll View (Scroll View tends to be more convenient while using the MIDI Split window, though both views will work). Choose the MIDI Tool and double-click the measure containing the four quarter notes to open the MIDI Tool Split window. It will appear on the top half of your screen and display MIDI data for several measures. To edit the MIDI data for this region, first choose the type of MIDI data from the MIDI Tool menu (see Figure 14.16).

Figure 14.16

Click and drag to enclose the notes or region you want to edit in the MIDI Tool Split window

If you want to highlight more than one non-consecutive region in the graph area, Shift-click and drag. If you are editing Key Velocities or Note Durations, you can also highlight the handles to select individual notes in the staff below the Split window (Shift-click to select non-consecutive notes). Now, from the MIDI Tool menu, choose the type of modification (Set to, Scale, Add, etc.). Enter the desired value and click OK. The MIDI display portion of the MIDI Tool window updates to display your changes.

To navigate in the MIDI Tool Split window:

* Use the scroll bar on the bottom to move horizontally through your score. Use the scroll bar on the right to move up or down between staves.
* Use the layer select buttons on the lower left of your screen as you would normally to switch layers.
* From the MIDI Tool menu, choose Show Selected Notes to isolate the selected notes in the MIDI Tool Split window.

To playback the region without leaving the MIDI Tool window, from the MIDI Tool menu, choose Play.

Copying MIDI Data

You can copy MIDI data from one region and apply it to any other region of your score with the MIDI Tool. This feature works just like drag-copying with the Mass Edit Tool. To copy MIDI data:

1. Click the MIDI Tool.
2. Highlight a region of your score containing MIDI data you want to copy.

CHAPTER 14

3. From the MIDI Tool menu, select the type of MIDI data you want to copy.

4. Click and drag the highlighted region to the destination region. If the destination region is out of view, Ctrl/Option-Shift-click the first measure of the destination region. The Copy MIDI Data (Mac: Copy) dialog box appears.

5. Enter the number of times you want to copy the MIDI data. For example, if you are copying a single measure and want to apply the same MIDI data to the next five measures, enter "5" here.

6. Click OK.

Defining Other Markings for Playback

Although Human Playback redefined Finale's ability to generate a convincing MIDI performance quickly and easily, there is no shortage of techniques for manually adding playback effects. Holding true to Finale's reputation of customizability, with enough time and inclination you can tweak just about anything to your precise specifications, and editing playback is no exception. In this section, you'll learn how to manually define an accellerando or ritardando, and use some of Finale's other tools to create other types of playback effects.

Defining Ritardandi and Accelerandi with Executable Shapes

The following example is not recommended unless you insist on defining a ritardando or accelerando to an exact duration and/or tempo adjustment. Most agree that Human Playback does a sufficient job interpreting these markings in the score for you automatically. Most of all, the following instructions illustrate one of the murky secrets of Finale that only a power user would ever care to investigate: executable shapes. An executable shape is a diagram constructed in the Shape Designer that acts as a graphical representation of a playback effect. Using this method, you can scale a change in volume or tempo a specific amount over a specific duration.

In this example, you'll learn how to create a ritardando marking as an expression and define it for playback. You can apply the same principles to create an accelerando.

NOTE

Before going through the following steps, you might first try using the JW Tempo plug-in to define gradual tempo changes. With this plug-in, all you need to do is select a region and then define an opening and closing tempo for the region. See www.jwmusic.nu/freeplugins/index.html.

1. With the Expression Tool selected, double-click the score where you would like to begin the ritardando. The Expression Selection dialog box appears.

2. Scroll down and click the "*Rit.*" marking to select it.

3. Click Edit. The Text Expression Designer appears.

4. Click the Playback tab to show the playback options.

5. For Type, choose Tempo. Then choose the main beat from the drop-down menu to the right. At this point, you could click OK, Select, and OK to return to the score and use Finale's default "*Rit.*" playback definition. In the following steps, I'll show you how to specify your own custom gradual tempo adjustment.

6. After Effect, choose Execute Shape, and then click the Select button to the right. The Executable Shape Selection dialog box appears.

7. Click to select line number 4 (the line slanting downwards—for an accelerando, you would choose a line slanting upwards).

8. Click Duplicate, and then click Edit. The Executable Shape Designer dialog box appears as shown in Figure 14.17.

Figure 14.17

Edit the duration and degree of an executable shape in the Executable Shape Designer dialog box

9. Click the Shape ID button to open the Shape Designer dialog box. This is where you will define the basic duration and degree of your tempo change.

10. From the Shape Designer menu, choose Rulers and Grid. The Rulers and Grid dialog box appears.

11. Choose Eighth Notes. Then for Grid Marks Every, enter "4" and click OK

12. From the Shape Designer menu, choose Show, and then Grid.

13. The Shape Designer window should now contain grid markers (see Figure 14.18). Each horizontal grid marker (from left to right) equals four eighth notes, or a half note's duration. In this example, the line extends over two grid markers horizontally, so the ritardando is defined to last for one measure in 4/4 time. Each vertical grid marker (from top to bottom) equals one beat per minute. Since the line slopes down over two markers, the tempo will slow down two beats per minute from the original tempo over the course of the tempo change. In the future, use the Selection Tool to adjust the slope and length of the line as needed. For now, multiply the duration and number of beats per minute of the tempo change.

14. Click OK to return to the Executable Shape Designer.

15. Now, you can edit the duration and number of beats per minute in the Time Scale and Level Scale text boxes. You will be entering a ratio that adjusts the executable shape you defined in the Shape Designer. For Time Scale, enter "2:1." A ratio of 2:1 tells Finale to multiply the duration by 2—in this case increasing the duration to two measures. For Level Scale, enter "10:1." A ratio of 10:1 tells Finale to multiply the number of beats per minute by 10—in this case increasing the tempo change to 20 beats per minute. In the future, use any desired ratio to edit the executable shape you have defined in the Shape Designer.

CHAPTER 14

Figure 14.18
Edit the duration and degree
of an executable shape in the
Shape Designer dialog box

Duration

Beats Per Minute

16. Click OK, Select, OK, Select, and OK to return to the score. The "*Rit.*" marking appears.
    Play back your score to review your tempo change. To resume a specific tempo at any point
    in your score, follow the previous instructions for Setting a Tempo. Remember, HP must be
    set to None in order to hear any playback effect applied with an expression.

The TGTools Smart Playback Plug-In

The Smart Playback plug-in is an alternative to manually defining a playback effect from scratch if you are
not using Human Playback, or want to create your own playback effect for a portion of your score. You can
simply set your parameters in the Smart Playback plug-in, and Finale will adjust the corresponding MIDI
data, or add hidden playback notes for you accordingly. Use these examples as a guide to easily define trills,
glissandi, and hairpins for playback. The Smart Playback dialog box is modeless, so you will always be able
to apply the current settings without leaving the dialog box.

The Smart Playback plug-in adds MIDI data to your score much like the Apply Human Playback plug-in. The
Smart Playback plug-in, however, allows you to specify parameters for a single type of marking.

CAUTION
The Smart Playback plug-in is defined to override HP by default. There is no need to set HP to None to
hear playback effects applied with the Smart Playback plug-in (as long as Override Human Playback is
checked in the Smart Playback dialog box).

To prepare for this section, open a new default document (File > New > Default Document). Use this as a scratch document while going through the following steps.

Glissandi

When you define a glissando for playback with the Smart Playback plug-in, Finale also creates continuous data (pitch bend) that increases the pitch of the starting note a certain number of times per quarter note until reaching the destination note. The successive pitch changes are so frequent that the playback gives the effect of a glissando. To define glissandi for playback using the Smart Playback plug-in

1. Enter two notes on different pitches into the first measure of your scratch document. Then, click the Smart Shape Tool and choose the Glissando Tool from the Smart Shape Palette. Double-click the first note to extend a gliss to the second. Your first measure should look something like the example shown in Figure 14.19.

Figure 14.19

Use the Smart Playback plug-in to define a glissando such as this one for playback

2. Choose the Mass Edit Tool.

3. Highlight the first measure.

4. From the Plug-ins menu, choose TGTools > Smart Playback. The Smart Playback dialog box appears as shown in Figure 14.20.

Figure 14.20

Set parameters for trills, glissandi, and hairpin playback in the Smart Playback dialog box

5. In the Smart Playback dialog box, make sure Glissandi is checked. For now, leave Number of Steps per Quarter Note at 20 (an indistinguishable distance between note changes at most tempos). You can decrease this value in the future for a more jagged glissando (for piano perhaps) or increase this value for a finer transition at extremely slow tempos.

6. Click Go. You shouldn't see any changes to your notation. Play back the region to review the glissando.

TIP

Human Playback uses pitch bend MIDI controller data to produce very convincing pitch bends that are delayed slightly so that the majority of the playback effect occurs later in the glissando (as is standard performance practice).

Hairpins

When you define a hairpin crescendo or decrescendo for playback, Finale creates continuous data scaling the volume (controller #7) at the degree you specify. To define hairpins for playback using the Smart Playback plug-in

1. Enter a passage of eighth notes into the first two measures of your scratch document. Then, click the Smart Shape Tool and use the Crescendo and Decrescendo Tools in the Smart Shape Palette to create a crescendo under measure one and a decrescendo under measure two as shown in Figure 14.21.

Figure 14.21

Define crescendo and decrescendo hairpins such as these for playback using the Smart Playback plug-in

2. Choose the Mass Edit Tool.

3. Highlight the first two measures.

4. From the Plug-ins menu, choose TGTools > Smart Playback. The Smart Playback dialog box appears.

5. Click the Hairpins tab. Leave Volume Changes per Quarter Note at 15 and leave Set Volume to 64 at beginning of piece checked.

6. Click Go. Play back the region to review the crescendo and decrescendo.

To see the continuous data you have created, click the MIDI Tool. From the MIDI Tool menu, choose Continuous Data, set Controller Data to "Volume: 7," and click OK. Double-click one of the measures. This opens the MIDI Tool window with the volume data visible (see Figure 14.22). Click and drag to highlight the region, and then choose one of the editing options under the MIDI Tool menu to adjust the controller data.

NOTE

In the Smart Playback plug-in, when you choose Set Volume to 64 at the beginning of a piece while defining a hairpin for playback, you may notice the document sounds quieter during playback. To restore the original volume while keeping the defined hairpin playback, try setting the Base Key Velocity to 127 in the Playback Settings (Windows: click the Playback Settings icon in the Playback Controls; Mac: Expand the Playback Controls).

Figure 14.22

Use the MIDI Tool to edit controller data defined by the Smart Playback plug-in

Trills and Drum Rolls

To define trills for playback using the Smart Playback plug-in

1. In your scratch document, enter two whole notes in consecutive measures.

2. Enter a trill articulation over the first one and a trill Smart Shape over the second as shown in Figure 14.23 (the Smart Playback plug-in will generate a sounding trill from either of these markings). Of course, in the future, add a trill articulation or Smart Shape to any note before using this plug-in.

Figure 14.23

Before defining trills for playback, enter either a trill articulation or trill Smart Shape over the desired notes

3. Choose the Mass Edit Tool.

4. Highlight the measures containing the notes with trill markings.

5. From the Plug-ins menu, choose TGTools > Smart Playback. The Smart Playback dialog box appears.

6. Click the Trills, etc. tab.

7. Now, define your trill. For now, leave the trill check boxes and text boxes alone (the defaults will work fine). In the future, use these parameters to adjust the frequency of your trill and the presence of unmeasured tremolos. Under Trill Interval, choose the interval of the trill. The setting you choose will produce a trill alternating either one semi-tone higher or one whole tone higher with the original pitch.

8. Click Go. Hidden notes appear (if Show Hidden Notes and Rests is checked under the View menu). Play back the region to review the playback you defined.

You can also use the trill settings in the Smart Playback dialog box to generate repeated pitches (for drum rolls, for example). For this example, start a new percussion staff. From the File menu, choose New > Document with Setup Wizard. Click Next, add a Snare Drum staff, and then click Next, Next, and Finish to open a new snare drum document. Here is how to notate and define drum rolls for playback.

1. In your scratch document, enter notes with subdivision markings like those shown in Figure 14.24.(Use Articulation metatools 6,7, and 8 to quickly add the subdivision marks).

Figure 14.24

Generate playback of drum rolls with the Smart Playback plug-in

2. Choose the Mass Edit Tool and highlight the region.

3. From the Plug-ins menu, choose TGTools > Smart Playback. The Smart Playback dialog box appears.

4. Click the Trills, etc., tab.

5. In this example, there are three "unmeasured tremolos," each entered on a quarter note. Make sure Three slashes = unmeasured tremolo is checked. Then, after Trill/unmeasured tremolo speed, enter the number of strikes per quarter note (a higher number = tighter roll). In the text box next to Start trill after what percentage of duration, enter "0" (since you want each roll to begin immediately).

6. Click Apply. To turn off the display of hidden notes, from the View menu, uncheck Show Hidden Notes and Rests.

7. Play back the region to review the playback you defined. You will hear the subdivision indicated by the number of slashes, and notes with three slashes subdivided according to your settings for unmeasured tremolo.

Fermatas

Human Playback applies fermatas by slowing the tempo with the Tempo Tool during the fermata. You could apply the same Tempo Tool data manually, but the Tempo Tool isn't required to define this effect.

Defining a fermata for playback manually is best achieved with two tempo expressions, one to slow the tempo for the held note and then a hidden one to return to the original tempo. To prepare for the following steps, enter four quarter notes into a measure. You'll add a fermata on the third beat and define it for playback.

Remember, HP needs to be set to None, or the Tempo setting in HP Preferences needs to be set to No HP Effect to hear any manually defined tempo adjustments.

1. Click the Expression Tool and double-click on the third quarter note in the measure. The Expression Selection dialog box appears.

2. Make sure Note Expression is selected at the bottom of this dialog box.

3. Click Create to open the Text Expression Designer dialog box.

4. Click Set Font. The Font dialog box appears.

5. For Font, choose Maestro. For Size, choose 22.

6. Click OK to return to the Text Expression Designer.

7. In the text box, type "U" (capital U).

8. Click the Playback tab.

9. For Type, click the drop-down menu and choose Tempo.

10. For Set to Value, choose a slower tempo. For example, if the tempo of your piece is quarter = 96 beats per minute, enter "48" to decrease the tempo by half (doubling the duration of the note).

11. Click OK, Select, and then OK to return to your score. The fermata should appear above the note.

12. Now, you need to create an expression attached to the next note that tells Finale to return to the original tempo. Double-click on the note directly following the held note to open the Expression Selection dialog box.

13. Click Create to open the Text Expression Designer. Leave the text field blank (or use a hidden text style).

14. Click the Playback tab. For Type, click the drop-down menu and choose Tempo.

15. For Set to Value, choose the original tempo. For example, if the tempo of your piece is quarter = 96 beats per minute, enter "96."

16. Click OK, Select, and OK to return to the score.

17. Play back the region for review. Notice the scroll bar slows at the tempo change and then returns to the original speed after the held note. To increase the duration of the held note, right-click the handle of the fermata and choose Edit Text Expression Definition. Then decrease the number of beats per minute in the Set to Value text box.

CHAPTER 14

Rolled Chords

In piano music it is common to see a wavy line next to a chord telling the performer to "roll," or play each note of the chord in rapid succession, beginning with the lowest written note. Human Playback uses Note Durations to stagger the start times of notes in rolled chords. You can use the MIDI Tool to edit these start and stop times manually, but it's easier to create a rolled chord marking and define it for playback simultaneously with the Articulation Tool.

TIP

To use Human Playback's interpretation for all aspects of playback besides rolled chords (and other duration changes), in the Playback Settings/Playback Controls, choose the desired Human Playback style, then click HP Preferences. For Start/Stop Time, click the drop-down menu and select No HP Effect, and then click Save.

To create rolled chord marking and define it for playback

1. Enter a tall chord in a scratch Finale document with the Simple or Speedy Entry Tool.

2. Click the Articulation Tool.

3. Click the bottom note of a chord to open the Articulation Selection dialog box.

4. Click to highlight the Rolled Chord articulation (number 31 by default).

5. Click Edit to open the Articulation Designer dialog box.

6. In the Playback Effect section, notice that Change Attack is selected, and the setting for Bottom Note Value is –256. These settings tell Finale to play the bottom note of the chord 256 EDUs prior to the beat followed by the remaining notes in ascending order. The top note will sound directly on the beat (since Top Note Value is set to 0). If you want to begin the roll on the beat, set the Bottom Note Value to 0 and the Top Note Value to 256. To increase the overall duration of the roll, set the number for Bottom Note Value to less than –256 if the roll starts before the beat, or set the number for Top Note Value to greater than 256 if the roll starts on the beat.

7. Click OK and Select to return to the score. Click the top handle and drag to position the articulation. Click and drag the lower handle up or down to change the length of the roll marking.

TIP

Use the "R" metatool to quickly enter a rolled chord. With the Articulation Tool selected, simply hold down R and click the chord.

15

INTEGRATING FINALE WITH THE WEB AND OTHER PROGRAMS

Finale files are extremely versatile. You can e-mail a Finale file to anyone or post it on a Web site. The recipient can open it in NotePad, Finale's free, downloadable counterpart. You can save your Finale file as a MIDI file to edit in a MIDI sequencer, save it as an MP3 to distribute online or as a WAV file to burn to a CD. These are just a few examples of Finale's ability to transfer your music into other formats. With the help of third-party programs and plug-ins, you can perform even more tasks, such as converting a Finale file to MusicXML format to transfer to other music programs or even earlier versions of Finale.

Here's a summary of what you will learn in this chapter:

* How to share files online
* How to transfer music between programs
* How to enhance Finale with FinaleScript and third-party plug-ins

Sharing Files Online

There are two ways to post a Finale file on the Web. If you want to share your sheet music over the Web without playback capabilities, you can convert a Finale file into PDF format. Secondly, you can simply post a file in Finale format so that others can open it in Finale or any of the Finale Notation products. Visitors who don't own Finale can always download a free, basic version of Finale, called Finale NotePad, which is capable of opening any Finale file. In this section, you will learn how to use the above methods to integrate Finale with the Web.

Finale NotePad

You may want to transfer a Finale file over your Web site or by e-mail, with the intention of allowing those who receive the file full access to print, save, or even make minor changes to the file. You may be a music educator sending a musical example or homework to your students. If this is the case, recipients of the file may not own Finale (or its most recent version). That's okay. Tell them to download Finale NotePad.

Finale NotePad is MakeMusic!'s baby notation product. It offers a considerable amount of power considering the price (free). Here are some of NotePad's features:

* Open, save, and print any Finale file. That includes any file created in any version of Finale, Finale Allegro, Finale PrintMusic!, Finale Guitar, or Finale NotePad. You can also create new files from scratch with up to eight staves.

* Using Simple Entry, edit or create notation.

* Transpose to any key.

* Add basic elements to your score, including articulations, expressions, lyrics, text blocks, slurs, and hairpins.

* Save as a SmartMusic Accompaniment.

To download Finale Notepad, visit MakeMusic!'s Web site at www.finalemusic.com. A link on their home page will direct you to the NotePad download page (you can't miss it).

NOTE

If you are using Finale for Macintosh and you intend to e-mail a file, make sure to check Append File Extension in the Save As dialog box. As long as the .MUS extension appears after the file name, the file will open on Finale for Windows.

Saving as a PDF File

The PDF file format is great for transferring files over the Web or by e-mail. PDF files can be opened using the Adobe Acrobat Reader (available for free at Adobe's Web site, www.adobe.com) or, on Macintosh, PDFs can also be opened with Preview. Note that Adobe Reader is installed with Finale and used to view the Finale User Manual (which is in PDF format.) What exactly is a PDF file? Here's some text from their Web site that sums it up nicely:

"Adobe® Portable Document Format (PDF) is the open de facto standard for electronic document distribution worldwide. Adobe PDF is a universal file format that preserves all the fonts, formatting, graphics, and color of any source document, regardless of the application and platform used to create it. Adobe PDF files are compact and can be shared, viewed, navigated, and printed exactly as intended by anyone with free Adobe Acrobat® Reader® software. You can convert any document to Adobe PDF using Adobe Acrobat software." (See www.adobe.com/products/acrobat/adobepdf.html.)

If you are using a Macintosh computer, OS X offers the ability to print directly to a PDF. If you are using Windows, some additional steps are necessary.

To save a Finale file in PDF format on Macintosh

1. From the File Menu, choose Print. If the Page Setup dialog box appears, set up the page size and layout as you would normally. Click OK.

2. The Print dialog box appears. Click Save As PDF. (At this point, you could also choose Output Options from the pop-up menu, check Save As File, and specify PDF (or PostScript to create a .PS file).

3. Enter a name, specify a location, and click OK.

To save a Finale file in PDF format on Windows:

> **NOTE**
> These steps require Adobe Distiller, which can be purchased from Adobe. If you do not own Adobe
> Distiller, you could also investigate less costly PDF generation tools, such as PDF995 (www.pdf995.com).

1. First set up the Adobe Distiller as a printer. See your Adobe Acrobat instruction manual for instructions on how to do this.
2. Then, from the File menu, choose Print. In the Print dialog, click the Setup button.
3. Click the Printer/Name drop-down menu and choose the Adobe PDF. Then click OK to return to the Print dialog box.
4. Check Print to File.
5. Click OK.
6. The Save As dialog box appears. Name the file, choose a destination, and click Save to save the PDF file.

If you like, you can also generate a PostScript file to be converted to a PDF later. To do this, from the File menu, choose Compile PostScript Listing. The Compile PostScript Listing dialog box appears. Make any necessary changes to page size and format and click Compile. In the Compile/Save PostScript File As dialog box, name the file, choose a destination, and click Save. Now, to convert the .PS file to a PDF, simply drag it into the Adobe Distiller icon.

Transferring Music between Programs

You may want to take a file you have created in a MIDI sequencer (such as Cakewalk or Cubase) and open it in Finale to generate sheet music, or even copy excerpts of music back and forth between these programs using the MIDI clipboard. In this section, you will learn how to do this. I'll also explain a method for opening new Finale files in earlier versions (as far back as Finale 2000) and how to convert a Finale file into MP3 or WAV format for online sharing or to be burned to a CD.

MIDI Files

If you want to use a MIDI sequencer program to open a Finale file, you could save it from Finale as a MIDI file. To do this, click the File menu and choose Save As. On Windows, for Save As Type, choose MIDI File; on Macintosh, for Format, choose Standard MIDI File. Enter a file name and click Save. You will then see the Export MIDI File Options dialog box as shown in Figure 15.1.

You will probably want to choose Format, which will designate your staves into tracks. This is by far the most common MIDI file format. If you want to place all of your music into one track, choose Format-0. Click OK to save as a MIDI file.

If you want to open a file from another program, such as a MIDI sequencer, first save the file in Standard MIDI format from the sequencer. Then, in Finale, choose the File menu and then Open. On Windows, for Files of Type, choose MIDI File, (on Mac, choose Standard MIDI File from the Enable popup menu), then double-click the MIDI file, and you will see the Import MIDI File Options dialog box as shown in Figure 15.2.

Figure 15.1

The Export MIDI File Options dialog box

Figure 15.2

The Import MIDI File Options dialog box

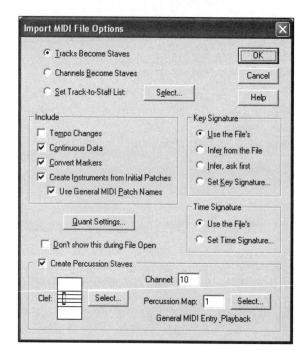

In this dialog box, you can tell Finale how to interpret the MIDI file. Make any desired changes and click OK to open the MIDI file into a Finale document.

Copying Music between Programs with the MIDI Clipboard

Like copying music from measure to measure in Finale, you can also move selected regions of music between documents in other programs that support the MIDI clipboard. The other program could be any MIDI sequencer or any program with MIDI editing capabilities. To move music (MIDI data) from Finale to another program, do the following:

1. Open Finale and the other MIDI program.

2. In Finale, click the Mass Edit Tool.

3. Highlight a region of music.

4. From the Edit menu, choose Export MIDI to Clipboard.

5. Move to the other MIDI program with the file you want to work with open.

6. Select a region of one of the MIDI tracks (or equivalent). See documentation of the MIDI application for more details (precise instructions for selecting a region vary between programs).

7. Press Ctrl/Command-V to paste MIDI data into the selected region.

Similar steps can be used to copy MIDI data from another MIDI program to Finale. In the other MIDI program, select a region of a MIDI track and press Ctrl/Command-C. Then, in Finale, highlight a region of measures with the Mass Edit Tool. From the Edit menu, choose Import from MIDI Clipboard. You will see the Import MIDI Data from Clipboard dialog box as shown in Figure 15.3.

Figure 15.3

Customize Finale's interpretation of MIDI data in the Import MIDI Data from Clipboard dialog box

While copying MIDI data between programs, the results you get will depend on the quantization settings in the program of the destination document. In Finale, click the Quant Settings button in the Import MIDI Data from Clipboard dialog box to choose the smallest note value and make other settings for the imported MIDI data (refer back to Chapter 4 for more information about quantization in Finale). Click OK to return back to the score to see the MIDI data as notes in a Finale staff. Hold down the Shift key while choosing Import MIDI Data from Clipboard from the Edit menu to bypass the Import MIDI Data from Clipboard dialog box. Consult the user manual for the other MIDI program for information on how to configure its quantization settings.

In addition to copying notes from other MIDI programs, you can also copy MIDI data such as volume changes and pitch bends. Just make sure the source region in the other MIDI editing program doesn't contain MIDI note data, then copy and import the MIDI information into the desired region in Finale. You'll find more information on Finale's MIDI capabilities in Chapter 14.

{ **TIP**
While attempting to review results from copying MIDI data between programs, you may find that playback in Finale or the other MIDI program may not work if they are both open at the same time. Close both programs (make sure to save any files you want to keep), then open the program you want to play back with first.

Backwards Compatibility and MusicXML (Windows Only)

Many programs, such as Microsoft Word, allow you to save documents so that they are compatible with earlier versions of their software. For example, you can save a document from Microsoft Word 2000 in Word 97 format. Then, open the file on a different computer that has only Word 97. This makes the program "backward compatible." Finale does not support backward compatibility, so files created in Finale 2005 cannot be opened directly in Finale 2004 or any earlier version of Finale. There are always too many new features in Finale that control placement of slurs, articulations, and other items that did not exist in earlier versions. Therefore, older versions of Finale would not be able to read this information, and many items would be misplaced in translation.

> **NOTE**
> Though files created in newer versions of Finale cannot be opened in any older version, the latest version of Finale will open any Finale file created in any earlier version.

In the past, the best way to transfer documents to earlier versions was by saving and opening a MIDI file. This method is unacceptable most of the time because all text and formatting gets lost while generating the MIDI file. Today, a new universal music file format has been developed, called MusicXML. Unlike MIDI files, the Music XML format does retain text and musical symbols. You can use the Recordare's Dolet plug-in to export and import files in MusicXML format. The full version of their Dolet plug-in is compatible with Finale versions back to Finale 2000. Therefore, you can use this plug-in to export a MusicXML file, then use the Dolet plug-in to import the file in Finale 2004, 2003, 2002, 2001, or 2000. A 30-day full-featured demo version of the Dolet plug-in is available at www.recordare.com/finale.

To transfer a file backward to an older Finale version (as far back as Finale 2000)

1. Download and run the Dolet installer. When prompted, choose to install to the Finale folder containing the older version of Finale. Then, install this plug-in to all versions of Finale you plan to transfer documents between. Finale 2005 already contains the MusicXML plug-in, so you will not have to install the Dolet plug-in if you are exporting your file from Finale 2005 (or 2003/2004).

2. Open the Finale file you want to export.

3. From the Plug-ins menu, choose MusicXML Export. The Dolet Light MusicXML Exporter dialog box appears as shown in Figure 15.4.

Figure 15.4

Specify a path for your MusicXML file in the Dolet (Light) MusicXML Exporter dialog box

4. Click the Browse button to choose a destination. The Save MusicXML window appears. Choose a path for your file here (like the desktop, for simplicity) and enter a name for your file. Click Save to return to the MusicXML Exporter dialog box.

5. Click OK to generate the MusicXML file.

6. Now, open the older version of Finale.

7. Make sure a new default document is open. If not, open a new default document (File > New > Default Document). If you used a template to create the original file, you could also open the template before importing for the most accurate layout in the translated file.

8. From the Plug-ins menu, choose MusicXML Import. The Dolet Light MusicXML Importer dialog box appears as shown in Figure 15.5. This is the plug-in you installed earlier. If you do not see the MusicXML Import option under the Plug-ins menu, run the Dolet installer again and be sure to specify the folder containing the older version of Finale.

Figure 15.5

Specify a path for your MusicXML file in the Dolet (Light) MusicXML Importer dialog box

9. In the File Type section, make sure MusicXML is checked.

10. Click the Browse button, and then navigate to your desktop (or wherever you saved the file).

11. Double-click the XML file to return to the Dolet Light MusicXML Importer dialog box. The path to the file should now appear in the File to Import text field.

12. Click OK. After some processing, the MusicXML file opens into the Finale document.

After importing the MusicXML file, you will need to make some changes since the music is essentially dropped into the empty Finale document.

Here are some suggestions for editing files imported from MusicXML:

❋ From the File menu, choose File Info. Here, enter the title, composer, copyright, and description. Then use text inserts to put this info into your document. Select the Text Tool, double-click on your file and choose Text > Inserts > Title, etc.

❋ Use the Page Layout Tool to edit the layout of the document (see Chapters 2 and 11 for more information on laying out the page)

❋ If you have more than one staff in your document, you may have to respace your staves. Click the Staff Tool, and then, from the Staff menu, choose Respace Staves. Enter a percentage or value to revert your staff spacing back to that of the original document.

❋ You will find that your score reverts to the default fonts. To specify a new music font, from the Options menu, choose Set Default Music Font. Then, to change other fonts, from the Options menu, choose Document Options and select Fonts.

CHAPTER 15

TIP
If your original score was in the Jazz Font, start by opening the Jazz Font Default file before importing from MusicXML. From the File menu, choose New > Document From Template. Double-click the file "Jazz Font Default.FTM" found in your Component Files folder.

Saving As an MP3 or WAV File

The ability to save a Finale document as an audio file was perhaps the most popular feature request from Finale customers for years. In Finale 2004, MakeMusic! listened and added a Save As Audio File feature under the File menu, and now, in Finale 2005, you can also save directly to MP3. Creating an MP3 audio file for sharing on the Internet, or saving on your computer or digital music player couldn't be easier.

To save as an MP3 or WAV/AIFF file:

1. First, you will want to preview how the audio file will sound. Finale uses its SmartMusic SoftSynth SoundFont to generate the audio file, so you'll need to choose that as the MIDI playback device. Windows users: From the MIDI menu, choose MIDI Setup, and then, for MIDI Out, choose SmartMusic SoftSynth. Then click OK. Macintosh users: From the MIDI menu, choose Internal Speaker Playback, and then SmartMusic SoftSynth playback.

2. Play back the score. Note that Finale will also use the Human Playback style selected in the Playback Settings/Playback Controls while generating the audio file. Refer back to Chapter 14 for more info on Human Playback. Now, save the file.

3. From the File Menu, choose Save Special, and then Save As Audio File. The Save As Audio File dialog box appears as shown in Figure 15.6.

Figure 15.6

Specify whether you want to save as an MP3 or WAV/AIFF file in the Save As Audio File dialog box

4. Name the file, and then for Windows users choose WAV. Mac users, choose AIF if you intend to burn the file to a recordable CD; otherwise, choose MP3.

5. Specify a location and click Save.

That's all there is to it. What you heard during Finale playback has been converted to a file you can play back just like any other digital audio file. If you created a WAV or AIFF file you intend to burn to a CD, follow the instructions that came with your CD-writing software to do so.

Saving a Finale File as a SmartMusic Accompaniment

The SmartMusic intelligent accompaniment program is MakeMusic!'s rising star product. With this application, you can play your solo along with, for example, a full symphony orchestra that actually follows your spontaneous tempo changes while you play. You can also control the accompaniment by pressing a foot pedal to resume after a fermata, caesura, or the like. With a library of over 50,000 accompaniments, all readily available, it is becoming increasingly popular among music students and educators. It can accompany brass, woodwind, and vocal performers (see www.smartmusic.com for details). For our purposes, its most exiting feature is the ability to perform custom accompaniments created with Finale!

NOTE
To use SmartMusic Studio accompaniments created from Finale, you need to first subscribe to SmartMusic Studio at www.smartmusic.com. SmartMusic version 7 or greater is required to use SmartMusic accompaniments created with Finale.

You can create a full-featured SmartMusic accompaniment with Finale 2005. You can even define markings such as rehearsal letters, pauses, and repeats using SmartMusic Performance Markers. Finale even includes a wizard you can use to get started. Here are the basics for saving a Finale file as a SmartMusic accompaniment:

1. From the File menu, choose New, and then SmartMusic Accompaniment Wizard. Page 1 of the SmartMusic Wizard appears. Here, leave Create a New Finale File selected. In the future, you could also open an existing Finale file, or start a file for use with SmartMusic's assessment feature from here.

2. Click Next. Choose Solo with Accompaniment if you want to create a standard SmartMusic accompaniment file that will follow the soloist. If you choose Ensemble, you will be able to mute instruments from within the SmartMusic application, but the intelligent accompaniment feature will not be available.

3. Under Select a Solo Instrument, choose the instrument that will be performing the solo. Then specify the title, composer, and copyright.

4. Click Next. Here, select the accompaniment staves. The rest of the wizard is the same as the Document Setup Wizard, so just follow the directions until the score appears.

5. Begin entering the solo and accompaniment notation.

6. During the performance, SmartMusic sometimes needs cues from the performer to, for example, resume playback after a fermata. This cue could be in the form of a note played by the soloist or triggered by the foot pedal. In addition, SmartMusic displays elements of the score during the performance, such as rehearsal markings and repeats (e.g., the pass of the repeat you are currently playing). You can add all of these indications using the Add SmartMusic Markers utility. From the Edit Menu, choose Add SmartMusic Markers. The Add SmartMusic Markers dialog box appears as shown in Figure 15.7. (See the Edit menu of the Finale 2005 User Manual for specific instructions on adding these markers).

Figure 15.7

Use the Add SmartMusic Markers dialog box to add pauses, rehearsal markers, repeats, and other items that apply to the performance in SmartMusic Studio

---

{ **TIP**

If there are repeats in your score, in the Add SmartMusic Markers dialog box, choose Repeats on the left and then click Create/Update Repeat Markers. If your repeats are defined properly, you will see the correct playback route here. If you see a problem, refer back to Chapter 6 for information on defining repeats.

---

7. When you have added all desired SmartMusic Markers, from the File Menu, choose Save Special, and then Save As SmartMusic Accompaniment. (If the SmartMusic Accompaniment Information dialog box appears, click OK.) The SmartMusic Accompaniment Options dialog box appears as shown in Figure 15.8.

Figure 15.8

Confirm your SmartMusic Accompaniment settings in the SmartMusic Accompaniment Options dialog box

8. Click OK (if you started with the Wizard, this dialog is set up for you). Then, name and choose a location for the SmartMusic Accompaniment and click Save.

9. Save the document as a standard Finale file. Once you save as a SmartMusic Accompaniment, the generated .SMP file cannot be opened in Finale. So, it's important to "backup" your accompaniment in .MUS format whenever you save an .SMP file.

10. Now, open SmartMusic. From the File Menu, choose Open SmartMusic Accompaniment. Choose the Finale Family Generated Files tab. Navigate to your file, select it, and click Open. The file opens in SmartMusic ready for your performance.

For more information, including detailed information on preparing a Finale file for SmartMusic, go to the Index of the Finale User Manual and go to the SmartMusic Accompaniment Options dialog box. Then click the link, To Prepare a File for SmartMusic Studio.

NOTE
To preview how a Finale file will sound as a SmartMusic Accompaniment, simply choose the SmartMusic SoftSynth as the playback device (see Chapter 14) and play back the file. Human Playback settings are also retained when you save a file as a SmartMusic Accompaniment.

Creating a File for Finale Performance Assessment

Introduced in Finale 2005, Finale Performance Assessment (also called FPA) is a program that listens to a live solo performance and assesses its accuracy by comparing what was played to the written solo notation. In other words, you can play a solo into your computer's microphone and FPA shows you the notes or rhythms you played correctly or incorrectly. This application is designed primarily for music educators and students and can be a great way to hone technical and sight reading skills.

FPA can assess woodwind and brass instruments played into a microphone attached to the computer. It can also assess a MIDI keyboard performance as shown in Figure 15.9. FPA is installed along side Finale 2005, and is also available as a free download on the MakeMusic! Web site (www.finalemusic.com). While using FPA, the notation to be assessed appears on-screen, so paper sheet music is not necessary. The performer plays along with a metronome click as FPA listens.

NOTE
Finale comes with some FPA sample files you can use to get started. Look in the Finale 2005 folder. These files are also available for download at www.finalemusic.com. Also, be sure to check the MakeMusic! Web site for updates to FPA.

In Finale you can create the solo line to be assessed, and then open it in FPA. Here's how:

1. To create a file for FPA, you must use the Assessment Wizard. Click FPA Wizard in the Launch Window, or, from the File Menu, choose New > Performance Assessment File. Page 1 of the Assessment Wizard appears.

Figure 15.9

After assessment, FPA immediately displays your results

2. At the top, note the three options. You can create a new document from scratch, use Finale's Exercise Wizard to create an exercise to be assessed, or open an existing file. If you choose to create an exercise, you will see options for generating the exercise (scales, arpeggios, etc.) in the next two pages. For now, leave Create a New Document selected.

3. Under Select a Solo Instrument, choose the instrument that will be performing the solo. Then specify the title, composer, and copyright.

4. Click Next. Specify the time and key and click Next. Then, specify a tempo and pickup measure and click Next. Page 4 appears, which lists the elements that FPA does not support. If any of these items appear in the Finale file, you will not be able to save in FPA format.

5. Click Finish. Your document opens, ready for you to start entering the solo line.

6. Enter the notation. Remember to keep it simple. FPA does not support durations of a 32nd note or smaller, grace notes, repeats, trills, manual positioning, and everything else listed on page 4 of the Assessment Wizard.

7. When you are ready to save the file, from the File menu, choose Save. The Save dialog box appears. Enter a name, choose a location, and click Save. If there are any conflicts, you will be prompted with the Assessment File Compatibility dialog box (see Figure 15.10)

8. You must resolve all conflicts before you are allowed to save in FPA format. You can leave the Assessment File Compatibility dialog box open as you modify your file. Double-click a conflict in this dialog to quickly go to the measure containing the conflict. After resolving the conflicts in your file, click Check Again to see if any conflicts remain. Repeat this process until all warnings are gone. This can be easier said than done, particularly if you have opened an existing file. Here are some tips for resolving FPA conflicts:

   ❋ If you see the warning, "Manual positioning of notes," do the following: From the Options menu, choose Document Options and then, on the left, select Music Spacing. Click the Manual Positioning drop-down menu, choose Clear, and then click OK. Choose the Mass Edit Tool, press Ctrl/Cmd-A, and press the 4 key to apply music spacing. Manual positioning is cleared.

Figure 15.10

All conflicts that appear in the Assessment File Compatibility dialog box must be resolved before you can save as an FPA file

* If you see the warning, "Data in layer 2 (3 or 4)," use the Move/Copy Layers dialog box. Select a region with the Mass Edit Tool, and then from the Mass Edit menu, choose Move/Copy Layers. You may need to add a scratch staff and some creative partial measure copying to get the notes you want in the solo line. You can also choose Show Active Layer Only from the Options Menu to display a layer you want to remove, and then use the Mass Edit Tool to clear it.

* If you see the warning, "Page *x* has a different margin," do the following: Choose the Page Layout Tool. From the Page Layout menu, choose Redefine Pages and then All Pages.

* If you see the warning, "Default music font is not Maestro," do the following: From the Options Menu, choose Set Default Music Font. For Font, choose Maestro and click OK.

9. When all conflicts are resolved, you will be able to save the FPA file. To open the file in FPA, first close Finale. (Finale and FPA cannot be running at the same time.) Navigate to the FPA file and double-click it to open the FPA application. The solo is now ready to be assessed.

NOTE
Finale can open FPA files directly. If you want to edit your FPA file, you can do so by opening the file from within Finale (File > Open).

Supplementing Finale with Third-Party Plug-Ins and FinaleScript

Finale offers anyone with programming experience in C or C++ (and their own development tools) the ability to create Finale plug-ins. In this way, code-savvy users can produce their own Finale "features" for use in their work. A number of third-party plug-in developers have created a large amount of helpful utilities and even sell their plug-ins to users anxious to get the very most out of Finale. Many professional engravers rely on third-party plug-ins in their Finale work, and any Finale user can easily benefit from them.

As much as developing your own plug-in can increase efficiency, you don't need to be a programmer to automate complex procedures. Introduced in Finale 2004, FinaleScript allows you to specify a sequence of commands that can be applied to one or many documents. In this section, you will learn how to incorporate the available third-party plug-ins into your Finale repertoire, and how to create your own time-saving scripts using the FinaleScript plug-in.

NOTE

If you are a programmer interested in Finale plug-in development, you can download the Plug-in Development Kit (PDK) from MakeMusic!'s download page (visit www.makemusic.com, and then click Downloads to run a search). Note that MakeMusic!'s technical support department specializes in the Finale program itself and does not answer questions specific to plug-in development. Visit the PDK Users Forum, also available from MakeMusic!'s Web site, to interact with other plug-in developers.

TGTools

The TGTools plug-in set is a collection of supplemental plug-ins created by third-party plug-in developer Tobias Giesen. You have already seen a limited version of his plug-ins under Finale's Plug-ins menu (Plug-ins > TGTools). These have been included with the Finale package since version 2002. The full version of TGTools offers many additional features including utilities for expression management, music spacing, lyrics, playback, and more (over 60 commands total). To purchase TGTools, or to download a demo version, visit www.tgtools.de. A full-featured 30-day demo is available. If you haven't installed this demo already, do so now. In this section I'll provide a brief overview of TGTools and explore some ways to incorporate them into your Finale work. For complete information on TGTools, download the PDF Manual available at www.tgtools.de.

After you have installed TGTools, you will see a TGTools menu item at the top of your screen. Under this menu you can find all of the TGTools utilities (see Figure 15.11).

Figure 15.11

After installation, you will see the TGTools menu on the top of your screen where you can access all of the TGTools plug-ins

You can use TGTools to manipulate entries, selected regions, or your entire document. Most commands will require selection of a region of measures with the Mass Edit Tool. To select partial measures, from the Edit menu, choose Select Partial Measures. Feel free to experiment with the TGTools commands. Any change to your score can be undone by pressing Ctrl/Command-Z.

Expression Browser (Windows Only)

You may have noticed that expressions you create in Finale always appear at the bottom of the Expression Selection window. While adding many expressions to the list, you may find yourself struggling to find each expression, even if you have reordered them manually. For more control over your expressions, use the TGTools Browser for Text Expressions plug-in. From the TGTools menu, choose Browser. The TG Browser for Text Expressions dialog box appears as shown in Figure 15.12.

Figure 15.12

Manage text expressions easily with the TGTools Browser for Text Expressions

Notice all of your expressions appear neatly within the window with assigned metatools on the right side of each box. Click Larger in the lower left to zoom in on the list or Smaller to zoom out.

Here are some ways to manage text expressions in the TGTools Browser for Text Expressions:

* To edit any item, click the box and type your new text. Click again to activate the editing cursor or drop-down menu. Make your changes and then click outside the box. Use the font character maps (Help > User Manual) to find the keystroke for any characters in Finale music fonts.

* In the Show section to the right, you can specify certain types of expressions to display in the window by checking the desired options. To search for an expression, click Search For and enter the search text in the text field beneath. The window updates automatically.

❋ Sort your expressions. In the Instant Sorting section, click the Options button to open the Text Expression Sorter where you can choose a priority for ordering based on family, size, and style.

❋ Click the New button at the bottom to create a new expression, or choose the Duplicate button to duplicate the selected expression.

Double-click, or click the X in the upper-right corner to close the Expression Browser. Any changes will be reflected in the Expression Selection dialog box.

Select Text Expression (Macintosh)

On Macintosh, the Select Text Expression feature lies in place of the Expression Browser (see Figure 15.13). This is a good way to manage metatool assignments for your text expressions. From the TGTools menu, choose Select Text Expression. The Select Text Expression dialog box appears containing all text expressions and their metatool assignments. To assign a metatool, type the key you want to assign so it appears in the Assign to Key text box. Then, click the text expression on the left. You return to your score with the expression clicked assigned to the key you entered.

Figure 15.13

Easily manage metatool assignments with the Select Text Expression dialog box on Macintosh

Smart Explosion of Multi-Part Staves

Often, while creating a score, several parts in an instrumental section are entered on a single staff to minimize the number of staves necessary in the system. This works well for the full score, but such staves can be confusing to the performers while reading the extracted part. You can use the Smart Explosion of Extracted Parts plug-in to "explode" a staff containing multiple voices into two or more independent parts. This plug-in will even recognize keywords such as "tutti" or "a2" to intelligently place the correct notes into the generated staves (see Figure 15.14). This is a more comprehensive utility than the Process Extracted Parts plug-in available in the standard Finale 2005 TGTools package.

Figure 15.14

Use the Smart Explosion of Multi-Part Staves plug-in to generate two or more parts from a single staff

To explode a multi-part staff into two or more parts, each on its own staff

1. Open any document containing a staff containing multiple parts. The staff can display the voices in the form of different layers, the same layer, or using voice 2.

2. From the Options menu, choose Program Options and select the View category. Make sure Show Defined Measure Numbers is selected. Click OK to return to the score.

3. From the View menu, make sure Show Active Layer Only is turned off.

4. Select the Mass Edit Tool, and click to the left of the staff to highlight it (or select any region of the staff you would like to explode).

5. From the TGTools menu, choose Parts > Smart Explosion of Multi-Part Staves. The Smart Explosion of Multi-Part Staves dialog box appears as shown in Figure 15.15.

Figure 15.15

Choose from a number of settings for your exploded parts in the Smart Explosion of Multi-Part Staves dialog box

6. Most of the time, the default settings here will work fine. Make sure Finale's Program Option, "Show defined measure numbers," is checked (Options > Program Options > View).

7. Click Go. A dialog appears telling you not to touch the mouse or keyboard while the plug-in is working. Click OK and wait until things settle down. When a dialog pops up, click OK.

Your parts are now neatly separated into individual staves. To undo these changes, you'll have to undo several times (from the View menu, choose Undo/Redo lists, select TG Smart Explosion of Multi-Part Staves and everything above, and then click OK). You can find more detailed information regarding exploding parts and even entire groups at once in the TGTools User Manual PDF (available at www.tgtools.de).

The Patterson Plug-In Collection

Robert Patterson is a third-party plug-in developer whose work appears both in supplemental plug-ins you can download from his Web site, www.robertgpatterson.com, and within the Finale program itself. Patterson Beams is also one of Robert's creations and has shipped with Finale since version 2002 (you can find more information on Patterson Beams in Chapter 10). The plug-ins offered at his Web site are free of charge for 30 days and can be activated with a single, modest registration fee. You can also find the evaluation version of his plug-in collection on http://robertgpatterson.com/-fininfo/finmain.html. You can find detailed instructions for installing the plug-in collection from the Web.

You can find a complete description of all plug-ins included in the Patterson Collection in the User Help section of the Patterson Plug-in collection Web site. I recommend reading the user help for each plug-in before putting it to use as you will find a wealth of valuable information (see http://robertgpatterson.com/-fininfo/finmain.html and click the User Help link).

Mass Copy

You may have noticed that you cannot copy items attached to notes (expressions, articulations, Smart Shapes, etc.) without copying the notes themselves if Select Partial Measures is turned on (under the Edit menu). The Patterson Mass Copy plug-in is basically a new way to copy items without having to copy the notes they are attached to. This plug-in will copy such items to and from partial measures.

Before going through the following steps, make sure the plug-in file "MassCopy" (Windows: with the extension .FXT) exists in your Finale/Plug-ins folder. If you would like to copy to and from partial measures, from the Edit menu, choose Select Partial Measures.

Here is the basic procedure for using the Mass Copy plug-in:

1. Choose the Mass Edit Tool.

2. Highlight the region containing note-attached items (or measure-attached Smart Shapes) you want to copy.

3. From the Plug-ins menu, choose Mass Copy. The Mass Copy dialog box appears as shown in Figure 15.16.

4. Click Set Source. Any time you click Set Source, the highlighted region will be set as the source region (the precise region is indicated to the right of this button). If a region is selected upon invoking the Mass Copy dialog box, the highlighted region will be selected automatically.

5. Check the items you want to copy from the selected region.

Figure 15.16

Choose the items you want
to copy in the Mass Copy
dialog box

6. Highlight the destination region and click Paste. Items from the source region appear in the highlighted destination region provided there is a corresponding entry available for the note-attached item.

NOTE
The Mass Copy plug-in will copy items only within a single document.

Staff Sets

Chapter 7 explained how to define specific staves for viewing in Scroll View using Staff Sets. The Patterson Staff Sets plug-in expands this concept to offer additional features for staff viewing including defining a view percentage for each staff set. With this plug-in, you can also save settings for each staff set you define allowing you to define an unlimited number of Staff Sets (instead of the eight offered in Finale proper).

Before going through the following steps, make sure the plug-in file "StaffSet" (Windows: with the extension .FXT) exists in your Finale/Plug-ins folder.

To define staff sets with the Patterson Staff Sets plug-in

1. Move to Scroll View (View > Scroll View).

2. From the Plug-ins menu, choose Staff Sets. The Staff Sets dialog box appears as shown in Figure 15.17.

3. Select the staves you want to include in the staff set. Ctrl/Command-click the desired staves.

4. Check Set View Percentage, and choose a desired view percentage. If you would like to use a view percentage other than the ones available, you will need to use a macro program to define the custom percentage (see the User Help for the Staff Sets plug-in accessible from www.robertgpatterson.com for additional info).

Figure 15.17

Define staves to include in a staff set and a desired view percentage in the Staff Sets dialog box

5. For Use Finale Staff Set, choose the staff set (1–8) you want to define. Note that you can define several staff sets for each Finale staff set by choosing the Save Settings option (see the User Help Web site for details).

6. Click OK. You return to the score with the selected staves isolated on the screen.

Staff Sets you define in the Staff Sets plug-in will be accessible from the View menu (View > Select Staff Set). To view all staves, from the View menu, choose Select Staff Sets and choose All Staves.

JW Plug-Ins

There are a number of freeware plug-ins available online created by Jari Williamsson. These include JW Tempo for easily defining gradual tempo changes, JW Search and Replace, JW Playback, and several others. Jari has posted a collection of links to sites containing his own and other available third-party plug-ins. Visit www.finaletips.nu and click the Plug-ins link on the left. This site is also a good resource for helpful Finale productivity tips. The following are descriptions of some JW plug-ins, where to get them, and how to use them.

JW Tempo

The JW Tempo plug-in offers an easy solution for defining accelerandi and ritardandi. This plug-in is freeware available for download at www.jwmusic.nu/freeplugins/index.html. Download the file from this site, and copy the enclosed file "jwtempo2000.FXT" into your Finale/Plug-ins folder. Then, launch Finale. (Note that HP must be set to None in the Playback Settings/Playback Controls in order to hear any tempo effects applied with this plug-in.)

To define accelerandi and ritardandi with the JW Tempo plug-in

1. Select the Mass Edit Tool.

2. Select the region of measures to which you want to apply a gradual tempo change.

3. From the Plug-ins menu, choose JW Tempo. The JW Tempo dialog box appears as shown in Figure 15.18.

Figure 15.18

Define the opening and closing tempo for the selected region in the JW Tempo dialog box

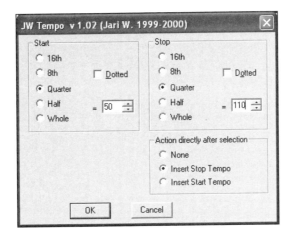

4. In the Start section, enter the original tempo of the region. Select the main beat from the radio buttons (check Dotted if necessary). Then enter the number of beats per minute in the text box (or use the up and down arrows). You can enter any value between 20 and 600 beats per minute.

5. In the Stop section, enter the number of beats per minute you want to define for the tempo at the end of the region.

6. Under Action Directly After Selection, choose Insert Stop Tempo if you want to continue using the tempo reached at the end of the selection. Choose Insert Start Tempo if you want to revert to the tempo at the beginning of the selected region.

7. Click OK. Your tempo changes gradually from the Start to the Stop tempo over the course of the selected region.

JW Playback (Windows only)

You can easily specify staves, groups, selected measures, or even staff sets for playback while reviewing your score by using the JW Playback plug-in. This plug-in is also freeware available for download at www.jwmusic.nu/freeplugins/index.html. Download the file from this site, and copy the enclosed file "jwplayback2000" into your Finale/Plug-ins folder. Then, launch Finale and open a document you want to play back. This plug-in is most beneficial in scores with many staves. To use this plug-in, no selection is necessary. From the Plug-ins menu, choose JW Playback. The JW Playback dialog box appears as shown in Figure 15.19.

Click the drop-down menu at the top to select a region of staves. To select any combination of staves for playback, choose Specific Staves, and then click any number of staves on the right. Under Start At, choose the measure to start playback. Under Stop At, choose a measure to stop playback. Click Play to begin playback. Click at any time to stop playback.

FinaleScript

FinaleScript is Finale's most customizable and, arguably, most powerful plug-in. It is a tool that allows you to specify a list of commands and apply them to the score, or to many documents, with a single click. In the body of these scripts, you can call tools, menu items, and even other plug-ins. Perform operations like

Figure 15.19

Choose specific staves, staff sets, and selected regions, and set other parameters for playback regions in the JW Playback dialog box

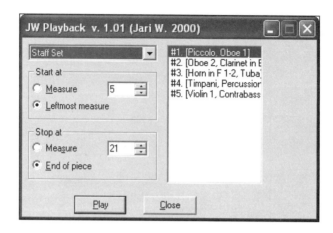

creating a score from parts, or transfer all or some document options to other documents The reach of this plug-in is really limited only by the commands available and your own imagination. Now, let's investigate the potential of FinaleScript.

1. From the Plug-ins menu, choose Miscellaneous, and then FinaleScript Palette. The FinaleScript Palette appears as shown in Figure 15.20.

Figure 15.20

The FinaleScript Palette includes a Commands Reminder, interface details, and several example scripts

2. The first two scripts in this list are a description of the controls and a list of commands. You'll find these convenient resources to reference as you design your own scripts. Double-click Command Reminder to open the FinaleScript Editor. The // characters at the beginning of each line indicate a comment. When you write your own scripts, any time you want to leave a note to yourself, just type // and then your comment. Since this is just a list of the commands, all lines are commented out. Click Cancel to return to the FinaleScript Palette.

3. Notice the text field at the bottom of the FinaleScript Palette. (If you don't see it, click the expand arrows on the right). You can enter any of the FinaleScript commands here. Enter "new default doc" and press Enter. Finale opens a new default document.

4. Type the following and, after each command, press Enter: "add staff," "select staff 1," "delete staff," "select 1 11," "fit music 3," "delete." You just added a staff, deleted the top staff, selected measure 1 through 11, fit those measures to 3 per system, and then deleted them.

This text field can be a good way to test a command to see if it will work. Most commands are intuitive and can be applied several ways. For example, to select the Mass Edit Tool, you can type "mass edit tool," "mass edit," "mass mover," and others.

TIP

You can choose any menu command in FinaleScript. Type "execute menu item *"menu item name"*" (with the name of the menu item in quotes). For example, to apply Display in Concert Pitch, type the following: "execute menu item "display in concert pitch"".

5. A script is just a list of commands like the ones you just entered that FinaleScript applies in the order written. Now, create a simple script. Click the New Script icon (it's the one to the right of the trash can). The FinaleScript Editor dialog box appears (see Figure 15.21). For the title, enter "Change to Horn in F, E Major." You'll create a script that will change your default staff to a Horn staff and set the key to E major.

Figure 15.21

Type a list of commands in the FinaleScript Editor dialog box

6. Type the following (one command per line as shown in Figure 15.21): "select staff 1," "instrument transposition f," "key signature e major," "staff name "Horn in F"".

TIP

FinaleScript commands are not case sensitive. You need not capitalize unless you are specifying text to be added to the score (as is the case with "Horn in F" here).

7. Click Save and Close. You return to the FinaleScript Palette with the script you just created selected.

8. Click the green Play button (leftmost icon) to run the script. Notice that the staff changes key and transposition, and adds "Horn in F" as the staff name. The Report button is blinking; click it to view a report on the script you just ran. To apply this script to a different staff, simply open the script and change "select staff 1" to "select staff #" (where # is the number of the staff counted from the top).

When you save a script, you will be able to use it in future Finale sessions (it is saved to a file called "FinaleScript.DAT" in the Component Files folder). Like Finale's existing scripts, those you create yourself can be edited at any time in the FinaleScript Editor. To apply a script to multiple documents, simply click the Browse for Folder button (second from the right) and select the folder containing the files you want to change. Then use the "batch process folder" command to instruct FinaleScript to process all Finale files in the selected folder. This can be especially useful for transferring document options to many other documents (as described in Chapter 13 under "Moving Document Options from One Document to Another."

After creating and running a new script, the rest is a matter of familiarizing yourself with the available commands. Use the existing scripts as models. You'll notice that several commands have attributes. For example, you can type "first clef treble" to change the opening clef to treble clef. Typing "first clef bass" changes it to a bass clef. (You can also use "tenor" or "alto.") You can find a full list of all FinaleScript commands and their attributes in the appendix of the Finale 2005 User Manual.

TIP

Visit the FinaleScript forum to get helpful advise from other Finale users experienced with FinaleScript. Go to www.finalemusic.com/forum, and then go to the "FinaleScript Plug-in" public forum.

Index